AF702128

Medieval History and Archaeology

General Editors

JOHN BLAIR HELENA HAMEROW

Silver, Butter, Cloth

MEDIEVAL HISTORY AND ARCHAEOLOGY

General Editors

John Blair Helena Hamerow

The volumes in this series bring together archaeological, historical, and visual methods to offer new approaches to aspects of medieval society, economy, and material culture. The series seeks to present and interpret archaeological evidence in ways readily accessible to historians, while providing a historical perspective and context for the material culture of the period.

RECENTLY PUBLISHED IN THIS SERIES

KINGSHIP, SOCIETY, AND THE CHURCH IN ANGLO-SAXON YORKSHIRE
Thomas Pickles

ANGLO-SAXON FARMS AND FARMING
Debby Banham and Rosamond Faith

THE OPEN FIELDS OF ENGLAND
David Hall

PERCEPTIONS OF THE PREHISTORIC IN ANGLO-SAXON ENGLAND
RELIGION, RITUAL, AND RULERSHIP IN THE LANDSCAPE
Sarah Semple

TREES AND TIMBER IN THE ANGLO-SAXON WORLD
Edited by Michael D. J. Bintley and Michael G. Shapland

VIKING IDENTITIES
Scandinavian Jewellery in England
Jane F. Kershaw

LITURGY, ARCHITECTURE, AND SACRED PLACES IN ANGLO-SAXON ENGLAND
Helen Gittos

RURAL SETTLEMENTS AND SOCIETY IN ANGLO-SAXON ENGLAND
Helena Hamerow

PARKS IN MEDIEVAL ENGLAND
S. A. Mileson

SILVER, BUTTER, CLOTH

Monetary and Social Economies in the Viking Age

Edited by
JANE KERSHAW
AND
GARETH WILLIAMS

Consultant editors
SØREN SINDBÆK
AND
JAMES GRAHAM-CAMPBELL

OXFORD
UNIVERSITY PRESS

OXFORD
UNIVERSITY PRESS

Great Clarendon Street, Oxford, OX2 6DP,
United Kingdom

Oxford University Press is a department of the University of Oxford.
It furthers the University's objective of excellence in research, scholarship,
and education by publishing worldwide. Oxford is a registered trade mark of
Oxford University Press in the UK and in certain other countries

© Oxford University Press 2019

The moral rights of the authors have been asserted

First Edition published in 2019

Impression: 1

All rights reserved. No part of this publication may be reproduced, stored in a retrieval system, or transmitted, in any form or by any means, without the prior permission in writing of Oxford University Press, or as expressly permitted by law, by licence or under terms agreed with the appropriate reprographics rights organization. Enquiries concerning reproduction outside the scope of the above should be sent to the Rights Department, Oxford University Press, at the address above

You must not circulate this work in any other form
and you must impose this same condition on any acquirer

Published in the United States of America by Oxford University Press
198 Madison Avenue, New York, NY 10016, United States of America

British Library Cataloguing in Publication Data
Data available

Library of Congress Control Number: 2018947663

ISBN 978–0–19–882798–6

Printed and bound by
CPI Group (UK) Ltd, Croydon, CR0 4YY

Links to third party websites are provided by Oxford in good faith and
for information only. Oxford disclaims any responsibility for the materials
contained in any third party website referenced in this work.

Preface

Silver, Butter, Cloth: Monetary and Social Economies in the Viking Age is the third volume of proceedings from a series of symposia which have sought to explore the character of economy in the Viking Age through the combination of archaeology and numismatics. This approach has grown out of a long-term collaboration between the Department of Coins and Medals at the British Museum and the Institute of Archaeology, UCL, in which both institutions have worked to integrate numismatics more closely with archaeology, in both the classical and early medieval contexts. One area in which links have been particularly close is that of Viking silver, where Professor James Graham-Campbell's interests in Viking hoards, and in Viking silver more generally, overlapped with those of my predecessor Marion Archibald and myself. When I was developing the exhibition *Paid in Burnt Silver: Wealth and Power in the Viking Age* at the British Museum (April–August 2000), James was characteristically generous with advice from an archaeological perspective, and we decided that it would also be interesting to organize a symposium at UCL to coincide with the exhibition, inviting a number of specialists working on different aspects of Viking silver, with a specific view to encouraging archaeologists and numismatists to engage with each other.

A variety of circumstances beyond our control meant that publication of the proceedings was delayed until 2007, when they appeared as *Silver Economy in the Viking Age* (Left Coast Press). Despite the title, it was already apparent that there was not one single silver economy, but several overlapping economies, including both monetary and social transactions, and including the monetary or quasi-monetary use of both coin and bullion, and the use of a variety of precious-metal objects in different forms of social exchange. The appearance the following year of the second volume in the Kaupang Excavation Project series, *Means of Exchange: Dealing with Silver in the Viking Age* (Aarhus University Press), edited by Dagfinn Skre, further stimulated discussion of these themes, and a second symposium on the subject was organized in Aarhus in 2008, to coincide with the end of James Graham-Campbell's time as Honorary Professor of Medieval Archaeology at the University of Aarhus. This was again organized in conjunction with the British Museum and UCL, and was again planned by James and myself, together with Søren Sindbæk of the University of Aarhus, involving several of the contributors to the Kaupang volume, and maintaining a combination of archaeologists and numismatists. This resulted in the publication in 2011 of *Silver Economies, Monetisation and Society in Scandinavia* AD *800–1100* (University of Aarhus Press). A key element in this symposium and its proceedings was the introduction of discussion of 'commodity-money' alongside silver, and a growing recognition that a focus on silver alone, or even silver and gold, risked missing out on an understanding of important elements in Viking Age economy and exchange.

The appointment of Jane Kershaw to a British Academy postdoctoral fellowship at UCL, working on the bullion economy of Viking England, provided the opportunity to organize a third symposium, to coincide with the exhibition *Vikings: Life and Legend* at the British Museum (March–June 2014). The heavy programme around that exhibition, including the scheduling of a live cinema broadcast for one of the days of the symposium itself, meant that although the symposium was planned jointly by Jane, Søren, and myself, with continued support and advice from James Graham-Campbell, the burden of organizing the symposium fell much more heavily onto Jane than on the rest of us. Other commitments also meant that Søren Sindbæk was unable to be as heavily involved in editing the volume as originally planned. Jane has, therefore, had the lion's share of the work in editing this volume, and I would like to thank her for all her efforts in producing what I feel is a very worthy successor to the previous volumes. Thanks are also due to James Graham-Campbell and Søren Sindbæk for their valuable input.

As the title of the book suggests, the symposium picked up where the last one left off, investigating silver alongside other forms of currency media. Developments in scientific analysis have meant that it has been possible to include more detailed discussion not only of the uses of silver, but its sources in the Viking Age, while the economic uses of gold, cloth, and butter are also discussed in more detail, taking forward the discussion of commodity-money and its relationship to more monetized economies. As ever, answering some questions raises more, and this continues to be a field in which more research is needed, but the chapters in this volume contribute to a more nuanced view of the range of economies in the Viking Age than ever before.

Gareth Williams
British Museum

Contents

List of Illustrations

List of Tables

Notes on Contributors

Florent Audy recently completed his PhD at the Department of Archaeology and Classical Studies, Stockholm University. His research focuses on the interface between archaeology and numismatics, particularly the reuse of coins.

James H. Barrett is Reader in Medieval Archaeology at the McDonald Institute for Archaeological Research, University of Cambridge. He researches medieval archaeology and historical ecology, with a particular focus on migration, political economies, and maritime societies from the Viking Age to the medieval period.

Mateusz Bogucki is Assistant Professor in the Institute of Archaeology and Ethnology, Polish Academy of Sciences. His research specialism is Viking Age archaeology and numismatics in the Baltic region.

Aaron J. Critch completed his PhD at the Department of Archaeology and Anthropology, University of Cambridge. He researches the archaeology of the North Atlantic, specializing in 'ring-money' from Viking Age Scotland.

Jacek Gruszczynski is a commercial archaeologist. He recently completed his PhD at Oxford on the social, political, and ritual contexts of hoard deposition in the Baltic zone during the Viking Age.

Svein H. Gullbekk is Professor in the Archaeology Section of the Museum of Cultural History, University of Oslo. His research covers Norwegian and European coins from the Viking Age onwards.

Jennifer F. Harland is Lecturer at the Archaeology Institute, University of the Highlands and Islands. She researches the zooarchaeology of the North Atlantic, with a particular focus on the identification and analysis of fish remains.

Michèle Hayeur Smith is a Research Associate at the Haffenreffer Museum of Anthropology at Brown University. Her research harnesses archaeological textiles from Iceland and the North Atlantic to investigate cultural change, gender roles, and trade relationships from the Viking Age to *c.*1800.

Gitte Tarnow Ingvardson is Curator of the Coin collection at the Historical Museum, Lund University, and a PhD Fellow at Bornholm University and the Saxo Institute at the University of Copenhagen. Her PhD topic is the Viking Age silver hoards of Bornholm and their archaeological context.

Marek Jankowiak is an Early Career Fellow in the Centre for Byzantine, Ottoman and Modern Greek Studies, University of Birmingham. He is interested in various aspects of the history of the Byzantine state, economy, and society and recently completed a large-scale study of the slave system that connected northern Europe, Byzantium, and the Islamic world in the ninth and tenth centuries.

Lauri Joosu is an Applied Geologist at the Department of Geology, University of Tartu, Estonia, with active research interests in petrology, mineralogy, and geochemistry.

Jane Kershaw is a Leverhulme Early Career Research Fellow at the Institute of Archaeology, Oxford University. She researches the archaeology of Viking Age Britain and Scandinavia, with a particular focus on metalwork.

Ivar Leimus is Curator of the Coin Collection at the Estonian History Museum. His academic research encompasses Estonia's history of money from the early medieval to modern period, with a special focus on Islamic coinage from the Viking Age.

Stephen Merkel is a Research Fellow in Archaeometry at the Institute of Archaeology, Ruhr University, Bochum. He recently completed a PhD on Viking Age silver and the silver economy at Hedeby.

Ester Oras is a post-doctoral researcher in the Department of Archaeology, University of Tartu, Estonia. Her PhD focused on wealth deposition in the eastern Baltic from the first to the ninth century. Her current research spans archaeological science, material cultural studies, and the archaeology of ritual and religion.

Guillaume Sarah has a PhD in Chemistry and is a researcher at the CNRS, IRAMAT-Centre Ernest Babelon, University of Orléans. He specializes in ancient coin analysis as well as provenance studies of metal, principally from the early medieval period.

John Sheehan is Senior Lecturer in the Department of Archaeology, University College Cork. His research specialism is Viking Age silver hoards in Britain and Ireland and the ecclesiastical archaeology of early medieval Ireland.

Gareth Williams has been a curator at the Museum since 1996, with responsibility for British and European coinage (*c.* AD 500–1180). Within this area he specialises in Anglo-Saxon and Viking coinage. Much of his work focuses on the use of coinage as evidence within broader historical and archaeological studies.

Andrew R. Woods is Curator of Numismatics at York Museums Trust. He researches the numismatics and archaeology of Ireland and the Irish Sea region, with a special focus on coinage and the economy of Late Viking Age Ireland.

Introduction

Economy, Currency, and Value in the Viking Age

Jane Kershaw

New economic and social practices led to profound changes in the use of monetary media in the Scandinavian world of the Viking Age (*c.*AD 800–1100). While the early Viking Age was dominated by a 'display' economy, based on the public show of silver wealth, the ninth century witnessed the increasing use of silver as a means of exchange, first as bullion and then as coin. Such changes elucidate the nature of payment and exchange in a society characterized by growth in long-distance networks and market centres, but they also provide a framework for studying social relationships and concepts of wealth and value broadly defined. This book examines the use of silver and other commodities (gold, butter, cloth) to explore the nature and complexity of Viking economic systems during this age of change. It aims to deepen understanding of contemporary economic practices and to advance new definitions of wealth, value, and money in the ninth to twelfth centuries.

The current book builds on the publication of two earlier volumes (Graham-Campbell & Williams 2007; Graham-Campbell, Sindbæk, & Williams 2011), both of which focused on developments in the use of silver in Viking Age Scandinavia. Together with the publication of the important silver and weight assemblage from Kaupang, Norway (Skre 2008c), these works demonstrated the existence of multiple, overlapping forms of silver economy, some characterized by commercial exchange and others by primarily social or ritualistic practices. They have been highly influential, revealing the pivotal role played by emerging urban communities in the development of the bullion (weighed silver) economy and demonstrating beyond doubt that silver was used in sophisticated transactions before the widespread circulation of coinage (for reviews, see Hoover 2008; Gaimster 2013; Kershaw 2013; Naismith 2013). The geographic focus has, for the most part, been mainland Scandinavia, although the 2007 volume also addressed silver (and gold) economies in the British Isles, Ireland, and Normandy.

Chapters in other volumes have explored silver and commodity-currencies in Viking Age Iceland (Graham-Campbell 2011; Gullbekk 2011b), while the monetary functions of silver in the West Slavic area have been addressed in a recent edited volume (Bogucki & Rębkowski 2013).

In the current book, we develop the theme of silver economies by addressing the monetary and social/ritual roles of silver, as manifest through practices such as fragmentation, hoarding, and demonetization. At the same time, we deliberately promote a broader and more rounded view of both currency and economy. Whereas, in the earlier volumes, there was a tendency to treat economy separately from society (Williams 2011, 337–8; for notable exceptions, see Gaimster 2007; Kruse 2007; Sindbæk 2011), here most of the contributors view economy as a reflection of social relations. In doing so, they uphold a 'post-substantivist' approach, as formulated recently by Dagfinn Skre: an approach that seeks to dissolve the long-held dichotomy within economic theory between formalism and substantivism through recognition that, with pre-industrial societies, just as in contemporary ones, 'it is within the compass of human possibility to trade as both an economic and a social agent' (Skre 2008a, 333–5). In other words, trade is embedded in social relations, while 'all exchanges of goods in every social situation will have an economic element' (Skre 2008a, 334). Consequently, a recurring theme in this book is how political, gendered, religious, and other social praxes structured the use of silver within Viking Age economies. Moreover, the concern with economy is not focused exclusively on the exchange of precious metal (Skre 2011, 85) (in this volume, see Jankowiak; Kershaw), but also incorporates its acquisition and production (Sarah; Merkel; Woods; Oras, Leimus, and Joosu, this volume) along with its consumption (Sheehan; Ingvardson; Gruszczynski, this volume).

The current volume differs from the preceding works in two further, important ways. The limitations of focusing on silver for understanding of Viking economic practice were recognized in the 2011 volume (Williams 2011, 338; Skre 2011; Gullbekk 2011a). Here, we consider the role of silver alongside that of other commodity-currencies, developing new methodologies for the identification of commodity-monies in the archaeological record. For the first time, currencies of butter, cloth, and gold can be shown to have played a significant role as monetary media in a variety of settings. Finally, we extend the geographic scope of the area under investigation beyond the core Scandinavian countries. Accordingly, we include new archaeological data and wider syntheses from both the eastern and western reaches of the Scandinavian overseas settlements.

The Monetary and Quasi-Monetary Functions of Silver

Within the current volume there are four main themes. Chapters in the first section harness new data to progress understanding of the monetary and quasi-monetary functions of silver. They combine to support the current model of the developing use of fragmented silver as currency from the mid to late ninth century, whilst generating new insights into the handling traditions that structured the use of silver as payment, particularly in the Baltic region.

A dominant theme in these early chapters is fragmentation. The deliberate fragmentation of both minted and unminted silver is a geographically widespread, though regionally and chronologically varied, phenomenon during the Viking Age, which occurs first in south Scandinavia and in the southern Baltic region (particularly at Truso) in the mid-to-late ninth century (Hårdh 1996; Williams 2011, 349). Although primarily social motives for the practice have been proposed (for instance, Spangen 2005, 116–17; Urbańczyk 2009), the prevailing interpretation of hack-silver is an economic one. Hack-silver has been widely regarded as an intermediary stage in the development of a coined-money economy, with the degree of fragmentation thought to signal the intensity with which silver circulated as a means of exchange and, by implication, the state of advancement of the local economy (Hårdh 1996, 84–6, 182; Kiersnowski 1961).

However, consonant with the emerging post-substantivist definition of economy, two studies show that silver fragmentation, alongside other handling traditions, could have both economic and social significance. Marek Jankowiak (Chapter 1) charts an increase in the rate of dirham fragmentation in an anticlockwise direction around the Baltic Sea. He maintains that the degree of dirham fragmentation reflects not local monetary circulation, as is often assumed in studies of hack-silver, but the distance of dirhams from their source as manifest through the number of transactions in which they changed hands. An important new observation is that the same hoard sometimes contains two or more fragments of the same dirham, a finding that undermines the commonly held view that hack-silver pieces were dispersed as local currency (Hårdh 2008, 98). In short, fragmentation took place when dirhams passed hands, but those fragments were occasionally kept together. While the fragmentation of dirhams thus reflects the trading systems linking the Baltic and Islamic lands, it may also have symbolic significance: fragmentation demonstrated the good silver content of a batch of dirhams at the point at which they passed into new ownership and thus served to authenticate transactions between merchants.

Fragmentation is one of a number of silver-handling traditions also considered by Gitte Ingvardson (Chapter 2) in her analysis of 'mixed' silver hoards (containing both coin and non-minted silver) from the Baltic island of Bornholm. Conventionally, the ratio of coin to non-minted silver within a hoard is taken to indicate the state of the local economy, with an increase in the proportion of coin over time signalling economic advancement and paving the way for the introduction of domestic coin (Hårdh 1996, 86). In this context, the extended presence of mixed hoards on Bornholm into the twelfth century may be interpreted as a sign of a primitive local economy. Yet Ingvardson shows through an in-depth narrative of six hoards that their composition reflects varying depositional and, in turn, economic contexts. Hoards deposited within a central settlement area have a different make-up, and display different patterns of fragmentation and testing, from hoards deposited on the outskirts of a settlement or in areas without other traces of human activity. They can be shown to occupy different economic spheres, relating to the monetary, productive, and ritual use of silver respectively, with hoards tentatively connected to silversmithing displaying a particularly pronounced level of fragmentation. It is clear, then, that silver-handling traditions cannot be viewed as a uniform phenomenon, but reflect local context.

The evidence for varying local and regional patterns of silver handling prompts questions about the representativeness and cross-compatibility of datasets, particularly regarding very small pieces of silver (Blackburn 2008, 65). To what extent do different methods of recovery affect the discovery and recording of hack-silver? Recent excavations have demonstrated that the use of different archaeological techniques can impact on the nature of data obtained even within the same site. At sites in the region of the White Lake (Beloe Ozero) on the Upper Volga, for instance, the recent introduction of fine wet sieving has enabled the identification of very finely fragmented dirhams, not detected in earlier excavations (Marakov 2012, 225–7). At Kaupang, Norway, dirham fragments recovered through excavation employing metal-detecting and partial sieving were moderately lighter than those recovered through metal-detecting alone (Blackburn 2008, 31, 65–6, table 3.14).

In this volume, Mateusz Bogucki (Chapter 3) shows how different methods of recovery can have a profound impact on the nature of recorded data in a case study of the Mózgowo hoard from Poland. This early eleventh-century hoard was recovered in three, chronologically separate stages, each employing a different method of recovery. Through detailed reconstruction of the hoard assemblage, Bogucki demonstrates that the size of the silver pieces recorded reflects their method of retrieval. Large fragments and whole coins dominate the assemblage discovered in the nineteenth century. The finest silver pieces were recorded through the excavation of thin layers of the topsoil in conjunction with systematic metal-detecting, whereas metal-detecting alone led to the recovery of slightly larger fragments. The implication is that data relating to both older discoveries and recent metal-detected hoards will contain biases that must be borne in mind in metrological studies.

Thus far, the monetary function of silver has been explored in relation to silver bullion in the East. Andrew Woods's chapter (Chapter 4) moves the discussion on to the role of Viking Age coinage in a western settlement context, through study of the Hiberno-Scandinavian coinage of Dublin. This coinage has conventionally been perceived as inferior to the developed coinage of the Anglo-Saxons, which it imitated at its outset. Yet Woods shows through close study of the Dublin coinage's weight, silver fineness, and currency renewal that the coinage developed independently, constituting a well-regulated currency that was effectively monitored by successive kings of Dublin. An important conclusion, focusing on the production of the Dublin coinage, is that while various renewals re-established coin weight and silver fineness, they did not correspond temporally with a change of ruler, and were thus not overtly political. Instead, the renewals appear to have been motivated by commercial viability, with the aim of facilitating trade around the Irish Sea. Unlike in Norway, where coinage renewals came about with the succession of a new ruler, the Dublin coinage seems not to have been harnessed primarily for political goals. Such findings serve to highlight the fact that not all Viking coinages were produced for the same reasons or were intended to serve the same functions.

The Non-Monetary Functions of Precious Metal

The second theme of the book is the role of precious metals in primarily non-monetary contexts. In such situations, silver (and gold) were transacted and consumed principally to transform social relationships, rather than to further the material exchange of goods, although it is recognized that such exchanges may also have had a commercial element (for instance, the distribution of tribute among military followers; payments made on the conclusion of treaties). Here, the aim is to integrate study of precious-metal bullion and coin with its social, cultural, and symbolic context. The focus is not the more familiar arena of gift-exchange (for which, see Gaimster 1991, and, for non-precious metals, Sheehan 2013), but how silver and gold were appropriated, exchanged, consumed, and deposited as a valuable metal for maintaining a variety of social relationships (Sindbæk 2011).

The chapter by Svein Gullbekk (Chapter 5) exemplifies this approach by highlighting the role of silver coins within the 'spiritual economy' of late Viking Age and medieval Scandinavia. Finds of coins beneath the floorboards of Scandinavian churches reveal that Christian parishioners made regular offerings of (low-denomination) coins in exchange for salvation, thus revealing the transformation of coins from monetary to devotional objects. Gullbekk shows that this practice can be dated to the later eleventh century, at a time when Scandinavian society was increasingly monetized. He argues further that the expanding Christian church actively embraced and propelled the emerging market economy: in this light, devotional offerings in coin became one means for the church to raise essential revenues. Coins took on new values and meaning as they passed from circulation within society, to ritual use within sacred contexts, to being gathered and used by the church.

In this volume, John Sheehan (Chapter 6) offers another example of silver use within the religious sphere, in relation to the acquisition and consumption of Scandinavian wealth by the Irish church from the mid ninth century. By considering the deposition of Viking Age silver hoards on church-owned land, rather than simply within ecclesiastical sites, Sheehan suggests that the Irish church owned far more Scandinavian silver than previously thought. He argues compellingly that secular Irish elites obtained this wealth from the Scandinavians via trade, alliance, tribute, and plunder, and then gifted it to the church, with whom they often had close dynastic connections. Shifting attention onto the consumption of silver, Sheehan argues that this wealth, while sometimes hoarded, was also used to fund church building, the foundation of high crosses and other sculptural traditions, potentially through the payment of silver (bullion) wages. Here, then, the acquisition of silver through multiple different means, its gifting as ecclesiastical patronage and its subsequent use as stored wealth and, potentially, as wage payment, reveals the multifaceted uses of silver within overlapping political, commercial, and spiritual economies.

The non-monetary function of silver in the Viking Age is particularly well elucidated by the demonetization of coinage, one tangible sign of which is in the physical transformation of coins into jewellery. In his chapter, Florent Audy (Chapter 7) considers the reuse of coins as pendants, a phenomenon affecting around 3 per cent of all coins from Viking Age Scandinavia. Audy argues that coins were repurposed as items of female jewellery not primarily for their iconographic content, since few reused coins show consistent patterns of orientation when suspended as pendants. Instead, he suggests, coin-pendants were valued for their silver content: they served as a guarantee of (bullion) value, enabling women to literally wear their wealth. Indeed, coin-pendants were sometimes recontextualized for a third time, by being deposited in hack-silver hoards as items of exchangeable bullion. The foreign origins and accumulated life histories of coin-pendants also likely conferred status on their wearers. Notably, in Scandinavia (unlike in England) the fashion for coin-pendants was not matched by a corresponding fashion for coin-like jewellery (such as nummular brooches) until the very end of the Viking Age, suggesting that it was indeed the object of the coin itself that held symbolic and material meaning.

A further instance of coin demonetization and reappropriation as ornament is provided by the Arabic dinar-turned-pendant from the small gold hoard from Essu, northern Estonia, a location on the Vikings' *Austrvegr* (eastern route) linking Scandinavia with north-west Russia. Alongside this coin-pendant, the Essu hoard contained five other, ornamental gold pendants, likely dating to the late ninth or early tenth century. In this volume, Ester Oras, Ivar Leimus, and Lauri Joosu present this hitherto overlooked hoard in full for the first time (Chapter 8). Following detailed stylistic, technical, and use-wear analysis, the authors demonstrate that the pendants were made in Scandinavia and likely formed part of a female necklace, a context of use that characterizes finds of Arabic gold dinars in Scandinavia more broadly. The recovery of the pendants from a bog suggests that the assemblage was originally deposited in a watery context. The Essu hoard thus illustrates the prominence of gold (including demonetized gold coins) within the Viking Age display economy, but it also has significance from a gender perspective. The hoard appears to relate to a wider group of early Viking Age ritual deposits comprising female gold or gilded jewellery sets, particularly necklaces (cf. the late ninth-century Hoen hoard, Fuglesang & Wilson 2006; Kilger 2008b). Such 'themed deposits', to adopt Kilger's terminology, are easily differentiated from the more numerous silver bullion hoards and may reflect a continuation of earlier, Migration-period practices of hoarding gold female jewellery in wetland contexts. They, like the Essu hoard, suggest a link between women's display of gold jewellery and the ritual or sacred sphere.

Thus far, the contributions have demonstrated the complex and nuanced ways silver and gold could be deployed in predominantly social economies, primarily through analysis of the precious metal itself. Consideration of the context of deposition also casts important light on the intended functions of hoards, as Graham-Campbell and Sheehan have recently demonstrated in relation to Viking Age hoards from watery locations in Ireland (2009).

In his chapter focusing on Gotland and Pomerania, Jacek Gruszczynski (Chapter 9) shifts attention onto hoard containers, interpreting the absence of containers as a sign that hoards were not intended for recovery, and thus equating containerless hoards with primarily ritual deposits. By integrating hoard data with recent research into rural archaeology on Gotland, Gruszczynski finds that the majority of Gotlandic hoards (58 per cent) were small, containerless hoards associated with newly 'broken fields', that is, farms that were newly established in the Viking Age. The implication is that the practice of symbolically deposited hoards on newly acquired land was widespread. Gruszczynski further finds that, on Gotland, hoards were more likely deposited in containers when they weighed over 600 g, whereas in Pomerania, the 'tipping point' was the lighter sum of 250 g. The sum of 600 g, equivalent to three marks of silver, is of note, since it represents the standard amount payable in fines and social obligations according to Gotlandic law. It may be, then, that these 'savings' hoards, kept at the average Gotland farm, acted as a 'portable but standardised medium for the payment of social obligations' (Bradley 1987, 358, quoted in Gruszczynski, this volume; see too Bradley 2016).

Sources of Silver

The widespread use of silver in the Viking Age, encapsulating both monetary or quasi/non-monetary purposes, fuelled a new demand for precious metal from the ninth century (Williams 2011, 352; cf. Sawyer 2013). How was this silver sourced? While the dominant sources of the silver used in Scandinavian contexts, namely western European and Islamic coinages, are known, their relative contribution to Viking wealth remains uncertain, particularly before the arrival in Scandinavia in the early-to-mid tenth century of substantial numbers of Samanid dirhams. Since the Scandinavians routinely melted down foreign coin into native forms of ingot and ring, the only means of addressing the relative input of different silver sources is through metallurgical analysis.

Two chapters in this volume address the question of silver source(s) from an archaeometric perspective. In his chapter, Guillaume Sarah (Chapter 10) presents a theoretical and methodological framework for 'fingerprinting' early medieval silver, here utilising minimally destructive mass spectrometry by laser ablation to obtain trace element (in particular, gold and bismuth) data and thermal ionization mass spectrometry (TIMS) for lead isotope data. Taking as a case study Carolingian coins from Toulouse, Sarah demonstrates that successive coinages of the late eighth to late ninth century possessed different gold and bismuth profiles, suggesting a shift in the sources of silver over the period. This is confirmed by the lead isotope data, which shows that the mine of Melle supplied some coinage from the 840s, but that both earlier and later coinages also utilized silver from another, as yet unidentified, source. Such findings demonstrate the importance of combining both elemental and isotopic analysis to generate the complete fingerprint of a silver object.

Stephen Merkel (Chapter 11) applies the same dual archaeometric approach to Viking silver coins and objects from Hedeby. He exploits known differences in the trace element compositions and lead isotope ratios of Anglo-Saxon, Carolingian, and Islamic coin to determine the origin of silver used in the Malmer KG7 coinage, produced at Hedeby in the first two decades of the tenth century. Mass spectrometry analysis of a wide range of silver items from Hedeby reveals that the silver forming this coinage did not originate principally in western Europe, nor does it match the signature of Samanid silver from Central Asia and Afghanistan. Rather, in both lead isotope ratios and its gold and bismuth contents, it appears to correlate with silver of eastern origin, which reached southern Scandinavia and the Baltic region prior to the large-scale influx of Samanid silver in the early-to-mid tenth century. Notably, this same silver source also characterizes a significant hack-silver assemblage from Hedeby, including bar ingots, which may have been produced locally. The fact that both locally produced coinage and hack-silver seems to originate from a common silver stock points to the concurrent use of both coined and bullion currency, raising interesting questions about the control of minting at Hedeby in the early tenth century.

Non-silver Currencies

As the contributions to this volume thus far demonstrate, silver has been at the forefront of studies of Viking Age economic systems. Given the substantial number of silver hoards, as well as increasing numbers of single and settlement finds from this period, this focus is understandable. But has the archaeological visibility of silver led to too narrow an understanding of currency and economic practice during the Viking period? The final three chapters in this volume suggest that it has. Collectively, they broaden our view of money and exchange in the Viking Age by moving the focus away from silver to other, diverse forms of monetary media.

It is now widely recognized that medieval Scandinavia was home to a flourishing commodity-money system, in which certain commodities with a utilitarian value came to adopt the primary functions of money, namely a unit of account and a means of exchange (Skre 2011; Gullbekk 2011a). Norwegian land-purchase documents from the thirteenth and fourteenth centuries record that both cattle and silver served as widely recognized units of account, but the actual payment media used was much broader, encompassing, alongside silver coin, cattle, grain, butter, flour and coarse flour, different varieties of hides/furs, dried fish, raw copper, salt, horses, and Icelandic *vaðmál* (a heavy woollen cloth) among other media, all payable in standardized units of length, weight, volume, or number (Gullbekk 2009, 217, 343–53).

The question is whether a commodity-money system, so well elucidated through medieval written records, can be traced back to the Viking Age. The paucity of written records for the Viking period means that the status of the Scandinavian commodity-money system prior to the twelfth century is obscure, although most scholars concur that its existence here, as in other areas of early medieval Europe, is highly likely (Williams 2011, 350; Gullbekk 2011a, 103; cf. Davies 2002; Kilger 2008a, 270–1, table 8.3). Indeed, as Dagfinn Skre has noted, there is a chronological gap between the origins of Scandinavian proto-urban sites dedicated to long-distance trade, and the introduction of silver currency, and this gap points to the use of other, non-silver forms of currency by the first generations of town dwellers (Skre 2008b, 352). The critical issue is how to identify potential commodity-money currencies in the archaeological record. As Skre has commented, 'silver money speaks for itself. Conversely, the cow bones found in a midden, the iron ingots in a deposit, or the scant remains of a woollen dress in a grave carry no mark of once having formed part of payment for grain, as they might actually have been' (2011, 76).

The chapters presented here are instrumental in developing new methods for recognizing the potential monetary role of commodities in the material record. Complete gold ornaments are normally viewed within the context of the display economy. Yet Jane Kershaw (Chapter 12) shows how hitherto neglected evidence for weight adjustment to a common Scandinavian standard, combined with evidence for the testing of complete gold objects, hints at a role for gold rings as a form of money in large units in Viking Age England. A monetary role for gold in England is also supported by an increasing corpus of hack-gold, primarily associated with the activities of the Viking Great Army in the late ninth century. It is possible that an increase in the availability of gold, acquired through raids in western Europe, encouraged a shift in its use from ornament to payment media within a multi-metallic bullion currency (for the potential monetary use of copper in Viking Age England, see Pestell 2013, 249–50).

In her archaeological analysis of the heavy, homespun woollen fabric known as *vaðmál*, Michèle Hayeur Smith (Chapter 13) stresses the importance of standardization in tracing the emergence of legal cloth money in Iceland.

While the use of *vaðmál* both as a unit of account and as an actual medium of exchange is recorded in Icelandic written documents from the medieval period up to the seventeenth century, its origins as cloth currency have remained obscure. Examining an assemblage of over 1,000 Viking Age and medieval textile fragments preserved in Iceland's farm middens and burials, Hayeur Smith pinpoints a marked shift towards the use of a standardized, twill cloth, with a set spin direction and thread count, from the late eleventh century. This standardized cloth can be distinguished from both earlier and later textile remains, which encompass a variety of fabric types of differing quality, coarseness, and decoration, and appears to meet the description of legal cloth currency provided in later written sources. Importantly, archaeological evidence indicates that it was widely produced and consumed across Iceland. In effect, there was 'a mint on virtually every farm' (Einzig 1966, 261).

The identification in the archaeological record of perishable foodstuffs used in payments presents even greater challenges, requiring innovative approaches. In medieval Scandinavia, written sources indicate that butter served as both a unit of account and a means of exchange, with 2 *laupa* (baskets) of butter worth the equivalent of 2 pounds of grain and 1 *kýrlag* (cow) (Skre 2011, 74). From the eleventh century, documents also attest the existence in Norway and elsewhere of a butter skat, in which taxes, levied first on land and then on cattle, were payable in 'lispunds' (30–2 lb) of butter. Butter, then, appears to have served as a payment medium in commercial contexts. Does the archaeological record substantiate this documentary evidence? In their chapter on the Orkney farm of Quoygrew, Aaron Critch, Jennifer Harland, and James Barrett (Chapter 14) identify a period of surplus dairy production from the eleventh to thirteenth centuries, which, notably, corresponds with a decline in the local availability of silver. The authors find evidence among the farm's extensive animal bone assemblage for an increase in cattle neonatal death, alongside an overall rise in the relative ratio of cattle to sheep. This shift towards intensified dairying may have been a response to meet a growing demand for butter skat.

How were these commodity-monies given value as currency? As staple products meeting essential household needs, both butter and cloth are likely to have acquired monetary value when, through frequent trade, they acquired stable value relations relative to other commodities. Gold is, of course, not a staple good, but its increased availability in the ninth century will have given it a stable worth relative to silver, enabling it to be exchanged at a standard rate within a bullion economy. Also critical to the process of monetization is the existence and enforcement of quality standards (Gullbekk 2009; 2011a, 104–5). In silver, likewise in gold as Kershaw demonstrates in this volume (Chapter 12), levels of precious-metal purity could be monitored by nicking and by the shaping of metal into recognizable, trusted and sometimes weight-adjusted forms of ring and ingot. Equivalent standards equally applied to other forms of commodity. Medieval Icelandic laws required that in order to be accepted as legal tender, cattle had to be between three and ten years in age; they had to be capable of bearing calves and producing milk (Gullbekk 2011a, 105). Hayeur Smith (Chapter 13) notes that the same laws also heavily regulated cloth currency. Only panels of *vaðmál* meeting a certain quality and measuring two ells in width and six ells in length were considered legal tender, while the existence of measuring tools suggests that standards were routinely enforced. Without these assurances of quality safeguarding standardization, it is difficult to see how commodities could have circulated monetarily.

The emphasis on the standardized production of commodity-currencies is also notable from a social perspective, since the production of both cloth and butter were likely predominantly female activities. As such, the production of regulated monetary media provides an important, yet hitherto overlooked, example of women's economic agency in the Viking Age (see especially Hayeur Smith, Chapter 13). Such agency in commercial environments is otherwise indicated by extensive finds of weights in female graves in Scandinavian contexts, both rural and urban (Kershaw forthcoming), the dual role of coin-pendants as female jewellery and bullion (Audy, this volume) as well as by literary and documentary references to female coin use and ownership and distribution of capital wealth (Waitz 1884, 55; Gustin 2004, 229–30; Jochens 1995, 152). Of potential significance here is the fact that, within urban settlements, silver currency and weights are found within both public and domestic settings, prompting the question whether women were directly involved in the sale of goods that they themselves produced at home (see, for instance, Pedersen 2008, 159, 162). Clearly, the gender dynamics underlying Viking Age exchange is a subject in critical need of further investigation.

The emergence of both butter and cloth currencies appears to be correlated with a decrease in the local availability of silver currency. Yet the relationship between different commodity-currencies and coined and uncoined silver is likely to have varied according to context. What is clear is that the use of commodity-currencies was not confined to cases where silver currency failed. The various commodity-monies of medieval Norway survived the introduction of domestic coinage in around 1000 (Gullbekk 2011a). In Scandinavian England during the late ninth and tenth centuries, a thriving silver bullion currency based on weighed-out hack-silver operated alongside that of official Viking coinages produced in York and East Anglia (Kershaw 2017). In this volume, Critch, Harland, and Barrett point out that butter skat continued to operate in Orkney even after Orkney was transferred to Scotland in the late fifteenth century, despite the fact that the Scottish crown had been issuing coin since the 1130s (Chapter 14). Indeed, the growing number of single coin finds from Viking Age Scotland, including from Norse settlements in Orkney, suggests the common use of coins within an unregulated monetary economy from the early tenth century, culminating with the introduction of Norwegian coinage in the mid eleventh century (Williams 2006). Commodity-monies could coexist and interact with coinage.

In fact, the concurrent use of two or more different monetary media is a widespread historical phenomenon (Kershaw 2017). Seen in the light of a multiplicity of payment options, the question becomes not whether two different forms of currency could coexist, but what governed choice in monetary media (Skre 2011, 73). Of course, choice may be restricted by availability, particularly in the case of agricultural money products, naturally affected by seasonality. We might also contrast the quality of the monies themselves: a demand for high-denomination media (cattle or horses, for instance) with a demand for small-denomination currency in different geographical settings (rural vs urban contexts). Yet it is also likely that, to quote Akinobu Kuroda, one money could do what another could not (2008, 7). Convention may have dictated the use of certain payment media in particular transactions. It is also likely that buyers and sellers exercised subjective preferences in choosing a means of exchange, trading off factors such as one's ability to test for quality, immediate need, long-term storage requirements, portability, and future convertibility (Skre 2011, 73). For some, choice of money media may also be a question of identity, a choice to use weighed silver bullion rather than local coinage, for instance (Kershaw 2017), or an agricultural product of particular familiarity. All these factors may have governed choice in payment media. They, like the diverse monies themselves, reveal the complexity of the means of exchange during the Viking Age.

REFERENCES

Blackburn, M.A.S. 2008. 'The Coin-Finds'. In Skre (ed.), 29–74.

Bogucki, M. & M. Rębkowski 2013. *Economies, Monetisation and Society in the West Slavic Lands 800–1200 AD*. Szcecin: Institute of Archaeology and Ethnology Polish Academy of Sciences.

Bradley, R. 1987. 'Stages of the Chronological Development of Hoards and Votive Deposits'. *Proceedings of the Prehistoric Society* 53: 351–62.

Bradley, R. 2016. *A Geography of Offerings: Deposits of Valuables in the Landscapes of Ancient Europe*. Oxford: Oxbow.

Davies, W. 2002. 'Sale, Price and Valuation in Galicia and Castile-León in the Tenth Century'. *Early Medieval Europe* 11: 149–74.

Einzig, P. 1966. *Primitive Money in its Ethnological, Historical, and Economic Aspects*. Oxford and New York: Pergamon Press.

Fuglesang, S.H. & D.M. Wilson 2006. *The Hoen Hoard: A Viking Gold Treasure of the Ninth Century*. Rome: Bardi Editore.

Gaimster, M. 1991. 'Money and Media in Viking Age Scandinavia'. In *Social Approaches to Viking Studies*, ed. R. Samson, 113–22. Glasgow: Cruithine Press.

Gaimster, M. 2007. 'Viking Economies: Evidence from the Silver Hoards'. In Graham-Campbell & Williams (eds), 123–34.

Gaimster, M. 2013. 'Review of Silver Economies, Monetisation and Society in Scandinavia AD 800-1100, ed. J. Graham-Campbell, S.M. Sindbæk & G. Williams'. *European Journal of Archaeology* 16.3: 561–5.

Graham-Campbell, J. 2011. '"The Serpent's Bed": Gold and Silver in Viking-Age Iceland and Beyond'. In Sigmundsson et al. (eds), 103–31.

Graham-Campbell, J. & J. Sheehan 2009. 'Viking-Age Gold and Silver from Irish Crannogs and Other Watery Places'. *Journal of Irish Archaeology* 18: 77–93.

Graham-Campbell, J., S.M. Sindbæk, & G. Williams (eds) 2011. *Silver Economies, Monetisation and Society in Scandinavia,* AD *800–1100.* Aarhus: Aarhus University Press.

Graham-Campbell, J. & G. Williams (eds) 2007. *Silver Economy in the Viking Age.* Walnut Creek: Left Coast Press.

Gullbekk, S.H. 2009. *Pengevesenets Fremvekst og Fall i Norge i Middelalderen.* Copenhagen: Museum Tuscalanums Forlag.

Gullbekk, S.H. 2011a. 'Norway: Commodity Money, Silver and Coins'. In Graham-Campbell et al. (eds), 93–111.

Gullbekk, S.H. 2011b. 'Money and its Use in the Saga Society: Silver, Coins and Commodity Money'. In Sigmundsson et al. (eds), 176–88.

Gustin, I. 2004. *Mellan Gåva och Marknad: Handel, Tillit och Materiell Kultur under Vikingatid.* Stockholm: Almqvist & Wiksell International.

Hårdh, B. 1996. *Silver in the Viking Age: A Regional-Economic Study.* Stockholm: Almqvist & Wiksell International.

Hårdh, B. 2008. 'Hacksilver and Ingots'. In Skre (ed.), 95–118.

Hoover, O.D. 2008. 'Review of Silver Economy in the Viking Age, ed. J. Graham-Campbell & G. Williams'. *American Numismatic Society Magazine* 7.2: 55–9.

Jochens, J. 1995. *Women in Old Norse Society.* Ithaca and London: Cornell University Press.

Kershaw, J. 2013. 'Review of Silver Economies, Monetisation and Society in Scandinavia AD 800–1100, ed. J. Graham-Campbell, S.M. Sindbæk & G. Williams'. *Early Medieval Europe* 21: 227–9.

Kershaw, J. 2017. 'An Early Medieval Dual-Currency Economy: Bullion and Coin in the Danelaw'. *Antiquity* 91: 173–90.

Kershaw, J. forthcoming. 'Beyond Metrology: New Approaches to Viking-Age Regulated Weights'. In *Weights and Their Identification: Methodological Challenges in the Study of Ancient Weights and Metrological Systems*, ed. L. Rahmstorf.

Kiersnowski, R. 1961. 'Coin Finds and the Problem of Money Hoarding in Early Medieval Poland'. *Wiadomości Numismatyczne* 5: 35–56.

Kilger, C. 2008a. 'Wholeness and Holiness: Counting, Weighing and Valuing Silver in the Early Viking Period'. In Skre (ed.), 253–325.

Kilger, C. 2008b. 'Kombinationer av Föremål. De Vikingatida Mittspännedepåerna'. In *Facets of Archaeology: Essays in Honour of Lotte Hedeager on Her 60th Birthday*, ed. K. Chilidis, J. Lund, & C. Prescott, 323–38. Oslo: Oslo Academic Press.

Kruse, S.E. 2007. 'Trade and Exchange Across Frontiers'. In Graham-Campbell & Williams (eds), 163–76.

Kuroda, A. 2008. 'What is Complementarity Among Monies? An Introductory Note'. *Financial History Review* 15.1: 7–15.

Marakov, N.A. (ed.) 2012. *Rus' v IX–X Vekakh: Arkheologicheskaia Panorama [Rus in the Ninth and Tenth Centuries: An Archaeological Panorama]*. Moscow: Vologda.

Naismith, R. 2013. 'Review of Silver Economies, Monetisation and Society in Scandinavia AD 800-1100, edited by J. Graham-Campbell, S.M. Sindbæk & G. Williams'. *The Economic History Review* 66.1: 374–5.

Pedersen, U. 2008. 'Weights and Balances'. In Skre (ed.), 119–78.

Pestell, T. 2013. 'Imports or Immigrants? Reassessing Scandinavian Metalwork in Late Anglo-Saxon East Anglia'. In *East Anglia and its North Sea World in the Middle Ages*, ed. D. Bates & R. Liddiard, 230–55. Woodbridge: Boydell Press.

Sawyer, P. 2013. *The Wealth of Anglo-Saxon England*. Oxford: Oxford University Press.

Sheehan, J. 2013. 'Viking Raiding, Gift Exchange and Insular Metalwork in Norway'. In *Early Medieval Art and Archaeology in the Northern World: Studies in Honour of James Graham-Campbell*, ed. A. Reynolds & L. Webster, 809–23. Leiden: Brepols.

Sigmundsson, S., A. Holt, G. Siguurðsson, G. Ólafsson, & O. Vésteinsson (eds) 2011. *Viking Settlements and Viking Society, Papers from the Proceedings of the Sixteenth Viking Congress, Reykjavik and Reykholt, 16–23 August, 2009*. Reykjavik: Hið Íslenzka Fornleifafélag & University of Iceland.

Sindbæk, S.M. 2011. 'Silver Economies and Social Ties: Long-Distance Interaction, Long-term Investments - and Why the Viking Age Happened'. In Graham-Campbell et al. (eds), 41–65.

Skre, D. 2008a. 'Post-substantivist Towns and Trade AD 600–1000'. In Skre (ed.), 327–41.

Skre, D. 2008b. 'Dealing with Silver: Economic Agency in South-Western Scandinavia AD 600–1000'. In Skre (ed.), 342–55.

Skre, D. (ed.) 2008c. *Means of Exchange: Dealing with Silver in the Viking Age*. Kaupang Excavation Project Publication Series 2. Aarhus: Aarhus University Press.

Skre, D. 2011. 'Commodity Money, Silver and Coinage in Viking-Age Scandinavia'. In Graham-Campbell et al. (eds), 67–92.

Spangen, M. 2005. 'Edelmetalldepotene i Nord-Norge. Komplekse Identiteter i Vikingtid og Tidlig Middelalder'. Master's dissertation, University of Tromsø.

Urbańczyk, P. 2009. 'The Polish Discussion on Medieval Deposits of Hack-Silver'. *Historia Archaeologia* 70: 499–521.

Waitz, G. 1884. *Vita Anskarii (Scriptores rerum Germanicarum in usum scolarum)*, Monumenta Germaniae Historica, Hannover.

Williams, G. 2006. 'Monetary Economy in Viking-Age Scotland in the Light of Single Finds'. *Nordisk Numismatisk Årskrift* 2006 for 2000–2: 163–72.

Williams, G. 2011. 'Silver Economies, Monetisation and Society: An Overview'. In Graham-Campbell et al. (eds), 337–72.

1

Silver Fragmentation

Reinterpreting the Evidence of the Hoards

Marek Jankowiak

Hoards of hack-silver, or fragmented silver coins and objects, are among the most striking types of Viking Age finds from northern Europe. Those from the western Slavic lands (i.e. Poland and east Germany), frequently composed of amorphous silver fragments weighing fractions of a gram, are particularly spectacular (examples in Kmietowicz 1994; Friedland & Hollstein 2008; Novák 2010). Such finds raise the question of the purpose of silver fragmentation. Was it determined by economic needs, such as the demand for small change, by some ritual practices, the meaning of which eludes us today, or by the availability of silver?[1] On the basis of a simple statistical analysis of the numismatic evidence, this chapter will assess these possibilities and argue for a different answer, namely that fragmentation occurred in the course of commercial transactions related to long-distance trade. Data presented below suggests that monetary and non-monetary silver was cut or broken into smaller pieces when it was exchanged for other commodities, in the first place slaves. As a result, the degree of fragmentation of silver depended primarily on the number of times it changed hands.

The existing studies on silver fragmentation tend to focus on selected geographical areas, most often either Scandinavia or Poland.[2] However, our understanding of Viking Age silver economies cannot be complete without a global perspective that would take into consideration the entire zone of silver circulation and silver hoarding including Scandinavia, the British Isles, Slavic lands, Rus', and areas populated by speakers of Finnish and Baltic languages. Even if this short study cannot fully meet such a requirement—I will only briefly survey finds from Rus'

[1] See the summary of interpretations and their critique, from a different position, in Kilger (2008, 309–12).

[2] Hårdh (1996) includes Pomerania, but not the rest of Poland, whereas Brather's (2007) interesting conclusions are based on the material from the southern coast of the Baltic sea. Bogucki (2011, 140–5) usefully summarizes various positions taken by Polish numismatists.

and will leave out Norway and the British Isles—it attempts to provide a comprehensive overview of the material from the entire Baltic area.

I will consider only one category of objects found in the silver hoards: the dirhams. This choice is justified by their relative standardization, which facilitates the comparison of finds from different geographical areas, and by their precise dating, as even small fragments can usually be attributed to a ruler and a geographical area, if not to a specific mint and year. This makes it possible to follow the patterns of fragmentation with a precision that is unavailable for other types of coins or objects. I will look successively at changes in the weight of whole dirhams, at the chronological evolution of fragmentation and its geographical patterns, at the relation between the age of the coin and its weight, and finally at the existence of multiple fragments of the same coin within a single hoard. These observations, taken together, will shed some light on the vexed question of 'monetary circulation' in the North.

Average Weight of a Whole Dirham

The canonical weight of an Abbasid dirham is usually set at 2.97 g (for instance, Darley-Doran 2002). This does not mean, however, that every single coin was expected to follow this norm. In a study of the mint of Samarra, Luke Treadwell showed that although this notional standard was maintained during the period of its activity in the ninth and the tenth centuries (AH 224–333 = AD 838–945), a transition from an *al pezzo* to an *al marco* minting system (that is, a move from coins being weighed individually, to being weighed in batches) took place probably during the period of political anarchy in the 860s. Earlier dirhams deviated from the standard by 0.1–0.2 g, while a dirham produced in Samarra in the late ninth century could weigh anything between 2 and 4 g (Treadwell 2001, 153). Treadwell connects the deregulation of the system with the appearance of fragmented coins in hoards from the Islamic world (for which, see Ilisch 1990) and, more broadly, with a shift from counting to weighing silver coins in commercial transactions.

Judging from data gathered by Gert Rispling,[3] a similar transition from a rigorous to a relaxed weight standard took place in other major Abbasid mints, such as Madinat al-Salam and al-Muhammadiya, where the standard deviation of the weights of individual dirhams increased from 0.2 g at the beginning of the ninth century to almost 0.4 g at its end, even if this change appears to have taken place more gradually than in Samarra. The early Samanid coinage followed a similar trajectory: in the first two decades after its inception in AH 280 (AD 893/4),

[3] Rispling's database contains data on *c.*70,000 dirhams and dirham imitations, mostly from Swedish hoards kept in the Royal Coin Cabinet in Stockholm, but also from other northern European collections and from published finds.

the weights of individual dirhams clustered tightly around the ideal weight of 2.97 g, but moving forward in time the standard deviation for the main two mints of al-Shash and Samarqand increased from 0.2–0.3 g to over 0.5 g in the AH 320s (AD 930s).[4]

In the absence of metrological studies of tenth-century dirhams, it is difficult to ascertain how long the traditional weight standard survived the abandonment of *al pezzo* minting. Central Asian mints reactivated at various points in the course of the tenth century—such as al-Shash since AH 280 (AD 893/4), Bukhara since AH 335 (AD 946/7), and Farwan since AH 380 (AD 990/1)—initially conformed quite closely with the canonical weight of 2.97 g,[5] which points to the preservation of this standard throughout the century. But data for other mints contained in Rispling's database suggests an increase in the average weight: a total of 233 whole Buyid dirhams, for instance, weighed on average over 3.6 g in the second third of the tenth century.

In this context, the picture that emerges from aggregate data on dirham finds from Scandinavia, Poland, and Rus' is difficult to interpret. In Figure 1.1 only whole dirhams of the three main dynasties—the Umayyads, the Abbasids, and the Samanids—are included. The graph represents their average weight in relation to the number of extant specimens, which gives an idea of the statistical reliability of the data. Although the average weight of a dirham in the entire sample of over 18,000 dirhams[6] is of 3.00 g, i.e. very close to the canonical standard, it varied significantly over time. Abbasid dirhams probably conformed to a lighter standard of 2.82 g until the AH 210s (AD 825–35) (see, for instance, Rebstock 2008, 2260), and to the canonical weight of 2.97 g in the second third of the ninth century AD, but their weight increased thereafter and reached 3.2 g on average in the AH 270s (AD 880s). Samanid dirhams followed a similar trend: after a relatively short initial period of stability around 2.9–3.0 g, they began to put on weight and reached on average half a gram more in the AD 950s, when their inflow to Scandinavia virtually stopped.

Although this data is not entirely unproblematic—the sample may, for instance, contain some dirhams damaged on the edges or clipped—it is probably free from systematic errors that would distort the trends described above. Variations in average weight are naturally bigger whenever few coins are available, but the trends would appear clearly even if the analysis was limited only to the years with a large number of extant coins.

[4] Calculated for 827 whole coins from Madinat al-Salam and 358 from al-Muhammadiyya struck in the third century AH (AD 816–913), and for 6,348 coins from al-Shash and 3,026 from Samarqand struck between AH 280 and 329.

[5] Averages for the first twenty years of their production: al-Shash 2.97 g (Gert Rispling's database); Bukhara 3.10 g (Gert Rispling's database); Farwan 2.92 g (Ilisch et al. 2003).

[6] Only whole dirhams for which full data (i.e. dynasty, date, and weight) is available are included in the sample.

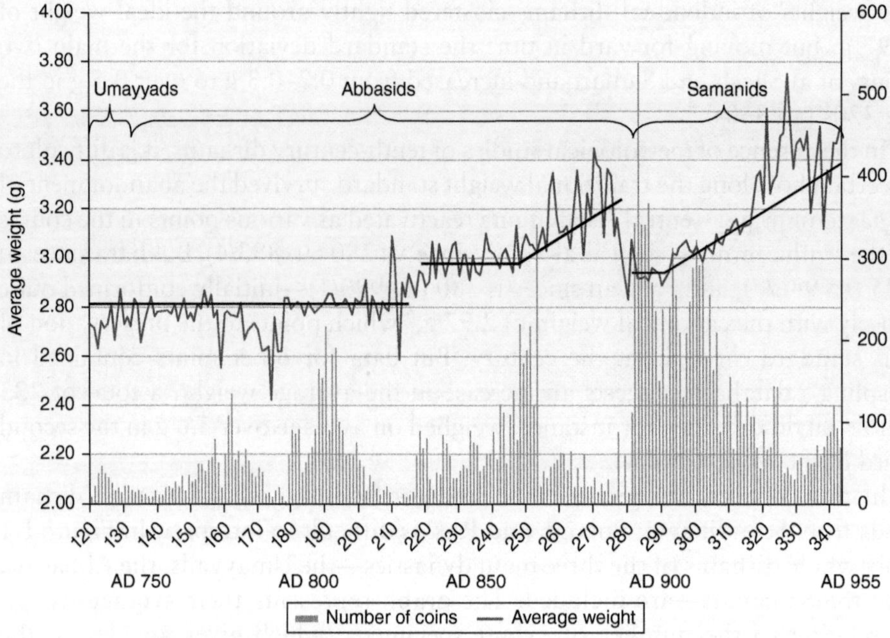

Fig. 1.1. Average weight of whole Umayyad, Abbasid, and Samanid dirhams from the northern hoards by Hijri year (line) in relation to the number of coins (bars). Only Samanid dirhams are included after AH 280 (AD 893/4). Total number of coins: 18,176.
Source: Gert Rispling's database.

As long as no large-scale metrological study of the Middle Eastern material is available, it is not possible to decide whether the observed upward trends resulted from an evolution of the standard within the Caliphate, or from deliberate selection of heavier coins by the Scandinavians. As we have seen, data for Samarra, less dependent on the Scandinavian material (Treadwell 2001, 141–2), and for the early issues of several Samanid mints suggests the maintenance of the notional weight standard of *c.*3 g until at least the mid tenth century, accompanied by an increasing dispersion of the weights of individual coins. This would point towards the latter interpretation, namely that the long-term increase in the weight of dirhams visible on Figure 1.1 resulted from a conscious selection of heavier coins by the Scandinavians from a broadening range of the available weights of dirhams. Assuming that heavy and light dirhams circulated alongside each other in the Caliphate,[7] the graph suggests that the Scandinavians accepted only the heavier ones. This implies that, despite variations in their individual weights, the coins were handled individually when Muslim and Scandinavian

[7] This assumption is supported by the important hoard from Susa in Iran (*tpq* AH 265 = AD 878/9, 1,130 coins): the 365 whole dirhams struck in the ten years before the *tpq* weigh anything between 2.06 and 4.52 g and are normally distributed around the average of 3.09 g. See Miles (1960, 134–6).

merchants were concluding their transactions: had they been weighed together, there would have been no incentive for selecting noticeably heavier dirhams.

Chronological Patterns

The supposed selection of heavier dirhams by the Scandinavians suggests, in turn, that dirhams were entering the northern world mostly as whole coins; a conjecture confirmed by the dominance of clipped dirhams, necessarily produced from whole coins, in southern Rus' (and only there), discussed further below. Dirhams were therefore divided somewhere on their way from the markets where Scandinavians met Muslim merchants, such as Bulgar on the Volga, to their final destinations, where they were deposited in hoards.

Can we detect any patterns in their fragmentation? A frequently used metric is the percentage of fragments in the total number of coins. It is easy to calculate, but it has the disadvantage of ignoring the size of the fragments. A more insightful indicator is the average weight of a dirham, whether whole or fragmented, in a given hoard. Such data is available only for a limited number of hoards: fragments were often discarded from the older finds, many small pieces of metal remained invisible to the finders until the advent of metal detectors (see Bogucki in this volume) and even the recent publications of hoards focus on coins that can be identified and rarely include the measurements of all the fragments. This is especially true for deposits of hack-silver from central Europe (Novák 2010 and FMP are exceptions). In addition, many hoards, in particular from Gotland, remain unpublished.

Figure 1.2 represents the average weight of a dirham, on the vertical axis, in relation to the *termini post quem* of ninety-four ninth- and tenth-century hoards from Gotland and the Swedish mainland, for which complete data on the weight of all the coins was available. Two groups of hoards are clearly distinguishable: the seventeen hoards buried in the second and third quarters of the ninth century are separated from a substantial group of finds dating to the tenth century by an almost empty quarter century (*c*.875–900). The two groups display different behaviours. In the ninth century, the later the hoard the heavier the average weight of a dirham: the earliest big hoards—such as Stora Tollby II (*tpq* 835) and Ocksarve I (*tpq* 840/1) in Gotland, or Sundveda (*tpq* 843/4) in Uppland—contain mainly fragments, whereas finds with *termini post quem* just before the 'silver crisis' of the late ninth century are mostly composed of whole dirhams. The only significant exception to this trend is the famous hoard of Spillings (*tpq* 870/1): although data on only a third of its monetary part is available, it appears that it was significantly more fragmented than other contemporary Gotlandic hoards (Östergren 2009, 28).

The picture for the tenth century is at first sight less clear. Unlike in the previous century, the average weights do not form a linear trend, but rather a broadening wedge with its upper limit at the constant level of 3 g—which

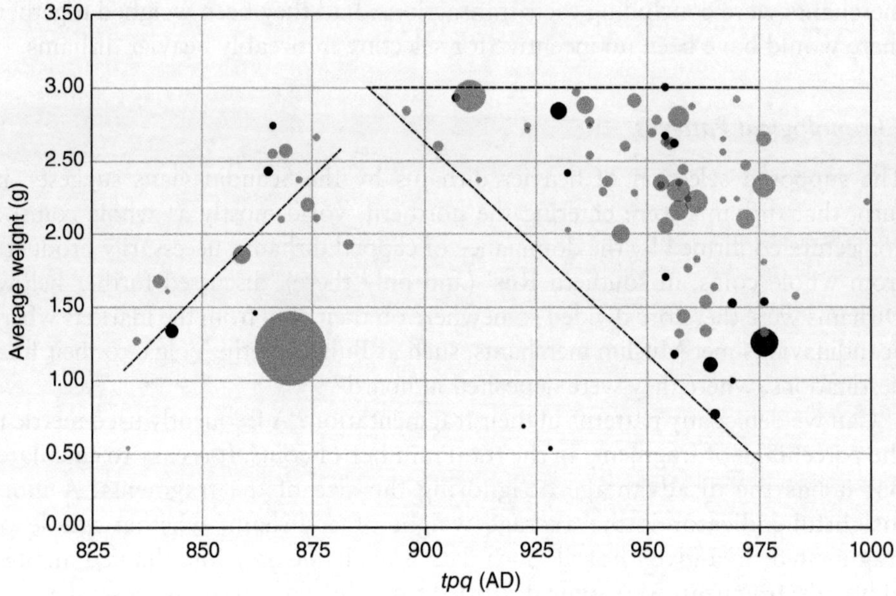

Fig. 1.2. Average weight of a dirham in ninth- and tenth-century hoards from Gotland (grey circles) and mainland Sweden (black circles). The size of the circle reflects the number of coins; the biggest represents the Spillings hoard (*tpq* 870/1).

Sources: CNS, listings kept at the Numismatic Institute of the University of Stockholm, Gert Rispling's database.

means that throughout the period hoards composed exclusively of whole dirhams continued to be deposited—and the lower border sloping down, which reflects not only the increased incidence of fragmented dirhams with time, but also the reduction in the weight of the average dirham fragment.

Two opposite trends were thus at work in Viking Age Gotland and mainland Sweden: a decrease in the degree of fragmentation in the ninth century, followed by an increase in the tenth. The first of these trends is particularly revealing, as it contradicts the view that prolonged inflow of monetary silver necessarily leads to an increase in economic complexity, reflected in an increased demand for small change, and therefore in a greater fragmentation of coins (as expressed, for instance, in Steuer, Stern, & Goldenberg 2002, 133–41). It rather appears that the Gotlanders and the Swedes who were initially using fragmented coins of the size of, on average, half a dirham progressed—or regressed?—towards the usage of whole coins. An opposite evolution took place in the tenth century. This suggests that there was little connection between the quantity of silver available in Gotland and mainland Sweden—or the 'monetization' of their economies—and the size of hoarded coins. In the absence of obvious internal reasons for the variations in the level of fragmentation of dirhams, it is necessary to look beyond Sweden in order to identify where on their way from the Islamic world dirhams were divided into smaller parts.

Geographical Patterns

Data on the average weight of dirham fragments aggregated at a regional level shows considerable differences between the major areas of hoarding.[8] Figure 1.3 illustrates this point for tenth-century hoards. Whole dirhams dominate in Estonia and, to a lesser degree, in Gotland. The coins are, on average, more fragmented as one moves to mainland Sweden, and even more so in the western Baltic area. The fragmentation of dirhams culminates in the western Slavic lands: no hoard from the emerging centre of the Piast state in Greater Poland contains dirhams of average size bigger than 1.2 g. The hoard of Dzierznica (*tpq* 983), for instance, the biggest silver hoard found in Poland, consists of 15 kg of hack-silver, including 18,200 fragments of dirhams weighing in total around 8 kg, which implies the average weight of a dirham of 0.44 g (Kmietowicz 1994). Finds to the south and west of Greater Poland are even more fragmented: dirhams in the hoard of Cortnitz (*tpq c.*1015) weigh on

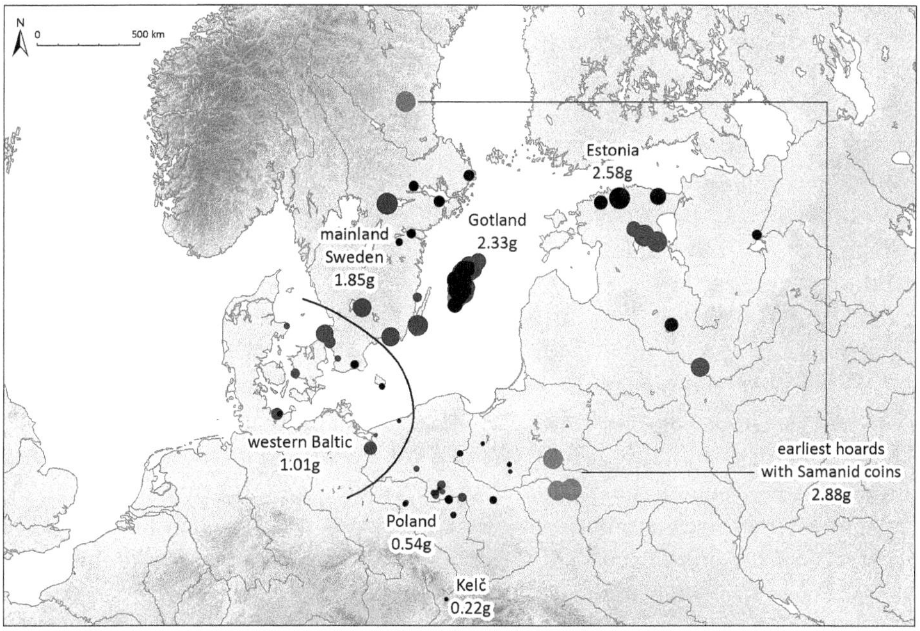

Fig. 1.3. Average weight of dirhams in tenth-century hoards (*tpq*s between AD 892 and 991). The size of the circle represents the weight of an average dirham in a given hoard; the darker the circle the later the hoard. Regional averages are calculated on the basis of hoards (not individual coins).

Sources: in addition to sources quoted for Fig. 1.2, Leimus (2007), Novák (2010), and FMP.

[8] The below calculations are based only on hoards for which a full record, unbiased by a selection of coins at any stage, is available.

average 0.33 g, while those in the find from Kelč (*tpq* 1010)—probably the most fragmented hoard currently known—0.22 g.[9]

This picture of an increasing fragmentation as one moves anticlockwise around the Baltic Sea is incomplete in that it does not include Rus'. The eastern Slavic lands display significant regional variations that need to be further investigated. Dirhams found on transit routes such as the Oka River are predominantly whole, whereas coins from urban centres such as Novgorod are more fragmented. Southern Rus' constitutes a system apart due to the prevalence of clipped coins that appear to have conformed to a decreasing weight standard in the course of the tenth century. Hoards of clipped dirhams are evidenced on a territory extending from the region of Kursk through eastern Ukraine (the recently published Bezliudovka hoard, *tpq* 935/6), probably Ukrainian Galicia (judging from the limited evidence available), to the borderlands of Hungary (the so-called Máramaros hoard, *tpq* 935/6).[10]

At the level of individual hoards, the picture is naturally more complex: on the coasts of mainland Sweden, for instance, finds with the predominance of both unfragmented coins and small fragments are attested. The latter are also attested in some, usually relatively small, Gotlandic hoards (e.g. Nygårds, *tpq* 957/8; Stora Vikers I, *tpq* 963/4), even if, on the whole, entire dirhams and fragments equivalent to one half and one quarter of dirham dominate on the island. Tiny pieces are found in big quantities in such 'productive sites' as Birka, Roma, and Truso, but this limited evidence for local fragmentation does not change the overall picture, characterized by significant regional differences.

The map illustrated in Figure 1.3 allows for several interpretations. A frequently held view relates the degree of fragmentation 'to the type of trade that was carried out in a region' (Hårdh 1996, 182). Dirhams were cut into smaller pieces in response to the local need for small change: the smaller the fragments, this reasoning goes, the higher the velocity of the local monetary circulation and, therefore, the more developed (or 'monetized') the market. A glance at the map shows that, in this interpretation, Greater Poland should have enjoyed the most monetized economy in the Baltic area in the Viking Age. This runs counter to the current state of archaeological evidence that does not as much as hint at the existence of this kind of advanced economy in the Piast state in the mid-tenth century (see, for instance, the evidence gathered in Kara 2009).

Another view relates the size of the fragments to the value of silver on a given market, which was a function of its availability (Kiersnowski 1961, 42–3; Suchodolski 1971, 24; *contra*: Hårdh 1996, 84). However, if we limit

[9] Kelč: Novák (2010); Cortnitz: information from the exhibition *900 Gramm Gehacktes. Oberlausitzer Silberschätze des 11. Jahrhunderts*, Landesmuseum für Vorgeschichte, Dresden, 8 May 2008–4 January 2009; see also Friedland & Hollstein (2008).

[10] Oka: Gomzin (2011, 74); Novgorod: Fomin (1992); Kursk: Lebedev (in prep.); Bezliudovka: Petrov (2014); Galicia and Máramaros: Fomin & Kovács (1987, 78).

our observations to Islamic coins, there is little correlation between the quantity of silver traceable in a given region and the average size of dirham. Estonia and Greater Poland, for instance, two areas comparable in terms of size, hoarding behaviours, and—judging from the hoards—the quantity of silver they attracted in the tenth century, are at the antipodes of dirham fragmentation.

Finally, the view that ritual behaviours and attitudes towards coins influenced the degree to which the dirhams were divided implies that they differed significantly between, say, Gotland and Denmark. This is, however, difficult to demonstrate; similarly, our minimal knowledge of Slavic religion and ritual (see, for instance, Komar & Khamaiko 2011) precludes any understanding of the observed difference between Scandinavia and the Slavic lands.

There remains the possibility that the degree of fragmentation was a simple function of the distance from the sources of coined silver. In the tenth century, most dirhams found in northern Europe originated in the Samanid emirate in Central Asia and were channelled to the North through the market of Bulgar on the Volga, the dominant role of which is demonstrated not only by the famous account of Ibn Fadlan, but also by the admixture of Volga Bulgar imitation dirhams in most hoards buried in the 930s or later.[11] Dirhams—as we have seen, probably mostly whole dirhams—were there acquired by Scandinavian warrior-merchants in exchange for slaves and furs. It appears that, at least in the period *c.*930–60, the main flow of dirhams bifurcated towards, on the one hand, the Kursk region and further west as far as western Ukraine, and, on the other, towards the Baltic area, which it reached through the rivers of north-western Russia, Novgorod (founded *c.*930), and the Gulf of Finland. The southern branch of the system was characterized, as mentioned above, by the clipping of the dirhams, whereas in the North the dirhams reached Estonia and Gotland substantially intact before undergoing fragmentation as they moved west- and southwards.

The fragmentation of dirhams in the Baltic area thus appears to be correlated with the degree to which their last owner's access to the market of Bulgar was mediated. It is likely, for instance, that the Piasts obtained dirhams through a long chain of intermediaries, such as merchants from Wolin and other Baltic emporia, the Danes, the Swedes from the mainland, and the Gotlanders.[12] They probably also had access to an alternative route via Mazovia (east-central Poland) and Kiev, but data on Ukrainian hoards is too fragmentary to offer full support to this hypothesis. The route of dirhams mirrored that of slaves, no doubt the main commodity exported by the Piasts. That captives changed hands multiple times on their way to the slave markets frequented by Muslim merchants is confirmed, *mutatis mutandis*, by the fate of an Irish saint, Findan, who,

[11] A catalogue of dirham imitations by Gert Rispling, Luke Treadwell, and myself is forthcoming.

[12] The admixture of a small quantity of Nordic coins in dirham hoards from Poland reinforces this view (I thank the anonymous reviewer for this comment).

after he had been kidnapped by a rival Irish clan and handed over to the Norsemen, was sold, 'as was their custom', four times before his owner decided to return to Scandinavia (Holder-Egger 1887, 503–4). Multiple transactions were thus probably the norm, and so too were transfers of captives between the main areas engaged in the slave trade.

A cluster of late ninth- and early tenth-century hoards from eastern Poland, the best known of which comes from Klukowicze (Jankowiak 2015, 47–50), seemingly contradicts this interpretation: although they were found deep inland and far from the main hoarding zones, they contain almost exclusively whole dirhams.[13] Being the oldest finds in Europe to contain Samanid dirhams, these hoards are the forerunners of the huge wave of Central Asian silver that would come to inundate the Baltic world in the first half of the tenth century. They have all the characteristics of consignments of silver brought directly from Central Asia: many coins are die-linked, they are mostly in a very good condition, and are remarkably tightly grouped chronologically. The appearance of these hoards unexpectedly far from the main river routes of eastern Europe can be explained by the dramatic change in the patterns of trade in the last quarter of the ninth century: upheaval both in the Abbasid Caliphate and in Rus' disrupted the old trade routes and temporarily shifted the flow of dirhams away from northern Russia (Jankowiak forthcoming). During this period of instability, silver appeared in areas where it had never been seen before. With time, however, routes were redirected to pass through an increasing number of intermediaries, which accounts for the increasing fragmentation of tenth-century dirhams.

Fragmentation in Relation to the Origin and Age of Coins

The argument that the degree of fragmentation of dirhams reflects the distance from the sources of Islamic silver—measured not in kilometres, but in the number of transactions in which a coin changed hands—gains additional support from the analysis of fragmentation in relation to the age of the coins. If the opposite reasoning was true, i.e. if coins were divided into smaller pieces in response to the intensity of monetary circulation within the area of hoarding, one would expect the older coins, which remained in circulation for a longer time, to be more fragmented than the more recent ones.

This was not the case. Data available for tenth-century hoards shows no significant relation between the size of dirham fragments and the age of the original coins, defined as the difference between the date of their minting and the *tpq* of the hoard to which they belonged, at least as long as the number of coins is significant (Fig. 1.4). The situation was no different in the ninth century, judging from the Spillings hoard. It appears that fragmented and whole dirhams have the

[13] The hoard from Viken (Hälsingland, Sweden, *tpq* 907/8) has similar characteristics to the Polish hoards.

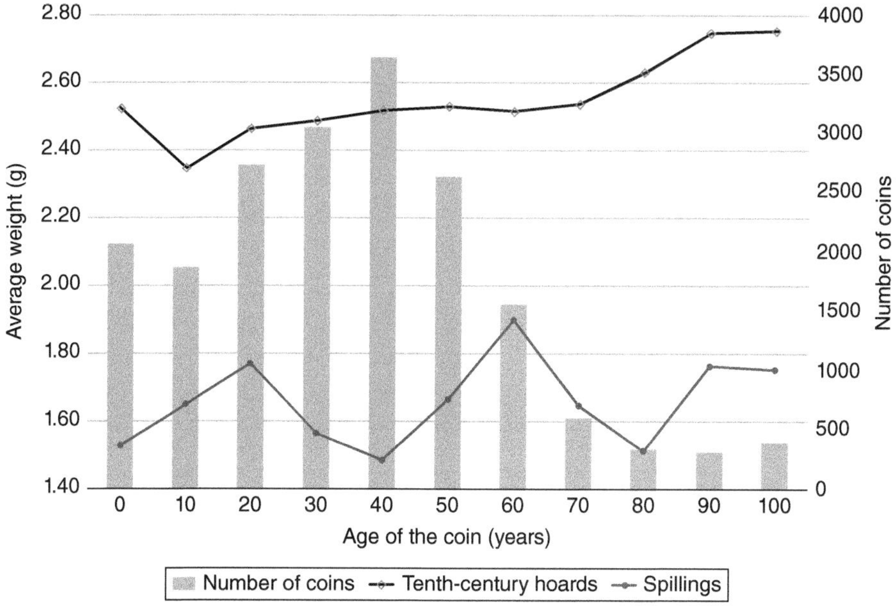

Fig. 1.4. Weight of an average dirham in relation to the age of the coin in tenth-century hoards (*tpq*s after AD 893) and in the Spillings hoard. The number of coins from tenth-century hoards for which the average has been calculated is represented by the bars.

Source: Gert Rispling's database.

same age profile, which suggests that coins of various ages circulated together and underwent division together. It is therefore hazardous to draw conclusions on the local circulation of silver from the size of the fragments, given that fragmentation occurred simultaneously for old and new coins.

Moreover, in the case of many hoards one gets the impression that the younger the coins, the more likely they were to be fragmented. In the hoard from Tjengvide, Gotland (*tpq* 954/5, 235 coins, CNS 1.1.8), for instance, the average weight of the thirty-seven coins struck in the fifteen years preceding the *tpq* is 2.30 g, while that of the older coins is 2.70 g.[14] The dirhams in the Ciechanów hoard (Mazovia, Poland, *tpq* 973, 82 whole dirhams and 3,769 fragments) are too fragmented to allow an analysis by year, but for the 431 coins on which the name of the Samanid emir can be read, the average weight clearly decreases with time, as illustrated in Table 1.1.

These examples, by no means isolated, disprove the view that fragmentation was related to the time during which a coin remained in circulation. They also contradict the connection between small fragments and low availability of silver: on the contrary, hoards such as Ciechanów suggest that the continuous inflow

[14] The fourteen imitations and the two lost coins are not included in the calculation.

Table 1.1. Average weight of the fragments of dirhams issued by successive Samanid emirs in the Ciechanów hoard.

Emir	Number of coins	Average weight (g)
Isma'il ibn Ahmad (892–907)	6	0.85
Ahmad ibn Isma'il (907–14)	5	1.24
Nasr ibn Ahmad (914–43)	127	0.97
Nuh ibn Nasr (943–54)	120	0.89
'Abd al-Malik ibn Nuh (954–61)	49	0.66
Mansur ibn Nuh (961–76)	124	0.67

Source: FMP 3.18.

Table 1.2. Size of the fragments of coins of various origins in the Ciechanów hoard.

Type of coin	Number of coins	Average weight (g)	Approximate weight of a whole coin (g)	Degree of fragmentation
Arabic	3,880	0.30	3.00	10%
Kreuzpfennige	11	0.22	0.80	28%
Half-bracteates	3	0.15	0.50	29%
Byzantine	11	0.83	2.60	32%
German	81	0.58	1.30	45%

Source: FMP 3.18.

of silver to Mazovia went hand in hand with the reduction of the size of fragments. It is easier to explain this phenomenon starting from the hypothesis that coins were divided as they were transiting between the successive trade centres. In this view, the decrease in the size of the fragments is indicative of the emergence of new intermediaries, keen to join the prosperous trade with the Islamic world. Indeed, an increasing compartmentalization of this trade system can be observed in the tenth century.

The final argument in favour of the interpretation of fragmentation as a proxy for the number of transactions separating the final owner of coins from their source is the different treatment of coins of various geographical origins in the same hoards. The observed pattern is that the more distant its origin, the more fragmented a coin is likely to be. To return to the Ciechanów hoard (Table 1.2), fragments of dirhams correspond to 10 per cent of their original size, while those of the Danish coins, the Kreuzpfennige, and the Byzantine coins are equivalent to roughly one-third of the whole coins; German issues of various cities of the Rhineland arrived at Ciechanów broadly speaking in halves. It is clear that coins of various origins were not adjusted to the same weight standard; to judge from the significant dispersion of their weights, neither were coins within the individual groups. It is difficult to see any logic behind the degree of their fragmentation other than geography or, to be more exact, the number of transactions that a given coin needed to reach its destination in northern Mazovia.

Why Were Dirhams Fragmented?

The above observations on the consistency of the average weight of dirham fragments in individual hoarding zones and the lack of unambiguous evidence for intense monetary circulation within them suggest that dirhams were divided when they moved between them, that is during transactions involving merchants from different zones. Various motives for the fragmentation of dirhams on their way from Bulgar westwards have been adduced, and more can be proposed. Pieces of coins may have been chipped off as taxes, such as those established by Olga of Kiev on the northern Russian rivers around 950 (Cross & Sherbowitz-Wetzor 1953, 81). The breaking or cutting of a coin may have served to authenticate its quality, in a way not dissimilar to that in which pecks, nicks, and notches are thought to have served a similar purpose in the ninth century. A study of how fragmentation relates to other methods of coin testing remains to be done, but one gets the impression that fragments do not bear too many marks of testing. Coins may also have been divided to remunerate multiple members of a group of merchants, as suggested by the dirham imitation from the Store Klintegårda hoard that was prepared for division into six fragments (Fig. 1.5): after all, the acquisition of the principal commodity that was traded for dirhams—slaves—required an organized effort.

But the relatively frequent occurrence of coins prepared for division and of two or more fragments of the same coin in the same hoard[15] perhaps speaks in

Fig. 1.5. A dirham imitation (Rispling S0756) from the Store Klintegårda hoard (Väskinde, Gotland, *tpq* 967/8) prepared for division into six fragments. GFC 9994:10.
Photo: Kenneth Jonsson.

[15] The following is a preliminary sample of such cases, mostly courtesy of Gert Rispling. Unless specified otherwise, two fragments of the same coin are meant: Bölske (six fragments of the same coin,

favour of motives that are usually labelled as 'ritual'. Symbolic annulment of the religious message of the dirhams might have been one, but it is perhaps more tempting to relate fragmentation to the authentication of transactions. The division of the coin not only allowed one to verify that it was not counterfeited, but perhaps also validated its transfer to a new owner (see Kilger 2006, 464, for a similar conclusion regarding the purpose of pecks).

Conclusions

The above analysis of the patterns of dirham fragmentation, although based on partial data, prompts several general observations. It appears, firstly, that there was a conscious selection of heavier dirhams by the Scandinavians, which speaks in favour of individual coin counting as the means of concluding transactions with the Muslim merchants. The decrease of fragmentation in the Swedish hoards in the course of the ninth century implies that there was no linear connection between the availability of silver and the way in which dirhams were treated. The variations in the average weight of dirham fragments in various hoarding zones are, in fact, difficult to correlate with any internal factors. The decreasing size of the fragments as dirhams moved away from Bulgar on the Volga rather suggests that fragmentation was a function of the distance from this main entry point of the dirhams into the Rus'–Scandinavian circuit. This interpretation is supported by the lack of relationship between fragmentation and the age of the coins, and by the strong connection between the place of the minting of the coin and the degree of its fragmentation in hoards containing silver of various geographical origins.

Taken together, these observations paint a picture of a system in which silver was above all a means of payment in transactions related to the long-distance trade in slaves and furs. The form in which it reached individual regions was to a large extent independent of local conditions. Silver was certainly used and exchanged locally—witness the 'productive sites' mentioned above—but local economies adapted to such forms of silver as were available (Kilger 2008, 298–321, offers an interpretation of the mechanisms of such adaptation). The main process of fragmentation, and its southern Rus' equivalent—clipping—resulted from commercial exchange between the main areas engaged in the long-distance trade, not within them.

This is no doubt the reason why fragmented coins all but disappear from the hoards in the early eleventh century, when the system of interlocking regional trade routes between the Baltic area and the market of Bulgar was replaced by

CNS 1.3.7.48); Bote III (KMK 102042); Hemängen (Bjärby) (CNS 1.3.34.13 and 14); Lunds II (three coins in two and one coin in three fragments, SHM 21734); Tjengvide (CNS 1.1.8.206 and 208, same coin according to Gert Rispling); Ytling (SHM 9533)—all from Gotland; Kleva, Västergötland (one coin in two and one coin in three fragments, SHM 4232); Wischendorf, Mecklenburg-Vorpommern (Štěpková 1962, coin 21). More certainly await identification.

more direct connections of the Scandinavians and the Slavs with the sources of silver in Germany and Anglo-Saxon England. The simplification of the patterns of trade was reflected in the simplification of the ways in which the means of payment were used. Rather than corresponding with a transition from a counted- to a weighed-silver economy, the episode of extreme fragmentation of dirhams in Central Europe resulted from external circumstances that disappeared with the collapse of trade with the Islamic world. But it remains to be seen to what extent these observations, based exclusively on the Islamic coins, can be supported by an analysis of other forms of silver hoarded in northern Europe in the Viking Age.

ACKNOWLEDGEMENTS

This chapter was written within the framework of the AHRC-funded project 'Dirhams for Slaves'. I am grateful to Luke Treadwell, Jacek Gruszczyński, Christoph Kilger, and the anonymous reviewer for their comments, to Mateusz Bogucki and Dorota Malarczyk for information on Polish hoards, to Kenneth Jonsson for granting me access to data on the Swedish hoards, and above all to Gert Rispling for putting at my disposal his database of coins from the Swedish finds. Needless to say, I am solely responsible for any misinterpretation of this data.

ABBREVIATIONS

CNS: Corpus Nummorum Saeculorum IX–XI qui in Suecia reperti sunt
FMP: *Frühmittelalterliche Münzfunde aus Polen: Inventar*
KMK: Kungliga Myntkabinettet, Stockholm
SHM: Statens Historiska Museet, Stockholm

REFERENCES

Bogucki, M. 2011. 'The Use of Money in the Slavic Lands from the 9th to the 11th Century—the Archaeological-Numismatic Evidence'. In *Silver Economies, Monetisation and Society in Scandinavia* AD *800–1100*, ed. J. Graham-Campbell, S.M. Sindbæk, & G. Williams, 133–51. Aarhus: Aarhus University Press.

Brather, S. 2007. 'Counted and Weighed Silver: The Fragmentation of Coins in Early Medieval East Central Europe'. In *Post-Roman Towns, Trade and Settlement in Europe and Byzantium*, ed. J. Henning, vol. 1: *The Heirs of the Roman West*, 451–71. Berlin: Walter de Gruyter.

Cross, S.H. & O.P. Sherbowitz-Wetzor 1953. *The Russian Primary Chronicle: Laurentian Text.* Cambridge, Mass.: Mediaeval Academy of America.

Darley-Doran, R.E. 2002. 'Wazn', *Encyclopedia of Islam.* New edition 11: 198–200.

Fomin, A.V. 1992. 'Novgorodskiie Klady Kuficheskikh Monet X v.'. *Numizmatika, Bonistika, Faleristika. Issledovaniia i Materialy. Numizmaticheskii Sbornik* 9: 32–44.

Fomin, A.V. & L. Kovács 1987. *The Tenth Century Máramaros County ('Huszt') Dirham Hoard*. Budapest: Magyar numizmatikai tàrsulat.

Friedland, S.N. & W. Hollstein 2008. 'Der Schatz im Acker—Ein Hacksilberfund des 11. Jahrhunderts aus Cortnitz, Stadt Weissenberg (Lkr. Bautzen)'. *Arbeits- und Forschungsberichte zur Sächsischen Bodendenkmalpflege* 50: 211–29.

Gomzin, A.A. 2011. 'Fragmentatsia Kuficheskikh Monet (Rezultaty Issledovaniia Materialov Srednego i Nizhnego Pooch'ia)'. *Rossiiskaia Arkheologiia* 4/2011: 64–76.

Hårdh, B. 1996. *Silver in the Viking Age: A Regional-Economic Study*. Stockholm: Almqvist & Wiksell International.

Holder-Egger, O. 1887. *Vita Findani*. In *Monumenta Germaniae Historica Scriptores* 15.1: 502–6. Hannover.

Ilisch, L. 1990. 'Whole and Fragmented Dirhams in Near Eastern Hoards'. In *Sigtuna Papers: Proceedings of the Sigtuna Symposium on Viking-Age Coinage 1–4 June 1989*, ed. K. Jonsson & B. Malmer, 121–8. London: Spink.

Ilisch, L., S. Lorenz, W. Stern, & H. Steuer (eds) 2003. *Dirham und Rappenpfennig. Mittelalterliche Münzprägung in Bergbauregionen*, Zeitschrift für Archäologie des Mittelalters, Beiheft 17. Bonn: Dr. Rudolf Habelt.

Jankowiak, M. 2015. 'Wer Brachte im 10. Jahrhundert die Dirhems in die Polnischen Gebiete und Warum?' In *Fernhändler, Dynasten, Kleriker. Die Piastische Herrschaft in Kontinentalen Beziehungsgeflechten vom 10. bis zum Frühen 13. Jahrhundert*, ed. D. Adamczyk & N. Kersken, 41–54. Wiesbaden: Wiesbaden Harrassowitz Verlag.

Jankowiak, M. forthcoming. 'The Flows of Dirhams to North-eastern Europe and the Rhythms of the Slave Trade with the Islamic World'. In *Viking-Age Trade: Silver, Slaves and Gotland*, ed. J. Gruszczynski, M. Jankowiak, & J. Shepard. London: Routledge.

Kara, M. 2009. *Najstarsze Państwo Piastów—Rezultat Przełomu czy Kontynuacji? Studium Archeologiczne*. Poznań: Instytut Archeologii i Etnologii Polskiej Akademii Nauk.

Kiersnowski, R. 1961. 'Coin Finds and the Problem of Money Hoarding in Early Medieval Poland'. *Wiadomości Numizmatyczne* 5: 35–56.

Kilger, C. 2006. 'Silver Handling Traditions During the Viking Age: Some Observations and Thoughts on the Phenomenon of Pecking and Bending'. In *Coinage and History in the North Sea World: c. AD 500–1250: Essays in Honour of Marion Archibald*, ed. B. Cook & G. Williams, 449–66. Leiden: Brill.

Kilger, C. 2008. 'Wholeness and Holiness: Counting, Weighing and Valuing Silver in the Early Viking Period'. In *Means of Exchange: Dealing with Silver in the Viking Age*, ed. D. Skre, Kaupang Excavation Project Publication Series, Volume 2, 253–325. Aarhus: Aarhus University Press.

Kmietowicz, A. 1994. 'Wczesnośredniowieczny Skarb Srebrny Dzierznica II. Uwagi o Historii Znaleziska i Jego Części Orientalnej'. *Wiadomości Numizmatyczne* 38: 161–7.

Komar, A. & N. Khamaiko 2011. 'Zbruchskii idol: Pamiatnik Epokhi Romantizma?' *Ruthenica* 10: 166–217.

Lebedev, V.P. in prep. 'Dirham Circulation in the Land of Severiane in the Tenth Century'.

Leimus, I. 2007. *Sylloge of Islamic Coins. Estonian Public Collections*. Thesaurus Historiae 2. Tallinn: Estonian History Museum.

Miles, G.C. 1960. 'A Ninth Century Hoard of Dirhams Found at Susa'. *Mémoires de la Mission Archéologique en Iran* 37: 67–145.

Novák, V. 2010. *The Kelč Hoard Revised: Fragments of Islamic Silver Coins*. Monumenta Numismatica 1. Prague: Institute of Philosophy of the Academy of Sciences of the Czech Republic.

Östergren, M. 2009. 'Spillings—the Largest Viking Age Silver Hoard in the World'. In *The Spillings Hoard—Gotland's Role in Viking Age World Trade*, ed. A.-M. Pettersson, 11–40. Visby: Gotlands Museum.

Petrov, P.N. (ed.) 2014. *Bezliudovskii Klad X v.: Materialy i Issledovaniia*. Kazan': Institut istorii im. Sh. Mardzhani Akademii Nauk Tatarstana.

Rebstock, U. 2008. 'Weights and Measures in Islam'. In *Encyclopaedia of the History of Science, Technology and Medicine in Non-Western Cultures*, ed. H. Selin, 2255–67. Berlin: Springer.

Štěpková, J. 1962. 'The Islamic Silver Coin-Hoard from Wischendorf (Wismar)'. *Annals of the Náprstek Museum* 1: 131–58.

Steuer, H., W.B. Stern, & G. Goldenberg. 2002. 'Der Wechsel von der Münzgeld- zur Gewichtsgeldwirtschaft in Haithabu um 900 und die Herkunft des Münzsilbers im 9. und 10. Jahrhundert'. In *Haithabu und die Frühe Stadtentwicklung im Nördlichen Europa*, ed. K. Brandt, M. Müller-Wille, & C. Radtke, 133–67. Neumünster: Wachholtz.

Suchodolski, S. 1971. 'Die Anfänge der Münzprägung in Skandinavien und Polen'. *Nordisk Numismatisk Årsskrift* (1971): 20–36.

Treadwell, L. 2001. 'Notes on the Mint at Samarra'. In *A Medieval Islamic City Reconsidered: An Interdisciplinary Approach to Samarra*, ed. C.F. Robinson, 141–56. Oxford: Oxford University Press.

2

As Long as it Glitters

A Re-evaluation of the Mixed Silver Hoards of Bornholm, Denmark

Gitte Tarnow Ingvardson

In Scandinavia and the Baltic countries, so-called 'mixed hoards' with both minted and non-minted silver were a common feature throughout the Viking Age. During the late Viking Age and the early Middle Ages, mixed hoards were succeeded by pure coin hoards. In southern Sweden, the portion of non-minted silver in the hoards diminishes from around 1025, whereas the hoards on Gotland contain both minted and non-minted silver throughout the eleventh century (Hårdh 1976, 130). In both present-day Denmark (except Bornholm) and in Poland, the economic changes took place in the second half of the eleventh century (Bogucki 2011, 137; Ingvardson 2010, 34), whereas on Bornholm, mixed hoards were deposited well into the twelth century (Grinder-Hansen et al. 2013, 149–51). The presence of mixed hoards is often interpreted as signifying a (somewhat primitive) metal-weight or bullion economy, within which coins, ingots, jewellery, and scrap silver were traded and treated equally as a means of payment.[1] Yet careful analysis of the composition and depositional context of six silver hoards from Bornholm reveals that mixed hoards could function in more diverse ways, and could occupy different economic spheres.

The Viking Age hoards from Scandinavia and the Baltic countries have previously been analysed with special focus on the non-minted silver (Hårdh 1976; 1996). According to Birgitta Hårdh, the weight and fragmentation of non-minted silver, together with the percentage of coins in relation to non-minted silver, can be used to reveal the role of silver, broadly defined: while complete objects primarily functioned as a means of display, highly fragmented silver principally served as low-value payment, paving the way for the introduction of

[1] This is, for example, the underlying thesis in many of the articles published in Graham-Campbell & Williams (2007).

coined currency by the eleventh century. In this chapter, a more individual approach to the hoards is applied. It is argued that the hoards reflect the people who collected and deposited them. The chapter will demonstrate that the composition of non-minted silver (both complete and fragmented) and coins within a hoard, together with the archaeological context, reflect the functions and, to some extent, the owners of the hoards. The raw material for the silversmith has a different composition and archaeological setting than the fortune of a merchant, the loot of a raider, or the female ritual deposit.

Compositions and Contexts

To comprehend the nature of the mixed hoards on Bornholm, we need to recognize the individuals that collected and deposited them. The silver hoards of Bornholm should not be seen as a uniform phenomenon, but as mirrors reflecting individual life stories. A way to unfold these biographies is to focus on the context of the hoards. Greatly inspired by the work of Fleur Kemmers and Nanouschka Myrberg, the hoard analysis is here divided into three contextual stages (Myrberg 2007, 157–9; Kemmers & Myrberg 2011, 89–95).

- The primary context—production time and production place. The analysis of when and where the objects in the hoard were produced paints a picture of the internal chronology of the hoard and its period of assembly. Was the hoard collected over a short or long period of time? Were the objects collected in one or several areas? Were the objects produced locally or imported?
- The secondary context—traces of use. The analysis of secondary features such as fragmentation, metal testing, and reworking reflects how the objects were used in the Viking Age. Fragmentation may reflect weight systems current in different regions (Hårdh 1996, 94–130) and patterns of test marks reflect circulation patterns (Ingvardson 2015, 131–3 with references). Secondary treatment can also illustrate a functional transformation. The piercing and looping of coins may indicate that the coins were used as jewellery and thereby removed from the economic sphere; conversely, cut-up jewellery was removed from the personal sphere and entered the economic sphere as hack-silver payments or raw material.
- The tertiary context—circumstances of the deposition. This stage of analysis gives an insight into the owner of the hoard, and the circumstances that led to its deposition. What is the nature of the site? Is it a manor, a craft site, or a plain agrarian settlement? Is the hoard deposited in one or several containers? Which other archaeological remains are present in the surrounding area?

Kemmers and Myrberg connect this approach to the study of coins, but the methodical approach is valid for any archaeological object as demonstrated in the analysis of the largest Viking Age hoard of Bornholm, the Nørremølle hoard (Ingvardson 2012). The interpretation of these different stages of context is determined by the narrative context, which could be described as the sum of our cultural and historical knowledge. How does the evidence of the hoards relate to our knowledge of Viking Age life on Bornholm?

The identification of objects in this chapter is based on preliminary surveys, and future research might revise the classifications of some coins and non-minted items. I have divided the minted silver into the major coin groups represented on Viking Age Bornholm: Kufic dirhams and German, English, and Scandinavian pennies. The last group, others/no ID, covers coins minted in, for example, Ireland, Byzantium, and Poland, as well as currently unidentified coins.

The non-minted silver in the hoards consists of different kinds of jewellery (arm-, neck-, ear-, temple-, and finger-rings as well as different forms of pendants), ingots, melts and other forms of silver, whose original function and form is not always detectable. The function of an object at the time of deposition may, to some extent, be reflected in its degree of fragmentation: a complete neck-ring may have been regarded as jewellery, for instance, whereas a fragmented neck-ring may have been regarded as payment. However, in this chapter it is suggested that not all kinds of fragmented, or hack-, silver hold the same qualities and that not all fragmented silver objects necessarily had the same function. A fragmented silver-foil bead was perhaps not preferred as raw material for the silversmith, who instead preferred a fragment of an ingot or a melt. A complete neck-ring, which might be expected to have functioned as jewellery, may also have functioned as payment, raw material, or/and as a ritual mediator at the time of deposition. Interpretation depends on context, regarding both the composition of a hoard and its archaeological setting.

A differentiated approach to the non-minted silver, including the fragments, brings us a step closer to understanding the people who collected and deposited the hoards. It is assumed that the silver objects functioned as one or more of the following purposes: means of payment, personal ornaments, raw material, and/or ritual mediator. In this light, the non-minted silver is divided into jewellery, ingots, and scrap silver. This categorization is not straightforward. As the aim of this study is to investigate the potential of a differentiated approach to the non-minted silver, including the fragments, it is necessary to primarily distinguish non-minted silver according to form. Fragments of identifiable jewellery are therefore included in the category of jewellery, and fragments of identifiable types of ingots are included in the category of ingot, whereas non-identifiable silver fragments such as wires, rods, and silver foil, as well as melts/lumps and drops are included in the scrap silver category. A certain group of melts is of special interest. Hårdh describes them as 'more or less round cakes of silver with a flat and coarse underside and a domed, shiny upper side' (2013, 529). She suggests that these melts should perhaps be seen as a primitive form of ingots produced in the West Slavic area and in the south-easternmost parts of Scandinavia (Hårdh 1976, 90 ff.; 2013, 530), hereafter melts of Slavic/Scandinavian type. Furthermore, Hårdh has suggested that these melt types show a different distribution pattern to irregular lumps, thus indicating a function as means of payment stored in hoards, whereas irregular lumps should be seen as workshop material (2011, 284–5). To investigate this question further, melts of Slavic/Scandinavian type are separated as a category. As complete jewellery may reflect a different function to that of fragmented jewellery, in the same way that a complete coin may reflect a different function to that of a fragmented coin, the presence of complete versus fragmented objects in the hoards is also considered.

The evidence of the hoards is interpreted in the light of their archaeological setting (the tertiary context). Bornholm Museum has undertaken archaeological excavations on thirty-six hoard sites (Ingvardson & Nielsen 2015, 27) (Fig. 2.1). Most excavations have provided data on the circumstances of deposition, either because a part of the hoard was found in situ or because a clear silver cluster was present. However small, these excavations offer detailed data on the circumstances of deposition and thereby provide an extra dimension in the interpretation of the hoards. The excavations sometimes give a picture of which structures the hoards are deposited in, and occasionally also provide evidence of the general structure of the sites. Preliminary analysis of the sites indicates that the deposition place of the hoards can be divided into three main categories (Ingvardson & Nielsen 2015, table 1):

1. Hoards deposited in the central part of a settlement area—often in a house.
2. Hoards deposited on the outskirts of a settlement area, perhaps in areas with production activity.
3. Hoards deposited in an area without other prehistoric remains.

This chapter presents a case study of six hoards. It asks if hoards within different categories display different compositional characteristics and reflect different depositional behaviour. It further aims to clarify if these elements reflect the function of the hoards. Before initiating the case study, the narrative context of the hoards is presented. The setting includes a short presentation of the general trends of the Viking Age hoards on Bornholm, a discussion of the nature and influence of metal-detector archaeology, as well as an outline of the trade and settlement structure of the island.

Viking Age Hoards and Detector Archaeology on Bornholm

Detector archaeology is widespread on Bornholm, and metal-detectorists regularly find Viking Age silver objects (Horsnæs et al. 2013, 7–8). The intensity of detector archaeology is clearly illustrated by the fact that more than 8,450 Viking Age coins have been registered since 1989 on an island that covers 589.16 km^2. In 1989 Bornholm Museum began a close cooperation with the private metal-detectorists in order to qualify the information of the hoards presented in G. Galster's 1980 catalogue of Viking Age coins from Bornholm

(Galster 1980). The campaign had two main focuses. First, to rescue what might remain of the hoards, and second, to locate the exact place of deposition of the hoards in Galster's publication. Archive analysis and detector surveys have enabled Bornholm Museum to review Galster's catalogue. At present, twenty-three of the thirty-one hoards in Galster's catalogue have been relocated, and new surveys have added more finds to the hoards (Ingvardson & Nielsen 2015, 27). One or two new Viking Age hoards are found every year on Bornholm. What often starts out to be a few single finds on a field found by metal-detecting often turns out to be a disturbed hoard scattered in the plough-soil. Based upon

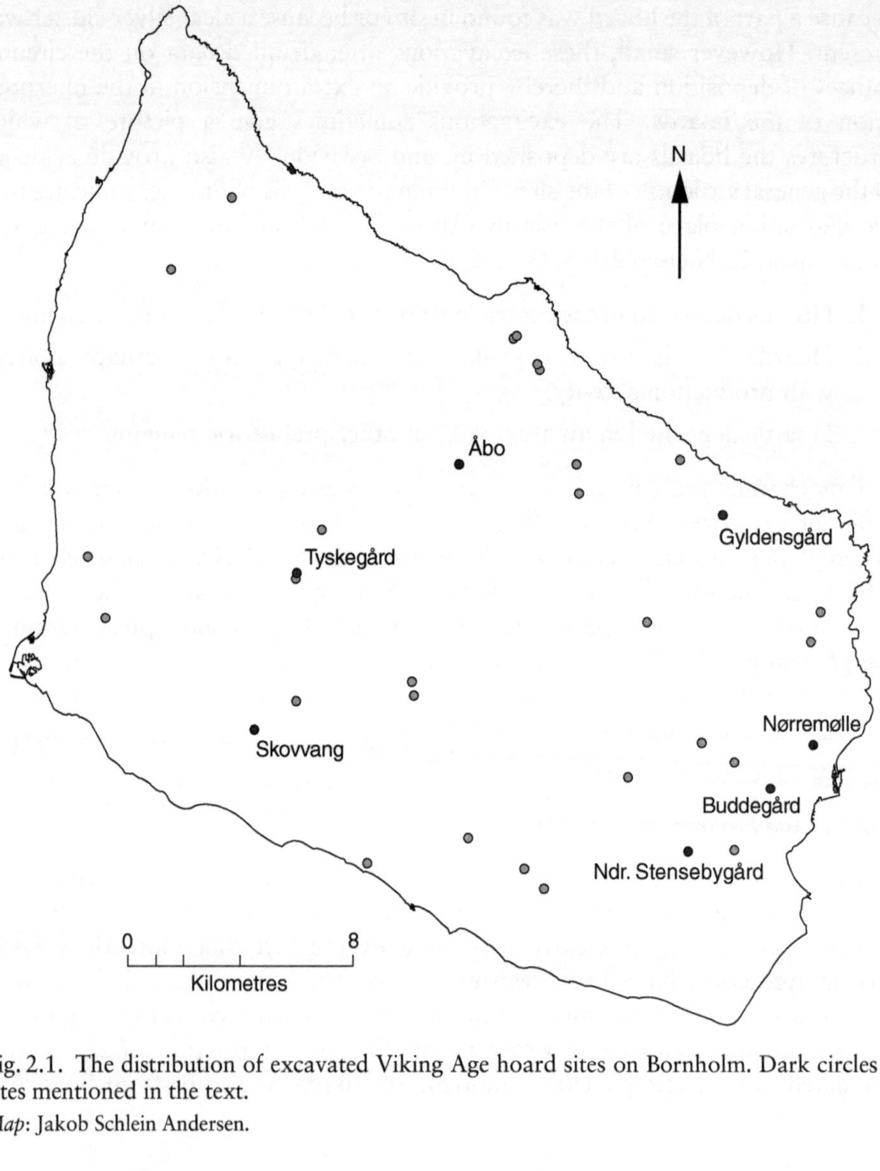

Fig. 2.1. The distribution of excavated Viking Age hoard sites on Bornholm. Dark circles = sites mentioned in the text.
Map: Jakob Schlein Andersen.

current experience, a concentration of five silver objects or more within an area of 15 × 15 m strongly indicates a disturbed hoard. Bornholm Museum seeks to undertake a small archaeological rescue excavation when a detectorist finds a concentration of silver objects. To date, thirty-six such excavations have been accomplished (Fig. 2.1). Forty-six locations await further investigation.

Background: Hoards, Trade, and Settlement Structure on Bornholm

As the Viking Age hoards of Bornholm constitute a fast-growing and dynamic archaeological find group it is difficult to give a complete and up-to-date picture of the body of hoards. Figure 2.2 gives an overview of the composition of Viking Age hoards on Bornholm. The oldest such hoard, the Skovsholm hoard with a *tpq* of 855, is the only hoard on Bornholm dominated by Kufic dirhams minted under the Abbasid dynasty (Horsnæs 2014, 65; Laursen & Ingvardson 2014). The remaining part of Kufic dirham hoards are dominated by Samanid coins and are deposited in the second half of the tenth century. At the turn of the eleventh century the dominant role of the Kufic dirhams in the Viking Age hoards of Bornholm fades in favour of western European coins. The hoards in the first half of the eleventh century are generally large, and characterized by English and especially German coins with a small influx of Scandinavian and Kufic coins. From the second half of the eleventh century, the hoards are normally small. They are dominated by German and English coins and some Scandinavian coins, whereas Kufic dirhams are very scarce (Horsnæs et al. 2013, 17–22; Ingvardson 2012, 293; Laursen & Ingvardson 2014). The presence of other silver objects such as wires, rods, melt/lumps, ingots, silver foil, and jewellery in many of the hoards well into the twelfth century suggests that other kinds of silver objects continued to play a role in the economic system of Bornholm.

Several factors point towards an evident reorganization of trade and settlement in tenth-century Bornholm. In the Migration period and in the early Viking Age, trade and power were concentrated in a few centres, Sorte Muld being the most important (Ingvardson 2014, 329–30; Nielsen 1994a, 125–9). After its heyday from the fourth to the seventh centuries, the dominance of the Sorte Muld complex fades. The find distribution demonstrates that the settlement area at Sorte Muld is limited to a few smaller areas in the ninth century; in the tenth and the early eleventh centuries, the site was reduced to a few individual farmsteads (Aarsleff 2009, 119; Watt 2009, 26–7). No new trading centre has yet been established on the island, but this does not mean an absence of trade-related finds. From the end of the tenth century a new settlement structure of individual farmsteads appears. The farmsteads are primarily recorded through reconnaissance and metal-detector surveys, and are characterized by finds of Baltic Sea ware, fragments of imported millstones from Central Europe, whetstone from south Norway, weights and coins (Aarsleff 2008, 21–2; Nielsen 1994a, 125–9). Settlement sites from the transitional period between the decline of the Sorte Muld complex and the rise of the new settlement structure are very scarce.

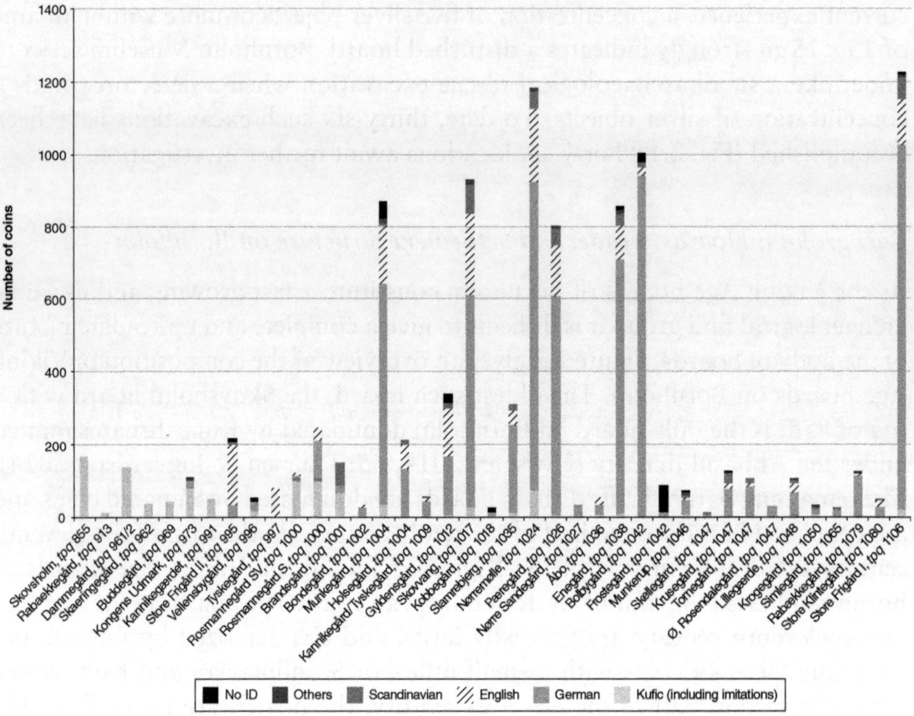

Fig. 2.2. The coin composition of Viking Age hoards on Bornholm. Data based on von Heijne 2004, updated with new finds provided by Helle Horsnæs (Ingvardson 2012, fig. 15) and the author.

The only known Viking Age hoard from the ninth century is the Skovsholm hoard (Fig. 2.2). Skovsholm contains around 170 coins minted AD 611–855 and is dominated by Abbasid dirhams. Most of the coins are fragmented in approximately halves or quarters; only twenty-two coins are complete (Horsnæs 2014, 65; Laursen & Ingvardson 2014; Ingvardson & Nielsen 2015, 29–30). The Skovsholm site is strategically well placed by the Skovsholm stream about 1.5 km southeast of Sorte Muld on a plateau tapering towards the east coast of Bornholm. The outlet of the Skovsholm stream into the Baltic Sea is flanked by two natural harbours with access to fresh water sources from natural springs. Small archaeological excavations by Bornholm Museum in 2013 and 2015 revealed that the hoard was likely deposited near a natural spring. However, the original place of deposition of the hoard was disturbed by the dismantling of a well in the area, and the coins were spread in the plough-soil in an area of approximately 30 × 15 m. Settlement remains were recorded in the area around the hoard, but the excavations did not give a clear view of the site structure. The strategic location, the proximity to the Sorte Muld complex, and the unusually early dating of the hoard imply that Skovsholm may be a key site to understand the radical changes that took place on Bornholm in the late Viking Age.

However, the function of the Skovsholm site is still unclear. Was Skovsholm an outpost of the shrinking Sorte Muld complex or was it part of a new power elite structure on Bornholm?

The presence of imports, weights, and coins on the new decentralized settlements can be seen as strong markers for trade, and it is therefore likely that these settlements played an important role in the organization of trade on Bornholm in the late Viking Age (Ingvardson 2014, 329–36). A decentralized trade structure is underlined by the distribution pattern of weight types on Bornholm. According to analyses made by I. Gustin and H. Steuer, polyhedral (cubo-octahedral) weights and spherical weights with flattened poles are primarily connected to Viking Age trade activity, and signal a development towards a standardization of trade using hack-silver as currency, whereas other weight types, as for example spherical, cylindrical, segment shaped, quadrilateral, and conical/biconical lead weights, dominate in areas with craft activity (although see Pedersen 2008 for a different view) (Gustin 2004; Steuer 1987). On Bornholm, polyhedral weights and spherical weights with flattened poles are dispersed on many sites with a few weights per site, whereas other weight types, although widespread, are especially numerous at Iron Age productive sites, including Sorte Muld. The distribution implies that sites with many weights are a pre-Viking Age phenomenon on Bornholm, whereas Viking Age sites only produce a few weights per site (Ingvardson 2014, 330–2). This scattered distribution thus seems to support the theory of a decentralized organization of trade in Viking Age Bornholm.

The hoards of Bornholm show a different structure to hoards from other regions in Denmark (von Heijne 2004, 155–67). This calls into question whether Bornholm belonged to the Danish kingdom in the late Viking Age, and suggests that the island functioned as an independent economic and perhaps also political unit (Ingvardson 2014, 334–6). Not only does non-minted silver continue in use well into the twelfth century, but the coin compositions in the hoards of Bornholm also display a contrasting economic situation compared to the more central parts of Denmark, as Zealand, Scania, Funen, and some parts of Jutland. During the eleventh century, the hoards in these central parts of Denmark change from a dominance of foreign coins to a dominance of Danish coins, and later to a dominance of national domestic coins (Grinder-Hansen 1994, 106; Ingvardson 2010, 27; Jensen 2006, 161 ff.). On Bornholm, by contrast, foreign coins continue to dominate the hoards throughout the eleventh century (Fig. 2.2).

If Bornholm functioned as an independent economic and perhaps also political unit, it is likely that the influx of silver to Bornholm was connected to individual initiatives and that the variation in the composition of the hoards signals an unregulated economy, beyond the control of a central power. This theory is supported by the signs of a decentralized trade system, the absence of a new powerful trading centre after the importance of Sorte Muld was diminished in the tenth/eleventh century, and the fact that many of the eleventh-century hoards were deposited on what appear to be more or less ordinary settlement sites (Ingvardson 2012, 305–9).

Six Hoards, Six Life Histories

In the following six case studies of hoard sites I interpret the combined evidence of coins and non-minted silver contained within the hoards in relation to other archaeological finds and features at the hoard sites. All the hoards belong to the late Viking Age—the late tenth or eleventh century—and were selected because they display a notable variation in the composition of minted and non-minted silver as well as variation in the circumstances of deposition.[2] The case studies include two hoards interpreted as deposits in the central part of a settlement area (category 1): Gyldensgård and Nørremølle; two hoards interpreted as deposits in the outskirts of a settlement area (category 2): Nordre (Ndr.) Stensebygård and Åbo; and two hoards interpreted as deposits in areas without other archaeological indicators (category 3): Buddegård and Tyskegård.[3]

Category 1: Hoards Deposited in the Central Part of a Settlement

Gyldensgård, north-east Bornholm, hoard deposited after c.*1010*

The Gyldensgård hoard was located by metal-detector surveys in February 2002. Part of the silver objects were preserved in situ and surrounded by a black organic material, interpreted by the excavator as the dissolved remains of a purse. In order to rescue the remains, Bornholm Museum initiated a small excavation (255 m^2).[4] This revealed that the hoard was deposited in the northern part of a three-aisled house, 0.70 m from a roof-bearing post. The house was 6.15 m wide. Due to limited funding the house was only partly unearthed and the length was not established. A contemporary ditch was excavated only a few metres north of the house. The ditch formed an excellent environment for preservation of organic material, and a very large amount of fish bones was recovered. The absence of otoliths (found in the inner ear) among the bone material implies that the fish were brought to the site without heads. The ditch also contained iron needles and nails, hammer scales, Baltic Sea ware

[2] The six hoards presented in the case study are part of an ongoing PhD project, which includes all excavated Viking Age hoards on Bornholm. When finalizing the project, the chronological aspects of the hoarding practice on the island will of course be discussed. However, this aspect is not the focus of the present chapter.

[3] The presentation of sites is based on small archaeological excavations and field surveys (both with and without metal detectors). Field surveys exclusively produce archaeological finds from the plough-soil, which have been removed from their original archaeological context, often as a result of agricultural activities. While this factor, together with the small size of the excavated areas, makes it difficult to offer detailed interpretations of the structure and activity of the sites, the finds do reflect past activity at the site. Of course, future excavations and surveys might alter the present picture.

[4] The excavations presented in this chapter were funded by the Danish Agency for Culture unless stated otherwise.

pottery, loom weights, and a silver coin. The large number of loom weights (thirty-one fragments) is notable: they were found not only in the ditch but also in connection to the house (Thorsen 2003). The hoard is interpreted here as being deposited in a house on the central part of a settlement area, although the large number of loom weights does suggest craft activity.

Silver objects (147): 140 coins and 7 pieces of non-minted silver were found in situ. A total of 340 coins (375.9 g), consisting of 5 Kufic dirhams, 165 German, 130 English, 14 Scandinavian, and 26 others/no ID pennies, as well as 3 pieces of jewellery, 6 ingots, 1 Slavic/Scandinavian melt, and 15 pieces of scrap silver (non-minted silver in total: 58.7 g) are at present attributed to the hoard, although a widespread distribution pattern indicates that some objects may belong to other depositions (Fig. 2.3). A detailed analysis of the chronological sequence of the hoard has not yet been established, and around fifty coins are still not identified in detail. The oldest coin so far identified is a Samanid dirham minted in 937/8; the youngest is a Konrad II penny minted 1027–39. Preliminary surveys show a marked concentration of coins minted in the last three decades of the tenth century and the first decade of the eleventh century. With the widespread

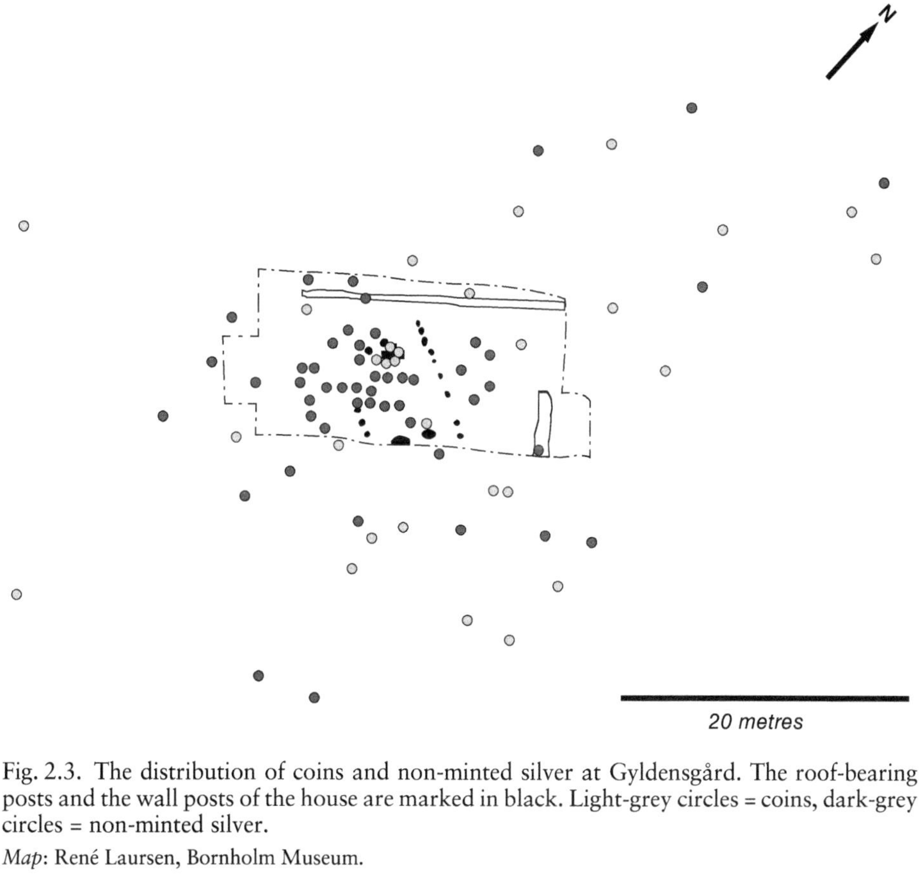

Fig. 2.3. The distribution of coins and non-minted silver at Gyldensgård. The roof-bearing posts and the wall posts of the house are marked in black. Light-grey circles = coins, dark-grey circles = non-minted silver.

Map: René Laursen, Bornholm Museum.

distribution in mind, it is therefore possible that the Konrad II penny does not belong to the hoard. Time of deposition is therefore estimated to be shortly after *c.*1010. All ingots and the Slavic/Scandinavian melt are fragmented, one piece of jewellery is a complete foil bead (perhaps originally part of a larger jewellery assemblage), and the two remaining pieces are fragmented. Three out of six melt/lumps are fragmented, while the majority of the coins (71 per cent) are complete (Fig. 2.4).[5] A total of 308 coins (91 per cent) bear test marks and/or are bent, and 13 out of the 25 pieces of non-minted silver objects are bent and/or often heavily test marked. Individual items of non-minted silver weigh between 0.5–6.1 g, with an average weight of 2.35 g.

Nørremølle, east Bornholm, hoard deposited after 1024

The Nørremølle hoard was located by metal detector in 2006. Part of the hoard was preserved in situ in the lower part of a ceramic vessel of Baltic Sea ware. In 2007 Bornholm Museum initiated a small excavation (425 m^2), which revealed

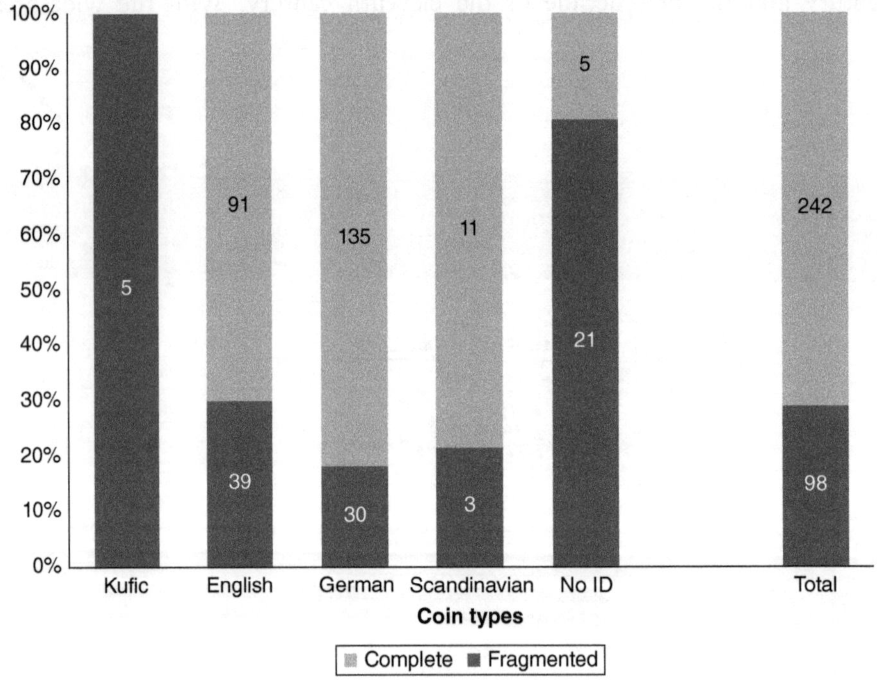

Fig. 2.4. The distribution of fragmented and complete coins in the Gyldensgård hoard.

[5] T.B. Christensen and M.E. Christensen kindly allowed me access to unpublished material produced in connection with their Bachelor projects from 2009: *En analyse og diskussion af Gyldengårdsskattens nedlæggelse og kontekst* and *En bearbejdning og analyse af det numismatiske materiale*, Copenhagen University.

that the hoard was deposited near a large stone. Settlement remains such as trenches, pits, and postholes were found near the deposition. A pair of roof-bearing posts just a few metres north of the deposition contained Baltic Sea ware, sherds of a soapstone vessel, a miniature vessel, a fragmented amber bead, and some fragmented iron items. The objects date to the late Viking Age, and the house may be contemporary with the hoard. The postholes were filled with charcoal and large amounts of fragments of burnt wattle-and-daub and charred grains. It is therefore likely that the house was burnt. The dimensions of the house cannot be established as it was not fully excavated. The material culture of the site indicates an agrarian settlement with Baltic Sea ware, bones from domesticated animals, a small amount of slag, fragments of wattle-and-daub, and a single loom weight. Besides sherds of a soapstone vessel and the miniature vessel, the only extraordinary finds are an iron arrowhead found in the top of a posthole and a small pit with a large amount of animal bones (Ingvardson 2012). The Nørremølle hoard is interpreted as being deposited in the central part of a settlement area, just outside a dwelling house (category 1).

Nørremølle is the largest Viking Age hoard on Bornholm with a total of 1,194 coins (1388.83 g), divided into 72 Kufic dirhams, 846 German, 204 English, 45 Scandinavian, and 27 others/no ID pennies, as well as 38 Slavic/ Scandinavian melts (130.14 g), 9 ingots (108.88 g) and 40 pieces of scrap silver (90.43 g) (Ingvardson 2012). The chronology of the hoard is broad, as the oldest coin in the hoard is from the Umayyad dynasty minted 661–750, while the youngest is a Lüneburg penny minted 1024–45 by Duke Bernhard II. However, the majority of the coins cluster in the decades around 1020, and 65 per cent of all coins are minted after 980.

Like Nørremølle, the hoards of south Scandinavia are dominated by Otto-Adelheid pennies, though with a relatively high proportion of English and Scandinavian coins. In hoards deposited in the Slavic area, the Otto-Adelheid penny is succeeded by the Saxon penny (*Randpfennig*) as the dominant coin type around 1020, and there are very few English and Scandinavian coins in the Polish hoards (von Heijne 2004, 23; Kilger 2000, 127; Kluge 1981). The coin composition in the Nørremølle hoard thereby indicates an influx of coins from Scania and Zealand. By contrast, the jewellery shows strong contact with the Slavic area, where the majority of the items was produced.[6] The melts of Slavic/ Scandinavian type are characteristic for the hoards from Poland, Bornholm, and Eastern Sweden (Hårdh 2011, 289). Thus, the analysis of the primary context shows a surprisingly clear-cut division between coins and jewellery, demonstrating a coin influx from Scania and Zealand, and a jewellery influx from the Slavic area (Ingvardson 2012, 289–94).

[6] Slavic jewellery is a common element in the late Viking Age Bornholm hoards, especially on the southern parts of the Island, see Czonstke 2011.

Only 2 of the 170 pieces of jewellery are complete: an earring/temple ring produced in the West Slavic area and an earring/temple ring produced in the area covering present-day Hungary, Serbia, and Romania. Among the jewellery are two beads that have most likely been part of identical earrings/temple rings (Fig. 2.5). This indicates that identical earrings/temple rings had been fragmented—perhaps by the owner of the hoard—and suggests that the two complete earrings/temple rings were not saved as jewellery but as raw silver. Seven out of nine ingots and all thirty-eight melts of Slavic/Scandinavian type are more or less fragmented, whereas the majority of the coins (78 per cent) are complete (Fig. 2.6). Ninety-seven per cent of the objects in the Nørremølle hoard (both coins and non-minted silver) are tested either by bending and/or by test marks (Ingvardson 2012, 296–7). The average weight of objects in the Nørremølle hoard is 1.3 g. The majority (93.5 per cent) of the objects—including the coins—weigh less than two grams; 35.5 per cent less than one gram. Among the non-minted silver items, 74 per cent weigh less than two grams and 50 per cent less than one gram (Ingvardson 2012, 297–9).

Category 2: Hoards Deposited on the Outskirts of a Settlement

Åbo, central Bornholm, hoard deposited after 1036

Eight coins and two Slavic/Scandinavian melts found within a 12 × 12 m area of a field in 2010 were the first signs of the Åbo hoard. During a small rescue excavation in 2013–14, part of the hoard was found in situ within the posthole of a roof-bearing post of a house. In order to ascertain the size of the house,

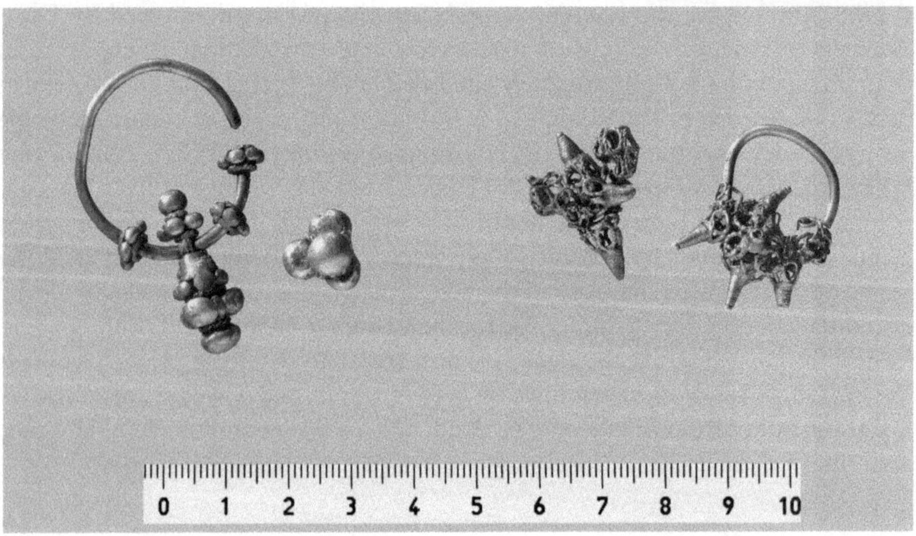

Fig. 2.5. Two complete earrings/temple rings together with beads from the Nørremølle hoard. *Photo*: John Lee, the National Museum of Denmark.

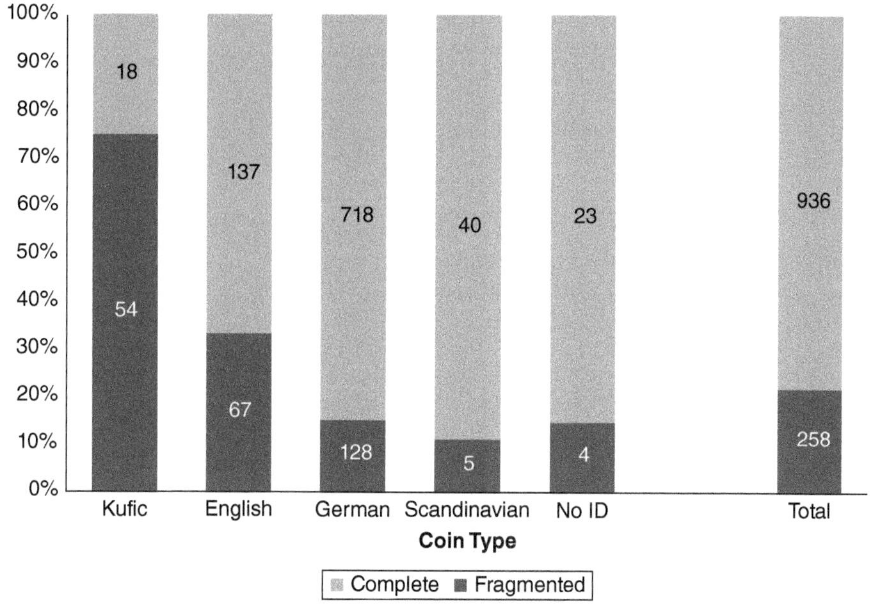

Fig. 2.6. The distribution of fragmented and complete coins in the Nørremølle hoard.

Bornholm Museum continued the excavation in 2014 and uncovered a 14 m long house surrounded by a trench/drainage. The house is situated in an area with settlement remains in several phases. The limited size of the house suggests that it might have functioned as a stall-house/economy building (Ingvardson & Nielsen 2015, 30). The house is situated in a natural depression in the landscape, and reconnaissance and metal-detector finds suggest that the central part of the settlement is situated on a ridge north of the hoard. Soil samples were gathered from the postholes of the house, and hopefully future macro fossil analysis will give an insight into the function of the house. The hoard is interpreted as deposited in the outskirts of a settlement area (category 2).

The hoard consists of twenty-three German and nineteen English pennies, as well as nine Abbasid and one Samanid dirhams, totalling fifty-two coins (73.04 g), in addition to eight Slavic/Scandinavian melts (47.96 g), and three melts (31.35 g) and one foil bead (1.20 g) probably produced in the West Slavic area during the eleventh century. Two Abbasid dirhams minted by Harun al-Rashid in 805/6 constitute the oldest coins in the hoard, while two Cnut the Great short cross pennies and a Konrad II *nachprägnung* place the time of deposition to the 1030s; 46 per cent of the coins are minted 1010–40. Two out of three melts and all Slavic/Scandinavian melts are fragmented, while 81 per cent of the coins are complete (Fig. 2.7). The foil bead is folded; however, because of its fragile nature it is difficult to determine if it is due to a deliberate action, or due to its stay in the earth. The finder of the Åbo hoard, Frank Pelle, has suggested that the bead had functioned as a form of closure to a now dissolved purse. All but one coin bear test

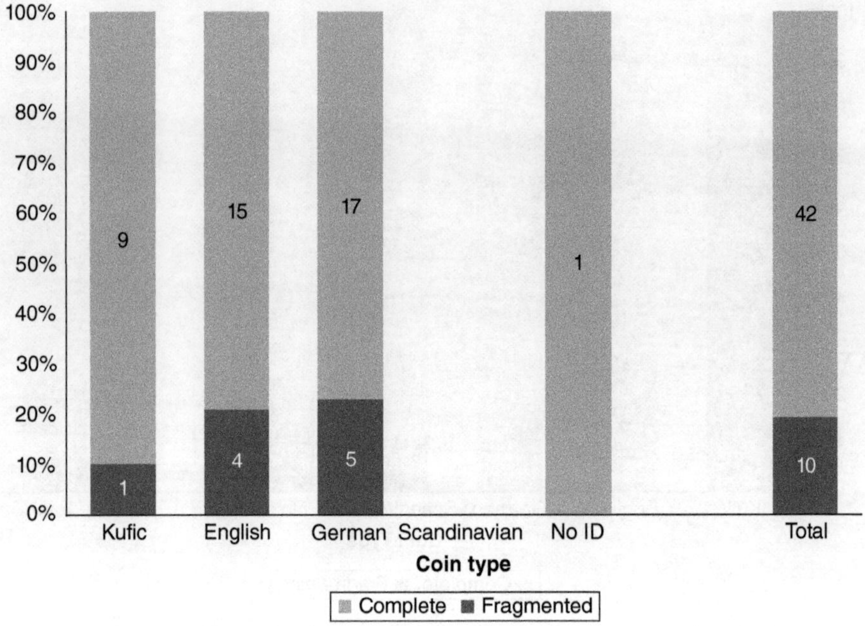

Fig. 2.7. The distribution of fragmented and complete coins in the Åbo hoard.

marks and/or is bent and all but one melt and one Slavic/Scandinavian melt bear test marks. The average weight of all objects in the Åbo hoard is 2.39 g; within the non-minted silver the average weight is 6.68 g. There is a marked correlation between types of objects and weight. Perhaps not surprisingly objects below two grams are dominated by western European coins, while Kufic dirhams are the dominant object type weighing between 2–4 g. Of special interest is the distinction between Slavic/Scandinavian melts and other melts, as Slavic/Scandinavian melts weigh between 4–7 g, while other melts clearly constitute the heaviest objects in the hoard weighing 9.30 g, 9.82 g, and 15.35 g (Fig. 2.8).

Ndr. Stensebygård, east Bornholm, hoard deposited after 1047

The first record of the hoard was in 1820 in connection with excavations of the passage grave Hallebrøndshøj. The excavator, Lieutenant Jansen, noted that six Viking Age coins were found south of the mound (Galster 1980, 54–5, no. 22). Fifty years later, the farmer of Stensebygård found three more coins (Galster 1980, 78–9, no. 27). In 1993 the depositional location of the hoard was established by metal-detector surveys resulting in the discovery of thirty coins and six pieces of non-minted silver. The next year, another successful metal-detector survey brought forth thirty coins and two pieces of non-minted silver. The hoard had been disturbed by continuous agricultural activity since 1820 and was now spread over a large area of 70 × 20 m, but with a clear cluster within an

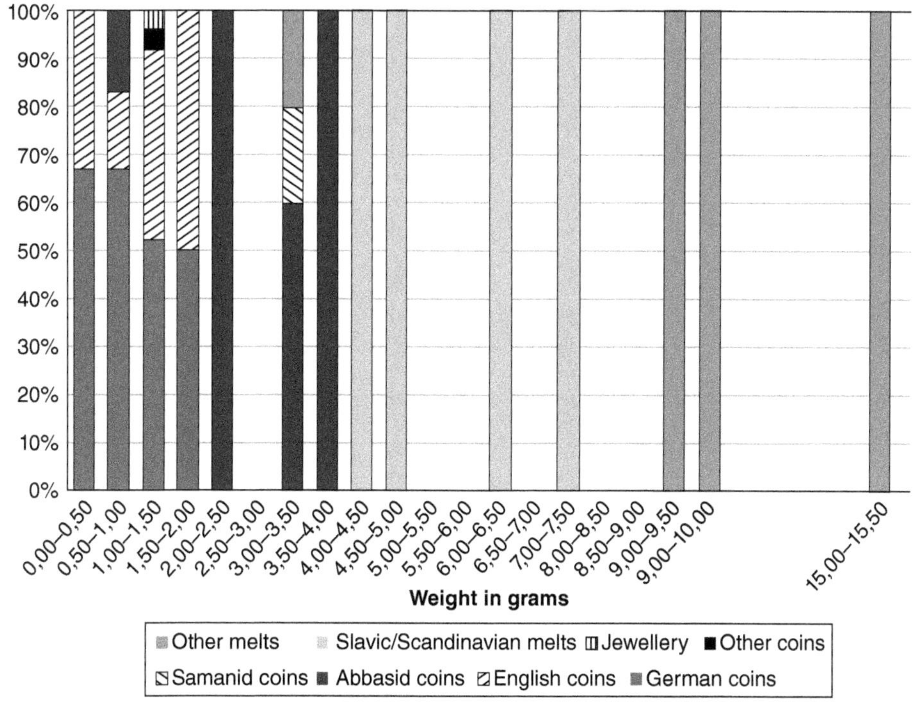

Fig. 2.8. The weight distribution of objects and coins in the Åbo hoard.

area of 18 × 12 m. Burnt wattle-and-daub and fragments of Baltic Sea ware indicated that the hoard was deposited in a settlement area, and an excavation (400 m^2) was initiated by Bornholm Museum in 1994. Several postholes were recorded in the area, but were unfortunately not excavated, which complicates any interpretation of the house construction. A further sixteen coins and four pieces of non-minted silver were found during the excavation, but no objects were preserved in situ. However, the excavation indicated that the hoard was originally deposited in a silversmith's pit, as the coin cluster was centred on the pit. The remains of two vessels of Baltic Sea ware placed on top of the pit were interpreted by the excavator as the original deposition place of the hoard. Beneath the vessels a fragment of a Viking Age silver bracelet, small silver melts, and a fragmented melting pot with a partially melted silver coin were found (Nielsen 1994b). The clear connection to a silversmith's pit places the Ndr. Stensebygård hoard in category 2.

Subsequent to the excavation, a few silver objects have been found by metal detector. At present the total number of objects is thirteen pieces of non-minted silver consisting of one piece of jewellery (2.92 g), one ingot (1.46 g), and eleven pieces of scrap silver (17.06 g), as well as 107 coins, including 2 Abbasid and 1 Samanid dirhams, 81 German, 12 Scandinavian and 8 English, and 3 other/no

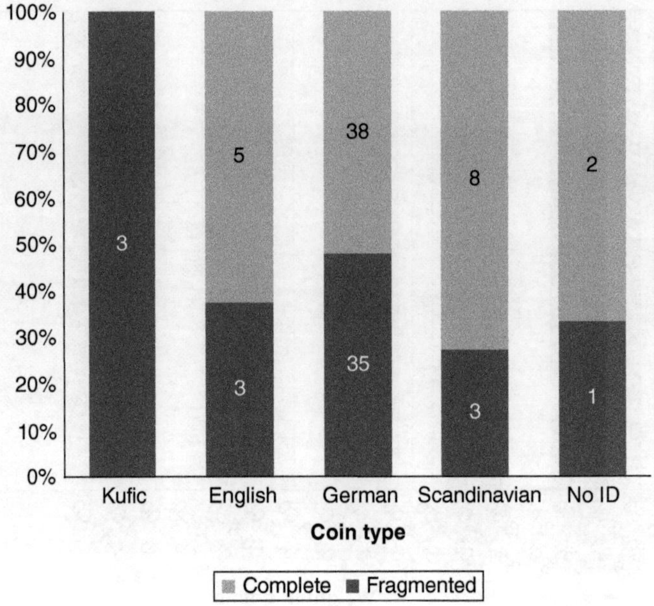

Fig. 2.9. The distribution of fragmented and complete coins in the Ndr. Stensebygård hoard.

ID pennies (>86.45 g).[7] The ingot, the jewellery, and 43 per cent of the available coins are fragmented (Fig. 2.9). The coins are heavily test marked and bent: only one complete coin and seven small fragments are not bent or test marked. The poor state of the coins makes it difficult to create a clear picture of the chronological sequence of the hoard. Two Abbasid dirhams dating back to the 780s and 790s are the oldest coins, while three Danish Svend Estridsen (1047–74) pennies constitute the youngest.

Category 3: Hoards Deposited in Areas Without Other Archaeological Indicators

Tyskegård, south-west Bornholm, hoard deposited after 997

In 1876 farmer A. Hansen found thirty-four Æthelred II long cross coins spread within an approximately 1 × 1 m area on his field near a very large stone. Thirty-three of the coins (one had gone missing) were sent to the Royal Collection of Coins and Medals in Copenhagen, twelve of these are preserved to the present day (Galster 1980, 48–51). With the purpose of relocating the place of deposition of the hoard, the fields of Tyskegård were surveyed by metal detector in

[7] Unfortunately, the current whereabouts of some of the coins is unknown. Only ninety-eight coins are included in the analysis of secondary treatment.

1993. Ten coins were recovered and in 1994 a further eighteen coins were found. A small excavation in 1996 (300–400 m^2) brought forth nineteen new coins, but no other prehistoric remains were located in the area around the coin cluster (Wagnkilde 1996a). Only 300 m south of the Tyskegård hoard the remains of a burnt-down house were excavated. Another hoard, named Kannikegård, was found spread near a bedrock 20 metres from the burnt-down house. A few ceramic sherds of late Viking Age type were found in the postholes of the house. The Kannikegård hoard was deposited after 1009 and consists of forty-eight coins, primarily of German origin, and three pieces of scrap silver. Many coins are fragmented and bear test marks (Wagnkilde 1994). At present, a connection between the two hoards cannot be established. The absence of other archaeological finds and structures in the area around the deposition places the Tyskegård hoard in category 3.

Only sixty of the eighty-two Æthelred II long cross pennies that can be attributed to the hoard are preserved today. Descriptions of the twenty-one now lost coins are available in the register of the Royal Collection of Coins and Medals, whereas the only available information about the coin that was lost before submission is that it was of the same type as the rest of the coins (Galster 1980, 48; Moesgaard 2006, 406). The total weight of the remaining sixty coins is 99.89 g. At least half of the ten fragmented coins display freshly made fractures, presumably caused by modern farming, whereas four of the five fragmented coins are chipped, also indicating that the fragmentation was not done deliberately. Only three coins bear test marks, two coins have one peck, and one coin has two pecks. Eighteen coins are bent once. As Moesgaard has pointed out, the applied test method is very similar, as the coins are bent in almost identical angles: this implies that the testing was done at one time, and by the same person (Moesgaard 2006, 408). The Tyskegård hoard is interpreted as a deposition of Danegeld, as the hoard consists exclusively of Æthelred II long cross coins minted in *c.*997–1003. The few signs of wear indicate that the hoard was deposited soon after its acquisition (Moesgaard 2006, 405–19).

Buddegård, south-east Bornholm, hoard deposited after 969

A silver trefoil brooch (30.4 g) and a fragment of an arm-ring (14.5 g) together with thirty-five Kufic dirhams were found by metal-detector surveys in 1995 in a field with few other archaeological finds. An excavation (675 m^2) the following year confirmed that the hoard had been deposited in an area without settlement remains, near a stream (Wagnkilde 1996b). A further twelve dirhams and a missing fragment of the trefoil brooch were found during the excavation, and one coin was later recovered by metal detector.

During cataloguing I refitted two fragments into one coin and three fragments into another coin. The total number of coins is hereafter forty-five (122.71 g), divided between eight Abbasid and thirty-one Samanid dirhams as well as six dirham imitations. The oldest coin in the hoard is an Abbasid dirham minted in al-Basra in Iraq in 749–62, and the youngest coin is a Samanid dirham minted in Bukhara in Uzbekistan in 946/7. Another Bornholm hoard, Kannikegærdet, holds the only known parallel to the trefoil brooch, and it is therefore possible that the brooch is locally produced. Notably, the Kannikegærdet hoard also contains a parallel to the arm-ring (Nielsen 1996). Parallels to the arm-ring are otherwise found on Gotland.[8] The majority of the coins (thirty-one) are complete. Of the fourteen fragmented coins, five coins display fresh fractures: they have clearly been damaged after deposition, an interpretation supported by the five refitted fragments. Many coins (twenty-one) are pierced or looped; together with the low degree of fragmentation, this suggests that the coins should perhaps be considered as jewellery. The trefoil brooch is bent and in three fragments, but may well have been complete (but bent) at the time of deposition. Neither the brooch nor the arm-ring bear test marks. Thirty-four coins are bent, but of these a large proportion (twenty) are only bent once: this is unusual as many coins in the Bornholm hoards are bent several times. Furthermore, only four coins bear test marks. The coins thereby display few signs of secondary treatment, with the exception of piercing/looping. The combination of the trefoil brooch and complete looped/pierced dirhams suggests that Buddegård should be included in the group of Scandinavian jewellery hoards with specially selected objects connected to the female sphere.[9]

Evaluation of the Compositions and Archaeological Settings of the Mixed Hoards

The six investigated hoards display differences in their compositions, which may relate to their archaeological setting. A general trend is that all hoards are dominated by coins (in number); only in the Åbo hoard does the non-minted silver weigh more than the coins (Fig. 2.10).

The two hoards, Gyldensgård and Nørremølle, deposited in the central part of a settlement area (category 1) show great diversity both in coin types and in non-minted silver objects. In both hoards most of the non-minted silver is fragmented into rather small pieces, while the majority of the coins are complete. The majority of the coins and non-minted silver are test marked and/or bent, indicating that they were used as a means of payment in a weighed metal (bullion) economy. The coin composition shows that most of the coins in both hoards

[8] My deepest thanks to Professor B. Hårdh for identifying the jewellery, and for drawing my attention to the parallels in the Kannikegærde hoard. Parallels to the arm-ring are found in Norrkvie in Grötlingbo parish, Häggvalls in Gerum parish, and Mallgårds in Alskog parish on Gotland.

[9] This hoard type appears with different combinations during the Iron Age and the early medieval period, as described by Kilger (2008, 325–35) and Myrberg (2007, 163–70).

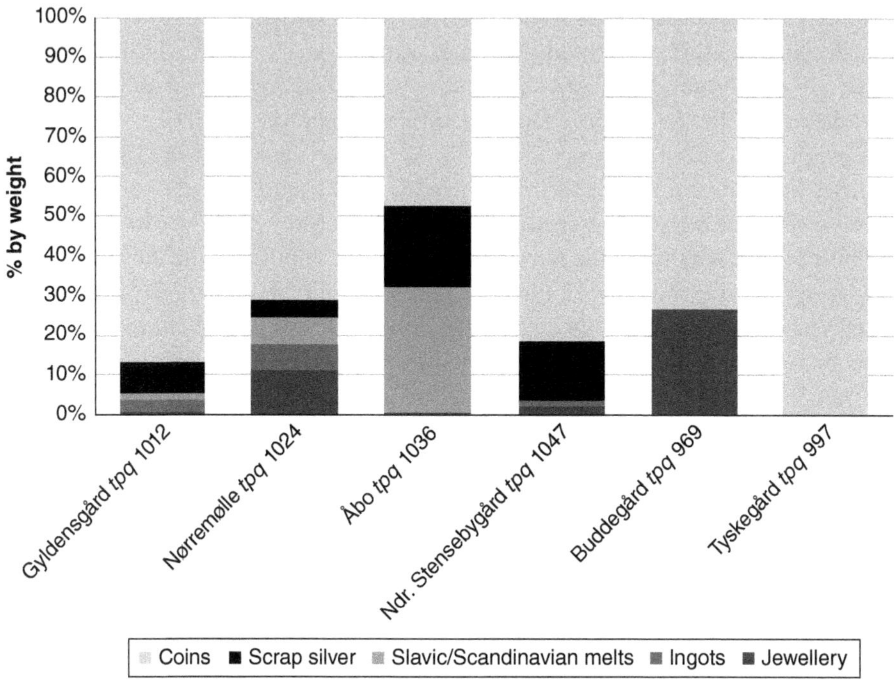

Fig. 2.10. The weight distribution of minted and non-minted silver in the six hoards included in the case study.

were minted within a forty-year period, perhaps indicating a collection phase corresponding to the career of one person. M. Östergren has shown that some of the Gotlandic hoards were most likely deposited on the floor level of a house, meaning that the hoards may have been accessible over an extended period of time (1989, 61). With this in mind, I would like to suggest that hoards like Gyldensgård and Nørremølle should be characterized as 'active hoards', where the owner had continuous access to the hoard, and where objects were continuously removed and recycled (although it is noted that the Nørremølle hoard was deposited close by, rather than within, a house, and may thus have been 'inactive' during its final, deposition phase). The diverse composition of the hoards supports the view that objects were collected in many different areas: objects in the Nørremølle hoard were probably collected both north and south of Bornholm (Ingvardson 2012, 287–93). When the owner had continuous access to the hoard, objects could be added/removed many times, which may account for the diversity of objects in the hoards. The hoards' composition, treatment, and archaeological setting (their primary, secondary, and tertiary contexts) may thus point to trade as the key origin of their silver. As it is described above (the narrative context), Bornholm was characterized by a decentralized settlement and trading structure at the time when the two hoards were deposited. It is therefore likely that the Gyldensgård and Nørremølle hoards, presumably like many of the other hoards of the island, are the result of individual merchants exploring the ideal geographical position of Bornholm in the middle of the Baltic Sea (Ingvardson 2014, 334–6). The interesting presence of large amounts of partly cleaned fish and the high number of loom weights at the Gyldensgård sites might be indications of some of the trade goods (fish and cloth) that were traded for the silver in the hoards.

The two hoards, Ndr. Stensebygård and Åbo, deposited on the outskirts of settlement areas (category 2) show other characteristics in their primary, secondary, and tertiary contexts. The Ndr. Stensebygård hoard stands out as the only hoard among the many Viking Age hoards of Bornholm that can be securely connected to a silversmith's work place. The hoard is therefore interpreted as raw material for silver smithing. This is supported by the primary and secondary context of the objects, as the hoard holds a very high portion of scrap silver among the non-minted silver, while the almost destructive nature of the secondary treatment of the coins gives the impression that the coins were perhaps also regarded as scrap silver at the time of deposition. As mentioned, the Åbo hoard stands out as the only one out of the six investigated hoards in which the non-minted silver (almost exclusively melts) weighs more than the coin group (Fig. 2.10). Notably, all the melts are cut into smaller pieces; where the division is made the edges are sharp and the surfaces straight, indicating that the division was done while the silver was still soft. A difference in weight between the (lighter) Slavic/Scandinavian melts and (significantly heavier) 'other' melts was noted above (Fig. 2.8), and may indicate a functional difference. It is possible that the Slavic/Scandinavian melts are products of the cupellation process (where silver was refined in hearths lined with bone-ash material) and should be interpreted in the context of silver smithing: refined, practical, workable pieces of silver for the smith, made from very small pieces of silver, as wires, rods, and silver foil, as well as small pieces of Slavic jewellery (Gustafsson 2013, 93–4). However, it must be stressed that the Slavic/Scandinavian melts are present in many hoards on Bornholm—also in hoards that are not interpreted as raw material for silver smithing (e.g. the Nørremølle hoard, Fig. 2.11). The analysis of the secondary context shows that many of the melts from the Åbo hoard, as well as from other Bornholm hoards not connected to silver smithing, carry test marks. These are traditionally interpreted as signs of trade, but it must be presumed that the silversmith was most likely also interested in the silver alloy.

Category 2 hoards should be interpreted as raw material for the silversmith. This is supported by the primary and secondary contexts, both in regard to the marked presence of Slavic/Scandinavian melts, which perhaps should be connected to a form of a smithing/cupellation process, and in the presence of heavily fragmented and almost destroyed coins particularly in the Ndr. Stensebygård hoard. The presence of objects representing a refining process makes sense in an

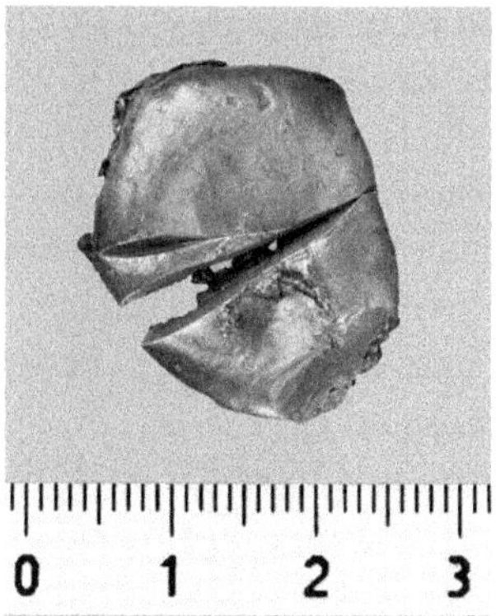

Fig. 2.11. Cut melt of Slavic/Scandinavian type from the Nørremølle hoard.
Photo: John Lee, the National Museum of Denmark.

area like Bornholm, where objects of many different qualities were collected and hoarded well into the twelfth century. In a bullion economy, the Slavic/Scandinavian melts may have functioned as a form of trusted standard: practical both as raw material for the silversmith and as payment.

The composition of both the Tyskegård and Buddegård hoards, deposited in areas without any other archaeological activities, is unusual in relation to most other Viking Age hoards. The Tyskegård hoard is the only hoard consisting solely of coins (Fig. 2.10). As the hoard consists exclusively of Æthelred II long cross pennies, with very few secondary traces, the primary and secondary context indicates that it was most likely collected over a very short period of time, probably through raids in England, and that the hoard was deposited soon after it was collected. The Buddegård hoard, with its combination of a trefoil brooch and high proportion of complete and pierced/looped dirhams, is the only Bornholm hoard so far to be connected to a group of hoards with specially selected objects centred on trefoil brooches, which seem to relate to the female sphere (Kilger 2008, 325–35). Both hoards thus consist of apparently carefully selected items, which were perhaps intentionally withdrawn from the economic sphere. Given the hoards' apparently deserted deposition place, signalling a careful selection of the landscape context surrounding the deposition act, it is reasonable to speculate that both hoards might represent ritual depositions.

Conclusions

These case studies demonstrate that the silver hoards of Bornholm cannot be viewed as a uniform phenomenon. The actors and processes behind the hoards are visualized by combining the evidence of coins and non-minted silver in their archaeological context. The analysis suggests that hoards with different compositional characteristics (primary and secondary context) display different depositional behaviour (tertiary context), and that the combined evidence of the primary, secondary, and tertiary context to some degree reflects the owners and functions of the hoards. Furthermore, the study supports the notion that a differentiated approach to the large group of non-minted silver might shed new light on the different functions of mixed hoards of Viking Age Scandinavia. The conclusion must be that the collection and deposition of the hoards was facilitated by different people with different backgrounds, desires, preferences, opportunities, and goals, and as such each hoard is unique. However, the potential of the method presented here is not limited to interpreting individual hoards in a micro perspective. In light of the narrative context, similarities in the combination of silver objects and in hoarding practices allow us to make some general observations. The case studies associate the six hoards with three essential activities in Viking Age society: trade, silver smithing, and ritual deposition. When applied to the vast number of other Viking Age silver hoards from the island, the method will no doubt bring us closer to an understanding of the economic, political, and social organization of Viking Age Bornholm.

ACKNOWLEDGEMENTS

I would like to thank Lea Cunliffe and Jane Kershaw for language revision of the text, and René Laursen for help and support.

REFERENCES

Aarsleff, E. 2008. 'Velstandens Ø'. *Skalk* 4 (2008): 18–25.

Aarsleff, E. 2009. 'Viking Age Finds'. In Adamsen et al. (eds), 118–22.

Adamsen, C., U.L. Hansen, F.O. Nielsen, & M. Watt (eds) 2009. *Sorte Muld: Wealth, Power and Religion at an Iron Age Central Settlement on Bornholm*. Rønne: Bornholms Museum.

Bogucki, M. 2011. 'The Use of Money in the Slavic Lands from the Ninth to the Eleventh Century: The Archaeological/Numismatic Evidence'. In Graham-Campbell et al. (eds), 133–55.

Czonstke, K. 2011. 'Biżuteria Słowiańska z Wczesnośredniowiecznych Skarbow Bornholmskich' (Slavic Jewellery from Early Medieval Hoards in Bornholm), *Materiały Zachodniopomorskie*, Nowa Seria VI/VII, 2009/10: 167–202.

Galster, G. 1980. 'Vikingetids Møntfund fra Bornholm'. *Nordisk Numismatisk Årsskrift* 1977–8: 5–248.

Graham-Campbell, J., S.M. Sindbæk & G. Williams (eds) 2011. *Silver Economies, Monetisation and Society in Scandinavia* AD *800–1100*. Aarhus: Aarhus University Press.

Graham-Campbell, J. & G. Williams (eds) 2007. *Silver Economy in the Viking Age*. Walnut Creek: Left Coast Press.

Grinder-Hansen, K. 1994. 'Mønter som Kilde til Middelalderens Økonomiske Historie—En Præsentation af Kildematerialet'. *Fortid og Nutid* 2: 101–33.

Grinder-Hansen, P., M. Märcher, F.O. Nielsen, S. Nygaard, & P. Pentz 2013. 'Skatten fra Østermarie'. *Nationalmuseets Arbejdsmark* 2013: 140–55.

Gustafsson, N.B. 2013. *Casting Identities in Central Seclusion: Aspects of non-ferrous metalworking and society on Gotland in the Early Medieval Period*. Stockholm: Stockholms Universitet.

Gustin, I. 2004. *Mellan Gåva och Marknad. Handel, Tillit och Materiell Kultur under Vikingatid*. Stockholm: Almqvist & Wiksell International.

Hårdh, B. 1976. *Wikingerzeitliche Depotfund aus Südschweden. Probleme und Analysen*. Acta Archaeologica Lundensia, Series in 8° No.6, Stockholm: Almqvist & Wiksell.

Hårdh, B. 1996. *Silver in the Viking Age: A Regional-Economic Study*. Stockholm: Almqvist & Wiksell International.

Hårdh, B. 2011. 'Viking-Age Silver from Hoards and Cultural Layers'. In Graham-Campbell et al. (eds), 281–308.

Hårdh, B. 2013. 'The Silver Hoard from Skovvang, Bornholm'. In *Early Medieval Art and Archaeology in the Northern Worlds: Studies in Honour of James Graham-Campbell*, ed. A. Reynolds & L. Webster, 527–39. Leiden: Brill.

von Heijne, C. 2004. *Särpräglat. Vikingatida och Tidig Medeltida Myntfynd från Danmark, Skåne, Blekinge och Halland (ca 800–1130)*. Stockholm: Stockholms Universitet.

Horsnæs, H.W. 2014. 'Changing Hands: The Skovsholm Dirham Hoard'. In *The World in the Viking Age*, ed. S.M. Sindbæk & A. Trakadas, 65. Roskilde: Viking Ship Museum.

Horsnæs, H.W., M. Märcher, & M. Vennersdorf 2013. 'A Stepping Stone in the Baltic Sea: Two Millennia of Coin Finds and Coin Use. A Case Study of Vester Herred, Bornholm'. *The Journal of Archaeological Numismatics* 3: 1–65.

Ingvardson, G.T. 2010. *Møntbrug. Fra Vikingetid til Vendertogter*. Aarhus: Aarhus Universitetsforlag.

Ingvardson, G.T. 2012. 'Nørremølle—The Largest Viking Age Silver Hoard of Bornholm (Denmark)'. *The Journal of Archaeological Numismatics* 2: 281–346.

Ingvardson, G.T. 2014. 'Trade and Power—Bornholm in the Late Viking Age'. In *Northern Worlds—Landscapes, Interactions and Dynamics: Research at the National Museum of Denmark. Proceedings of the Northern Worlds Conference, Copenhagen 28–30 November 2012*, ed. H.C. Gulløv, 325–37. Odense: University Press of Southern Denmark.

Ingvardson, G.T. 2015. 'Traces of Use'. In *King Harold's Cross Coinage: Christian Coins for the Merchants of Haithabu and the King's Soldiers*, by J.C. Moesgaard, 127–38. Odense: University Press of Southern Denmark.

Ingvardson, G.T. & F.O.S. Nielsen 2015. '100 Viking Age Hoards of Bornholm—Status, Challenges and Perspectives'. In *Small Things—Wide Horizons: Studies in Honour of Birgitta Hårdh*, ed. L. Larsson, B. Helgesson, F. Ekengren, & B. Söderberg, 27–34. Oxford: Archeopress.

Jensen, J.S. 2006. 'Thc Introduction and Use of Runic Letters on Danish Coins Around the Year 1065'. In *Runes and Their Secrets: Studies in Runology*, ed. M. Stoklund, M. Lerche Nielsen, B. Holmberg, & G. Fellows-Jensen, 159–68. Copenhagen: Museum Tusculanum Press & University of Copenhagen.

Kemmers, F. & N. Myrberg 2011. 'Rethinking Numismatics: The Archaeology of Coins'. *Archaeological Dialogues* 18: 87–108.

Kilger, C. 2000. *Pfennigmärkte und Wärungslandschaften. Monetarisierungen im Sächsische-Slawischen Grenzland ca. 965–1120. Commentationes De Nummis saeculorum IX–XI in Suecia repertis*, Nova Series 15. Stockholm: Royal Swedish Academy of Letters, History & Antiquities.

Kilger, C. 2008. 'Kombinationer av Föremål—De Vikingatida Mittspännedepåerna'. In *Facets of Archeology: Essays in Honour of Lotte Hedeager on her 60th Birthday*, ed. C. Prescott, K. Chilidis, & J. Lund, 323–38. Oslo Archaeological Series 10. Oslo: Unipub.

Kluge, B. 1981. 'Das Angelsächsische Element in den Slawischen Münzfunden des 10. bis 12. Jahrhunderts. Aspekte einer Analyse'. In *Viking-Age Coinage in the Northern Lands*, ed. M. Blackburn & M. Metcalf, 257–327. BAR Int. Ser. 122. Oxford: Archeopress.

Laursen, R. & G.T. Ingvardson 2014. 'Skovholm—en Bornholmsk Stormandsgård'. In *Vikingetidens Aristokratiske Miljøer. Arkæologi på Saxo-Instituttet*, ed. H. Lyngstrøm & L.C.A. Sonne, 55–8. Copenhagen: Saxo-Instituttet.

Moesgaard, J.C. 2006. 'The Import of English Coins to the Northern Lands'. In *Coinage and History in the North Sea World c.500–1250: Essays in Honour of Marion Archibald*, ed. B. Cook & G. Williams, 389–434. Leiden: Brill.

Myrberg, N. 2007. 'The Social Identity of Coin Hoards: An Example of Theory and Practice in the Space Between Numismatics and Archaeology'. In *Coins in Context I. New Perspectives for the Interpretation of Coin Finds. Colloquium Frankfurt a. M., October 25–27, 2007*, ed. H.M. von Kaenel & F. Kemmers, 157–71. Studien zu Fundmünzen der Antike 23. Mainz: von Zabern.

Nielsen, F.O.S. 1994a. 'Middelaldergårde på Bornholm'. *Hikuin* 21: 125–38.

Nielsen, F.O.S. 1994b. Archaeological Excavation Report, Museum of Bornholm, BMR 2151 Ndr. Stensebygård.

Nielsen, F.O.S. 1996. Archaeological Excavation Report, Museum of Bornholm, BMR 2292 Kannikegærdet.

Östergren, M. 1989. *Mellan Stengrund och Stenhus. Gotlands Vikingatida Silverskatter som Boplatsindikation*. Theses and Papers in Archaeology 2. Stockholm: Institute of Archaeology, University of Stockholm.

Pedersen, U. 2008. 'Weights and Balances'. In *Means of Exchange: Dealing with Silver in the Viking Age*, ed. D. Skre, 119–79. Kaupang Excavation Project Publication Series, Volume 2. Aarhus: Aarhus University Press.

Steuer, H. 1987. 'Gewichtsgeldwirtschaften im Fruhgeschichtlichen Europa. Feinwagen und Gewichte als Quellen zur Wahrungsgeschichte'. In *Untersuchungen zu Handel und Verkehr der Vor- und Fruhgeschichtlichen Zeit in Mittel- und Nordeuropa. Teil IV. Der Handel der Karolinger- und Wikingerzeit*, ed. K. Duwel, 405–27. Gottingen: Vandenhoeck & Ruprecht.

Thorsen, M.S. 2003. Archaeological Excavation Report, Bornholm Museum, BMR 3194 Gyldensgård SV.

Wagnkilde, H. 1994. Archaeological Excavation Report, Bornholm Museum, BMR 2174 Kannikegård.

Wagnkilde, H. 1996a. Archaeological Excavation Report, Bornholm Museum, BMR 2150 Tyskegård.

Wagnkilde, H. 1996b. Archaeological Excavation Report, Bornholm Museum, BMR 2306 Buddegård.

Watt, M. 2009. 'Sorte Muld—Past and Present'. In Adamsen et al. (eds), 16–27.

3

On Silver Fragmentation

How Reliable is Metrological Data? A Case Study Based on the Mózgowo Hoard, Poland (tpq *1009*)

Mateusz Bogucki

Silver Fragmentation in Poland

Silver fragmentation is one of the characteristic traits of Viking Age coin and jewellery finds. Hoards of fragmented silver have been recorded across the entire Viking world—from Ireland to Russia. The term 'hack-silver hoards' used to describe mass finds of this type is thus justified. Finds defined by this term are, of course, chronologically and geographically diverse, but have been generally interpreted as collections of currency, with the high degree of fragmentation of silver seen as a product of the intense use and circulation of silver as a form of payment (Kiersnowski 1960; Hårdh 1996; 2008, 99; Suchodolski 1971; 2012, 135–9; Bogucki 2004, 61–2; but see now Jankowiak this volume). In this chapter, alongside a brief presentation of this phenomenon using the example of Polish lands, focus will be given to another aspect of research on the fragmentation of silver in the Viking Age. The main topic is the question of whether available data relating to silver fragmentation is representative.

Silver fragmentation in Poland occurs as early as the beginning of the ninth century. Deliberately fragmented Arabic dirhams from this period are found exclusively in the trade emporium Truso (Bogucki 2007) and on several sites in Western Pomerania (Pomerania comprising the southern shore of the Baltic Sea area in modern-day northern Germany and Poland), primarily in the vicinity of Kołobrzeg, north-west Poland (Łosiński 1988). However, although present, fragmentation remains a rare phenomenon in Poland until the mid tenth century. The most intensive silver fragmentation in Polish hoards appears from *c.*970/80 to *c.*1020 (for older literature see Bogucki 2011, 135–8).

Within Polish literature there are several theses that try to explain the phenomenon of silver fragmentation in the early Middle Ages. As they were presented and discussed in the literature, it is sufficient to list them here:

- Importing already fragmented oriental silver from the Islamic Empire (Ilisch 1990);
- Obtaining small monetary units for payments as counted money (Kiersnowski 1960; Suchodolski 2004; 2013);
- Obtaining silver pieces of low weight for use in weight exchange (Suchodolski 2004; 2013; Bogucki 2011, 140–5);
- Religiously motivated intentional destruction(?) of silver (Duczko 2002; Urbańczyk 2002; 2009).

When discussing the problem of the fragmentation of silver, some authors (including the current writer—Bogucki 2004; 2005) have erroneously treated fragmentation, and pecking and nicking, as a manifestation of the same phenomenon or as very similar occurrences. Today, the author is convinced that those two practices had different backgrounds and should be separated and interpreted individually. They could, and probably did, interpenetrate, but the main reasons behind them were different. While fragmentation can probably be regarded as an economic activity—as a means of obtaining low-weight silver for metal-weight exchange, pecks, nicks, hammering, and other destructive actions carried out on silver had a non-economic, customary-ritual-magical motivation (Duczko 2002; Kilger 2006; Czwojda 2007; Bogucki 2011, 140–5).

Searching for a Small Unit

Assuming that fragmentation was motivated by the need to obtain pieces of silver of low weight for use in weighed metal transactions, the available material can be searched for some metrological regularities. Such attempts have been undertaken for a long time. The main focus has traditionally been to find the smallest unit of weight that would show the amount of silver taken as usual means of payment in everyday situations (Kiersnowski 1960; Suchodolski 1971; 2012, 135–9; Bogucki 2004, 61–2).

Table 3.1 provides the weight units of silver fragments found in hoards from Pomerania, Great Poland, and Mazovia (central north-east Poland) from AD *c.*970–1020. It shows that there are two dominating groups of fragments. It is quite obvious that the weight of the most commonly found pieces of silver diminishes the further towards the south-east they are found. Additionally, it is worth stressing that pieces of coins and silver in Scandinavia are heavier still, so that the thesis of diminishing weight along a south-eastern direction (in the

Table 3.1. The weight groupings of silver fragments found in hoards from Pomerania, Great Poland, and Mazovia, AD 970–1020.

	Pomerania	Great Poland	Mazovia
1st small unit	0.3–0.4 g	0.2–0.3 g	0.1–0.2 g
2nd small unit	0.7–0.8 g	0.6–0.7 g	0.5–0.6 g

Baltic area) seems very plausible (Tambor 1989, 16–24; Hårdh 1996, 84–130; Nowakiewicz 2003, 281–5; Bogucki 2004, 62, see Jankowiak this volume). It is assumed that the basic amount of silver used for everyday payments in early medieval Poland at the turn of the tenth and eleventh centuries was 0.2 g (disregarding local discrepancies depending on the availability of silver). In addition to statistical analyses, the widespread use of this weight is confirmed by two other kinds of sources. Firstly, Danish half-bracteates of the tenth century (Malmer types KG 9–12), produced for the Scandinavian local market, have an average weight of *c*.0.15–0.5 g (Malmer 1966; Suchodolski 2013), while the cross types of the late tenth century weigh *c*.0.2–0.35 g (Moesgaard 2015, 45), which corresponds to the average weight of silver (*c*.0.2 g) in Poland. Secondly, support can be found in written sources. Ibrahim ibn Yaqub noted in the 960s that for one *kinšar/kirat* (European denier) in Prague one could buy ten chickens, wheat for one man for one month or barley for one horse for forty nights (Kowalski 1946). This means that the price for one chicken was 1/10 of a denier, which equals *c*.0.15–0.2 g of silver. The arguments presented above show that *c*.0.2 g of silver appears to have been a commonly used sum in the late tenth and early eleventh centuries from southern Denmark to southern Poland (Bogucki 2004, 61–2).

Despite the fact that statistical analyses are supported both by the metrology of a chosen group of coins and by written sources, the question has to be raised about the representativeness of the available source material—the weight of silver pieces from early medieval hoards. The history of the discovery of the Mózgowo hoard (Fig. 3.1), the modern-day reconstruction of its assemblage, and the continued discovery of new elements through metal-detecting and excavation can contribute to this discussion. The case study demonstrates that our knowledge of early medieval hoards, and silver weights, may often be based on incomplete data. Similar analyses should be carried out on a larger number of rediscovered hoards. Such 'rediscoveries' are increasingly common both in Poland and in Scandinavia (primarily on Gotland).

The Mózgowo Hoard

The first finds of early medieval coins and jewellery belonging to this hoard were unearthed in the vicinity of Mózgowo, commune and county Iława, northern Poland (formerly Mosgau, Kreis Rosenberg) in October 1868 during ploughing, on a field belonging to Benjamin Beyer from Kisielice (formerly Freystadt, Kreis Rosenberg). Already the first note about the hoard includes information about German coins of the Emperors Otto III and Henry II (collectively 983–1024), English coins of Æthelred II (978–1013 and 1014–16), and Czech coins of Boleslaus II (972–99). At that time, coins from Cologne, Strasburg, and Augsburg were identified and the date of deposition of the hoard was determined at *c*.AD 1000 (Bergau 1868). This part of the hoard never belonged to a public collection, but was distributed among several private collections.

Fig. 3.1. Part of the Mózgowo hoard.
Photo: author.

More precise information was soon published by Herman Dannenberg (1876, 47), who had the opportunity to analyse the collection belonging to the director of the city archives in Magdeburg, von Mülverstedt, comprising some 2,000 coins from the Mózgowo hoard. A description of this part of the hoard figures as number 11 on H. Dannenberg's list (1876). Because this description has the character of a primary source, it is quoted here unabridged:

11) Mosgau (bei Rosenberg, West-Preussen[1]). [Ca. 1010]

a) Deutsche: Metz (Adalbero II., Theodorich II.), Verdun (Haimo), Masstricht (Otto, Heinrich II.),

incert. *Rf.* Heinricus moneta, Thuin (? Mém. IV, S. 59), Viset (Otto III.), Köln (Ottonen), Herzog Theodorich EIL CIV, Deventer (Otto)—Otto & Adelheid, Herzog Bernhard (nur mit Kopf), Hildesheim (Otto, Bernward), Magdeburg, Halberstadt (Arnolf), Dortmund (Otto, Heinrich), Wendenpf. grosse und kleine (letztere Nachahmungen der Magdeburger)—Schwaben Herzog Otto (?ac pacif.), Breisach (Otto), Esslingen, Strassburg (Otto, Heinrich II., B. Widerold), Basel (K. Konrad 937–993), Constanz, Augsburg (Liutolf, Siegfried, Bruno, nur vom älteren Typus)—Neuburg NIVVAN ClVITAS (König Heinrich II.), Regensburg, ausser Otto auch Herzog Heinrich (985–995) und H. rex vom alten (Portal-) Typus, aber auch mit Kopf (*Rf.* VECCHO), Salzburg (Herzog Heinrich IV).

b) Böhmen, Boleslaw, Jaromir—Verona (Otto III.)—Æthelred—Norwegen (Erik Jarl 1000–1015)—Bruchstücke von arabischen Dirhems.

Unter allen kein Konrad H., ja nicht einmal ein Heinrich 11. mit Kaisertitel, kein Ulrich von Böhmen (1012–37) und kein Knut (1010–35), auch kein Regensburger Heinrich V. mit dem Schriftkreuze. Wir kommen also etwa auf dieselbe Zeit wie bei den beiden vorigen Funden, höchstens vielleicht wegen des häufigeren Auftretens der Heinricus rex—Denare 1–2 Jahre später.

[1] Nach gefälliger Mittheilung des Hrn. Archivrats v. Mülverstedt in Magdeburg, dem dieser Fund grösstentheils zugefallen, betrug derselbe etwa 2000 Stück. Möglich, dass manches in der mir vorgelegten Auswahl gefehlt hat.

In the second volume of his work, H. Dannenberg corrected the interpretation of one coin, namely the denier of Graf Heinrich von Stade, which had been originally attributed to the Norwegian Jarl Eric (1894, 521). In addition, several coins from Mózgowo have been mentioned in works by Eduard Fiala and several other authors, who repeated (sometimes erroneously) the information of H. Dannenberg (Fiala 1891, 31, no. 28; 1895, 161, no. 29; Gumowski 1905, 62; 1953, 91; Markov 1910, 114; Chmielecki 1907, 36, no. 8; Kujot 1913, 258; Suhle 1926, 82; 1928, 226; Łęga 1930, 588, no. 106; Langenheim 1933, 282, no. 34; La Baume 1938, 53; Jammer 1952, 145, no. 230; Albrecht 1959, 170, no. 292; Żak 1963, no. 132; Cach 1970, no. 114; Gajewski 1982, 26; Kócka-Krenz 1993, 276; Ilisch 1998, 19, 109). An article by E. Fiala from 1922 is exceptional for its description of a Czech denier of Boleslaus III with the mint master name JOHAN ETL. This coin was, according to Fiala, bought 'many years ago' by a person called Vávr in Frankfurt am Main, together with many German, several Italian, English, and Norwegian deniers, hacked-up dirhams and several deniers of Boleslaus and Jaromir (Fiala 1922, 181–2).

Until the late 1990s, the most up-to-date published information about the Mózgowo hoard was a list published in the second volume of *Polskie Skarby Wczesnośredniowieczne* (Kiersnowscy & Kiersnowscy 1959, 72–3, no. 107), while the fate of the coins from the hoard remained unknown. However, the hoard was identified by Wolfgang Hahn in the 1970s in the Herzog Anton Ulrich-Museum in Braunschweig, Lower Saxony, Germany. Thirty years later, Borys Paszkiewicz prepared a preliminary description of the hoard, and finally, in 2013, Peter Ilisch identified and attributed all the coins. According to the museum records, the coins were purchased from a man called Mülverstedt from Magdeburg in 1902. Another piece of information states that the second part of the hoard had been in the ownership of Wiggert, director of a gymnasium, and was later sold to Emil Bahrfeldt.[1] There is little doubt that the Mülverstedt

[1] A letter from the director of the numismatic cabinet at the Herzog Anton Ulrich-Museum in Braunschweig, Professor Wolfgang Leschhorn, from 2013: 'Teile des Fundes sind im Jahre 1902 von einem Herrn von Mülverstedt aus Magdeburg angekauft worden. Der Vorname des Verkäufers ist uns nicht mehr bekannt. Ich finde in unserem Inventarbuch den Hinweis, dass die zweite Hälfte des Fundes

mentioned in the recordings of the museum is the same as the director of the city archives in Magdeburg, mentioned earlier by Dannenberg.

This person was Johan George Adalbert von Mülverstedt, born in Gdańsk, educated in Tylża and at the university in Königsberg, interested not only in genealogy, which was the main topic of his studies, but also in numismatics. In addition to collecting coins, he published a book entitled *Magdeburgisches Münzkabinett des neuen Zeitalters* (Herfurth 1997, 516–17). Considering his origins, he must have had contacts among collectors and antiquarians in Western Prussia that enabled him to purchase a significant part of the coins discovered in Mózgowo.

Johan von Mülverstedt died in 1914 and it is almost certain that the numerous German, several Italian, English, and Norwegian denarii, pieces of dirhams and several denarii of Boleslaus and Jaromir, together with the JOHAN ETL denarius, which according to E. Fiala had been purchased 'many years ago' by Vávr, were previously part of the collection of J.G.A. von Mülverstedt (the part belonging to Wiggert, the gymnasium director, was most probably sold before 1902 to Emil Bahrfeldt; his collection was sold to several buyers as late as 1921). As only 459 coins from Mózgowo are present in the museum in Braunschweig, and as J.G.A. von Mülverstedt sold his coins to several purchasers, a comparison of Braunschweig coins with the list of Dannenberg cannot be fully consistent (see Table 3.2).[2]

In September 2010, a further part of the hoard from Mózgowo was discovered by members of the Society of Researchers of History Deutsch Eylau 'Ylavia'. Through an analysis of old maps and cadaster data, they were able to identify the original place of the hoard's discovery and, with the use of metal detectors, found in the topsoil 834 elements of the hoard: 717 coins or pieces of coins and 117 pieces of jewellery. All finds were handed over to the Muzeum Warmii i Mazur in Olsztyn, north-east Poland.

Finally, a third part of the Mózgowo hoard was discovered during regular excavation works led by the Muzeum Warmii i Mazur in Olsztyn in August 2012; 374 finds were discovered during those works, including 337 whole

von Mosgau zunächst bei Gymnasialdirektor Wiggert lag, dann an S. Bahrfeldt ging. Die arabischen Münzen sollen 1902 an einen Herrn German in Niederlössnitz gegangen sein. Das Herzog Anton Ulrich-Museum gab eine Reihe angelsächischer Münzen Ethelreds ab und einen Denar Arnulfs von Halberstadt.'

[2] A problem with the identification of coins from Mózgowo in the museum collection is caused by the fact that the museum is in possession of numerous denarii from the tenth and eleventh centuries from Mózgowo, along with other deposits from Poland. At least thirty-one coins from the hoard from Lisówek have been identified with certainty. They found their way to the museum through the collection of Emil Bahrfeldt (1921). Additionally, there are several early medieval coins in Braunschweig which most probably come from unidentified hoards from Poland or eastern Germany. They were previously part of the collection from Palace Friedenstein in Gotha, where coins had been collected at least from the eighteenth century onwards (Eberle 2012). Despite all reservations, it must be stated that the coins presented below, except for the dirhams (which were sold in 1902—see note 1 above) and some rare Lorraine and Swabia deniers, are a representative part of the Mózgowo hoard discovered in 1868.

Table 3.2. The composition of various parcels of the Mózgowo hoard, and a summary of all recorded elements. In the last column, 'X' means that the coins were present in the hoard, but in unknown numbers.

Coin/Object type	Region	Mint	Literature	Braunschweig	2010	2012	TOTAL
Dirhams			X	2	196	84	282+X
Germany		Remiremont		2	1	—	3
		Verdun	X	4	—	—	4+X
		Toul		1	—	—	1
	Upper Lorraine	Metz	X	2	—	—	2+X
		'Eyl'	X	1	—	—	1+X
		Upper Lorraine		1	—	—	1
		Tuin	X	1	—	—	1+X
		Namur		1	—	—	1
		Maastricht	X	1	—	—	1+X
		Ciney		1	—	—	1
		Visé	X	2	—	—	2+X
		Köln	X	7	20	3	30+X
		Deventer	X	8	3	1	12+X
	Lower Lorraine	Hamaland		1	1	—	2
		Boulogne?		1	—	—	1
		Western Flanders		2	—	—	2
		Western Lower Lorraine		9	—	—	9
		Low Countries		5	—	—	5
	Frisia	Frisia		20	1	—	21
		Dortmund	X	7	3	1	11+X
		Soest		1	—	—	1
		Münster		1	—	—	1
		Stade	X	—	—	—	X
		Lüneburg		16	7	—	23
	Saxony	Hildesheim	X	—	—	—	X
		Otto & Adelheid	X	38	101	19	158+X
		Magdeburg	X	1	—	—	1+X
		Halberstadt	X	—	—	—	X
		Quedlinburg		4	1	—	5
	Thuringia	Erfurt		4	—	—	4
		Meissen		—	1	—	1
		Würzburg		6	—	—	6
	Franconia	Mainz		32	7	1	40
		Worms		10	3	—	13
		Speyer		2	7	—	9
		Strassburg	X	13	5	—	18+X
		Breisach	X	—	—	—	X
	Swabia	Ulm		1	—	—	1
		Esslingen	X	4	1	—	5+X
		Basel	X	—	—	—	X
		Zürich		1	—	1	1

(continued)

Table 3.2. Continued

Coin/Object type	Region	Mint	Literature	Braunschweig	2010	2012	TOTAL
		Konstanz	X	—	—	—	X
		Augsburg	X	12	2	—	14+X
		Regensburg	X	32	4	1	37+X
		Freising		1	—	—	1
	Bavaria	Nabburg		4	—	—	4
		Neuburg	X	—	—	—	X
		Salzburg	X	2	2	2	6+X
Cross pennies				44	102	43	189
Italy			1	4	1	—	6
Bohemia			X	30	39	16	85+X
Hungary				1	—	—	1
England			X	31	39	22	92+X
Denmark				13	9	13	35
Slavic imitations				20	—	—	20
Unattributed				19	161	130	310
Ornaments			1	—	117	37	154
TOTAL				**426**	**834**	**374**	**1634+X**

and/or fragmented coins and 37 pieces of jewellery. During those excavations, topsoil was removed in thin mechanical layers and searched with the use of specially tuned metal detectors.

A comparison of coins from the museum in Brunschweig with those known from older publications and with those discovered in 2010 and 2012 (Table 3.2) indicates that the coins from Braunschweig must have been specially selected. Within the Braunschweig collection whole coins dominate, while dirhams and jewellery are almost absent. Of note is the relatively small number of Otto and Adelaide denarii, cross denarii, and Speyer coins, and the presence of fragmented coins from particular groups only—Czech and English. At the same time, the Braunschweig collection includes many rather rare coins, primarily from Upper and Lower Lorraine. This, however, may also be connected with the fact that the majority of the museum's collection is composed of whole coins, while the discoveries from 2010 and 2012 consist primarily of small pieces of coins, many of which are difficult to identify.

A complete analysis of the chronology and composition of the Mózgowo hoard is provided elsewhere (Bogucki, Ilisch, & Kulesza 2013; Malarczyk 2013; Nowakiewicz 2013; Bogucki et al. 2016, 79–108, no. 27). Here, it can be stated that the hoard from Mózgowo was deposited after AD 1009. However, considering the presence of numerous cross denarii of type II and an Otto and Adelaide denarii of type Hatz IV, 10m, the date of deposition can be set at approximately AD 1015.

The Metrology of European Coins and the Problem of Representativeness of Data

The hoard from Mózgowo is a typical example of early eleventh-century deposits from the Polish lands. The majority of coins and jewellery that constituted the hoard were fragmented. The Mózgowo hoard is also a good case study for metrological analyses, because, due to different methods of prospection and acquiring finds, we can assume that the known part of the hoard constitutes a representative sample. As in the case of many other similar hoards (Suchodolski 1971; 2012, 135–9; Bogucki 2004, 61–2), elements of relatively low weight, between 0.1 and 0.2 g, are most common (18.72 per cent). The next group of coin fragments, between 1.1 and 1.2 g, constitute the second largest group (6.63 per cent). An interesting feature is the absence of another group, known from other deposits from this period, representing elements weighing approximately 0.5–0.6 g (Bogucki 2004, 62). At the present stage of research, it is difficult to explain such a weight composition of silver. An explanation will require wide-scale metrological research based on a larger number of well-documented hoards. Such an analysis is far beyond the scope of this chapter. However, the key requirement for such a study is the presence of reliable, numerous, and representative samples of comparative material. And it is exactly this aspect to which the hoard from Mózgowo, or rather the story of its discovery, contributes important data.

A comparison of the weight composition of European coins from all three parts of the hoard, i.e. from the museum in Braunschweig and from the parts discovered through targeted metal-detecting in 2010 and excavation in 2012, proves that data from older literature and data concerning hoards discovered during ploughing is entirely unreliable. Comparing the weight structure from the three parts (Fig. 3.2), it becomes apparent that whole coins dominate in the collection from Braunschweig, with a particularly high representation of coins weighing between 1.1 and 1.2 g (13.31 per cent) and heavier (in total over 50 per cent). Coin fragments weighing less than 0.5 g constitute 19 per cent of the collection and coins weighing below 1 g 45 per cent. This is undoubtedly the result of a selection of coins and is also reflected in the typological structure of the coin collection.

In the part of the hoard discovered in 2010 by members of the 'Ylavia' society with the use of metal detectors, small pieces of coins are notably more numerous. The largest group are pieces weighing between 0.1 and 0.2 g (30.65 per cent), while coins weighing more than 1 g are less numerous (a total of 16.47 per cent). Most surprising, however, is the weight distribution of coins found during regular excavation works in 2012. As might be anticipated, the frequency of whole coins is lower than among finds from 2010. However, a very high percentage (over 50 per cent) of small coin fragments weigh less than 0.1 g. This is an entirely new discovery. Among the finds from 2012, 87.61 per cent weigh below 0.5 g and 93.33 per cent below 1 g, while only 6.66 per cent were heavier than 1 g. Such a

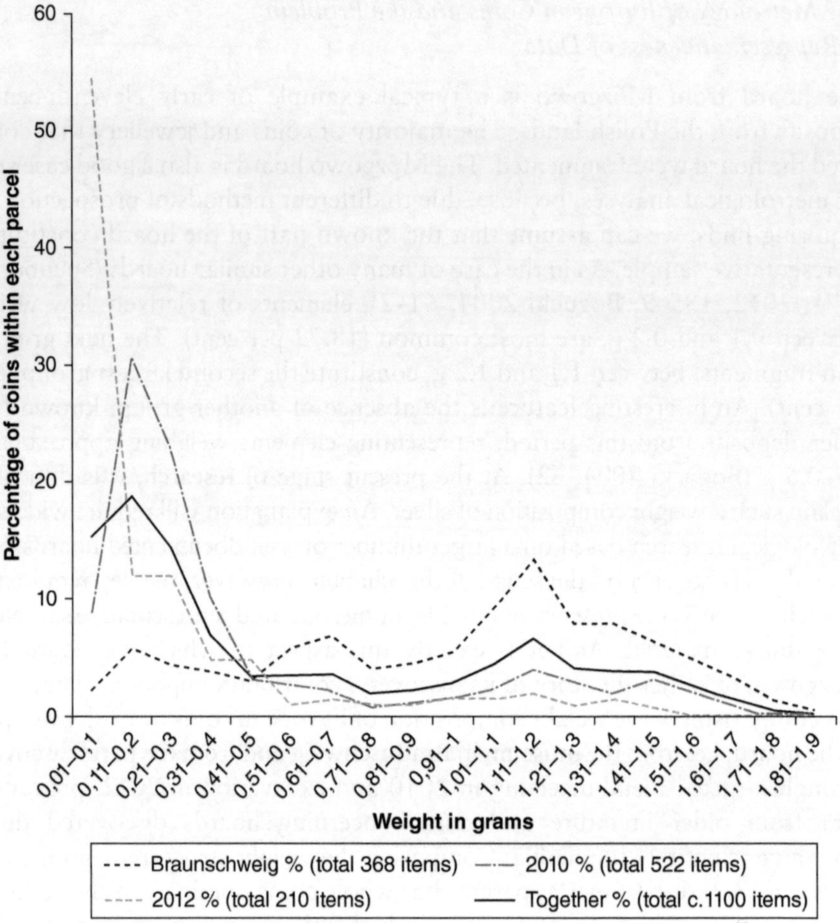

Fig. 3.2. Weight distribution of the European coins from the Mózgowo hoard, showing the percentage within each part of the hoard.

significant percentage of very small fragments results from the implemented excavation methods—within the topsoil earth was removed in 5–10 cm thick layers, the surface of the trench was kept even and flat and metal detectors were tuned in order to signal even the smallest electromagnetic anomalies. Thus, numerous very small pieces of silver were discovered that would normally remain undetected, as they were producing signals resembling those of small lumps of iron.

The comparison provided above leads to important conclusions regarding both the methodology of excavating 'hack-silver' hoards and the representativeness of source material used to gather information about the metrology of early medieval 'hack-silver'. With regard to methodology, it has to be stated that data about the degree of fragmentation drawn from older sources is, on the whole, likely to be unreliable (with the exception of hoards discovered in situ, ideally in whole containers, during archaeological excavations). Hoards discovered today, with the use of metal detectors, likewise cannot be treated as an absolutely reliable source for studying the metrology of 'hack-silver', as, as a rule, metal detectors are set on *default mode*, which makes it impossible to detect smaller pieces of silver. This applies above all to hoards found on farmland, where small, modern iron objects are abundant and tend to obscure signals of silver. Only during regular archaeological works, when a site is unearthed in thin layers and specially tuned metal detectors operated by professionals are implemented, is it possible to detect even the smallest possible finds.[3] Only under such conditions is the acquired source material complete, representative, and conclusive.

Discussion

Although the hoard from Mózgowo reveals the incompleteness of data that was hitherto used for statistical analyses leading to the determination of small units of weight, it does not, in itself, provide much information which could explain how such small units functioned. It would seem that a combination of all three parts of the Mózgowo hoard would result in a statistically valid sample for analysis. Yet, comparing the weight charts of particular parts with the combined end-chart we can see that each part is clearly reflected within the end-chart (Fig. 3.2). This applies to the selected Braunschweig part, in which whole coins are almost exclusively present (thus a somewhat higher percentage of coins weighing *c.*1 g in the end-chart), as well as to the 2012 finds, comprised almost entirely of very small fragments (thus the highest percentage of pieces lighter than 0.3 g). The weight structure of the Mózgowo hoard is thus atypical; undoubtedly, relatively numerous pieces are missing. Those missing coins are probably primarily halved and quartered coins that must have been discovered in the nineteenth century. Due to their low attractiveness for collectors they were excluded from the Braunschweig collection and presumably, in accordance with the custom of the day, melted down. Therefore, the 'second small unit', of pieces weighing *c.*0.5 g, is lacking. Those reservations do not alter the fact that, in the Mózgowo hoard, the 'first small unit' consists of pieces weighing 0.1–0.2 g (18.73 per cent), as is common in hoards from nearby Masovia. However, a new feature to emerge is the very significant amount, 15.27 per cent, of lighter fragments, weighing between 0.01–0.1 g.

At this point we may question the possible function of such small pieces of silver. Some researchers, especially P. Urbańczyk, argue that small pieces of

[3] Here it needs to be stated that a significant majority of professional archaeologists in Poland are unfamiliar with the use of metal detectors. Even those few that use them in their research only operate them on a basic level. The vast majority of the smallest finds discovered during the 2012 excavations were detected only due to the involvement of two professional metal-detector operators—Artur Troncik and Piotr Szyngiera.

silver could not perform economic functions, because at that time there was no market exchange. He has argued further that these fragments are too small to be handled in a practical sense (Urbańczyk 2002; 2009). By contrast, I have elsewhere argued that exchange markets functioned in early medieval Poland at the turn of the tenth and eleventh centuries, as confirmed by written, archaeological, and numismatic sources (Bogucki 2004; 2005; 2011; see too Suchodolski 2004; 2013). With regard to the convenience of using such small pieces of coins and ornaments, it is sufficient to state that contemporary balance weights were sensitive enough to detect weight differences of 0.01 g (Hårdh 1996, 26). In my opinion, the dominant reason for fragmenting silver was economic—the need for small units to make payments. The question is whether they were accepted by weight or were counted out by number, or indeed whether the system was mixed. At this stage of research, it is impossible to say whether the appearance of fragments weighing less than 0.1 g reflected changes in the value of the metal or whether it reflected adjustments in the size and weight of the fragments for the purpose of making the smallest change.

Combining data from published sources with coins from Braunschweig and finds from 2010 and 2012, we can present a more or less detailed list of 1,516 coins and coin fragments from the Mózgowo hoard. At least 2,000 coins and one whole necklace were discovered in 1868. Adding the 1,047 coins found in 2010 and 2012 we reach the number of 3,047 coins. Originally, there must have been many more, as there is no information about the size of the collection owned by Wiggert, the director of a gymnasium. Even careful estimates allow us to state that the hoard from Mózgowo could have originally included some 4,000–5,000 coins, coin fragments, and items of jewellery.

The weight of coins discovered in 1868 remains unknown, but considering the average weight of coins from Braunschweig and those discovered in 2010: 0.66 g (finds from 2012 are excluded as it is impossible that such small pieces were found earlier), we can estimate that those 2,000–3,000 coins had the weight of *c.*1,300–2,000 g. No data is available about the weight of the necklace, but it could have been 100–200 g. The weight of coins and jewellery discovered in 2010 and 2012 gives the total of 406.93 g of silver (dirhams 83.33 g + denarii 282.72 g + jewellery 40.99 g). Thus, the combined weight of silver from the Mózgowo hoard could be estimated at *c.*2–2.5 kg.

The calculations provided above allow us to place the hoard from Mózgowo within the group of relatively large early medieval deposits. It is, at the same time, the largest early medieval hoard from Warmia and Masuria. Significantly larger deposits have been discovered in other areas (such as Dzierznica, Lisówek, and Słuszków in Great Poland, Karczmiska in Little Poland, and Łupawa in Pomerania), but the vast majority of early medieval hoards contained no more than several hundred coins. An interesting question is the estimated value of the Mózgowo hoard. Because of the lack of sources about the prices in the tenth and eleventh centuries, all estimates will be speculative. However, based on the results of studies on the value of money in the Middle Ages, such a guess can be justified. The basis for such conclusions is a unit called *trofa*, a biological unit of the value of money that describes the cost of products needed for one man to survive one day (3,000 calories).[4] We do not know the exact value of a *trofa* in the eleventh century, but it is assumed that it was approximately 0.2 g of pure silver (Żabiński 1981, 8–15, 27–37; Suchodolski 1997, 151–8; 2012, 257–8). A simple calculation leads to the statement that the hoard from Mózgowo could be worth between 10,000 and 12,500 *trofa*.

REFERENCES

Albrecht, G. 1959. *Das Münzwesen im Niederlothringischen und Friesischen Raum vom 10., bis zum Beginnenden 12. Jahrhundert.* Hamburg: Museum für Hamburgische Geschichte.

Bahrfeldt, E. 1921. *Münzen des Deutschen Mittelalters, Sammlung Dr. Emil Bahrfeldt, Berlin.* Frankfurt am Main: Hess.

Bergau, J.N. 1868. 'Münzfunde aus Westpreussen'. *Altpreusisiche Monatschrift* V: 557.

Bogucki, M. 2004. 'Dlaczego we wczesnym średniowieczu powstawały skarby złomu Srebrnego? Uwagi na marginesie prac Jacka Kowalewskiego i Przemysława Urbańczyka'. *Wiadomości Numizmatyczne* XLVIII/1 (177): 49–76.

Bogucki, M. 2005. 'Reasons for Hiding Early Mediaeval Hack Silver Hoards'. In *XIII Congreso Internacional de Numismática. Madrid—2003. Acta—Proceedings—Actes*, Vol. II, ed. C. Alfaro, C. Marcos, & P. Otero, 1151–7. Madrid: Ministerio de Cultura.

Bogucki, M. 2007. 'Coin Finds in Viking Age Emporium at Janów Pomorski (Truso) and the "Prussian Phenomenon"'. In *Money Circulation in Antiquity, the Middle Ages and Modern Times: Time, Range, Intensity. International Symposium on the 50th Anniversary of Wiadomości Numizmatyczne. Warsaw, 13–14 October 2006*, ed. S. Suchodolski & M. Bogucki, 79–108. Warszawa-Kraków: Wydawnictwo Avalon.

Bogucki, M. 2011. 'The Use of Money in the Slavic Lands from the 9th to the 11th Century—the Archaeological-Numismatic Evidence'. In *Silver Economies, Monetization and Society in Scandinavia, 800–1100*, ed. J. Graham-Campbell, S. M. Sindbæk, & G. Williams, 129–48. Aarhus: Aarhus University Press.

Bogucki, M., P. Ilisch, & M. Kulesza 2013. 'Monety zachodnioeuropejskie w skarbie z Mózgowa'. In *Znaleziska średniowiecznych skarbów srebrnych z terenu Pojezierza Iławskiego w zbiorach Muzeum Warmii i Mazur*, ed. E. Jelińska, 14–139. Olsztyn: Muzeum Warmii i Mazur.

Bogucki, M., D. Malarczyk, P. Ilisch, M. Kulesza, J. Piniński, & T. Nowakiewicz 2016. 'Frühmittelalterliche Münzfunde aus Ermland und Masuren'. In *Frühmittelalterliche Münzfunde aus Polen. Inventar*, Band V, ed. M. Bogucki, P. Ilisch, & S. Suchodolski, 19–186. Warszawa: Instytut Archeologii i Etnologii PAN.

Cach, F. 1970. *Nejstarší České Mince.* Prague: Česká Numismatická Spolěcnost.

[4] The term *trofa*, originating from Greek τροφή—sustenance—has no equivalent in English numismatic literature. The closest are the Big Mac Index used by 'The Economist' or Purchasing Power Parity.

Chmielecki, K. 1907. 'Wykopaliska monet i srebra: Maszenice, Nieciszewo, Poczałkowo w świetle najnowszych badań'. *Roczniki Towarzystwa Naukowego w Toruniu* 14: 3–44.

Czwojda, L. 2007. 'A Tentative Interpretation of Peck Marks upon Coins of the Viking Age'. *Wiadomości Numizmatyczne* LI/1 (183): 1–28.

Dannenberg, H. 1876. *Die Deutschen Münzen der Sächsischen und Fränkischen Kaiserzeit I*. Berlin: Weidmann.

Dannenberg, H. 1894. *Die Deutschen Münzen der Sächsischen und Fränkischen Kaiserzeit II*. Berlin: Weidmann.

Duczko, W. 2002. 'Test or Magic? Pecks on the Viking-Age Silver'. In Paszkiewicz (ed.), 193–208.

Eberle, M. 2012. *Gothas Gold—300 Jahre Münzkabinett*. Gotha: Stiftung Schloss Friedenstein.

Fiala, E. 1891. *Beschreibung Böhmischer Münzen und Medaillen*. Prague.

Fiala, E. 1895. *Česke Denary*. Prague.

Fiala, E. 1922. 'Johan Etl'. *Věstník Numismatickě Společnosti Česko-Slovenské v Praze* IV/2: 181–2.

Gajewski, L. (ed.) 1982. *Skarby Wczesnośredniowieczne z obszaru Polski. Atlas*. Wrocław: Wrocław Zakład Narodowy im. Ossolińskich.

Gumowski, M. 1905. *Wykopaliska monet polskich X i XI wieku*. Kraków: Nakładem Akademii Umiejętności.

Gumowski, M. 1953. *Polskie skarby monet X–XI wieku (Materiały)*. Warszawa.

Hårdh, B. 1996. *Silver in the Viking Age: A Regional-Economic Study*. Stockholm: Almqvist & Wiksell International.

Hårdh, B. 2008. 'Hacksilver and Ingots'. In *Means of Exchange: Dealing with Silver in the Viking Age*. Kaupang Excavation Project Publication Series, vol. 2, ed. D. Skre, 95–118. Aarhus: Aarhus University Press.

Herfurth, A. 1997. 'Mülverstedt, Johan George Adalbert von'. *Neue Deutsche Biographie* Band 18: 516–17.

Ilisch, L. 1990. 'Whole and Fragmented Dirhams in Near Eastern Hoards'. In *Sigtuna Papers: Proceedings of the Sigtuna Symposium on Viking-Age Coinage 1–4 June 1989, Commentationes de Nummis Saeculorum IX–XI*, Nova Series 6, ed. K. Jonnson & B. Malmer, 121–31. Stockholm and London: Spink.

Ilisch, P. 1998. 'Die Münzprägung im Herzogtum Niederlothringen I: Die Münzprägung in den Räumen Utrecht und Friesland im 10. Und 11.Jahrhundert'. *Jaarboek voor Munt- en Pfenningkunde* 84–5 (1997–8): 43–7.

Jammer, V. 1952. *Die Anfänge der Münzprägung im Herzogtum Sachsen (10. und 11. Jahrhundert)*. Hamburg: Museum für Hamburgische Geschichte.

Jelińska, E. (ed.) 2013. *Znaleziska średniowiecznych skarbów srebrnych z terenu Pojezierza Iławskiego w zbiorach Muzeum Warmii i Mazur*. Olsztyn: Muzeum Warmii i Mazur.

Kiersnowscy, T. & R. Kiersnowscy 1959. *Wczesnośredniowieczne skarby srebrne z Pomorza,* Materiały. Polskie Skarby Wczesnośredniowieczne. Inwentarze II, Polskie Badania Archeologiczne 4. Warszawa: Zakład Narodowy im. Ossolińskich, Wydawnictwo Polskiej Akademii Nauk.

Kiersnowski, R. 1960. *Pieniądz kruszcowy w Polsce wczesnośredniowiecznej*. Warszawa: Państwowe Wydawnictwo Naukowe.

Kilger, C. 2006. 'Silver-Handling Traditions during the Viking Age—Some Observations and Thoughts on the Phenomenon of Pecking and Bending'. In *Coinage and History in the North Sea World c.500–1250: Essays in Honour of Marion Archibald*, ed. B. Cook & G. Williams, 449–65. Leiden: Brill.

Kócka-Krenz, H. 1993. *Biżuteria północno-zachodnio-słowiańska we wczesnym średniowieczu*. Poznań: Wydawnictwo Naukowe Uniwersytetu im. Adama Mickiewicza.

Kowalski, T. 1946. *Relacja Ibrahima ibn Jakuba z podróży do krajów słowiańskich w przekazie al-Bekriego*. Monumenta Poloniae Historica, Nova Series 1. Kraków: Gebethner i Wolff.

Kujot, S. 1913. *Dzieje Prus Królewskich*, Vol. I, Roczniki Towarzystwa Naukowego w Toruniu XX. Toruń: TNT.

La Baume, W. 1938. 'Die Silberhortfunde des Frühen Mittelalters aus dem Gebiet an der Unteren Weichsel'. *Altpreussische Forschungen* 15: 42–62.

Langenheim, K. 1933. 'Spuren der Wikinger um Truso'. *Elbinger Jahrbuch* 11: 262–83.

Łęga, W. 1930. *Kultura Pomorza we wczesnym średniowieczu na podstawie wykopalisk*. Toruń: Towarzystwo Naukowe.

Łosiński, W. 1988, 'Chronologia napływu najstarszej monety arabskiej na terytorium Europy'. *Slavia Antiqua* XXXI: 93–181.

Malarczyk, D. 2013. 'Monety arabskie w skarbie z Mózgowa'. In Jelińska (ed.), 140–57.

Malmer, B. 1966. *Nordiska Mynt före år 1000*. Bonn and Lund: Habelt/Gleerup.

Markov, A. 1910. *Topografija Kładov Vostočnykh Monet*. St Petersburg.

Moesgaard, J.C. 2015. *King Harold's Cross Coinage: Christian Coins for the Merchants of Haithabu and the King's Soldiers*. Studies in Archaeology & History, Jelling Series vol. 20:2. Copenhagen: National Museum of Denmark.

Nowakiewicz, T. 2003. 'Ozdoby i srebro siekane z wczesnośredniowiecznego skarbu srebrnego z Ciechanowa'. In *Studia Galindzkie* I, ed. W. Wróblewski, 261–318. Warsaw: Instytut Archeologii Uniwersytet Warszawski.

Nowakiewicz, T. 2013. 'Niemonetarna część skarbu z Mózgowa'. In Jelińska (ed.), 158–88.

Paszkiewicz, B. (ed.) 2002. *Moneta Mediaevalis. Studia numizmatyczne i historyczne ofiarowane Profesorowi Stanisławowi Suchodolskiemu w 65. rocznicę urodzin*. Warszawa: Wydawn. DiG.

Suchodolski, S. 1971. 'W sprawie intensywności wymiany lokalnej na ziemiach polskich w X–XI wieku'. *Archeologia Polski* XVI: 503–15.

Suchodolski, S. 1997. 'Zasoby pieniężne "Szarego Człowieka" w Polsce wczesnośredniowiecznej'. In *Człowiek w społeczeństwie średniowiecznym*, ed. R. Michałowski, 151–8. Warszawa: Wydawnictwo DiG.

Suchodolski, S. 2004. 'Aus Welchen Gründen Hat Man in der Wikingerzeit im Ostseeraum Münzschätze Deponiert?' In *Fundamenta Historiae. Geschichte im Spiegel der Numismatik und Ihrer Nachbarwissenschaften. Festschrift für Niklot Klüßendorf zum 60. Geburtstag am 10. Februar 2004*, ed. R. Cunz, 107–16. Hannover: Schmidt.

Suchodolski, S. 2012. *Numizmatyka Średniowieczna. Moneta źródłem archeologicznym, historycznym i ikonograficznym*. Warszawa: Wydawnictwo Trio.

Suchodolski, S. 2013. 'Warum Hat Man im Frühen Mittelalter Schätze Deponiert?' In *Economies, Monetisation and Society in West Slavic Lands 800–1200 AD*, ed.

M. Bogucki & M. Rębkowski, 89–107. Wolińskie Spotkania Mediewistyczne II. Szczecin: Instytut Archeologii i Etnologii, Polskiej Akademii Nauk.

Suhle, A. 1926. 'Angelsächsische Münzen in den Grösseren Schatzfunden Östlich der Elbe von ca. 950 bis ca. 1150 n. C.' *Blätter für Münzfreunde* III/1: 80.

Suhle, A. 1928. 'Angelsächsische Münzen in Nordostdeutsche Funden'. *Blätter für Münzfreunde* 63/3: 225–30.

Tambor, J. 1989. 'Pieniężne funkcje biżuterii srebrnej na ziemiach polskich w X–XI wieku'. *Wiadomości Numizmatyczne* XXIII (127–30): 12–43.

Urbańczyk, P. 2002. 'Wczesnośredniowieczne skarby złomu srebrnego'. In Paszkiewicz (ed.), 209–24.

Urbańczyk, P. 2009. 'The Polish Discussion on Medieval Deposits of Hack-Silver'. In *Historia Archaeologica*, ed. S. Brather, D. Guenich, & C. Huth, 501–23. Berlin and New York: De Gruyter.

Żabiński, Z. 1981. *Systemy pieniężne na ziemiach polskich*. Kraków: Zakład Narodowy im. Ossolińskich.

Żak, J. 1963. *'Importy' Skandynawskie na ziemiach Zachodniosłowiańskich od IX do XI w. 1. Katalog*. Poznań: Państwowe Wydawnictwo Naukowe.

4

Royalty and Renewal in Viking Age Ireland

Andrew R. Woods

Introduction

It has been argued that coinage has a clear connection to royal authority in the early medieval period (for example, Williams 2007; Blackburn 2009). Kings who could create and maintain an effective coinage have been interpreted as powerful. This power is demonstrated by their ability to effectively oversee production, call upon an effective administration, marshal economic resources, and deploy imagery associated with kingship. Perhaps the classic example of a well-ordered, administered, and symbolically rich coinage being suggestive of a powerful state can be found in late Anglo-Saxon England. Here, a national system of mints maintained good control over the weight and fineness of the coinage with a series of symbolically rich coinages renewed every few years (cf. Naismith 2012, 88).

However, these various elements were not necessarily present in all early medieval coinages. Coinages could have clear symbolic power without extensive administrative control. The apparently limited circulation and use of the symbolically loaded coinage struck in Anglo-Scandinavian York would certainly suggest as much (Blackburn 2004). Conversely, many eighth-century coinages give an impression of being well produced but without the same administrative or symbolic focus (Metcalf & Op den Velde 2009). In the current context, the focus will be on the Hiberno-Scandinavian coinage of Viking Age Ireland.[1] Struck between *c*.995 and 1170 in Dublin, the coinage was originally classified by Michael Dolley, who described some of the coinage as 'debased and degraded imitations' (Dolley 1966, 139). While not his original intention, it has created an unhelpful perception of a chaotic and unordered coinage with subsequent implications for understanding the level of economic and political sophistication in Viking Age Ireland (Blackburn 2008, 116).

[1] The term 'Hiberno-Scandinavian' will be preferred to terms such as 'Hiberno-Norse' or 'Hiberno-Danish' (see Sheehan, Stummann Hansen & Ó Corráin 2001, 93–4). The 'Viking Age' is here defined in its broadest Irish form as AD 795–1170.

The following will offer a reappraisal, discussing what the organization and administration of the Hiberno-Scandinavian coinage suggest about royal power in the Viking Age. While the primary focus will be on Viking Age Ireland, comparison will also be drawn with other contemporary areas, particularly with Norway and England, to highlight the variety of forms that coinage could take at the time, and the implications for royal authority. When considering coin production, the overall focus is the extent of royal oversight and manipulation of the coinage as expressed through levels of consistency in weight and alloy content (silver fineness). The administration of the coinage will be discussed in light of evidence for the exclusion from circulation of foreign coin and for the occasional renewal of the coinage.

Background

Raiding commenced in Ireland in 795, escalating during the course of the ninth century (Sheehan 2008, 282). Ship camps (*longphuirt*) were soon established upon major river routes, which facilitated increasingly inland raiding activities. One of these ship camps grew to form Dublin, the largest settlement in Ireland at the time, while significant Viking Age settlement occurred in a number of other towns. The urban aspect to Viking settlement in Ireland must be stressed with relatively small-scale settlement focused primarily upon coastal areas and towns (Bradley 1988). The outward-facing aspect of the Scandinavian presence in Ireland is also visible with settlement in Ireland forming part of an interconnected Irish Sea region, comprising the Isle of Man and the coastal regions of south-west Scotland, north-west England, and north Wales (Griffiths 2010).

Before the Viking Age, there is little archaeological evidence for the economic use of silver in Ireland. This situation changed over the course of the ninth century, particularly from around AD 850, as hoards attest to the adoption of the use of bullion for economic purposes (Sheehan 2000; 2007). Hoards deposited in this time combine whole objects, hack-silver, ingots, and coins in differing combinations based upon chronology and geography. During the course of the tenth century, all of the coinage used in Ireland was imported, with the overwhelming majority of coins coming from England. Coinage became much more significant as a means of exchange from the mid tenth century, as attested by increasing numbers of single finds of coinage and a growing proportion of silver in hoards in coined form (Blackburn 2007; Bornholdt-Collins 2010; Woods 2014, 298–302).

This gradual increase in the proportion of coined silver relative to bullion suggests that coinage was likely to have been valued above its intrinsic bullion worth and was accompanied by the adoption of a coin-using mentality in some areas of Ireland. This probably emerged as the product of regular mercantile contact between England and Ireland, which encouraged the use of coinage in the latter (Woods 2015). However, it must be stressed that the adoption of coin use in Ireland was a complex process, which likely saw a degree of flexibility when it came to using silver. Choice of silver currency depended on when, where, and with whom exchange took place. This is most clear when considering the geography of coin use given its limited distribution, centred upon Dublin and parts of the Irish midlands (Woods 2014, 302–12; Blackburn 2009, 66–8).

The situation altered during the mid 990s when Dublin began to strike its own coinage. Following this decision, Ireland had its own distinctive coin history until the arrival of the Anglo-Normans in AD 1170. This coinage, typically referred to as 'Hiberno-Norse' or 'Hiberno-Scandinavian', was extensively classified in the 1960s (Dolley 1966; for a review of previous literature, see Blackburn 2008, 112–14). Recently, the current writer reassessed the coinage (Woods 2013), suggesting a new chronology and typology.

Production

The act of striking coinage provided a means for early medieval rulers to bolster their authority, not only in practical, financial terms but also symbolically as it represented a royal act, being a privilege reserved almost exclusively for kings (Blackburn 2004, 333). It follows that the consistency of coinage provides a means of assessing the levels of royal oversight and the ability of rulers to enforce certain standards of production. It is generally assumed that when coins were produced both a specific weight and fineness were targeted. This is highlighted in contemporary law texts where the importance of maintaining silver standards is stressed (Naismith 2012, 156; Screen 2007). Where a coinage is well maintained, it may be suggested that there was both a widely known weight and fineness standard, and sufficient royal authority and oversight to ensure that it was met. The situation is slightly complicated by the fact that weight and fineness could be manipulated, either officially, for economic or political purposes, or illicitly, by those working at the mint. For instance, weight standards were altered in tenth-century Scandinavian York for political purposes, to stress its independence from contemporary West Saxon coinage and to bring it into line with other Anglo-Scandinavian coinages of the southern Danelaw (Blackburn 2004, 339–40). The fineness of Harald Hardråde's coinage was seriously debased in the 1040s and 1050s (Skaare 1976, 79–85; Gullbekk 2009, 147). Harald's changes would have had the effect of increasing profits of mint and king at the expense of the coin user.

Weight

Discussion of the declining weight of coinage in Ireland has usually focused on the long term where, in general, the coinage became lighter during the course of the eleventh and twelfth centuries (Dolley 1966, 134–5). This can lead to the perception of a poorly organized or administered mint. However, it can be suggested that the mint was well organized and controlled if a comparison is made of the weights of 'die-linked' coins. Comparing the weight of coins struck using the same die allows an examination of how closely weights were maintained within a very short period of time, namely the life of one die. Where studies have pursued this approach in the past, they have been considered by counting the number of die-duplicates that are within certain, gradated weight ranges of one another, namely 0.03 g, 0.06 g, and 0.09 g (Petersson 1969, 142–4; Blackburn 2008, 125–6, Table 5).[2] This approach is less helpful when working on coinage with a light weight, because these measures represent a significant proportion of coins weighing less than one gram. Here, a more useful approach is to quantify the variation amongst die-duplicates as a percentage of the total weight. In this case, a higher percentage indicates greater variation and a smaller percentage suggests greater control.

Table 4.1 summarizes the variation in weight between Hiberno-Scandinavian coins struck using the same dies. The difference in number of comparisons is due to differing survival rates amongst coins of the various periods. The data suggests that there was a general consistency in the levels of control over the weight of coins being struck using the same dies in Dublin. With the exception of the late eleventh century, specifically from *c.*1075, most coins were struck within 10 per cent of the weight of their die-duplicates. This is not a large difference, representing at most 0.14 g, especially when the weight of coins may have been affected by post-deposition factors.

Comparing these figures with contemporary coinages elsewhere, the Dublin coins can be seen to fit a broader pattern. In the Norwegian ruler Harald Hardråde's *Triquetra* coinage (*c.*1047–66), the median difference (0.09 g) between die-duplicates is 10 per cent of their median weight (0.87 g) (based on data drawn from Skaare 1976). In England, the control of weight at the mint appears to have been slightly more stringent. Data exists from Lincoln in the period 1056–1180 and it shows that some die-linked coinages were quite precisely maintained, such as in William I's type v with a variation of only 3 per cent (median difference 0.04 g with a median weight of 1.38 g, based on data drawn from Mossop 1970). However, this was not the case for all Lincoln coinages as Edward the Confessor's *Hammer Cross* type has a variation of 9 per cent (median difference 0.13 g with a median weight of 1.32 g) and William I's type ii has a variation of 16 per cent (median difference 0.19 g with a median weight of 1.15 g). On the whole, the level of precision in England was slightly greater than in Ireland but this may speak of a longer-established minting tradition, capable of greater precision, as well as suggesting a greater degree of royal oversight. By way of comparison, the well-regulated mints of thirteenth-century England had an acceptable variation of around 7 per cent (Allen 2012, 147–8). Thus, the mints of Ireland and Norway, whilst not quite reaching the standard of contemporary England, were executing a well-maintained coinage.

[2] In the text, Blackburn (2008) erroneously gives these figures as 0.3, 0.6, and 0.9 g. The figures of 0.03, 0.06, and 0.09 g given in the table are correct.

Table 4.1. Weight differences between Hiberno-Scandinavian die-duplicates. Data drawn from Woods 2013.

Group	Period		Number of comparisons	Median weight (g)	Weight range (g)	Median difference in weight (g)	Median difference (as % of median weight)
A	*c.*995–7	*Crux* Imitations	57	1.53	1.10–1.79	0.12	8%
B	*c.*997–1003	*Long Cross* Imitations	65	1.42	1.10–1.76	0.09	6%
C	*c.*1003–9	*Helmet* Imitations	25	1.22	1.02–1.42	0.11	9%
D	*c.*1009–18	*Last Small Cross* Imitations	4	1.02	0.95–1.10	0.10	10%
E	*c.*1018–20	*Quatrefoil* Imitations	12	0.99	0.83–1.10	0.14	14%
F	*c.*1020–40	Long Cross with pellets reverse	221	1.07	0.57–1.64	0.08	7%
G	*c.*1040–60	Long Cross with hands reverse	873	0.89	0.58–1.24	0.07	8%
H	*c.*1060–5	'Scratched Cross' reverse types	841	0.78	0.49–1.44	0.07	9%
I	*c.*1065–75	Long Cross with sickles and related types	831	0.88	0.62–1.01	0.05	6%
J	*c.*1075–80	Imitation of 1070s Anglo-Norman types	21	0.67	0.53–0.84	0.09	13%
K	*c.*1080–5	'Bird' and associated types	163	0.63	0.43–0.96	0.07	11%
L	*c.*1085–90	*Paxs* Imitations, derivatives and related types	135	0.82	0.59–0.97	0.09	11%
M	*c.*1090–5	Small Flan	31	0.65	0.53–0.89	0.13	19%
N	*c.*1095–1100	Stylized facing and profile busts	26	0.60	0.47–0.73	0.05	8%

Silver Fineness

Fairly precise control over the production of coinage is also suggested when the alloy of the Hiberno-Scandinavian coinage is considered. Figure 4.1 is a plot of the silver fineness of the Hiberno-Scandinavian coinage. This draws upon the work of Heslip and Northover (1990) but also combines more recent, and currently unpublished results.[3] Figure 4.1 reveals that, from the outset of the coinage, and throughout the eleventh century, there was a consistently high silver standard. There is a median figure of 93 per cent fine and a mean of 91 per cent, with the latter affected by a small minority of coins from the second half of the eleventh century, which appear to be significantly debased, with fineness between 50 per cent and 70 per cent. The picture is certainly one of a well-maintained alloy, with a standard just in excess of 90 per cent fine, quite consistently achieved throughout most of the period in question. In this regard, the Hiberno-Scandinavian coinage can be compared favourably to coinage struck in England, where extensive fineness analyses have been conducted, and where results show that an average silver fineness of 93 per cent was achieved in England's mints in the first half of the eleventh century (data from Metcalf & Northover 1986; 2002).[4] A precisely maintained silver alloy was also achieved around the Irish Sea, in the Hiberno-Manx coinage (Bornholdt 1999). Indeed, it

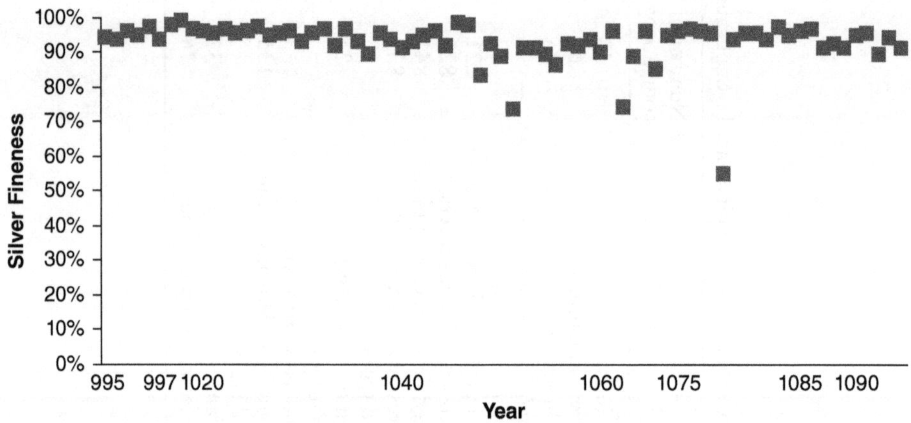

Fig. 4.1. Silver fineness of Hiberno-Scandinavian coins.

[3] For a full discussion of methods and the validity of combining datasets see Woods 2013, 154–7.

[4] The high level of silver attained in the Hiberno-Scandinavian coinage is not simply a result of its source. While high-quality silver from England was the source for some of the Hiberno-Scandinavian coinage, it was not simply melted down and restruck once it reached Dublin. English coinage reveals a heterogeneous mix of trace elements, whereas trace elements in the Dublin coinage are fairly consistent. This pattern suggests the use of cupellation and the reintroduction of base metals to achieve a certain standard of silver in the Dublin coinage. For further discussion, see Woods 2013, 154–66.

is likely that this was a deliberate act, creating a coinage with the same fineness in order to facilitate regional exchange.

Combining the data from weight and silver fineness, it is apparent that there was both technical expertise and fairly consistent oversight in the Hiberno-Scandinavian coinage. Impressions of the coinage based upon a general, long-term trend of declining weights are misleading (cf. Dolley 1987, 816–18). It seems likely that at most points the Hiberno-Scandinavian mint had a weight standard with an acceptable margin of error of around 10 per cent and an even more precisely maintained alloy. This level of control suggests that the mint was reasonably precise when silver was processed into new coins, although it must be acknowledged that England maintained more consistent standards.

An explanation for the limited variation of weight within die-linked types must be sought elsewhere (Table 4.1). Generally speaking, it seems likely that weight standards were manipulated at various points, with lighter coins struck at the end of the type rather than at the beginning (Blackburn 2008, 118). It is possible to trace this within Groups B and F, summarized in Table 4.2, where some internal chronology can be applied to the coins. In the case of Group B (*c.*997–*c.*1003) the earliest coins are those which have the legend 'Sihtric Cununc'; these are followed by a large group with the legend 'Sitric Rex' and a smaller group which is late within the coinage which name the ruler as 'DYMN' (Blackburn 2008, 124). In Group F (*c.*1020–*c.*1040), early and late groups have been distinguished, as has a very late group with a distinctive 'E' on the reverse (Seaby 1984). In both of these cases, where chronology can be determined, it seems that the weight of the coinage gradually decreased. It is possible that the alloy was also manipulated, with a slight decrease in the silver fineness visible between *c.*1020 and *c.*1040 (Heslip & Northover 1990, 108). This is a pattern

Table 4.2. Summary of weight variation within Groups B and F. Weight data for group B is drawn from Woods 2013, and for Group F from Seaby 1984.

Group B	Median weight (g)
Sihtric Cunung	1.51
Sitric Rex	1.37
DYMN Rex	1.31
Group F	
Early	1.13
Late	0.97
'E' Coinage	0.62

which mirrors contemporary England (Petersson 1969; cf. Lyon 1976, 195–205). Debasement such as this should probably be interpreted within the context of political authority. It is likely to represent an attempt to increase mint profits across the period, rather than as any kind of failure in the mint (Lyon 2003, 71–2). Debased coins with the same nominal value would have proved lucrative for those producing them, as larger volumes of currency were produced from the same volume of silver (cf. Gullbekk 2009, 131–2).

Administration

It is widely accepted that the effective exclusion of foreign currency and an ability to renew currency, a process often known as *renovatio monetae,* are indicative of an effectively administered coinage (Naismith 2012, 181–3; Grierson 1981; Grierson 1962, x).

The Exclusion of Foreign Currency

It has been argued that there was a fairly effective exclusion of foreign coinage from Dublin, with slightly more variation outside areas surrounding the town (Blackburn 2008, 117). This pattern is clear from the evidence of single finds, which are likely to more accurately reflect the circulating currency than hoards, where a degree of selectivity is often introduced. All single finds in Ireland were struck overseas, overwhelmingly in England, until the 990s when Dublin began to strike its own coinage (Woods 2014). Following this, almost all foreign currency is excluded from Ireland. This is not instantaneous as there are small numbers of English coins found in Ireland until the 1030s. However, after two *Short Cross* coins of Cnut dated *c.*1029–*c.*1036, found in Co. Limerick and Co. Clare, there is no foreign single find in Ireland until a find from the High Street, Dublin, of a penny of Stephen, datable to *c.*1136–54 (Woods 2014, 313–29, especially cat. nos. 85, 86, and 159).

The evidence from hoards is slightly more equivocal given the fact that only the areas around Dublin saw significant coin use in the Viking Age (Woods 2014, 302–12). Hoards buried beyond this may not accurately reflect the circulating currency. Table 4.3 summarizes the coinage contained in Irish hoards between *c.*990 and *c.*1110 (for references see Woods 2013, 222–31). The standards of recording are variable, frequently relying on the reconstruction of antiquarian finds. The hoards are not evenly spread throughout the period, meaning that some periods are difficult to interpret. However, it can be confidently asserted that foreign coinage was fairly effectively excluded. While it represents the entirety of the circulating medium in the 990s it decreased in importance during the course of the eleventh century, playing a negligible role beyond 1050. Across the period in question, only in the Knockmaon hoard do foreign coins outnumber those struck in Ireland. In many ways, this is an unusual hoard, containing a mixture of hack-silver and French coinage, which is unparalleled in contemporary Ireland (Dolley 1966, 57).

Table 4.3. Summary of Irish coin hoards *c*.990–1110. 'x' indicates presence in uncertain numbers.

Hoard	Deposition date	Current Hiberno-Scandinavian type	Older Hiberno-Scandinavian type	Foreign
Castle Street (1)	*c*.990	–	–	79 (100%)
Kildare	*c*.990	–	–	34 (100%)
Castle Street (2)	*c*.995	–	–	242 (100%)
Werburgh Street	*c*.995	–	–	125 (100%)
Renewal 1—c.995				
Dundalk	*c*.995	1 (14%)	–	7 (86%)
Clondalkin (no. 2)*	*c*.995	37+ (100%?)	–	
Renewal 2—c.997				
Knockmaon	*c*.1000	1 (8%)	2 (16%)	11 (76%)
Derrymore	*c*.1000	5 (62%)	–	3 (38%)
Collinstown	*c*.1000	9 (82%)	–	2 (18%)
Renewal 3—c.1020				
Fourknocks	*c*.1030	27 (93%)	–	2 (7%)
Ballycastle (TF1)	*c*.1030	x	x	x
Tonyowen	*c*.1035	3 (100%)	–	–
Renewal 4—c.1040				
Kilkenny	*c*.1040	x (60%?)	x (20%?)	x (20%?)
Ballylinan	*c*.1050	12 (92%?)	–	1 (8%?)
Dunbrody	*c*.1050	x (70%?)	x (19%?)	x (11%?)
Baltinglass	*c*.1050	x	x	–
Limerick	*c*.1065	107 (100%?)	–	–
Clondalkin (no. 1)	*c*.1065	50+ (100%?)	–	–
Clonmacnoise	*c*.1090	5 (17%)	25 (83%)	–
Co. Meath	*c*.1090	x	x	–
Glendalough (no. 1)	*c*.1095	x	x	–
Dunamase	*c*.1100	x	x	–
Renewal 5—c.1100				
Christchurch Cathedral	*c*.1110	6 (86%)	1 (14%)	–
Armagh Cathedral	*c*.1110	3 (100%?)	–	–
Donaghenry	*c*.1110	33+ (100%?)	–	–

* Blackburn (2008, 123) says that upwards of seventy-five pennies came from this hoard; here, the number given is 37+. This reflects the difference between the numbers of coins originally known from the hoard (Blackburn) and the total for which we have accurate data regarding their type (given here).

In an English context, the ability to ensure that no foreign currency circulated has been termed a 'demonstration of effective royal power' (Campbell 2000, 32). The removal of foreign coinage has also been interpreted in the light of growing royal power in Norway, seen as instigated by Harald Hardråde (Gullbekk 1992; Skaare 1976, 106–7). It is appropriate to extend such arguments to Ireland, where a similarly consistent exclusion of foreign coinage was achieved. Blackburn argued that this exclusion of foreign coinage required both 'political and economic muscle' in Ireland (2008, 128). To this muscle, it is also possible to add that there must have been exceptional administrative abilities, ensuring that no foreign coinage was used in Dublin, as well as an effective political authority, capable of deciding upon and enacting a fairly significant level of economic control.

The Renewal of Currency (*Renovatio Monetae*)

Renovatio monetae goes a step beyond ensuring local currency is used, with an occasional demonetization of official currency and the issuing of a new type. A brief description can be found in the Edict of Pîtres, promulgated in 864 by Charles the Bald, which stated that 'no coins should be accepted anywhere in my kingdom except for those of the new coinage which are of good alloy and weight' (cited in Naismith 2012, 181). However, the precise mechanisms of this process are uncertain; the length of time it took and how authorities were able to compel people to exchange their coins are unknown (Stewart 1990, 463–8). Dolley and Metcalf have suggested (1961, 155) that in England business conducted in 'official' spaces, such as markets, would have required the most recent type of coinage to be allowed.[5] Grierson has likewise suggested that current coinage may have been required in certain situations such as fines, taxes, or compensations (1962; see too Stewart 1990, 467–8). It is quite difficult to ascertain the mechanisms of recoinage in England and there is certainly no simple model that can be applied to Ireland, where less supporting evidence survives.

Differing forms of coin renewal existed in the Viking Age. The first of these is what is often described as *periodic*, with coin renewed on a fairly regular basis every few years. Such a system is argued for Anglo-Saxon England, with gaps between coinages argued to be between two and seven years at various points in the late tenth and eleventh centuries (Stewart 1990, 460). The other form might be described as *regal*, with the coinage renewed upon the death of one king, the new coinage being that issued by his successor. Gullbekk has argued that this occurred in Norway in the latter half of the eleventh century, with Harald Hardråde removing earlier coins at the outset of his reign, a process repeated by his son Olaf Kyrre (2009, 60–5).

Absolute certainty regarding the renewal of the Hiberno-Scandinavian coinage is difficult given the number of hoards and their distance from Dublin. However, it can be argued that a form of *renovatio* did occur in Ireland at a number of points. The evidence for this is based upon the hoards, summarized in Table 4.3. From this basis, it is suggested that renewals may have occurred in *c.*995, *c.*997, *c.*1020, *c.*1040, and *c.*1100. In each case, the iconography of the coinage was altered with the new type, illustrated in Figure 4.2.[6]

[5] However, the requirement to use the current type is never explicitly stated in Anglo-Saxon law codes, where it might be expected to occur; cf. Stewart 1990, 466.

[6] The figure contains only the major types where it is argued that *renovatio* occurred. A large range of different designs was utilized in the period, including many between these renewals of the coinage. Most of the types are illustrated in Dolley 1966.

The clearest evidence for the demonetization of old coinage can be found at the outset of the Hiberno-Scandinavian coinage. The currency was very swiftly transformed from being almost entirely Anglo-Saxon to being locally made imitative *CRUX* pennies (Group A). This is most clear in the evidence from the Clondalkin (2) hoard, deposited *c.*995, composed exclusively of newly produced coins (Blackburn 2008, 123). This must have been deposited within a year or two of the Castle Street (2) or Werburgh Street hoards, and yet the currency it contained was entirely different, with both Castle Street (2) and Werburgh Street consisting entirely of foreign issues. It is difficult to envisage the mechanics of this change without suggesting demonetization, especially considering that the hoard appears to draw from a well-mixed currency pool, with coins struck from several different dies and naming different moneyers (Blackburn 2008, 123).

Following only a very brief period there appears to have been another renewal in *c.*997 where the *CRUX* imitations (Group A) were replaced by *Long Cross* imitations (Group B), with Dublin following the lead of Anglo-Saxon England. The two types are found together in the anomalous Knockmaon hoard, but not in either of the two other hoards from this period, Collinstown and Derrymore. Beyond Ireland, the two types are rarely found in conjunction, suggesting the latter was fairly successful at demonetizing the former (Blackburn 2008, 127).

Between *c.*1003 and *c.*1020, Dublin struck a number of different coin types (Groups C, D, and E) but none appear to have been accompanied by attempts to demonetize older types. This was changed in *c.*1020 when all of these older coinages were removed from circulation. Dublin struck coins with a *Long Cross* design (Group F) but with the addition of pellets in the reverse. The distinctive nature of this coinage has been emphasized in the past, with it being described as the first national coinage produced in Ireland (Blackburn 2008, 127–8). The success of this renewal is attested in the Fourknocks hoard, and perhaps in the tiny Tonyowen find (Table 4.3). However, against this must be balanced the uncertain evidence of the Ballycastle (2) hoard, which appears to have comprised new, old, and foreign currency in uncertain proportions.

The potential renewal of *c.*1040 is where evidence is least certain. There are four hoards which terminate during the period *c.*1040 and *c.*1060 when Group G coins with a *Long Cross* and 'hands' design circulated. Where these can be judged, each contains a majority of the 'new' type although sizeable minorities of old coinage appear alongside these. Most of these hoards were deposited some way from Dublin so it may be that the town was using a more uniform currency than these distant areas.

Caution must be exercised when trying to read anything into the various shadowy hoards of the first decade of the twelfth century, as records are not good. However, around *c.*1100 a period of iconographic heterogeneity was replaced by the single design (Group O) visible in Figure 4.2. The hoards of this period are almost exclusively of this type, with almost none of the variety of types that circulated in the late eleventh century surviving to be hoarded. The

Fig. 4.2. Imagery of Hiberno-Scandinavian *renovatio monetae* types. (Images kindly provided courtesy of the Committee of the Sylloge of Coins of the British Isles.)

evidence is somewhat uncertain but there may well have been another renewal around the year 1100.

In arguing for occasional renewals in Ireland it must be noted that these did not accompany every iconographic change. Between *c.*997 and *c.*1020 a number of different imitative types were issued—Groups C, D, and E copying *Helmet*, *Last Small Cross*, and *Quatrefoil* types of England—but their issue does not appear to have prompted the demonetization of earlier types. They were struck at the same mint, in Dublin, name the same ruler, and appear to have circulated alongside both one another and the older currency of Group B. Similarly, a variety of differing types were struck in the late eleventh century but none were accompanied by attempts at demonetization, with coins of Groups I to N mixing fairly freely. This can be seen in hoards with a very mixed character, which are common from the latter half of the eleventh century.

However, when *renovatio* occurred it appears to have been accompanied by a change in imagery on the coins. In most cases this was fairly clear; a variety of different symbols was added to the obverse alongside pellets on the reverse in *c.*1020, while hands were added to the reverse in *c.*1040. In *c.*1100, the variable iconography of the late eleventh century was replaced by a single standard design. This would have made the monetary change fairly clear to the users of the coinage. Thus while every renewal of the coinage was accompanied by some form of iconographic change, not every iconographic change represented a renewal of the coinage.

Alongside the iconographic change there also appear to have been attempts to restore the intrinsic silver quality of the coinage. Low weights, which accompany the end of the various coin types, were 'improved' with the striking of the new types. This can be seen in the difference between the late types of group F (Phase II) and the new coinage of Group G (Phase III) where the weight increased from around 0.62 g to somewhere around 0.88 g (data drawn from Seaby 1984; Dolley 1966). The weight also increased around *c.*1020 as *Quatrefoil* types, struck *c.*1018–20, were struck at a weight around 0.99 g, significantly less than the new types struck after the renewal. This situation is not unique to Ireland. In contemporary English coinage there also appears to have been gradual reductions in weight, which were then increased at the outset of the new type (Petersson 1969). It would suggest that gradual debasement and then renewal were a part of the mechanics of early medieval coinage.

Perhaps the most important element of *renovatio* in Ireland was its timing. While the evidence for the effectiveness of renewal is challenging to assess based upon a fairly small number of poorly recorded coins, it is possible to be much more confident over the issue of chronology. The dates suggested for renewal—*c.*995, *c.*997, *c.*1020, *c.*1040, and *c.*1100—could conceivably be shifted a year or two in either direction but are unlikely to be significantly wrong (Woods 2013, 74–117). This allows for their comparison with the historical evidence for the succession of kings in Dublin, and across Ireland more generally.

What becomes very clear is that there is no correlation between the changing monarchs of Dublin or Ireland and the renewal of the Hiberno-Scandinavian coinage. The first three renewals occur within the long reign of the Hiberno-Scandinavian king of Dublin Sihtric Silkenbeard (989–1036). Sihtric's death in 1036 does not appear to cause a renewal of the coinage. Nor does it seem that the conquest of Dublin by Diarmait mac Máel na mBó in 1052, the first time an Irish king had been able to claim effective authority over the town, led to any discernible change in its coinage (Duffy 1992, 96–7). Subsequent conquest by the Ua Briain dynasty from Munster also does not occasion a renewal of the coinage. Indeed, it is during the middle of the reign of Muirchertach Ua Briain, king of Dublin between 1094 and 1114, that another renewal of the coinage occurred (Duffy 1992, 111–13). Furthermore, none of these kings sought to add their name and titles to the coinage: this occurred only during the initial years of the coinage when Sitric is named on the coins. In short, decisions to renew coinage appear unconnected to the changes in royal control over Dublin, in contrast to other areas of Europe. Perhaps instead it might be possible to conceptualize the renewal of Dublin's coinage as primarily economically motivated. Each reform was preceded by a drop in weight, and perhaps fineness, of the coinage. *Renovatio monetae* increased these, restoring them to previous highs. It may have been with this aim in mind that the coinage was changed, rather than primarily as a statement of political intent.

Conclusions

A perception of inferiority, especially when compared to England, has coloured the interpretation of the coinage of Viking Age Ireland. This is unhelpful as an examination of its production suggests a well-maintained and effectively monitored coinage. The Hiberno-Scandinavian coinage was not quite as tightly weight-controlled as coinage in contemporary England but a margin of error of around 10 per cent is not atypical in a European context. The precision of the alloy, barring a few anomalous coins which may suggest debasement towards the end of some types, is also very marked, at a little over 90 per cent fine. This consistency speaks of careful maintenance and a desire to ensure that the same silver alloy was in use around the Irish Sea, and points to a sophisticated awareness of economic matters.

While there were debasements of the Hiberno-Scandinavian coinage, these were unconnected to failures at the mint. Instead they seem to indicate an awareness of the mechanics of early medieval coinage. Weights gradually debased within a type could yield increased profits for the king. The precise production and apparent manipulation of weights speak of a coinage administered by those with a clear understanding of how it functioned. It also presupposes a coin-using economy. While full discussion of this is beyond the scope of this chapter, it is possible to argue for monetary circulation within a geographically limited area within Ireland, and around certain other areas of the Irish Sea (Woods 2014, 302–12; Blackburn 2009, 66–8).

Where Ireland differs from other areas is in the issue of *renovatio monetae*. Renewals of the coinage have been suggested as occurring in Ireland, with older types demonetized at a number of points during the tenth and eleventh centuries. However, these are fundamentally different from those that occurred in either contemporary England or Norway. While the former might be described as *periodic* and the latter as *regal*, in Ireland it is perhaps more appropriate to describe them as *economic*. There was not the same desire to utilize coinage for overtly propagandist functions in Ireland. In contrast to either England or Norway, there is no correlation between the important political events that Dublin was a part of and the chronology of its coinage. Succession and conquest made no mark on Dublin's coinage, with recoinage occurring within the reigns of rulers, rather than at their beginning or end. It seems likely that the primary concern in renewing the coinage was in its 'improvement', particularly increasing its weight following gradual debasement within a type. This has an important implication for how the coinage is viewed as it can be argued that it was produced for more functional purposes, to facilitate trade around the Irish Sea.

This, in turn, impacts on how we view other coinages in northern Europe. Kings *could* use coinage for clear political purposes, legitimizing their rule through coinage. However, it does not necessarily mean that it *was* used as such. The king of Dublin exercised control over the mint and was presumably able to profit from reminted foreign silver, gradually debasing coin types and during the process demonetizing older silver at times of renewal. However, production of coinage in Ireland seems much more focused on commercial viability. This can be contrasted with England, where periodic renewal is suggestive of the importance placed on administration and/or regular minting profits. In Norway, the political element is clear, with coinage associated with new kings. This serves to highlight the fact that not all Viking Age coinages were the same. As with earlier bullion economies, coinage was produced and administered in a number of ways across the varying time and space of the period. As such, examining exactly when, where, and how coinage was produced and administered is crucial to understanding relationships between kings and their money in the Viking Age.

REFERENCES

Allen, M.R. 2012. *Mints and Money in Medieval England*. Cambridge: Cambridge University Press.

Blackburn, M.A.S. 2004. 'The Coinage of Scandinavian York'. In *Aspects of Anglo-Scandinavian York*, ed. R.A Hall, 325–49. York: Council for British Archaeology.

Blackburn, M.A.S. 2007. 'Currency Under the Vikings, Part 3. Ireland, Wales, Man and Scotland'. *British Numismatic Journal* 77: 119–49.

Blackburn, M.A.S. 2008. 'Currency Under the Vikings. Part 4. The Dublin Coinage *c.*995–1050'. *British Numismatic Journal* 78: 111–37.

Blackburn, M.A.S. 2009. 'Currency Under the Vikings. Part 5. The Scandinavian Achievement and Legacy'. *British Numismatic Journal* 79: 43–71.

Bornholdt, K.A. 1999. 'Myth or Mint? The Evidence for a Viking-Age Coinage in the Isle of Man'. In *Recent Archaeological Research on the Isle of Man*, ed. P.J. Davey, 199–220. BAR British Series 278. Oxford: Archaeopress.

Bornholdt-Collins, K. 2010. 'The Dunmore Cave [2] Hoard and the Role of Coins in the Tenth-Century Hiberno-Scandinavian Economy'. In Sheehan & Ó Corráin (eds), 19–46.

Bradley, J. 1988. 'The Interpretation of Scandinavian Settlement in Ireland'. In *Settlement and Society in Medieval Ireland: Studies Presented to F.X. Martin, O.S.A*, ed. J. Bradley, 49–78. Kilkenny: Boethius.

Campbell, J. 2000. *The Anglo-Saxon State*. London and New York: Hambledon and London.

Dolley, M. 1966. *Sylloge of Coins of the British Isles, 8: Hiberno-Norse Coins in the British Museum*. London: Trustees of the British Museum.

Dolley, M. 1987. 'Coinage to 1534: The Sign of the Times'. In *A New History of Ireland II: Medieval Ireland 1169–1534*, ed. A. Cosgrove, 816–26. Oxford: Oxford University Press.

Dolley, M. & D.M. Metcalf 1961. 'The Reform of the English Coinage under Eadgar'. In *Anglo-Saxon Coins: Studies Presented to F.M. Stenton on the Occasion of His 80th Birthday, 17 May 1960*, ed. M. Dolley, 136–68. London: Methuen.

Duffy, S. 1992. 'Irishmen and Islesmen in the Kingdoms of Dublin and Man, 1052–1171'. *Ériu* 43: 93–133.

Graham-Campbell, J. & G. Williams (eds) 2007. *Silver Economy in the Viking Age*. Walnut Creek: Left Coast Press.

Grierson, P. 1962. 'Numismatics and the Historian'. *Numismatic Chronicle* (1962): i–xiv.

Grierson, P. 1981. 'The Gratia Dei Rex Coinage of Charles the Bald'. In *Charles the Bald: Court and Kingdom. Papers Based on a Colloquium Held in London in April 1979*, ed. M.T Gibson & J.T Nelson, 52–64. BAR Int. Series 101. Oxford: Archaeopress.

Griffiths, D. 2010. *Vikings of the Irish Sea*. Stroud: History Press.

Gullbekk, S.H. 1992. 'Renovatio Monetae i Norge i Middelalderen'. *Nordisk Numismatisk Årsskrift* (1992): 52–87.

Gullbekk, S.H. 2009. *Pengevesenets Fremvekst og Fall i Norge i Middelalderen*. Copenhagen: Museum Tusculanum Forlag.

Heslip, R. & J.P. Northover 1990. 'The Alloy of the Hiberno-Norse Coinage'. In *Sigtuna Papers: Proceedings of the Sigtuna Symposium on Viking-Age Coinage, 1–4 June 1989*, ed. K. Jonsson & B. Malmer, 103–11. London: Spink.

Lyon, C.S.S. 1976. 'Some Problems in Interpreting Anglo-Saxon Coinage'. *Anglo-Saxon England* 5.1: 173–224.

Lyon, C.S.S. 2003. 'Anglo-Saxon Numismatics'. *British Numismatic Journal* 73: 58–75.

Metcalf, D.M. & J.P. Northover 1986. 'Interpreting the Alloy of the Later Anglo-Saxon Coinage'. *British Numismatic Journal* 56: 35–63.

Metcalf, D.M. & J.P. Northover 2002. 'Sporadic Debasement in the English Coinage, *c.*1009–1052'. *Numismatic Chronicle* 162: 217–36.

Metcalf, D.M. & W. Op den Velde 2009. *The Monetary Economy of the Netherlands, c.690–c.760 and the Trade with England: A Study of the 'Porcupine' Sceattas of Series E*. Amsterdam: Koninklijk Nederlands Genootschap voor Munt- en Penningkunde.

Mossop, H.R. 1970. *The Lincoln Mint: c.890–1279*. Newcastle upon Tyne: Corbitt and Hunter.

Naismith, R. 2012. *Money and Power in Anglo-Saxon England: The Southern English Kingdoms 757–865*. Cambridge: Cambridge University Press.

Naismith, R., M.R. Allen, & E. Screen (eds) 2014. *Early Medieval Monetary History: Studies in Memory of Mark Blackburn*. Farnham: Ashgate.

Petersson, H.B.A. 1969. *Anglo-Saxon Currency*. Lund: Gleerup.

Screen, E. 2007. 'Anglo-Saxon Law and Numismatics: A Reassessment in the Light of Patrick Wormald's The Making of English Law I'. *British Numismatic Journal* 77: 150–72.

Seaby, W.A. 1984. *Sylloge of Coins of the British Isles, 32: Ulster Museum: Belfast. Part 2, Hiberno-Norse Coins*. London: British Academy.

Sheehan, J. 2000. 'Ireland's Early Viking-Age Silver Hoards: Components, Structure, and Classification'. *Acta Archaeologica* 71.1: 49–63.

Sheehan, J. 2007. 'The Form and Structure of Viking-Age Hoards: The Evidence from Ireland'. In Graham-Campbell & Williams (eds), 149–61.

Sheehan, J. 2008. 'The Longphort in Viking-Age Ireland'. *Acta Archaeologica* 79: 282–95.

Sheehan J. & D. Ó Corráin (eds) 2010. *The Viking Age: Ireland and the West Proceedings of the Fifteenth Viking Congress, Cork, 2005*. Dublin: Four Courts Press.

Sheehan, J., S. Stummann Hansen, & D. Ó Corráin 2001. 'A Viking-Age Maritime Haven: A Reassessment of the Island Settlement at Beginish, Co. Kerry'. *Journal of Irish Archaeology* 10: 93–119.

Skaare, K. 1976. *Coins and Coinage in Viking-Age Norway: The Establishment of a National Coinage in Norway in the XI Century, with a Survey of the Preceding Currency History*. Oslo: Universitetsforlaget.

Stewart, B.H.I.H. 1990. 'Coinage and Recoinage after Edgar's Reform'. In *Studies in Late Anglo-Saxon Coinage*, ed. K. Jonsson, 455–86. Stockholm: The Swedish Numismatic Society.

Williams, G. 2007. 'Kingship, Christianity and Coinage: Monetary and Political Perspectives on Silver Economy in the Viking Age'. In Graham-Campbell & Williams (eds), 177–207.

Woods, A.R. 2013. 'Economy and Authority: A Study of the Coinage of Hiberno-Scandinavian Dublin and Ireland'. PhD thesis, University of Cambridge.

Woods, A.R. 2014. 'Monetary Activity in Viking-Age Ireland: The Evidence of the Single-Finds'. In Naismith, Allen, & Screen (eds), 295–330.

Woods, A.R. 2015. 'Prelude to Hiberno-Scandinavian Coinage: The Castle Street and Werburgh Street Hoards'. In *The Vikings in Ireland and Beyond: Before and After the Battle of Clontarf*, ed. H.B. Clarke & R. Johnson, 355–72. Dublin: Four Courts Press.

5

The Rise of Spiritual Economies in Late Viking and Early Medieval Scandinavia

Svein H. Gullbekk

A Spiritual Economy

In Scandinavia, the introduction of Christianity brought about radical changes in attitudes towards material wealth and money. Whereas it seems that in pre-Christian religion the accumulation of wealth could be related to its use in the afterlife, the new religion promised a Heaven without materiality. Within Christian thought, money took on a new purpose: as a means for people to obtain salvation. At the same time, the establishment of national monetary regimes from the eleventh century meant that society as a whole was increasingly monetized, and the church embraced this wave of monetization, making it a backbone of their elaborate organization. Here, I sketch an outline of the emergence of a 'spiritual economy', developed and evolved from the early church through to the period under question. I do so through an exploration of how newly available coins were deployed in religious settings. What has become known as the 'economy of salvation' provides the foundation for one of the most important subjects in theological discourse: the activity of the creator God in the world to redeem a fallen and sinful humanity.[1] The medieval period, especially the period from the later eleventh to the early thirteenth centuries, witnessed a particularly important and sustained instantiation of this discourse.

Within the 'spiritual economy', financial contributions to the church could take a number of different forms, including devotional gifts for religious purposes, payments made during pilgrimages to sacred places, sales of land at favourable conditions, payment of dues exacted for religious purpose, trade in relics, and the building of churches, monasteries, and cathedrals. Such transactions represented a significant portion of the medieval economy as a whole.

[1] For a convenient modern theological statement on the economy of salvation see the *Cathechism of the Catholic Church*: www.vatican.va/archive/ccc_css/archive/catechism/index/e.htm (accessed 18 June 2017).

In this chapter, consideration of the phenomenon of money offerings in Scandinavian churches reveals how coins moved from being a means of payment to a means of salvation. The later eleventh century emerges as the key turning point in shifting attitudes towards wealth and coinage, marking the transformation of coins from monetary to spiritual objects in Christian contexts and revealing another dimension to the function of money in the northern world.

Wealth and Materiality in Pre-Christian Norse Religion

In pre-Christian, Norse religion, the sacrifice of wealth was central for the continued success of the deceased. The laws of burial, as decreed by the god Óðinn in a famous passage from *Ynglinga Saga*, make it clear that goods buried in the ground could be brought along into the afterlife:

> He ordained that all dead people must be burned and that their possessions should be laid on a pyre with them. He said that everyone should come to Valhalla with such wealth as he had on his pyre, and that each would also have the benefit of whatever he himself had buried in the earth. (Finlay & Faulkes 2011, 11)

The narrative of Odin's law comes from the first section of Snorri Sturluson's *Heimskringla*, written in the 1220s. Snorri thus based his telling on oral tradition working in a Christian context several centuries after the narratives he described supposedly took place. Nonetheless, the practical link between the material world and the afterlife in pre-Christian religion is attested in other sources, including in the saga of Egil Skallagrimsson (*Egil's Saga*) (Scudder 2004).[2] This describes a drinking feast in the hall of King Æthelstan, following his victory over a combined force of Norwegians and Scots at the battle of Brunanburh in 937. Egil, mourning his brother who was slain in the battle, appears as withdrawn, morose, and irritable. The king gives Egil a large gold ring and two chests full of silver. The silver is for Egil to bring back to Iceland for his father as compensation for the loss of his son (Scudder 2004, ch. 55). However, Egil never delivers the silver to his father. Many years later, he rides out to the moors escorted by two slaves carrying the chests, only to return home alone having killed the slaves. His motivations for the murders are not explicitly stated in the text. One interpretation is that Egil wanted to ensure that the slaves would not return and steal the silver, which was intended for his use in Valhalla (Scudder 2004, ch. 85).[3] This may, then, imply an understanding of silver as currency in Valhalla, either as spiritual or as material money.

[2] Snorri Sturluson was the author of *Heimskringla*, but several scholars studying *Egil Skallagrimssons's Saga* have also attributed this text to Snorri. If this attribution is correct, all the references to Odin's law discussed in this chapter derive from one hand.

[3] The saga of Olaf the Saint contains a story of Norwegian Vikings under the leadership of Tore Hund, who plunder a grave mound for silver and gold at a farm in Bjarmeland. Tore Hund relies on knowledge about the local customs, whereby wealthy men who died would be buried with half their wealth, sometimes less. He convinces his men that he knows the whereabouts of such buried wealth and they all agree to plunder (Finlay & Faulkes 2014, ch. 133).

The concern that buried treasure would be stolen, destroying the status of the grave and making the treasure unavailable to the owner for use in the afterlife, was real in the Viking Age. Numerous Viking Age grave robberies are attested archaeologically, including at the famous ninth-century Norwegian burial mounds of Tune, Borre, Gokstad, and Oseberg (Bill & Daly 2012, for the broader phenomenon of grave reopening in the Viking Age, see Klevnäs 2016). In spite of the extraordinary rich grave goods excavated from Oseberg and Gokstad, finds of precious-metal artefacts or coins have not been recorded due to grave robberies during the Viking Age (Bill & Daly 2012). Any consideration of relations between wealth and the afterlife seems to have been neglected. On the contrary, these grave robberies seem to have been acts of destroying symbols of power. By removing treasure, they also inflicted damage on the deceased's reputation in the afterlife.

In this, pre-Christian, period, buried treasure was perceived as an exploitable resource. This is portrayed as a fact in the sagas, as well as in later medieval laws. For instance, in the Norwegian Land Law (*Landsloven*) of 1274, the rights to unearthed treasure are divided three ways, between the king, the landowner, and the finder (Taranger 1962, ch. VI, 16). In *Heimskringla* it is stated that buried treasure was the property of the king. In Harald Hardråde's saga in *Morkinskinna*, an account is given of a disagreement between King Harald and Einar Tamberskjelve concerning a buried treasure that was unearthed (Anderson & Gade 2000, ch. 34). According to Einar Tamberskjelve, the treasure was originally the property of his father-in-law, Jarl Håkon Erikson, and therefore the legitimate inheritance of his wife and son who were direct heirs of the Jarl. In the saga, the treasure was buried in a coffin with the name of the owner Jarl Håkon inscribed in runic letters. The original owner was long since dead, and presumably living well in Valhalla. In the saga narrative, neither of the parties was concerned with the question of whether the removal of the hoard would create problems for Jarl Håkon in his existence in Valhalla.

What was buried in these hoards was, naturally enough, a reflection of what constituted wealth and money in society in general. Strikingly, in parallel with the process of Christianization, a transformation of the material economy took place from one based primarily on weighed silver to one where coined cash became the dominant measure of value and means of payment. This can clearly be seen in the composition of contemporary hoards: while, in the 980s, hoards in Norway and southern Scandinavia typically contain 80 per cent rings, hack-silver, and silver ornaments, by the 1050s, the ratio had shifted to 80 per cent coins, the vast majority of which were Norwegian, rather than foreign issues (Table 5.1) (Bendixen 1981, 410; Hårdh 1976, 140–3; Gullbekk 2009, 31–4). The economic logic seemingly present in pre-Christian Viking religion was one where material wealth constituted a strong asset in the afterlife.

Table 5.1. Coins and unminted silver in Norwegian hoards *c.*950–1100.

Tpq	Hoards	Weight of coins (g)	Percent of coined silver	Weight of unminted silver (g)	Percent of unminted silver	Total weight of silver (g)
978	Bråtveit	5	41%	7.2	59%	12.2
	Kvitberg	22	65%	11.7	35%	33.7
991	Tråen	126	14%	746.0	86%	872.0
991	Fuglevik	80	97%	2.8	3%	82.8
997	Bore	100	66%	51.1	34%	151.1
1002	Sløgstad	67	94%	4.1	6%	71.1
1002	Kaldal	289	68%	135.5	32%	424.5
1007	Ringnes	2	>1%	443.5	100%	445.5
1014	Jøsang	318	99%	3.8	1%	321.8
1017	Hårr	418	71%	174.4	29%	592.4
1018	Slethei	578	100%	1.8	>1%	579.8
1023	Nesbøen	416	79%	108.0	21%	524.0
1029	Årstad	1,849	97%	60.3	3%	1,909.3
1035	Dronningensgate 10	964	88%	136.4	12%	1,100.4
1050	Brøholt	381	86%	64.0	14%	445.0
1051	Foldøy	1,008	77%	294.0	23%	1,302.0
1060	Stavenesodden	23	100%	0	0%	23
1067	Nedstrand	7	100%	0	0%	7
1067	Nordrum	32	13%	207.0	87%	239.0
1067	Helgelandsmoen	218	50%	217.5	50%	435.5
1067	Tjora	19	100%	0	0%	19
1067	Skagen	16	?	?	?	?
1080	Måge	234	91%	24.0	9%	258.0
1080	Gresli	2,045	98%	50.1	2%	2,095.1
1080	Imsland	136	100%	0	0%	136
1080	Stange	11	100%	0	0%	11

Sources: Grieg 1929, 200–29; Skaare 1976, 127–76; Gullbekk & Sættem forthcoming. Only hoards containing coins are listed. For coinless hoards, likely dating to the late tenth or eleventh century, see Grieg 1929, 230–64. For coinless hoards from northern Norway which may date to the late tenth or eleventh century, see Spangen 2016.

Christianization and the Rise of Monetary and Spiritual Economies

The order of the world undoubtedly changed between the Viking and later periods. The coming of a new religion brought conceptual shifts (Garipzanov 2014), which included new attitudes towards wealth and money in religious contexts. The attitude towards economy in a Christian society was in many ways rooted in the concept of the Divine Economy: a spiritual economy with a different logic than the one prevailing in pre-Christian religion. Christian views on wealth and money were shaped through an already venerable tradition that rested on an institutionalized interpretation of biblical texts with a clear division between the worldly and the spiritual.[4] Material wealth had no place in God's Heaven, nor in the purgatorial passage to Heaven through which souls were purified.[5] When souls left this life, their bodies were left behind, together with their earthly belongings.

A major structuring principle of the Christian spiritual economy was that of sin. Sin takes something away from someone with no right to do so: it is a negation of right, of authority and responsibility, it creates loss, disorder, and dislocation. Adam and Eve, by disobeying the instruction of God not to eat fruit from the tree of knowledge, took what was not rightfully theirs to take. This creates original sin: a shattering dislocation of the original purpose of man's creation so destructive, so violent, and so intense, that it warped human nature for the rest of time (Wiley 2002). Sin therefore needs to be compensated for. In economic terms, this is what is referred to as the economy of salvation: the action needed to restore mankind, and, by extension, to create order (Tanner & Watson 2006).

Yet whilst eschewing worldly wealth, the emergence of a Christian, spiritual economy took place against a backdrop of quickening monetization, marked by the establishment of national coinage as legal currency (Gullbekk 2011, 101–2). While the role of money in eleventh-century Norway is yet to be fully established, it seems that the development of a national currency from the mid eleventh century gave rise to a general use of coinage. This is seen principally in the substantial size of the circulating coinage (Malmer 1989; 1997), with millions of coins being produced in Norway in the middle decades of the eleventh century (Gullbekk 2011, 101). The widespread use of coinage is suggested by the fact that even severely debased coins, such as those produced by Harald Hardråde in the 1040s and 1050s, appear to have been widely accepted (Skaare 1976, 79–85). Several studies of coinage and monetary

[4] See Anderson 2013. It is important to note the diversity of opinion on the moral perils, or not, of wealth that existed in the medieval period. See Naismith 2015.

[5] Le Goff 1981 remains the standard treatment, although it is not without flaws. While spatial and conceptual notions of purgatory extend from the New Testament onwards, the doctrinal clarification of purgatory was a later medieval phenomenon. See also Russell 1997.

circulation in the time of Hardråde's son Olaf Kyrre (ruled 1067–93) provide overwhelming evidence for successful recoinages (Skaare 1976; Gullbekk 2009). These removed foreign elements in the available currency, provided silver for coinage, and provided an opportunity for the proclamation of updated political and symbolic messages on new coins. The ability to organize and administer recoinages became a prerequisite for the administration of monetary regimes on a national scale. Again, it seems that the crown's issues were widely, if not universally, accepted among the Norwegian population (Malmer 1961; Skaare 1976; Gullbekk 2009).

There was, then, a tension between the increasing availability and use of cash and the Christian concepts of earthly wealth. What was the relationship between the growth in the use of coin as a means of payment and the emerging Christian spiritual economy? Certainly, circulating coinage acted as a medium for the display of Christian symbolism: it is well known that coinage produced in Scandinavia *c.*995–*c.*1030 frequently displayed Christian iconography, a practice that highlights the strong connections between Christianity, kingship, and coinage (Gullbekk 2015; Williams 2007). An arguably more novel approach is to explore how and when money entered the religious sphere.

As the church grew more powerful and became better organized in Scandinavia, and as part of a general cultural shift in the eleventh and twelfth centuries, attitudes towards money became more complex, balancing moral debates on the one hand and pragmatic responses on the other. The spiritual economy concerned with money being used for the purpose of salvation would be matched by the church engaging in a market economy. The activity of the church as it dealt with the secular world was wide-ranging, involving building processes, pastoral care, and general maintenance and upkeep of the ornaments, lighting, and fabric of church buildings, and the living expenses for a large number of clergy. In an increasingly monetized economy, the demand for money increased in line with an expanding church organization. This demand was met partly through collections of tithes, dues and taxes, fines, offerings, and donations. The latter became a major source of income, while the procurement by the church of enormous sums of cash provoked a variety of responses amongst churchmen and laity as to the morality of money as a means of payment (Gasper & Gullbekk 2012; Naismith 2015).

One pertinent question is: when was a spiritual economy introduced to all levels in society? In this matter the question of norms and common practices takes on a central importance. The church would expect and demand monetary offerings from the very onset of Christianization in Scandinavia. The response to this is not reported in any contemporary sources in any detail, but the custom of money offerings reflecting individual members of the congregation presenting coin offerings at Mass has produced material residues for us to study.

Money Offerings in Christian Contexts

In post Viking Age Norway, the intimate link between spiritual attitudes and material economies found expression in the phenomenon of money offerings within religious contexts. Money offerings can be understood as coins presented by members of the congregation as spiritual gifts to the church within a Christian liturgical and ritual framework (Klackenberg 1992; Gullbekk 2015). From the second half of the eleventh century, the medieval church encouraged everyone to make coin offerings, primarily as a means of absolving sin. The use of money in this spiritual context reflects transactions between man and God: the money offered becomes money transformed, from means of exchange to spiritual objects, while the coins themselves became a form of mediation between humanity and the court of Heaven.

Today, the phenomenon is witnessed materially by thousands of single coin finds retrieved from beneath the wooden floorboards of medieval Scandinavian churches. Broadly speaking, the finds are interpreted as accidental losses that occurred during offering rituals, rather than deliberate deposits. Archaeological surveys have revealed that the finds are spread over the entire church, with concentrations of finds in the chancel, around the triumphant arch, side altars, and entrances where offering boxes usually were placed. They appear, then, to represent offerings made primarily in relation to altars, shrines, and entrances, but also include offerings made in money-boxes and offering purses which circulated within the congregation, or were passed directly to the priest. A dominant feature of these money offerings is that they represent low denominations, that is, coins of the lowest worth. Following the introduction of a multi-denomination system in Norway in the 1270s and 1280s, farthings and halfpennies outnumber pennies by a ratio of 4 to 1. By contrast, foreign coins with a considerable higher value than local currencies in Scandinavia are hardly ever found in church contexts. They do, however, occur in contemporary hoards. In this sense, it is not the purchasing power of the coin or calibre of the offerings that was relevant, but the coin's ideological, ritual, or symbolic value.

When did the practice of money offerings commence and when did it become a common feature in society? Archaeological evidence offers insights into the chronology and development of coin offerings within a spiritual economy. To date, over 80,000 single finds of coins have been recorded within 650 Scandinavian churches. They date from the late eleventh century onwards, with an emphasis on the period from the late twelfth century onwards (Moesgaard 1987; Klackenberg 1992; Gullbekk 2009, 50–4; Zäch forthcoming). Notably, very few coin finds are known from late Viking Age churches. Despite the fact that Scandinavian kings adopted Christianity, and were instrumental in processes of conversion, church building and the development of church organization, coin finds from Norwegian churches dating from the eleventh or first half of the twelfth century number just *c.* twenty to thirty.

By contrast, from the last quarter of the twelfth century, 1,280 single finds of coins are recorded from thirty churches (Gullbekk & Sættem forthcoming). The reason for this radical upturn lies partly with the advances in church organization following the establishment of a Norwegian archbishopric in 1152/3 (Johnsen 1945), and partly with the contemporary increase in minting activity across northern Europe, resulting from the availability of fresh silver supplies in central Europe (Spufford 1988). In the rest of Scandinavia, coins from the eleventh century in church contexts are equally rare, if not rarer.

Notably, however, the pattern for the emergence of coin offerings varies considerably across Scandinavia. In Sweden, coin finds related to money offerings appear in significant number only from the second half of the thirteenth century (Klackenberg 1992). In Finland, the practice is later still (Ehrensten 2014). From the archaeological record, the same seems to have been the case in Danish churches where coin finds from eleventh- and twelfth-century contexts are scarce (Bendixen 1972). This pattern is in some ways surprising, since the process of Christianization and church organization was profoundly more developed in Denmark than in the rest of Scandinavia: for instance, Denmark had a diocese in the 1060s (Hybel & Poulsen 2007). However, from the records of coin finds in Scandinavian churches, the devotional practice of money offerings seems to have been applied in Norway before it became widely adopted in Denmark, Gotland, and mainland Sweden, albeit with significant variations on a regional and local basis in each of these realms.

Patterns of money offerings on the Baltic island of Gotland offer a case study of this chronological development. As many as 250,000 coins from the period *c.*800 to *c.*1125 have been recorded in Gotlandic hoards. In comparison, some 32,000 coins have been produced as single finds in churches from the island in the period *c.*1140 to *c.*1520. As single finds in archaeological contexts, this must be the highest number recorded from a region in the Middle Ages anywhere (Kilger forthcoming). A chronological analysis provides a rather surprising pattern: as many as *c.*30,000 coins belong to a group of so-called W-bracteates dated *c.*1350–*c.*1450.[6] In the previous period, the number of finds from church contexts is much less significant: just forty-eight coins can be dated to the period *c.*1140–1225.[7] The few finds recorded from the twelfth century stand in contrast to the enormous resources used in church building on Gotland during the same period. From the huge number of stone churches erected on Gotland in the late Viking and early medieval periods, it is clear that the island was a hub for international trade, attracting goods and monetary resources like few other places. Indeed, an observed decline in hoarding in the twelfth century, compared to the eleventh, has been interpreted as monetary savings being converted into

[6] Data from Fridh 2014 and recent excavations of St Olofs Holm (pers. comm. Dan Carlsson).

[7] For a discussion of the early coinage from Gotland, see Myrberg 2008. The coin finds from Gotlandic churches are surveyed by Moesgaard 1987 and Fridh 2014.

the building of churches, and thereby as providing vivid expressions of spiritual economy (Wienberg 2004). The evidence of single coin finds from churches suggests that a spiritual economy connected with the use of money as part of devotional practice emerged on Gotland on a significant scale only in the thirteenth century.

The contemporary, eleventh-century historical evidence for the use of money related to religious matters within Scandinavian society is limited to a few remarks in the History of the Archbishops of Hamburg-Bremen (*Gesta Hammaburgensis Ecclesiae Pontificum*) written by Adam of Bremen in the years between 1073 and 1076 (Tschan 2002). In this account, the Norwegian King Harald Hardråde (ruled 1047–66) is portrayed as a magnate with pagan attitudes: he tears down churches, executes Christians, and has an affiliation with witchcraft. On the basis of a letter sent from Archbishop Adalbert of Hamburg-Bremen to King Harald between the years *c.*1053–66, the king is accused of having stolen the money offerings that parishioners had presented to the shrine of St Olaf and of using this to pay the wages of soldiers in his retinue (Tschan 2002, ch. III). How many offerings were involved, and how large they were, is difficult to establish, but if the king was willing to violate the property of the shrine for his own gain, it suggests that the sum of offerings was substantial. Certainly, comparative evidence of offerings made to shrines in medieval England, including those of St Thomas in Canterbury and St James in Bury St Edmunds, suggests that offerings peaked shortly after the shrine was established or following celebrations related to the establishment of the cult (Nilson 1998). It is therefore notable that the cult of St Olaf emerged shortly after his martyrdom at the battle of Stiklestad in 1030.

This is the earliest source for money offerings in Scandinavia, and offers a vivid example of the transition of coins between monetary, demonetized, and (re)monetized spheres. In his treatise, Adam describes the Norwegians as decent people treating their priests and churches with great respect. On the other hand, he also complains that the Norwegian clergy were greedy for money and charged for performing the sacraments (Koht 1921, 79). The practice of charging for clerical services was also expressed as unwarranted in the Gulathing law, a regional law for the western part of Norway, in a version (the *Kristendomsbolken*) dating from the 1160s or 1170s. The prohibition is explicitly defined by saying that a priest must not 'operate within another priest's parish for the purpose of earning money' (Larson 1935, GT §23). Cash income from money-based church services seems to have been widespread from the reign of Harald Hardråde until the early twelfth century, when these payments were replaced by tithes (Helle 1974, 237–8).

In Scandinavian contexts, the spiritual injunction to make offerings from the mid eleventh century, later imposed with a stronger ecclesiastical organization from the late eleventh century onwards, created the first general demand on all inhabitants to make monetary payments for spiritual purposes. The universal demand upon the Scandinavian people to provide tithes and St Peter's Pence was established during the twelfth century, albeit at different times and places in the different ecclesiastical regions within Scandinavia (Holtzmann 1938, 359; Hybel & Poulsen 2007, 306–8). One important step in the development of church organization was the establishment of parish organizations that, in Scandinavia, would develop successively in the second half of the twelfth and first part of the thirteenth century (Sigurdsson 2003, 49–78). The evidence for parish churches receiving and distributing money provides evidence for significant differences between regions in Scandinavia. While money offerings can be observed in some regions in the first half of the twelfth century, a radical increase in the latter part of that same century can be seen in others. In many regions, the devotional use of money can first be observed from the middle or late thirteenth century. In recent scholarship, the transformation of churches from private to communal ownership and the rise of parish organizations have been seen as an explanatory model for the more intense use of money in relation to the Mass where members of the congregations would perform their devotional practices (Risvaag forthcoming; Myrberg Burström forthcoming).

The practice of money offerings demonstrates how the means of payment could be transformed into the means of salvation, but how deeply a changing attitude towards the materiality of money permeated society remains open to question. Here, it is worth noting that, within the medieval church, the Eucharist host or wafer appears to have been made in the image of a coin. This relationship between the Eucharist wafer and coin was observed by contemporary commentators. In his influential, late thirteenth-century commentary on Christian ritual and practice, *Rationale divinorum officiorum*, the liturgical writer William Durandus, echoing the sentiments of his twelfth-century predecessor, Honorius Augustodunensis (Honorius of Regensburg, d. 1151), noted that:

> The bread is thus formed in the manner of a denarius, first because the bread of life was betrayed for the sake of denarii, also because [the bread of life] ought to be given as a reward to those laboring in the vineyard. Also the name and image of our emperor is often written on this bread, since through him [Christ] we are reformed in the image of God and our names are written in the book of life. Some also represent a lamb there, first because he who is sacrificed is a true lamb, but also for the sake of the text, which reads [Exodus 29]: This is what you shall do upon the altar: you shall offer lambs continually and wine for the libation unto the lamb. (cited by Kumler 2011, 187)

From the eleventh century, wafers were made in the image of coins: they were round, flat, white, and two-sided. Like coins, they were mass produced (by means of an iron host press) and were sometimes engraved with religious imagery or liturgical phrases. This timing is significant: the emergence of coin-like wafers corresponds with the rise of monetary offerings in coin, suggesting a notion of the 'minting' of the Eucharist (Kumler 2011, 188). How parishioners in Norway viewed the host has yet to be investigated: in Scandinavia, surviving oblation-irons used to press the Eucharistic wafer date from the fourteenth century, although it seems likely that the practice of making wafers in the mould of current coins was widespread from the eleventh or twelfth century. We may speculate that people would have recognized the formal resemblance between the host and their coin offerings, leading to a 'confusion of their forms and values' (Kumler 2011, 190). Such recognition must have given coins used in ritual offerings additional layers of spiritual meaning.

Conclusions

Ritual acts of devotion have left tens of thousands of numismatic footprints below church floors. These footprints provide evidence for individual practices where the most intimate relationship between the individual and their beliefs was expressed. In this drama of devotional acts, played out in the framework of doctrinal traditions and regional adaptation, the identity of the Christian soul was shaped and constituted through the recurring message of Christianity; there is only one God, and only a life as a good Christian would secure a place in Heaven. In the search for a place beside Christ, medieval farmers, crafts people, and merchants would present their money offerings convinced that this was the right thing to do, an act connected to the sacraments and the Eucharist at the very heart of the devotional service.

ACKNOWLEDGEMENTS

The research for this chapter was made possible by the Norwegian Research Council, and was carried out under the aegis of the research project 'Human Sacrifice and Value: the Limits of Sacred Value' (project number 275947).

REFERENCES

Anderson, G. 2013. *Charity: The Place of the Poor in the Biblical Tradition*. New Haven: Yale University Press.

Anderson, T.M. & E. Gade (eds) 2000. *Morkinskinna: The Earliest Icelandic Chronicle of the Norwegian Kings*. Ithaca: Cornell University Press.

Bendixen, K. 1972. 'Middelaldermønter i de sidste 10 års Danske Kirkefund'. *Nordisk Numismatisk Årsskrift* 1972, 49–70.

Bendixen, K. 1981. 'The Currency in Denmark from the Beginning of the Viking Age until *c.*1100'. In *Viking-Age Coinage in the Northern Lands. The Sixth Oxford Symposium on Coinage and Monetary History*, BAR Int. Series 122, ed. M.A.S Blackburn & D.M. Metcalf, 405–18. Oxford: Archaeopress.

Bill, J. & A. Daly 2012. 'The Plundering of the Ship Graves from Oseberg and Gokstad: An Example of Power Politics?' *Antiquity* 86.333: 808–24.

Ehrensten, F. 2014. 'Mynten i Finlands Kyrkor'. *Nordisk Numismatisk Årsskrift* 2014 (2015): 153–200.

Finlay, A. & A. Faulkes (trans.) 2011. *Heimskringla. Vol. I The Beginnings to Óláfr Tryggvason*. London: Viking Society for Northern Research.

Finlay, A. & A. Faulkes (trans.) 2014. *Heimskringla. Vol. II Óláfr Haraldsson (The Saint)*. London: Viking Society for Northern Research.

Fridh, S. 2014. 'Mynten på Ön. En Studie av de Mynt från 1150–1699 som Hittats i Lösfynd och Hopade Fynd på Gotland'. Master's thesis in numismatics, Stockholm University.

Garipzanov, I. (ed.) 2014. *Conversion and Identity in the Viking Age*. Turnhout: Brepols.

Gasper, G.E.M. & S.H. Gullbekk 2012. 'Money and its Use in the Thought and Experience of Anselm, Archbishop of Canterbury (1093–1109)'. *Journal of Medieval History* 38: 155–82.

Gasper, G.E.M. & S.H. Gullbekk (eds) 2015. *Money and the Church in Medieval Europe, 1000–1200: Practice, Morality and Thought*. Farnham: Ashgate.

Grieg, S. 1929. *Vikingetidens Skattefund*. Universitets Oldsaksamling Skrifter. Oslo: Universitets Oldsaksamling.

Gullbekk, S.H. 2009. *Pengevesenets Fremvekst og Fall i Norge i Middelalderen*. Copenhagen: Museum Tuscalanums Forlag.

Gullbekk, S.H. 2011. 'Norway: Commodity Money, Silver and Coins'. In *Silver Economies, Monetisation, and Society in Scandinavia* AD *800–1100*, ed. J. Graham-Campbell, S.M. Sindbæk, & G. Williams, 93–111. Aarhus: Aarhus University Press.

Gullbekk, S.H. 2015. 'The Church and Money in Norway, *c.*1050–1250. Salvation and Monetization'. In Gasper & Gullbekk (eds), 223–44.

Gullbekk, S.H, C. Kilger, H. Roland, & S. Kristensen (eds) forthcoming. *Towards an Archaeology of Salvation: Coin Finds in Scandinavian, Icelandic and Central European Churches*. Oxford: Routledge.

Gullbekk, S.H. & A. Sættem forthcoming. *Norske Myntfunn ca.1050–1319. Kongemaktens Ressursgrunnlag, Monetarisering og Middelalderens Fromhetskultur*. Oslo: Dreyer forlag.

Hårdh, B. 1976. *Wikingerzeitliche Depotfunde aus Südschweden: Katalog und Tafeln*. Bonn: Rudolf Habelt.

Helle, K. 1974. *Norge Blir en Stat 1130–1319*. Oslo, Bergen, and Tromsø: Universitetsforlaget.

Holtzmann, W. 1938. 'Krone und Kirche in Norwegen im 12. Jahrhundert'. *Deutsche Archiv für Geschichte des Mittelalters* II: 341–400.

Hybel, N. & B. Poulsen 2007. *Danish Resources c.1000–1550: Growth and Recession*. Leiden: Brill.

Johnsen, A.O. 1945. *Nicolaus Brekespears Legasjon til Norden*. Oslo.

Kilger, C. forthcoming. 'Moving Money, Ritual Money—Studying Use of Coins in Bunge Church on Medieval Gotland, 12th–15th centuries'. In Gullbekk et al. (eds).

Klackenberg, H. 1992. *Moneta Nostra. Monetarisering i Medeltidens Sverige*. Lund: Lund universitet.

Klevnäs A. 2016. '"Imbued with the Essence of the Owner": Personhood and Possessions in the Reopening and Reworking of Viking-Age Burials'. *European Journal of Archaeology* 19.3: 456–76.

Koht, H. (ed.) 1921. *Historia Norvegiae*. Gamalnorske bokverk IV. Oslo.

Kumler, A. 2011. 'The Multiplication of the Species: Eucharistic Morphology in the Middle Ages'. *RES: Anthropology and Aesthetics* 59/60: 179–91.

Larson, L.M. (trans.) 1935. *The Earliest Norwegian Laws: Being the Gulathing Law and the Frostathing Law*. New York: Columbia University Press.

Le Goff, J. 1981. *La Naissance du Purgatoire*. Paris: Gallimard.

Malmer, B. 1961. *A Contribution to the Numismatic History of Norway during the Eleventh Century*. Lund: Berlingska Boktryckeriet.

Malmer, B. 1989. *The Sigtuna Coinage c.995–1005*. Commentationes de nummis saeculorum IX–XI, in Suecia repertis, Nova series 4. Stockholm: Kungl. Vitterhets Historie och Antikvitetsakademien.

Malmer, B. 1997. *The Anglo-Scandinavian Coinage c.995–1020*. Commentationes de nummis saeculorum IX–XI, in Suecia repertis, Nova series 9. Stockholm: Kungl. Vitterhets Historie och Antikvitetsakademien.

Moesgaard, J.C. 1987. 'Kirkegulvsmønter fra Gotland'. *Nordisk Numismatisk Unions Medlemsblad* 1987: 134–41.

Myrberg, N. 2008. *Ett Eget Värde. Gotlands Tidligaste Myntning, ca. 1140–1220*. Stockholm Studies in Archaeology 45. Stockholm: Stockholms Universitet.

Myrberg Burström, N. forthcoming. 'Building for Glory. The House of the Lord in Gränna and Arby, Småland, Sweden'. In Gullbekk et al. (eds).

Naismith, R. 2015. 'Turpe Lucrum? Wealth, Money and Coinage in the Millennial Church (*c.*975–1125)'. In Gasper & Gullbekk (eds), 17–37.

Nilson, B. 1998. *Cathedral Shrines of Medieval England*. Woodbridge: Boydell Press.

Risvaag, J.A. forthcoming. 'Echoes of the Mother Church in a Remote Valley: Høre Stave Church, Oppland Norway'. In Gullbekk et al. (eds).

Russell, J.B. 1997. *A History of Heaven: The Singing Silence*. Princeton: Princeton University Press.

Scudder, B. (trans.) 2004. *Egil's Saga*. London and New York: Penguin.

Sigurdsson, J.V. 2003. *Kristninga i Norden 750–1200*. Oslo: Samlaget.

Skaare, K. 1976. *Coins and Coinage in Viking-Age Norway*. Oslo, Bergen, and Tromsø: Universitetsforlaget.

Spangen, M. 2016. 'Circling Concepts: A Critical Archaeological Analysis of the Notion of Stone Circles as Sami Offering Sites'. PhD thesis, Stockholm University.

Spufford, P. 1988. *Money and its Use in Medieval Europe*. Cambridge: Cambridge University Press.

Tanner, N. & S. Watson 2006. 'Least of the Laity: The Minimum Requirements for a Medieval Christian'. *Journal of Medieval History* 32: 395–423.

Taranger, A. (ed.) 1962. *Magnus Lagabøters Landslov*. Oslo: Universitetsforlag.

Tschan, F.J. (trans. of Adam von Bremen) 2002. *History of the Archbishops of Hamburg-Bremen*. New York: Columbia University Press.

Wienberg, J. 2004. 'Medieval Gotland—Churches, Chronologies and Crusades'. In *The European Frontier: Clashes and Compromises in the Middle Ages*, ed. J. Staecker, 285–98. Lund: Almqvist & Wiksell International.

Wiley, T. 2002. *Original Sin: Origins, Developments, Contemporary Meanings*. New York: Paulist Press.

Williams, G. 2007. 'Kingship, Christianity and Coinage: Monetary and Political Perspectives on Silver Economy in the Viking Age'. In *Silver Economy in the Viking Age*, ed. J. Graham-Campbell & G. Williams, 177–214. Walnut Creek: Left Coast Press.

Zäch, B. forthcoming. 'Coin Finds In and Around Churches—A Survey of the Central European Evidence'. In Gullbekk et al. (eds).

6

Reflections on Kingship, the Church, and Viking Age Silver in Ireland

John Sheehan

This chapter considers the wealth of some of Ireland's kings, as represented by Viking Age silver hoards, and relates it to investment in the ecclesiastical sphere during the ninth and tenth centuries. While the rich Irish annals do not contain references to hoards or hoarding, there are some mentions of the phenomenon in early literary sources, and these relate to the church. In what follows, I argue that Viking Age silver hoards were deposited on church land with higher frequency than has hitherto been appreciated, and can therefore be seen to represent ecclesiastical, rather than secular, wealth. I consider a case study of Clann Cholmáin of Mide, the most powerful polity in tenth-century Ireland, and how its connections with the development of the monastery of Clonmacnoise may be related to its silver wealth, as evidenced by the Lough Ennell and Hare Island hoards. Finally, I briefly consider the status of the cross-marked ingot, which is suggested to be a product manufactured for use in Irish ecclesiastical contexts.

The Introduction of Viking Age Silver

Given the nature and duration of Scandinavian settlement and activity in Ireland it is no surprise that a large number of Viking Age silver hoards have been found there. In fact, over 130 hoards of ninth- and tenth-century date are now on record, representing a concentration of finds that is, in numerical terms, unequalled in the Viking world outside Scandinavia during this period. Just over half of these are 'coinless' hoards (comprising non-numismatic material, such as ingots and ornaments, only), while the remainder comprise either 'mixed' hoards (combining coin and non-numismatic material) or coin hoards (composed exclusively of coins) (Sheehan 2007). Given that just under half of Ireland's hoards contain coins, it may seem that there are good prospects for dating hoards as well as the various types of non-numismatic material that occur in them. Unfortunately, however, the matter is not so straightforward. It is complicated, for instance, by the fact that most of the mixed hoards were deposited during the mid to late tenth century while the coinless hoards have a wider date range, from the second half of the ninth century onwards. In addition, the wide range of the bullion values of the hoards, which vary significantly, contribute towards the complexity of the issue; many of the coin hoards are rather small finds, with the coinless examples tending to be significantly heavier. Consequently, it is the coinless hoards that account for the great bulk of the considerable amount of silver wealth that was present in Ireland during the ninth and tenth centuries, and many of these cannot be closely dated. As a result of these and other issues it is difficult to relate the hoards to historically attested events, or even to broad historical horizons of activities. It is more straightforward, however, to relate these finds to the Irish kingdoms in which they are found. This is because a large proportion of the finds are provenanced to a locality, combined with the fact that the broad extent and limits of the 185 or so kingdoms that existed around AD 900 are now identifiable as a result of recent work on Ireland's early medieval territorial, political, and economic divisions by Paul MacCotter (2008).

While it is not always possible to identify particular cultural contexts for Viking Age silver hoards from Ireland, it is nonetheless evident that there are sometimes discernible correlations between groupings of specific types of hoards and certain locations that are associated with the dominant dynasties of the Irish kingdoms (Purcell & Sheehan 2013, 37–41; Sheehan 2015). It is clear from both general patterns of distribution and from the tendency for many of these Scandinavian-type hoards to derive from Irish settlement sites, such as royal centres, ecclesiastical foundations, ringforts, and crannógs, that a great many of these finds represent Irish wealth. Reflection on how this was acquired usually focuses on the economic relationships that must have existed between the Irish and the Scandinavians (Graham-Campbell 1998, 106). While this view has merit, it does not take account of the importance of other potential mechanisms for silver exchange, such as the formation of political alliances, the practice of gift-exchange, the conventions of ransoming, and, perhaps most importantly in the Irish context, the exercise of tribute.

Silver of Scandinavian character begins to appear in Ireland during the mid ninth century, the same time as the *longphuirt* settlements, defined as 'fortifications . . . to protect fleets and to facilitate raiding and trading' (Kelly 2015, 55), begin to develop. However, the military capabilities of these sites were kept in check by the force of the Irish kings. As a result, unlike the Scandinavians in England, the Scandinavians in Ireland remained landless for the most part; they were therefore not normally in a position to use cattle, the main marker of wealth and medium of exchange in Ireland (Kelly 1997, 57–8; McCormick 2008, 209–11), to develop economically. Instead, in order to become relevant in Ireland, and to make it possible for them to become part of local political and economic systems, it seems the Scandinavians had to innovate and introduce an economic support system that was new to the country. Archaeologically, the evidence for this is the silver. It is now appreciated that a significant proportion of the coinless hoards from Ireland may belong to the second half of the ninth century, the main era of the *longphuirt* (Sheehan 2014, 210–11). This connects with the results of recent archaeological investigations at the *longphort* of Woodstown, Co. Waterford, which has demonstrated that silver and ingot-production were important facets of the economy at this site (Young 2014, 111–12; Sheehan 2014, 195–6). Woodstown has produced a metal-working furnace within which silver, as well as copper-alloy, was worked, and, in addition, it has produced crucibles, silver-assaying cupels, and many lead weights (Wallace 2014). What these finds seem to suggest is that a major innovation of the Scandinavians in Ireland at this time was the introduction of a silver-based system of exchange.

The majority of the silver hoards from Ireland have been found in Irish, as opposed to Scandinavian, contexts. In both societies gift-giving appears to have been part of elite culture (Sheehan 2013, 811–21), so perhaps the gifting of silver was perceived as one of the ways for the incoming Scandinavian leaders to try and establish themselves within the Irish elite. Indeed, it seems that establishing themselves within this grouping appears to have been an important aim from the outset. The historical sources reference both intermarriage and the formation of military alliances between the Scandinavians and the Irish from the mid ninth century onwards; in fact, the first recorded military pact of this type was in 842, within a year of the first recorded *longphuirt* (Purcell & Sheehan 2013, 41). Therefore, it may be argued that *longphuirt*, rather than being primarily regarded as assault bases, should be viewed as a result of cooperation between the Scandinavian leaders and some Irish kings. Indeed, it has been suggested that the foundation of the early *longphort* at Linn Ross (Rossnaree), a short distance from the royal centre of Knowth/Cnóbha, may have been established with the consent of the Brega kingship (Downham 2004, 238). It is evident from the literary and historical sources that the Scandinavian incomers were not perceived as being of inferior rank, and from an early stage the annalists recognize their status by frequently referring to them as 'sons of the King of Lochlann'; for instance, Amlaíb (ON Óláfr) is referred to in this manner in the Annals of Ulster *sub anno* 853. It seems on this basis, as well as on the basis of the archaeological evidence, which shows that silver was beginning to occur in Irish contexts, that the appearance of the *longphuirt* is correlated with the arrival of the Scandinavians as part of the Irish political scene, and not simply as alien pagan raiders. Far from being mere raiding bases, the *longphuirt* were developing trading and other economic functions using silver and other media. It appears that these sites were being invested in as mid-ninth-century power bases, as much to develop power in the future as in the present. It is not surprising, therefore, that during the following century Ireland's first towns developed in the same locations of some of the *longphuirt* (Kelly 2015, 91–2).

Cattle formed the basic unit of wealth in early medieval Ireland, resulting in livestock becoming the foundation of its wealth system (Kelly 1997, 57–8; McCormick 2008, 209–11). This appears to have begun to change from the ninth century onwards, during a period of significant political, social, and economic adjustment during which there was a notable shift from devolved to centralized power (Ó Corráin 1972, 28–32). These changes were not due to the Scandinavians, but the incomers had arrived on the scene at an opportune time, during a period of transformation. There are hints in the written sources that within native Irish society there is a move away from the cattle-based structure of wealth to one which also included silver as a means of exchange (Kelly 1997, 57–8). Clearly, the use of silver in this way must have resulted from the influence of the Scandinavians.

The Church

This mid-ninth-century period of transformation also involved the church, given its close relationship with kingship. While Christianity was introduced into Ireland in the late fourth/early fifth century, the eighth and ninth centuries marked the main period of the consolidation of the church. This was a time of expanding ecclesiastical power, evidenced by an increase in church building and the production of sculpture, metalwork, etc. This power was founded on the earlier growth of ecclesiastical estates, large agricultural demesnes that surrounded significant church establishments. These estates were granted to the church by local dynasties, often the same kin-groups that had founded the church sites, a connection which led to what has been described as 'an incestuous dynamic of ecclesiastical and secular politics' in which the church sites were 'the essential props of ambitious dynasties' (Ryan 1988, 33). In recent years UCC's *Making Christian Landscapes* project has been researching these ecclesiastical estates, using both historical and landscape approaches (Ó Carragáin 2014). It has shown that in some parts of the country, where the historical or archaeological evidence survives, these ecclesiastical estates could grow to occupy up to a third of the land mass. If we measure the importance of the church in this way, it should not be surprising to learn that a significant number of Viking Age silver hoards were deposited on church-owned land. Hoards, often coin hoards, occasionally turn up in early church sites, but the recognition that the distinction between 'secular' and 'ecclesiastical' settlement forms is a modern construct now indicates that the silver wealth of the church cannot be measured by these finds alone. Given that a significant proportion of ringforts, crannógs, and other settlement sites occur on church land, it has become evident that church-owned silver is not necessarily always going to be found solely on the ecclesiastical sites themselves and that the church probably owned more silver than has been previously supposed.

In what follows, I use the silver hoards of the ninth and tenth centuries to consider the relationship between the church, with its estates, the Irish kings, with whom the church had very close and often familial affiliations with, and the Hiberno-Scandinavians, who were responsible for introducing silver to Ireland and whose ambitions resulted in their interaction with these kings.

Historical and Literary Sources

References to Viking Age silver and silver hoarding do not occur in the Irish annals. This may appear surprising, given that the annals are such rich historical sources for a period when silver was so prevalent, but these sources normally focus on political and ecclesiastical events. Nevertheless, references to silver do occur in several literary texts, including in the Ulster Cycle, where the term is normally used in descriptions of the regalia of the mythical heroes of these tales (Mallory 1986). It is interesting to note, however, that some literary sources do relate to silver hoards and hoarding, sometimes involving the Scandinavians, and to an association between this silver and the church.

The first of these is particularly thought-provoking because it occurs specifically in connection with the discovery of a silver hoard and how this was subsequently used towards funding the building of a church, described as 'a great oratory, built of stone and extremely beautiful'. This narrative is in St Bernard's *Life of Malachy*, written in Clairvaux between 1148 and 1153, and it involves St Malachy's discovery of a hoard of silver and his use of it to fund the building of the church at Bangor, Co. Down (Meyer 1978, 79–80): 'Hence it was that when many pieces of silver were found Malachy did not put them back in their place, but took them out of their place; for he bade the whole gift of God to be spent on the work of God.' The hoard, which is very likely to have been of Viking Age date, is not interpreted as merely representing a chance find of old treasure but, rather, as a divine gift: 'For who else caused a treasure to be stored in that place, and being stored, not to be found till the time and work of Malachy?' While this source is of twelfth-century date, it may reflect an understanding and an appreciation in the Irish church that wealth from 'outside', and specifically silver, had been used to its direct benefit in earlier times.

Another literary source, of a different type, is *Ard na Scela, a mhic na ccuach*, a eulogy to Écnechán Mac Dálaig, king of Cénel Conaill, a kingdom in modern county Donegal, north-west Ireland, who died in 906 (Dobbs 1955). It is a long poem and is attributed to Flann mac Lonáin, who died in 918. Even though Ó Corráin dates it later, to the eleventh or twelfth century (1978, 32), and Downham assigns it to the twelfth or thirteenth century (2007, 39), it is nonetheless regarded as a source that provides important information on the Scandinavians' activities in this part of Ireland and on their interactions with the local rulers, particularly in relation to early tenth-century historical events that took place on the Fanad and Inishowen peninsulas (Graham-Campbell 1988, 109–10; Ó Floinn 1995, 101–3). These events are recorded in the Annals of Ulster, *sub anno* 921, and the Annals of the Four Masters, *sub anno* 919, and relate to the defeats of two Viking land-based fleets. The poem recounts details of these Viking coastal bases, forced marriage alliances between Viking leaders and Irish princesses in lieu of tribute demands, a runaway bride, and Viking treasures of gold and silver. Following their defeat by Écnechán, the wealth of the Vikings, which includes 'gold and pure white silver', is divided among the 'long-speared' Cénel Conaill dynasty, with 'ten ounces to every strong district' and 'five ounces to every great church', this division probably reflecting the early medieval concept of *tertia Deo*/'third to God' (Etchingham 1999, 271–88). It is worth noting that recorded hoards from, on, or close to the Inishowen peninsula represent one of the more noteworthy concentrations of Viking Age silver from within a geographically restricted area anywhere in Ireland (Purcell & Sheehan 2013, 50). Furthermore, these finds possess a number of features in common, each containing complete ornaments, few ingots, little or no hack-silver, and no coins, suggesting that they may represent a shared hoarding horizon dating to the same broad period. This apparent correlation between an archaeological distribution pattern and the location of incidents noted in early Irish literature is interesting, though in the present context what is of special significance is that the local church received no less than a third of Cénel Conaill's newly acquired silver wealth.

Scél Choirpri Chruim agus Móelsechlaind meic Móelrúanaid survives as a fifteenth-century religious saga tale (Wiley 2013), though it has been convincingly argued that it was first composed in the early tenth century (Kehnel 1997, 112–13). This is a story about the tormented spirit of Máel Sechnaill, the mid-ninth-century Clann Cholmáin king, which comes back from purgatory and visits the monastery of Clonmacnoise, one of the greatest ecclesiastical foundations in early medieval Ireland, which lies in his former kingdom. The spirit seeks help from Bishop Cairpre Cam, who prays and fasts for the post-mortem redemption of the king's soul and is eventually successful. When it is redeemed from torment, Máel Sechnaill's spirit revisits Clonmacnoise and, as a reward, shows the churchmen the spot where he had once buried a treasure of gold and silver which he had gained in a raid against the Dublin Vikings. Again, as in *Ard na Scela, a mhic na ccuach*, Scandinavian wealth has ultimately been acquired by the Irish church through the intervention of local kingships. As will be explored below, there is no doubt that Clonmacnoise benefited greatly from the patronage of Máel Sechnaill and subsequent Clann Cholmáin kings, particularly his son, Flann Sinna, who were extraordinarily silver-rich in the ninth and tenth centuries.

The main point about these literary sources is that they each relate connections between Viking silver and the church. While this association is not evident from the historical sources, it is already apparent from the recorded archaeological discoveries of gold and silver hoards on ecclesiastical sites, such as Monasterboice, Scattery Island, Rahan, Mungret, Dysart, Hare Island, Tynan, Dysert Glebe, Vesnoy, etc. One of the literary sources specifically relates to the discovery of a lost silver hoard, while the two others explain how silver was acquired by Irish kings as plunder from the Scandinavians. In one instance this wealth was then hoarded by the king, while in the other it was divided and redistributed. In both cases the church ultimately benefits, which is unsurprising given the close links, already noted, that existed between ecclesiastical and secular politics.

Southern Uí Néill and Clann Cholmáin

Some general trends emerge from the distribution patterns of recorded ninth- and tenth-century silver hoards within the context of Ireland's kingdoms and over-kingdoms. There are identifiable geographic concentrations in some areas that are clearly focused on the locations of important royal and ecclesiastical centres, and these sorts of concentrations seem to correlate with the place of deposition of much of the silver (Purcell & Sheehan 2013, 37–41; Sheehan 2015). However, the over-kingdom with the highest number of individual hoard find-spots, numbering almost fifty, and with by far the greatest total bullion value, is Southern Uí Néill (Fig. 6.1). The great silver wealth of this kingdom is unquestionable, and it is clear that the majority of these hoards represent Irish- rather than Scandinavian-owned wealth, albeit originally obtained from Dublin on its border zone (Kenny 1987, 512). Southern Uí Néill was an over-kingdom with sustained connections with the Viking town, whether through trade, alliance, tribute, ransom, loot, or other means. Some finds within the kingdom appear to be socially motivated, such as ornament hoards, others may have been more economically inspired and represent the use of silver as currency, such as hack-silver hoards, while others, such as large ingot hoards, appear more likely to signify tribute.

Southern Uí Néill was the most powerful polity in tenth-century Ireland, and the most significant of its three main septs was the Clann Cholmáin of Mide (Downham 2004). Over 60 per cent of the Southern Uí Néill's hoards are from the kingdom of Mide, forming the greatest number, by far, from a single kingdom in Viking Age Ireland. In bullion terms, however, most of it derives from a number of finds from around Lough Ennell, Co. Westmeath. This lake was the location of the Clann Cholmáin's royal centre from the eighth to the eleventh centuries, with its kings residing in a compact landscape comprising a platform ringfort, Dún na Scíath, a crannóg, Cró Inis, and an adjacent church site, Dysart.

Two of the Clann Cholmáin kings—Máel Sechnaill, who has already been noted above in relation to *Scél Choirpri Chruim agus Móelsechlaind meic Móelrúanaid*, and Flann Sinna, his son—made the somewhat conceptual high-kingship of

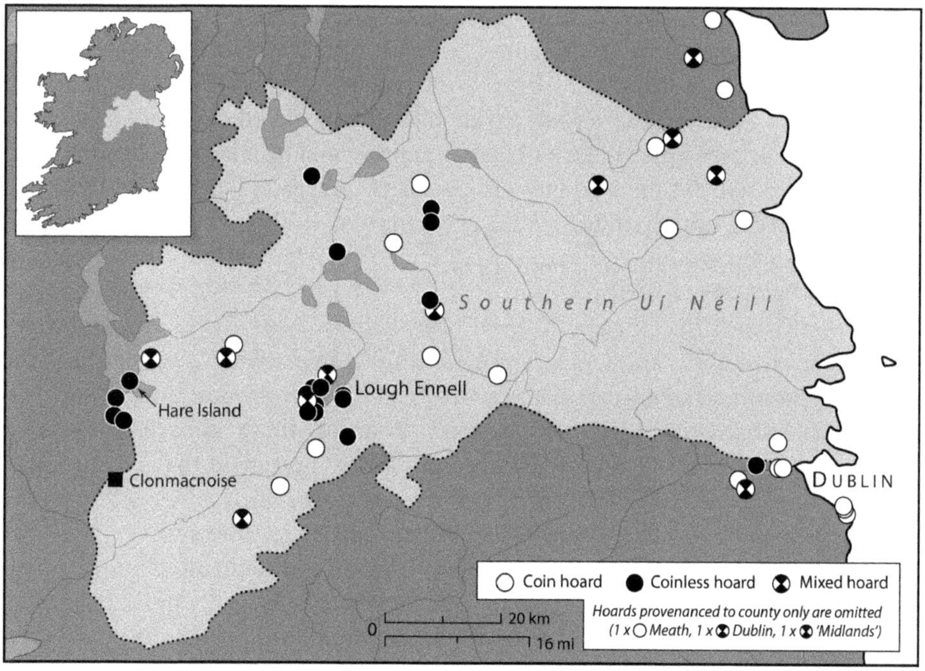

Fig. 6.1. The distribution of ninth- and tenth-century silver hoards in Southern Uí Néill, with Lough Ennell, Clonmacnoise, and Hare Island indicated.

Ireland, which they both held, into something more tangible (Byrne 1973, 264–5). The seventy-year period between the beginning and end of their periods of kingship (846–916) is also the formative period when *longphuirt* and noteworthy quantities of silver first appear in Viking Age Ireland. From the historical sources it is evident that these kings allied with the Dublin Vikings on occasion, sometimes through intermarriage, even if their relationship was usually one of enmity (Purcell & Sheehan 2013, *passim*). One way the importance of this connection can be quantified is by looking at the size and nature of the hoards deposited within the Clann Cholmáin territory.

Lough Ennell, the centre of Clann Cholmáin power, has produced a very impressive amount of Viking Age silver: eight hoards in all (Ryan et al. 1984; Maas 2015). Some are from islands and crannógs on the lake, some from its shoreline, one is from the Dysart ecclesiastical site, and another is from a crannóg, which may have been associated with Lynn, another important ecclesiastical site. Two of the finds are mixed hoards, dating to the tenth century, but the great bulk of the silver in the eight hoards is of non-numismatic form. Most of the finds are from the south and east side of the lake, where the hub of the royal landscape is located. The hoards are largely characterized by ingots and hack-silver, rather than ornaments, but they compensate for this apparent plainness in terms of their size and quantity. Some of the ingots are very large and, in terms of their form and weight, are not of Scandinavian character (Graham-Campbell & Sheehan 2009, 83), indicating that Clann Cholmáin were adept at making their own manner of ingots, even if the silver itself reached their hands as a result of Scandinavian activity. There is so much silver from the lake and its immediate environs, in fact, that the amount of wealth represented by it is paralleled in only a few other locations in the Viking world, such as Cuerdale, Lancashire (Graham-Campbell 2011), and Spillings, Gotland (Pettersson 2009). Together the hoards total a little over 50 kg of silver, amounting to over half of the total weight of Ireland's Viking Age hoards.

All of this wealth appears to have been accumulated by Clann Cholmáin during the later ninth and tenth centuries. It may be plausibly assumed that the massive amount of silver that has been recovered from around Lough Ennell is merely illustrative of what was actually hoarded there and, for whatever reasons, was left buried. It may also be reasonably presumed that Clann Cholmáin is unlikely to have left all of its silver hoarded in this way. Surely the dynasty also *used* its silver wealth, even if the evidence for how it may have done so is not inherent in the hoards themselves. Can we speculate on what this royal family was doing with its wealth? In order to do so the focus must be moved from the hoards towards the broader background of the Clann Cholmáin dynasty and its activities during the later ninth and tenth centuries.

Clann Cholmáin, and other Irish kingships, must have had multiple uses for their silver. These probably included paying mercenary allies, using it to strengthen social and political ties, as well as in trading, tribute, and gift-exchange. Silver was also used to facilitate the development of a series of experimental Irish ornament forms during the late ninth century, both secular and ecclesiastical, including the impressive penannular brooches of bossed and ball-types which were subsequently adopted and elaborated by the Hiberno-Scandinavians (Graham-Campbell 1983; Ó Floinn 1989, 89–90). In the case of Clann Cholmáin the acquisition of silver may even have been instrumental in furnishing the kingship with the ability to develop a fleet, for in *Chronicum Scotorum*, *sub anno* 910, it is recorded as having a fleet (*coblach*) on the Shannon lakes. Indeed, it is noted as gaining victory in this affair, the first recorded combat between Irish fleets (Etchingham 2015, 88), and this may have paved the way for the first maritime engagements between the Irish kingships and the Vikings. Some of the silver wealth was undoubtedly simply set aside and hoarded, perhaps in case it would be needed for future tribute or ransom payments. All of these types of silver uses—recycling, redistribution, and hoarding—are important, and deserve further consideration, but in the present context another use, connected to the relationship between Clann Cholmáin and the church is, perhaps, the most compelling. This is because there is historical, literary, art-historical, and archaeological evidence to show that this kingship developed into one of Ireland's foremost church patrons during its period of immense silver wealth.

Clann Cholmáin and the Church

In the past attention has been drawn towards the strong relationship that existed between Clann Cholmáin and the church, particularly in terms of the dynasty's patronage, even if it has not yet been considered in the context of its silver wealth. Ó Carragáin, for instance, noted that there is a remarkable concentration of pre-Romanesque stone churches in Southern Uí Néill, and he suggested that this relates to the commissioning of churches by Clann Cholmáin (2010, 121, fig. 131). There is one highly prestigious ecclesiastical site, however, with which Clann Cholmáin maintained a particularly intimate relationship from the mid ninth to the early eleventh century. This site, Clonmacnoise, Co. Offaly, belongs to a small group of high-ranking foundations that developed into centres of ecclesiastical and political power during the early medieval period, and study of its development during the Clann Cholmáin period shows that the dynasty went well beyond the limits of simply patronizing it by occasional church-building. The power and authority of a strong patron provided protection for an ecclesiastical site, and in this regard it is very interesting that not a single burning or plundering of Clonmacnoise, by either the Scandinavians or the Irish, is recorded during the reigns of either Máel Sechnaill (845–62) or Flann Sinna (879–916) (Ó Floinn 1998, 97). The burials here of both these kings were recorded in the annals, as well as of other members of their families, demonstrating that patronage of the site had already been taken over by Clann Cholmáin by 862, the year of Máel Sechnaill's death. The earliest piece of archaeological evidence for this patronage at Clonmacnoise is the high cross known as the South Cross, as this has an inscription which almost certainly bears the name of Máel Sechnaill (Ó Murchadha & Ó Murchú 1988, 61–3). This forms the earliest inscriptional evidence for what is clearly royal involvement in the setting up of high crosses, not just in Southern Uí Néill, but also elsewhere in Ireland, and it brings a new political dimension to understanding the background of these monuments. The South Cross must have been erected sometime during Máel Sechnaill's reign, probably during the 840s or 850s, the first decades of the *longphuirt*.

The best documented example of Clann Cholmáin's involvement in the patronage of church construction, however, is the building known as Clonmacnoise cathedral (Fig. 6.2). This is the largest surviving pre-Romanesque church in Ireland, was probably the first stone building at Clonmacnoise, and, in architectural terms, is an extraordinary building (Manning 1998; Ó Carragáin 2010, *passim*). It was consecrated in 909, and an entry in the Annals of the Four Masters, *sub anno* 904, attributes its building to Flann Sinna and abbot Colmán. It may be regarded as marking, in a monumental manner, the climax of a successful partnership between Clonmacnoise and the Clann Cholmáin dynasty, as well as an expression of the power and resources of both. However, there was more to this Clann Cholmáin investment in Clonmacnoise than just the

Fig. 6.2. Clonmacnoise cathedral, with the Cross of the Scriptures directly west of it (National Monuments Service, Department of Culture, Heritage and the Gaeltacht).

cathedral. A new high cross was also commissioned, the West Cross, also known as the Cross of the Scriptures, which bears the names of both Flann Sinna and Colmán on its inscription and was thus probably erected at the same time as the cathedral (Ó Murchadha 1980, 48–50). Ó Carragáin has demonstrated that this monument became one of three high crosses that were carefully arranged, or rearranged, to the north, south, and west of the cathedral, so that the axis of the overall scheme inscribes the Sign of the Cross over the building (2010, 44). Clearly, in the early tenth century Flann Sinna was closely associated with this large-scale, innovative, and sophisticated programme of architectural and sculptural development at Clonmacnoise. A similar cruciform arrangement of church and high crosses may have existed at Kells, Co. Meath, a site which also lies within Southern Uí Néill territory, and the patron of this scheme was most likely either Máel Sechnaill or Flann Sinna. Another link between Kells and Clonmacnoise is provided by their high crosses, as it seems the same master-sculptor was responsible for the early tenth-century examples at both sites (Stalley 2007, 159).

In addition to the development of the cathedral and high crosses, it is interesting to note that the first record of relics and shrines associated with Clonmacnoise date to the late ninth century, during the period of Clann Cholmáin's patronage, when the shrine of its founder, the *scrín Ciaráin*, receives mention in the Annals of the Four Masters, *sub anno* 894. It is not known who its patron was, but the likelihood that it may have been Clann Cholmáin is supported by records of similar donations to Clonmacnoise over the following century by subsequent kings of this dynasty, including that of a golden altar-frontal (Ó Floinn 1998, 93–7). Clann Cholmáin patronage also extended to the enshrinement of illuminated manuscripts, as Flann is recorded as having commissioned a *cumdach* or shrine for one of Ireland's most extraordinary manuscripts, the Book of Durrow, in the early tenth century (Meehan 1996, 13). Finally, a very large series of finely decorated cross-slabs was created at Clonmacnoise during the period of Clann Cholmáin patronage (Ó Floinn 1998, 92–3). Examples of this type are also found on other ecclesiastical sites within a radius of about 25 km of Clonmacnoise, which is an indication of the size of its ecclesiastical estate and influence. Interestingly, some of these slabs are ornamented with fret- and spiral-patterns of a type also found on the pinheads and terminals of the contemporary silver 'thistle brooches' of ball-type (cf. Johnson 2001, figs 17–22), raising the possibility that such Viking Age brooches may have been developed in artistic ecclesiastical settings which had access to silver, such as Clonmacnoise.

How might the patronage of Clonmacnoise, and of other important ecclesiastical foundations in Southern Uí Néill, be related to the wealth represented by Clann Cholmáin's Lough Ennell silver? Given the scale of investment in Clonmacnoise, and elsewhere, it seems likely that one of its uses of silver was to enhance and develop its status as church patrons. Did this mean they paid the *saer*, the master mason, and his builders, and other craftspeople, in silver bullion, or did they give silver wealth to Clonmacnoise and other establishments who could convert it to brooches or other forms of currency? The written sources indicate that church builders were paid in cattle (Ní Ghrádaigh 2007, 114), but is this just an outmoded euphemism by the tenth century? There is some evidence in the historical sources that silver bullion had already begun to displace cattle as a system of exchange and for reckoning values by the ninth century (Kelly 1997, 57–8; McCormick 2008, 209–11). Perhaps the arrival of silver, through the Scandinavians, gave rise to the emergence of independent professional craftspeople in Ireland, as in the Hiberno-Scandinavian towns, and that these included church builders, high-cross sculptors, and shipwrights.

Hare Island/Inis Aingin

It is perhaps noteworthy within the context of this chapter that the greatest recorded find of Viking Age wealth from Ireland, apart from the Clann Cholmáin group of hoards at Lough Ennell, comes from Hare Island, an ecclesiastical site. This large island, on the eastern side of Lough Ree, upriver from Clonmacnoise, is also located within Clann Cholmáin territory. Known in the annalistic sources as *Inis Aingin*, it has been identified as belonging to Clonmacnoise's ecclesiastical estate (Kehnel 1997, 71; Swift 2003, 117). It clearly was a site of considerable importance, for the Annals of the Four Masters, *sub anno* 894, record the holding of a synod there; in attendance were the senior ecclesiastics and bishop of Clonmacnoise, accompanied by the *scrín Ciaráin*. Kehnel suggests that the island may also have functioned as a trade harbour for Clonmacnoise (1997, 71). In this context, it is interesting to note that Scattery Island, in the Shannon estuary, another potential trade harbour, shares a hagiographical link with Clonmacnoise and that it too has produced a Viking Age silver hoard (Sheehan 2010). In 1802 two Viking Age hoards were discovered on Hare Island, one of gold and one of silver (Vallancey 1804; Graham-Campbell 1974; Graham-Campbell & Sheehan forthcoming). Both, unfortunately, were subsequently melted down, but drawings had been made of several of the hoards' components (Fig. 6.3). The weights of the ten armrings that comprised the gold hoard were recorded as amounting to 5 kg, making it the biggest gold hoard known from anywhere in the Viking world.

Hare Island is located close to the entrance of an inlet of the lake, known as Killinure, within which a number of other finds of Viking Age silver have been recorded. A large enclosure at Ballaghkeeran, at Killinure, has been interpreted as a *longphort* associated with the historically attested Scandinavian presence on Lough Ree during the first half of the tenth century (Fanning 1983; Kelly 2015, 61–3). This *longphort*, if it existed before these dates, which occur during the 920–30s, may have been established with the consent of the

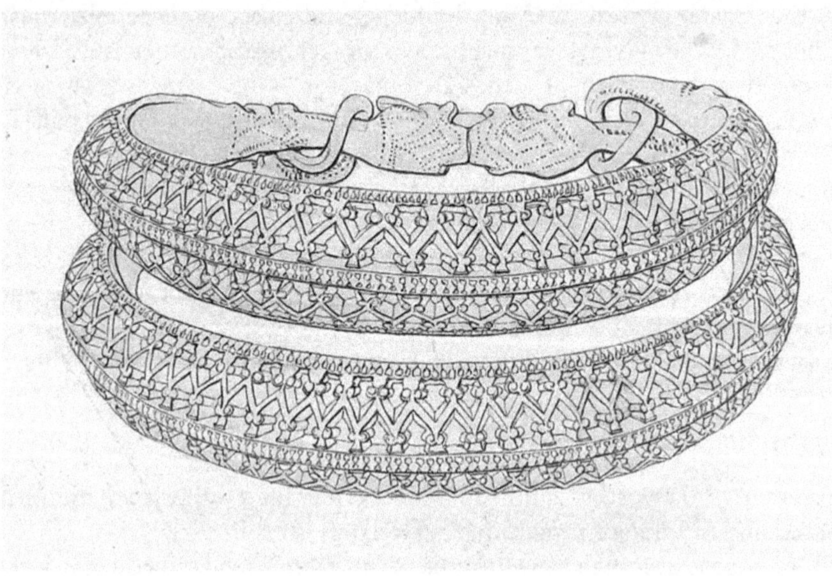

Fig. 6.3. One of the arm-rings from the gold hoard from Hare Island (The Society of Antiquaries, London).

Clann Cholmáin kingship and, in all likelihood, for its advantage. The Hare Island hoards represent a massive Viking Age treasure, found in Clann Cholmáin territory but on the Clonmacnoise estate, the deposition of which possibly dates to the same decade or so as the main Clonmacnoise developments outlined above. Was Clonmacnoise monastery hoarding its wealth on this island estate?

The Cross-marked Ingot

It appears that the Irish church was familiar with Viking Age silver, and with ownership of it. This raises the question, was church-owned silver, or silver destined for the church, ever distinguished in any way? The Hare Island silver hoard comprised ingots and arm-rings, samples of which were illustrated in scaled drawings prior to their loss (Vallancey 1804, fig. 1). These included a large ingot, *c.*8.9 cm in length and *c.*3.8 cm in width, with, on its upper face, a raised cruciform motif with expanded terminals. This ingot is broadly similar to the large cross-marked examples in the Cuerdale hoard (Kruse & Graham-Campbell 2011, 83, fig. 4.6), which average *c.*8.6 cm in length and *c.*2.7 cm in width (though it should be noted that there are also two other, much smaller, cross-marked ingots in this find). It is interesting to note that the larger Cuerdale ingots were cast in the same mould, even if some are cross-marked and some plain. We may draw parallels between these plain and cross-marked ingots and the process of wealth division between kings and the church that is described in *Ard na Scela, a mhic na ccuach*, and suggest that the Cuerdale cross-marked ingots may have been intended for the ecclesiastical sphere.

While in Britain ingots of this type are only represented in the Cuerdale hoard, it should be noted that among the substantial ingot component of the recently discovered Bedale find, from Yorkshire, are three examples with incised crosses (Ager 2012, nos. 6, 10, 19). These ingots, though they differ in size and weight from each other, seem to form a discrete subgroup as the crosses are of the same Latin type, have the same proportions, and are located in the same position on the ingots. Work in progress on the mixed hoard from Silverdale, Lancashire (PAS: LANCUM-65C1B4), deposited *c.*900–10, has revealed crosses on two of the ingots (Barry Ager, pers. comm.). In Ireland, apart from the Hare Island find, examples of ingots with raised crosses are on record from hoards at Newry, Co. Down (Fig. 6.4) (Bøe 1940, 107, fig. 73d), and an unpublished find from near Tyrrellspass, Co. Westmeath. The ingots from the latter find, which, incidentally, lies in the territory of Clann Cholmáin, are now missing, but were apparently very large, bigger than those from the Cuerdale find, and two of them featured crosses. The Newry example, at *c.*8.9 cm in length by *c.*1.6 cm in width, is not as broad as the Cuerdale examples, but it is of approximately the same length and its cross is of similar form. Given that cross-marked ingots are on record from three locations in Ireland, it is perhaps not surprising that

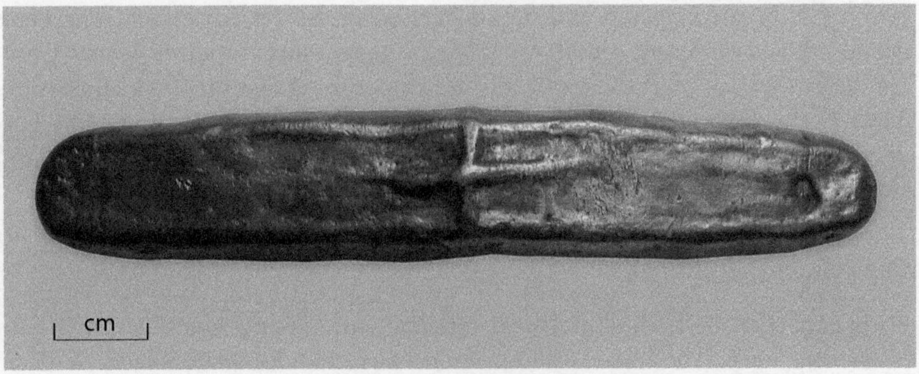

Fig. 6.4. Cross-marked ingot from Newry, Co. Down.

there are also two moulds for producing such ingots on record from there. One of these, in sandstone, is from Knowth/Cnóbha (Barton-Murray & Bayley 2012, 531, fig. 7.4:8), a royal site of Brega, in Southern Uí Néill, with strong Hiberno-Scandinavian connections (Wallace 2012). It would produce a large, broad ingot, of the same general form as the Cuerdale examples and, like the Cuerdale and Newry ingots, with a centrally positioned raised cross. The other occurrence is a soapstone mould from the excavations at Christchurch Place, Dublin (Fig. 6.5) (National Museum of Ireland registration number E122:16967), unfortunately broken, which would have produced a short, but thick and broad, cross-marked ingot.

There are locational contexts for three of the five occurrences of cross-marked ingots and ingot-moulds from Ireland. Apart from the Newry and Tyrrellspass hoards, about which little is on record, one of the others is from an ecclesiastical estate with royal connections, Hare Island, one is from an Irish royal centre, Knowth, and one is from Viking Dublin, which is essentially another type of royal centre. This apparent trend seems to imply that the background and contexts of cross-marked ingots are different to those of the more standard forms. They certainly appear to be a Hiberno-Scandinavian product, and it seems possible that some, at least, were specifically produced for use in Irish ecclesiastical circles.

Conclusion

This chapter considered how some of the wealth represented by Ireland's Viking Age silver, much of which was in the ownership of local and provincial kings, may have been put to use. Obviously, some of it was deposited in the ground as hoards, forming the body of evidence that is most easily recognizable archaeologically. On the other hand, some of the silver was recycled and used to facilitate the development of novel Irish ornament forms, including an impressive

Fig. 6.5. Soapstone mould for a cross-marked ingot from Christchurch Place, Dublin.

series of penannular brooches which were subsequently adopted and elaborated by the Scandinavians, while other quantities were presumably used in royal trading, tribute and gift-exchange. In this chapter, however, the evidence of literary sources is used as a platform for exploring the investment of silver wealth by kings in the patronage of the ecclesiastical sphere, with which they often had intense familial connections. Even though hoards are sometimes found on ecclesiastical sites, and thus represent this phenomenon archaeologically (as may the cross-marked ingots), it may be assumed, given the recent recognition of the magnitude of ecclesiastical estates in Ireland during the Viking Age, that some of the hoards associated with ringfort-type settlements actually represent ecclesiastical, rather than secular, wealth. Indeed, given the strong bond that existed between secular and ecclesiastical powers in early medieval Ireland, it may be challenging to distinguish between the wealth of the two. This bond, within the context of Viking Age silver, is illustrated by the powerful Clann Cholmáin of Mide. It is unlikely to be coincidence that this dynasty, on the evidence of the hoards the wealthiest in Ireland, was also the one that invested so heavily in church patronage.

REFERENCES

Ager, B. 2012. 'Hoard, Unique ID: YORYM-CEE620', Portable Antiquities Scheme. https://finds.org.uk/database/artefacts/record/id/504460. Retrieved April 2016.

Barton-Murray, R. & J. Bayley 2012. 'Metalworking', in Eogan, 526–33.

Bøe, J. 1940. *Norse Antiquities in Ireland. Viking Antiquities in Great Britain and Ireland* 3. Oslo: H Aschehoug & Co.

Byrne, F.J. 1973. *Irish Kings and High-Kings*. London: Batsford.

Clarke, H.B. & R. Johnson (eds) 2015. *Before and After the Battle of Clontarf: The Vikings in Ireland and Beyond*. Dublin: Four Courts Press.

Dobbs, M.E. 1955. 'A Poem Ascribed to Flann Mac Lonáin'. *Ériu* 17: 16–34.

Downham, C.E. 2004. 'The Vikings in Southern Uí Néill to 1014'. *Peritia* 17–18 (2003–4): 233–55.

Downham, C.E. 2007. 'St Bega—Myth, Maiden or Bracelet? An Insular Cult and its Origins'. *Journal of Medieval History* 33: 33–42.

Eogan, G. 2012. *Excavations at Knowth 5: The Archaeology of Knowth in the First and Second Millennia AD*. Dublin: Royal Irish Academy.

Etchingham, C. 1999. *Church Organisation in Ireland, AD 650 to 1000*. Maynooth: Laifin Publications.

Etchingham, C. 2015. 'Skuldelev 2 and Viking-Age Ships and Fleets in Ireland'. In Purcell et al. (eds), 79–90.

Fanning, T. 1983. 'Ballaghkeeran Little, Athlone, Co. Westmeath'. *Medieval Archaeology* 27: 221.

Graham-Campbell, J. 1974. 'A Viking-Age Gold Hoard from Ireland'. *Antiquaries Journal* 54: 269–72.

Graham-Campbell, J. 1983. 'Some Viking-Age Penannular Brooches from Scotland and the Origins of the "Thistle-Brooch"'. In *From the Stone Age to the 'Forty-Five: Studies Presented to R.B.K. Stevenson*, ed. A. O'Connor & D.V. Clarke, 310–23. Edinburgh: John Donald.

Graham-Campbell, J. 1988. 'A Viking-Age Silver Hoard from near Raphoe, Co. Donegal'. In *Keimelia: Studies in Medieval Archaeology and History in Memory of Tom Delaney*, ed. G. Mac Niocaill & P.F. Wallace, 102–11. Galway: Galway University Press.

Graham-Campbell, J. 1998. 'The Early Viking-Age in the Irish Sea Area'. In *Scandinavia and Ireland in the Early Viking Age*, ed. H.B Clarke, M. Ní Mhaonaigh & R. Ó Floinn, 104–30. Dublin: Four Courts Press.

Graham-Campbell, J. 2011. *The Cuerdale Hoard and Related Viking-Age Silver and Gold, from Britain and Ireland, in the British Museum*. London: British Museum Publications.

Graham-Campbell, J. & J. Sheehan 2009. 'Viking-Age Gold and Silver from Irish Crannogs and Other Watery Places'. *Journal of Irish Archaeology* 18: 77–93.

Graham-Campbell, J. & J. Sheehan forthcoming. 'The Viking-Age Hoards from Hare Island'.

Johnson, R. 2001. 'The Development of Irish Brooch Forms and Pins in the Viking Age, *c.*850–1170'. *Peritia* 15: 321–62.

Kehnel, A. 1997. *Clonmacnoise—the Church and Lands of St Ciarán: Change and Continuity in an Irish Monastic Foundation (6th to 16th century)*. Münster: Lit Verlag.

Kelly, E.P. 2015. 'The *Longphort* in Viking-Age Ireland: The Archaeological Evidence'. In Clarke & Johnson (eds), 55–92.

Kelly, F. 1997. *Early Irish Farming: A Study Based on the Law Texts of the 7th and 8th Centuries AD*. Dublin: School of Celtic Studies.

Kenny, M. 1987. 'The Geographical Distribution of Irish Viking-Age Coin Hoards'. *Proceedings of the Royal Irish Academy* 87c: 507–25.

King, H. (ed.) 1998. *Clonmacnoise Studies I: Seminar Papers 1994*. Dublin: Dúchas.

Kruse, S. & J. Graham-Campbell 2011. 'Classification of the Objects: Ingots'. In Graham-Campbell, 73–86.

Maas, J. 2015. 'The Viking Events of AD 902–19 and the Lough Ennell Hoards'. In Purcell et al. (eds), 251–62.

McCormick, F. 2008. 'The Decline of the Cow: Agricultural and Settlement Change in Early Medieval Ireland'. *Peritia* 20: 209–24.

MacCotter, P. 2008. *Medieval Ireland: Territorial, Political and Economic Divisions*. Dublin: Four Courts Press.

Mallory, J.P. 1986. 'Silver in the Ulster Cycle of Tales'. In *Proceedings of the Seventh International Congress of Celtic Studies, Oxford, 1983*, ed. D. Ellis Evans, J.D. Griffith, & E.M. Jope, 31–78. Oxford: Oxbow.

Manning, C. 1998. 'Clonmacnoise Cathedral'. In King (ed.), 57–86.

Meehan, B. 1996. *The Book of Durrow: A Medieval Masterpiece at Trinity College Dublin*. Dublin: Town House.

Meyer, R. (trans.) 1978. *The Life and Death of Saint Malachy the Irishman*. Kalamazoo: Cistercian Publications.

Moss, R. (ed.) 2007. *Making and Meaning in Insular Art*. Dublin: Four Courts Press.

Ní Ghrádaigh, J. 2007. 'A Legal Perspective on the *Saer* and Workshop Practice in Pre-Norman Ireland'. In Moss (ed.), 110–25.

Ó Carragáin, T. 2010. *Churches in Early Medieval Ireland: Architecture, Ritual and Memory*. New Haven: Yale University Press.

Ó Carragáin, T. 2014. 'The Archaeology of Ecclesiastical Estates in Early Medieval Ireland: A Case Study of the Kingdom of Fir Maige'. *Peritia* 24–5: 266–312.

Ó Corráin, D. 1972. *Ireland Before the Normans*. Dublin: Gill & Macmillan.

Ó Corráin, D. 1978. 'Nationality and Kingship in Pre-Norman Ireland'. In *Historical Studies XI: Nationality and the Pursuit of National Independence*, ed. T.W. Moody, 1–35. Belfast: Appletree Press.

Ó Floinn, R. 1989. 'Secular Metalwork in the Eighth and Ninth Centuries'. In *'The Work of Angels': Masterpieces of Celtic Metalwork, 6th–9th centuries AD*, ed. S. Youngs, 72–91. London: British Museum Publications.

Ó Floinn, R. 1995. 'Sandhills, Silver and Shrines—Fine Metalwork of the Medieval Period from Donegal'. In *Donegal History and Society: Interdisciplinary Essays on the History of an Irish County*, ed. W. Nolan, L. Ronayne, & M. Dunlevy, 85–148. Dublin: Geography Publications.

Ó Floinn, R. 1998. 'Clonmacnoise: Art and Patronage in the Early Medieval Period'. In King (ed.), 87–100.

Ó Murchadha, D. 1980. 'Rubbings Taken of the Inscriptions on the Cross of the Scriptures, Clonmacnois'. *Journal of the Royal Society of Antiquaries of Ireland* 110: 47–51.

Ó Murchadha, D. & G. Ó Murchú 1988. 'Fragmentary Inscriptions from the West Cross at Durrow, the South Cross at Clonmacnois, and the Cross of Kinnitty'. *Journal of the Royal Society of Antiquaries of Ireland* 118: 53–66.

Pettersson, A.M. 2009. *The Spillings Hoard: Gotland's Role in Viking Age World Trade*. Visby: The Gotland Museum.

Purcell, E., P. MacCotter, J. Nyhan, & J. Sheehan (eds) 2015. *Clerics, Kings and Vikings: Essays on Medieval Ireland in Honour of Donnchadh Ó Corráin*. Dublin: Four Courts Press.

Purcell, E. & J. Sheehan 2013. 'Viking Dublin: Enmities, Alliances and the Cold Gleam of Silver'. In *Everyday Life in Viking-Age Towns: Social Approaches to Towns in England and Ireland, c.800–1100*, ed. D.M. Hadley & L. Ten Harkel, 35–60. Oxford: Oxbow Books.

Russell, I. & M.F. Hurley (eds) 2014. *Woodstown: A Viking-Age Settlement in Co. Waterford*. Dublin: Four Courts Press.

Ryan, M. 1988. 'Fine Metalworking and Early Irish Monasteries: The Archaeological Evidence'. In *Settlement and Society in Medieval Ireland*, ed. J. Bradley, 33–48. Kilkenny: Boethius Press.

Ryan, M., R. Ó Floinn, N. Lowick, M. Kenny, & P. Cazalet 1984. 'Six Silver Finds of the Viking Period from the Vicinity of Lough Ennell, Co. Westmeath'. *Peritia* 3: 334–81.

Sheehan, J. 2007. 'The Form and Structure of Viking-Age Silver Hoards: The Evidence from Ireland'. In *Silver Economy in the Viking Age*, ed. J. Graham-Campbell & G. Williams, 149–62. Walnut Creek: Left Coast Press.

Sheehan, J. 2010. 'The Character and Cultural Context of the Inis Cáthaig/Scattery Island Hoard'. *The Other Clare* 34: 23–8.

Sheehan, J. 2013. 'Viking Raiding, Gift-Exchange and Irish Metalwork in Norway'. In *Early Medieval Art and Archaeology in the Northern World: Studies in Honour of James Graham-Campbell*, ed. A. Reynolds & L. Webster, 809–24. Leiden: Brill.

Sheehan, J. 2014. 'Silver'. In Russell & Hurley (eds), 194–222.

Sheehan, J. 2015. 'Fighting with Silver: The Woodstown Assemblage'. In Clarke & Johnson (eds), 161–76.

Stalley, R. 2007. 'Artistic Identity and the Irish Scripture Crosses'. In Moss (ed.), 153–66.

Swift, C. 2003. 'Sculptors and Their Customers: A Study of Clonmacnoise Grave-Slabs'. In *Clonmacnoise Studies, Volume 2, Seminar Papers 1998*, ed. H.A. King, 105–23. Dublin: Stationery Office.

Vallancey, C. 1804. 'Of Golden Implements and Ornaments of Gold and Silver Found in Ireland'. *Collectanea de Rebus Hibernicis* VI (ii): 237–89.

Wallace, P.F. 2012. 'Knowth and Dublin: A Comparison of Early Medieval Archaeologies'. In Eogan, 708–45.

Wallace, P.F. 2014. 'Weights'. In Russell & Hurley (eds), 222–55.

Wiley, D.M. 2013. 'A Medieval Irish Ghost Story'. *Zeitschrift für Celtische Philologie* 60: 239–74.

Young, T. 2014. 'Discussion of Metalworking Evidence'. In Russell & Hurley (eds), 103–13.

7

Beyond Economics

The Use of Coins as Pendants in Viking Age Scandinavia

Florent Audy

The reuse of coins as pendants in the Viking Age has gained increasing attention in the last two decades. This arises mainly from a strong desire to study coins from perspectives other than purely numismatic ones. As argued by Fleur Kemmers and Nanouschka Myrberg, 'monetary function is an essential aspect of coins, but not the only one' (2011, 93). Coins are, just as any other archaeological artefact, a part of material culture. It is therefore essential to move beyond economics and incorporate social, symbolic, and cultural variables into the discussion of coined money and its uses in the Viking Age.

The Viking Age coin-pendants lend themselves particularly well to such an approach. The coins of which they are made ceased, at least temporarily, to have a monetary function and acquired a new status as ornament. They were removed from circulation, physically adapted for suspension, and worn with other pendants in—often elaborate—female necklaces. A good example of this can be seen in the Vårby hoard, found in 1871 in the province of Södermanland, Sweden (Fig. 7.1). The hoard contained, among other things, two 'ball type' penannular brooches, five oriental belt mounts turned into pendants, nine openwork pendants with zoomorphic designs, and six looped Kufic coins (three of which are shown in Fig. 7.1). The reused coins were undoubtedly invested with a symbolic and ornamental function. All were gilded and formed part of a set of personal objects.

Although growing rapidly, research on the Viking Age coin-pendants is still in its early stages. The number of publications dealing with them is small and their scope limited. To date, only two articles have appeared which sketch a general outline of the phenomenon: one by Elina Screen (2014) on the coin-pendants found in Norway and one by Tuuka Talvio (2000) on the coin-pendants found in Finland. Both provide interesting insights into the reuse of coins as ornaments

Fig. 7.1. Ornaments from the Vårby hoard.
Photo: Swedish History Museum.

in the Viking Age, especially from a chronological point of view. Screen's article also offers a very useful discussion of the orientation of the pierced Anglo-Saxon coins, finding that in the period 980–1050, such coins were increasingly pierced so as to display a cross (Screen 2014, 369–70). Nevertheless, these works lack an integrated approach, leaving many questions unanswered: they pay too little attention to the contexts in which the coin-pendants occur and to the objects with which they are combined. Without such a contextual framework, it is not possible to determine how or by whom the coin-pendants were worn.

With the exception of these two articles, there is a tendency in the literature to focus on a limited number of finds, sites, and coin types, such as the Birka cemeteries (e.g. Audy 2011; 2012), the ninth-century Hoen, Norway, hoard (e.g. Blackburn 2006), or ninth-century Carolingian coins (e.g. Moesgaard 2004; Garipzanov 2005; 2008). As a result, the empirical evidence is often very fragmented and the different interpretations are hardly connected together. Another consequence is that a few coin-groups have been enhanced at the expense of others. We have, for instance, relatively many studies discussing the reused Carolingian coins, while the reuse of Islamic dirhams, though numerically dominant, is merely mentioned in passing. The eleventh-century Scandinavian coins reused as pendants, i.e. those minted when national coinages commenced in Denmark, Norway, and Sweden from around AD 1000, are also frequently excluded from the analysis (but see Screen 2014, 362–3).

In this study, I want to break down the divisions between the various coin groups and study the phenomenon as a whole. This is not to deny the diversity of the different coin groups in terms of their origins, iconography/design, and chronology, but to place the discussion on another level. Rather than emphasizing differences between coins selected for secondary reuse as pendants, the idea is to explore the role of the very object 'coin' in the practice of conversion into ornament and to discuss this common phenomenon. Why were coins in particular selected for conversion into pendants? How were they converted? And how were the inherent properties of the coins embodied in the pendants? This discussion aims to offer a starting point for understanding both how imported and locally minted coins were perceived in the Viking Age and how people engaged with them.

The Reuse of Coins as Pendants in the Viking Age: An Overview

How common were coin-pendants in the Viking Age? Coin-pendants occur in a range of different archaeological contexts, but a consideration of the numbers found in Viking Age hoards can be used to extrapolate overall numbers. A survey of coins from a sample of seventy-seven Scandinavian hoards buried between *c.*830 and *c.*1140, conducted by the current writer as part of a PhD, suggests that about 3 per cent of the coins known from Viking Age Scandinavia show signs of having been pierced or looped (Table 7.1).[1] Applying this figure over the corpus of Viking Age coin finds as a whole, this represents an estimated number of *c.*10,000 coin-pendants based on the most recent survey of Scandinavian coin finds (Jonsson 2015, 53). Providing an overview of all of them is not an easy task. The reasons for this are many, including the great scope of the phenomenon, its diversity, and the lack of published information on the reused coins. Despite these difficulties, it is possible to identify some basic patterns and to outline the essential properties of the Viking Age coin-pendants.

Firstly, almost all the Viking Age coin-pendants are made from coins originally intended to circulate as currency within the area in which they were produced. These coins were not manufactured to be used as ornaments; they were turned into pendants in a second phase of use. Because the coins to be transformed were selected among those available at the time, there is a strong correlation between the Viking Age coin stock and the coins collected for transformation. All the coin groups in circulation could potentially be

[1] This sample includes almost all the hoards with more than twenty coins found in Scandinavia after 1919. Because of the large number of hoards they have yielded, Bornholm and Gotland are only partly covered, respectively parishes A–F and A–N.

Table 7.1. Reuse as pendant within a sample of seventy-seven Scandinavian hoards, classified by geographical origin. Coin groups represented by fewer than fifteen coins in the sample are not included.

Origin	Coins	Reused	Rate
German	13,126	167	1.3%
Islamic	12,078	738	6.1%
English	6,985	122	1.7%
Danish	1,172	3	0.3%
Anglo-Scandinavian	404	11	2.7%
Blank	149	0	0.0%
Swedish	121	7	5.8%
Norwegian	77	0	0.0%
Sasanian	77	5	6.5%
Irish	55	1	1.8%
Bohemian	47	4	8.5%
Hungarian	20	0	0.0%
Byzantine	19	4	21.1%
Total	34,330	1,062	3.1%

Source: author's own PhD research.

reused (Table 7.1).[2] In the ninth and tenth centuries, most of the coin-pendants consist of Islamic coins, while in the eleventh century, most consist of imported English and German coins. This pattern can partly be explained by the fact that these groups dominate the circulating coin stock in their respective periods in overall numeric terms, but their reuse in large numbers also shows that they were greatly appreciated as ornaments. Yet it is also clear that some coin groups were particularly sought after as pendants, as suggested by their higher rates of transformation. The two most striking examples are the Carolingian and the so-called Hedeby coinages. These groups are not present in Table 7.1 because they almost never occur in hoards, a pattern which may indicate that their symbolic value, as items of display, was more important than their economic value as items of silver bullion. Within each of these coin groups, about 40 per cent of coins were transformed into pendants, while the average rate of transformation is around 3 per cent (cf. Garipzanov 2008; Malmer 1966). All the coin groups most frequently reused as pendants are relatively small in size and bear distinctive designs.

Remarkably this taste for reused coins did *not* stimulate the production of coin-like ornaments during most of the Viking Age. Within Scandinavia, it was not until the eleventh century that the fashion for such ornaments emerged, first in Denmark, probably in connection with the successful production there of

[2] Due to the sample size, not all types of pendants are represented. For instance, some Norwegian coin-pendants are known from hoards not covered by the sample (see Screen 2014, 362–3).

regal coinages (Jensen 1995, 102).[3] The only coin-like ornaments produced in Scandinavia before the eleventh century are a small group of uniface pendants made using various Umayyad and early Abbasid dirhams as dies. They occur in a few ninth-century graves scattered over mid-Scandinavia, such as grave 75 at Tuna, which contained fourteen specimens with beaded borders (Nylén & Schönbäck 1994, 60–2). This quasi-absence of coin-like pendants during most of the Viking Age is significant, and contrasts with the pattern in, for instance, England, where a fashion for coin-like brooches (although not pendants) existed within the framework of a coined economy (Williams 2001). It may indicate that, in Scandinavia, the imported coins were considered as ready-made decorative discs and that their reuse was mainly a matter of convenience and accessibility (cf. Williams 2006, 166). It may also indicate that it was important to wear a real coin rather than a pendant looking like one. In other words, the properties of the coin itself—its origins, materiality, and life history—took on heightened significance. These two explanations are not mutually exclusive.

Secondly, there is a strong technical homogeneity between the different groups of coins reused as pendants. All of them were transformed in a similar manner. After the coin was selected, it was provided with a simple means of suspension: an integral hole made by piercing; a 'sandwiched' loop where 'a strip of prepared metal is folded over leaving a cylindrical hoop, with its ends overlapping the edge of the coin, sandwiching it within the loop' (Blackburn 2006, 187); a ring formed from a piece of round-section wire; or a combination of any of them. The coin itself was very little modified and almost always retained its coin shape. The cross adapted from a German coin found in 2008 at Øster Vandet in Denmark is a very rare example of a coin reshaped into a non-circular pendant (in this case, a cross with splayed arms) (Price 2014, 189 no. 40; for a further example of a suspended dirham folded into a triangular shape, see Kleingärtner 2014, 75 no. 3). Some coin-pendants show traces of gilding on both sides, but it was highly unusual to further decorate them, for instance, with a frame or a border (see Blackburn 2006). Even the more elaborate forms of coin-jewellery that appear in the eleventh century—coin-chains in southern Scandinavia and coin-necklaces in Finland and Estonia—conform to these basic principles (for these phenomena, see Jensen 1992, 140; Jonsson 2009). The coins suspended from them were given little additional embellishment and remained central to the composition. Thus, from a technical point of view, the Viking Age coin-pendants all share a large degree of physical similarity, despite the many coin types involved in the practice.

[3] The reasons why coin-like jewellery began as a fashion in Denmark in particular are unclear, but may include Denmark's long tradition (dating back to the ninth century) of coin production and use, a stronger start to the regal coinage in Denmark compared to Norway, and the fact that, unlike in Sweden, coins were accepted at face value. It is also possible that the Danish practice of producing coin-like ornaments was influenced by Continental fashions. This is a phenomenon in need of closer detailed study.

Thirdly, from an archaeological point of view, there is no absolute separation between the various types of coin-pendants used in Scandinavia. The same find complex can combine coin-pendants of different origins or coins with different forms of suspension. A case in point is Birka grave 963, which can be dated to the middle of the tenth century (Arbman 1943, 386–8). This grave contained three coins: one Carolingian with a pierced hole; one Anglo-Saxon with a bronze loop; and one Scandinavian with a silver loop. They were found between two oval brooches, in combination with a shield-shaped pendant and several dozen beads. All the coin-pendants were originally strung together on a single necklace. Another interesting example is provided by the Valbo hoard in Sweden, deposited at the beginning of the twelfth century (Duczko 1986). The coins in the hoard, which span a period from 709/10 to 1066–87, form a disparate group. They consist of five Islamic, one Byzantine, one Swedish, one German, and five English coins. All these coins were turned into pendants, thus suggesting that they belonged to one and the same set. The fact that coin-pendants of different origins or coin-pendants mounted differently could be combined together suggests that they all appealed, to some extent, to the same realm of ideas. There was no fundamental difference between them. This fluidity between the types does not seem to disappear after the introduction of Christianity. Even in the eleventh–twelfth centuries, when almost all the coins in circulation in Scandinavia bear Christian symbols, a significant number of 'old' Islamic coins continue to be transformed and used as pendants. Good examples of this include the eighth-century Abbasid dirham found at Børglum, Denmark, with a loop made from a fragment of an English penny of Æthelred II, minted between *c.*997 and 1003 (Audy 2015, 102–3), or the looped Samanid dirham found at Sigtuna in a context dating to *c.*1200–30 (Roslund 2015, 44).

Finally, I would like to emphasize the fact that pierced and looped coins were used all over the Viking world and throughout the whole period. Their area of distribution extends from Iceland to Kievan Rus', encompassing the British Isles, Scandinavia, and the Baltic region. They are known from finds ranging from the very beginning of the ninth century to the first half of the twelfth century. There is, of course, considerable geographical and chronological variation. The coin-pendants seem to have been particularly appreciated in the eastern part of the Viking world, as shown by their frequent occurrence in Rus' graves (see Ravdina 1988) and in the Birka cemeteries (Audy 2012). They also seem to have been more fashionable in the early Viking Age than in the late Viking Age. As Figure 7.2 shows, the rate of transformation from coin to coin-pendant drops from about 6 per cent to about 2 per cent after *c.*980. This pattern probably reflects the fact that coins imported to Scandinavia no longer travelled through Rus' and Slavic territories, where, at an earlier date, some Islamic coins were pierced or looped (prior to their arrival in Scandinavia). It is worth noting that the coins reused as pendants are never completely absent in the Viking world, even in areas where they are not the norm. In England, though quite rare, several

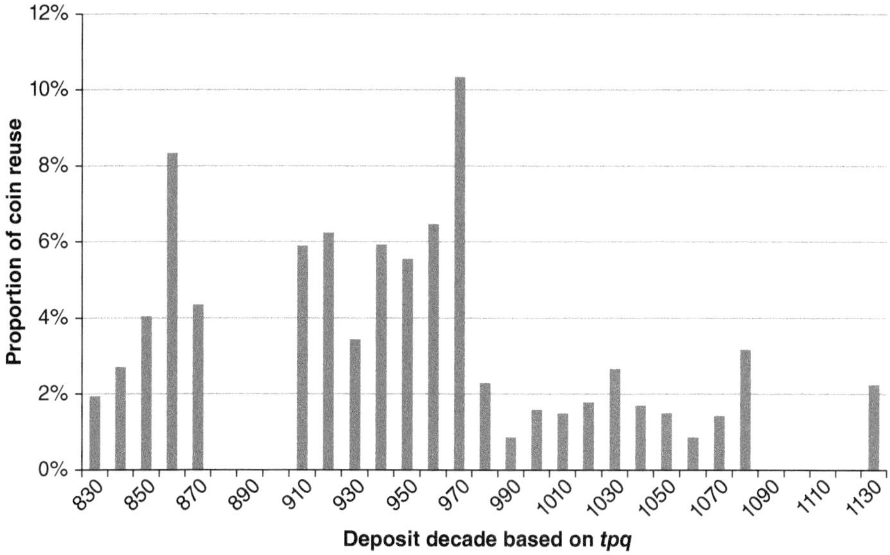

Fig. 7.2. Proportion of coin reuse by decade among the seventy-seven sampled hoards.

coins with Scandinavian-style loops attached have been reported recently in different parts of the country. A gilded silver coin of the Danish king Sven Estridsen (1047–75) was found at Mildenhall, Suffolk, in 1987 (Graham-Campbell 2011, 126, cat. no. 41, fig. 6.17) while a gilded silver Byzantine coin, which was likely pierced and gilded in Scandinavia, was found in the 'Ware-area', Hertfordshire, in 2007 (Kelleher 2013, 197–201).

The Viking Age coin-pendants seem to form a coherent category of material culture, despite some variation, especially in the eleventh century. They share many typological, technical, and contextual features, which suggests that the different types were not viewed as fundamentally different from each other. This does not mean that all the coin-pendants had the same meaning, but it is important to consider this common background when trying to understand them.

From Coin to Pendant: Transforming the Coin's Qualities

Turning coins into pendants is a fundamental process. It should be regarded as a stage of production in its own right, capable of generating new meanings, rather than simply as an adjustment. Physically, it is true that the impact of the transformation is often limited. It may consist, in its crudest form, of a single hole or a small loop. Conceptually, however, the changes involved by the transformation have important consequences with respect to function and value. The coin-pendants are thus to be seen as the result of a dramatic reincarnation, a pivotal moment in the life of the object (see, for instance, Appadurai

1986; Joy 2009). At the same time, it has to be kept in mind that many original features of the reused coins are permanent and enduring. As argued by Chris Gosden and Yvonne Marshall, 'renewals are never fully complete. They bring with them fragments of old lives, threads of earlier meanings' (1999, 177). When the coins were recontextualized and repurposed in the Viking Age, their original use and value were not totally erased. For instance, they retained a silver bullion value, as is indicated by the occurrence of pierced and looped coins as hack-silver in bullion hoards. A good example of this is the Byzantine coin from the Vålse hoard, deposited in *c.*991, which is both looped and fragmented (Horsnæs 2015, fig. 2). This continuity in function and meaning is essential for understanding how the coin-pendants were valued and perceived.

So far in the existing literature only one aspect of the transformation has been discussed in depth: the reinterpretation of the coin designs. Most scholars dealing with the Viking Age coin-pendants have tried to understand how people responded to the images, symbols, and writings appearing on them, by considering whether the orientation of the coin preserves the integrity, and thus potentially the intended meaning, of the iconography. The purpose has usually been to determine whether the coins, particularly those with cross designs, were worn as amulets and/or as Christian ornaments (for instance, Moesgaard 2004; Screen 2014).

In the Viking Age, very few groups of coin-pendants reveal regular patterns of orientation. The early Scandinavian coins of the pictorial type, issued at Hedeby in the first half of the ninth century, were systematically orientated so that one of the pictures could appear the correct way up (Audy 2012, 415). A parallel here can be drawn with the *Agnus Dei* coins, issued in the early eleventh century in Anglo-Saxon England. These were, for the most part, pierced/suspended so that either the obverse (featuring the Lamb of God) or, more commonly, the reverse (featuring a Dove, the symbol of the Holy Spirit) was correctly orientated (Keynes & Naismith 2011, 206–7). These two groups of coins feature pre-Christian (i.e. pagan—for instance, ships and masks) and Christian images respectively. Their selection was probably contingent, to a large extent, upon this meaningful iconography. Even if these two coin groups are exceptions, they support the hypothesis that a regular and systematic orientation is possible when the designs are well understood and regarded as significant by their owners. In some instances, though, the meaning the owner assigned to the design may have been different from the meaning intended by the issuer of the coin (see Talvio 1990, 84). For the *Agnus Dei* pennies adapted as pendants, it is remarkable that the Holy Dove, whose depiction resembles very closely that of birds often seen in Viking Age art and jewellery (see e.g. Ambrosiani 2001), is almost always preferred to the Lamb of God in instances when a lack of regular striking means that the two sides of the coin are not coordinated (Keynes & Naismith 2011, 206–7).

The interpretation of the other Viking Age coin groups found in Scandinavia is more problematic because of greater variation in coin orientation. This is especially the case with those bearing a cross. It is striking, for instance, that many of the crosses on coins are still not displayed correctly in the late Viking Age, even though Christianity was already well established in Scandinavia. A case in point is the orientation of Anglo-Saxon and Anglo-Norman pennies from Scandinavian collections struck between 1035 and 1100 (Table 7.2). Among these coins, the proportion of crosses oriented at irregular angles exceeds one quarter. Many also orient both the bust of the king and the cross, thus implying that some of the users may have responded to the former (since the crosses appearing on Anglo-Saxon coins are equal-armed crosses, it is possible to orientate the crosses without orientating the bust). This is not to say that the coin-pendants were *never* used as Christian symbols, just that the religious function cannot in itself explain the orientation of the cross. It must be emphasized that, even in obvious Christian contexts, the cross was not always displayed correctly. A notable example is the penny of William II found in grave 222 in the Swedish churchyard of Leksand, which orientates the cross as an X (Fig. 7.3) (Jonsson 1982).

Table 7.2. Orientation of the late Anglo-Saxon and early Anglo-Norman coins (1035–1100) reused as pendants in the Scandinavian collections, with a tolerance of up to 15° clockwise or counter-clockwise.

	Both sides	Only bust	Only cross	Neither sides	Total
Denmark	7 (36.8%)	1 (5.3%)	7 (36.8%)	4 (21.1%)	19
Sweden	18 (28.6%)	1 (1.6%)	27 (42.9%)	17 (27%)	63
Norway	0 (0%)	0 (0%)	5 (62.5%)	3 (37.5%)	8
Total	25 (27.8%)	2 (2.2%)	39 (43.3%)	24 (26.7%)	90

Source: Sylloge of Coins of the British Isles 11, 18, 40, 52, 54, and 66.

Fig. 7.3. Pierced coin of William II found in grave 222, Leksand churchyard.
Photo: author.

That there was an aesthetic intention behind the orientation of the Islamic coins has been pointed out by Mark Blackburn for the looped dinars in the Hoen hoard (Blackburn 2006, 192–3). In this late ninth-century gold hoard, the ten Islamic coins were not merely regarded as decorative discs. They were all arranged so as to display the ornamental lines of the Kufic inscription either horizontally or vertically. This pattern of orientation seems to be present in other Viking Age contexts. My examination of the Islamic coin-pendants found in Upplandic graves shows that many of them respect the design of the coin: out of thirty-three coins available for study, twenty-six had a horizontal or vertical alignment, three an irregular alignment, and four an indeterminate alignment.[4] Even though the Kufic inscriptions were not understood, their orientation was far from arbitrary.

Orientation seems to have been an individual matter and probably depended on many factors, such as the degree of familiarity with the images/inscriptions and the intentions of the owner. Under these circumstances, the variation observed among most of the coin groups is an indication that the coin-pendants were *not only* valued for their iconography. There was something else about coins that made them desirable to wear.

The fact that some of the designs were not displayed correctly should not lead to the conclusion that those designs were not playing any part at all in the practice. They probably were what made a coin a unique object in the eyes of their owners. It is no doubt for this reason that the unstruck flans (blanks) were not used as pendants (Table 7.1). Out of hundreds of unstruck flans found in Viking contexts, one of the few exceptions to have been converted comes from the hoard of Mannegårde, Gotland, deposited in *c.*1102. This unstruck flan, whose size and weight indicate an Islamic origin, was presumably transformed into a pendant because of the presence of a graffito representing a crescent moon. There is an apparent paradox here. The display of coins does not seem to depend fundamentally on their designs, but the absence of designs is exclusionary. This paradox can be solved by considering the coin designs from a different point of view.

Beyond their symbolic content, the coin designs were obviously associated with different types of ideas, and particularly with the idea of value. The conceptual link between coin design and standardized value/weight appears to have been clearly understood in the Viking Age. This is evidenced by the use of coin designs on a series of weight-calibrated objects produced in Scandinavia, including so-called regulated weights and late Viking Age silver arm-rings

[4] These figures are based on the following graves: Adelsö, Björkö, graves nos. 58, 367, 457, 707, 731, 834, 835, 843, 844, 954, 967 (KMK 101752); Alsike, Tuna, disturbed grave(s) (SHM 9404, 9818); Ekerö, Helgö, grave no. 23 (SHM 30710); Gamla Uppsala, Prästgården, grave no. 36 (UMF dnr 2/73); Löt, Fånö, grave (SHM 11763); Lovö, Söderby, grave no. 21 (KMK 103233); Skuttunge, Grävsta, grave no. 24 (SHM 19464); Stavby, Kommunalhuset, grave no. 28 (SHM 24988); Täby, Arninge, grave no. 4 (KMK 103677); Vaksala, Eke Äng, grave (SHM 25879).

from Gotland. These arm-rings (particularly Stenberger's 'Armbügel' Type 3: Stenberger 1958, 109–10) carry punched cross motifs reminiscent of the designs that appear on contemporary Nordic and western European coins, and have been interpreted as a means of conferring authority on the manufactured ring (Söderberg 2011). As argued by Anders Söderberg, 'there seem to have been certain traditions of providing credibility by the transferred use of coin symbols' (2011, 25). The most notable example is provided by a series of oblate-spheroid weights with designs on their upper surfaces imitating the 'barbarized' Arabic script carried on imitation dirhams struck by the Volga Bulgars (Schultzén 2009, 33). Although barbarized, the pseudo-Kufic inscriptions still contain the Arabic word *bakh*, a phrase which can be translated as 'of good quality' (Kilger 2008, 309). Throughout the Viking Age, it seems that the coin designs were perceived as a guarantee of value, even though the foreign coins on which they appeared were not accepted at nominal value in a Scandinavian context. By choosing to wear coins, owners were choosing objects whose quality was guaranteed and unmistakable, 'like wearing a designer watch', to borrow an analogy coined for rings by Gareth Williams (2007, 182). In this spirit, the coin-pendants can be seen as a form of bullion jewellery. It is significant that so many of them regained a currency role at a later point in their lives and were deposited in mixed (i.e. coin and non-numismatic artefact) hoards (Talvio 2000, 983).

Another idea associated with coin designs in the Viking Age seems to be that of foreignness. Among the many coin groups reused as pendants in Scandinavia, only one has designs which are deeply rooted in the local tradition: the early Scandinavian coins of the pictorial type as defined by Brita Malmer (1966). These designs were inspired by different foreign types, including Carolingian deniers and Frisian sceattas, but were incorporated into a Nordic iconographic repertoire, with the depiction of masks, snakes, stags, or cockerels (Malmer 1966; Varenius 1994). The choice of designs rooted in the Nordic, religious universe has been interpreted as an attempt to provide the coinage with legitimacy and credibility (Kilger 2008, 275–8). Remarkably, this very small group of coin-pendants is almost the only one showing a regular pattern of orientation. All the other coin groups have, by contrast, designs which were alien to the Nordic iconographic tradition or which were adopted locally at a late stage, such as crosses, busts, or Kufic/Latin inscriptions. Indeed, the coin itself was a foreign object during most of the Viking Age, in the sense that coins were rarely produced in Scandinavia before the turn of the first millennium. That this foreignness was significant is indicated by the difference in treatment between the imported coins and their Scandinavian imitations. It is striking, for instance, that the proportion of Byzantine silver coins (*miliaresia*) reused as pendants is around 30 per cent in Scandinavia, while the proportion of their local imitations reused as pendants does not exceed 10 per cent (Audy 2016, 164).

It is hard to say whether the owners of reused coins were able to identify their geographical origins, but there are cases where the area of minting seems to have been particularly meaningful. This is well illustrated by a grave find from Søndre Bø, Norway. The grave, dated to the second half of the ninth century, contained seven pierced and looped coins. Six of them are Carolingian deniers and one is an Anglo-Saxon penny (Aannestad 2015, 348, 357–8). According to Simon Coupland, the fact that the Carolingian coins at Søndre Bø come predominantly from the West Frankish kingdom, which is an unusual feature in Scandinavia, suggests that they were brought directly from this region as existing parcels. In the 830s and 840s, the coast of Aquitaine is known to have been plagued by Viking raids (Coupland 2011, 115). It seems plausible that the memory of these events was still vivid when the coins from Søndre Bø were transformed into pendants sometime in the second half of the ninth century. In other words, the special symbolic value attached to coin-pendants was also derived, to some extent, from the ability of objects to acquire biographies (see Joy 2009, 544). Indeed, from surveying the data, one gets the impression that many of the reused coins were already ancient when they were buried—in some cases, more than two hundred years old.

The long life of some of the coin-pendants has important consequences. Quite frequently, the reused coins are very damaged and no longer beautiful. They have, arguably, lost their ornamental value. This is the case of the looped Samanid coin from the hoard of Mannegårde, Gotland (Fig. 7.4). The coin, which is a dirham minted in Andaraba, Afghanistan, in AH 360 (AD 970/1), was deposited in the first decade of the twelfth century, more than 130 years after its production. Due to its constant rubbing on the clothing, the dirham's surface is badly worn. The inscriptions are almost completely illegible. The long use of the coin as pendant is further evidenced by the presence of at least one earlier suspension next to the loop. Another hole further away may also reflect an early stage in the life of the pendant. Obviously, this dirham had a special value for its users. It was kept in use over several generations, despite the fact that it was no longer beautiful. Under such circumstances, there are good

Fig. 7.4. Islamic coin-pendant from the hoard of Mannegårde.
Photo: author.

reasons to think that the coin was admired for qualities other than those related to its appearance.

It is clear that there was something about coins that made them desirable to wear in Viking Age Scandinavia, just as it did, for instance, in early Anglo-Saxon England (Williams 2006, 166). This probably had something to do with the nature of the object itself. As stressed by Richard Kelleher, 'coins were chosen to be adapted *because* they were coins' (2013, 24). An essential aspect here is the coin design. It was through it that the main qualities of the coins, such as their 'foreignness' or age, were expressed. With a few exceptions, the iconographic content of the designs seems to have been of varying importance, even though there was a marked aesthetic intention behind their orientation. The way the designs were perceived was probably very personal.

Viking Age Coin-pendants in Context: A Case Study

Viking Age coin-pendants appear in a variety of archaeological contexts, including hoards, cemeteries, churchyards, and settlement remains. Although they all provide useful information, only one of these contexts allows us to see how the reused coins were worn, displayed, and valued: inhumation burials. One such example of an inhumation burial with a coin-pendant is Birka grave 844. The grave, which contained a looped Abbasid dirham, offers perfect conditions for a contextual analysis by being well documented and fully illustrated.[5] This analysis will not be exclusively concerned with the archaeological context. According to the definition of Kemmers and Myrberg, 'context might be understood to refer to the various stages in the life of a coin, each of which can be studied' (2011, 89). It means that the production of the coin, its use, and its transformation also need to be situated (see also Ingvardson, this volume).

Birka was one of the major trading places of the Viking Age in Scandinavia. It was established on a small island in Lake Mälaren in the course of the eighth century and was deserted around 970. No fewer than sixty-three coin-pendants are known from the cemeteries surrounding the site. They were recovered from thirty-one female or double graves, most of which were richly equipped (Audy 2012, 416–17). The concentration of coin-pendants at Birka is unique. The cemeteries connected with the settlement account for more than one quarter of the Scandinavian graves with coin-pendants from the Viking Age. This may be due to the international character of the site, an idea supported by the exceptionally wide range of foreign coin types reused as pendants here (Audy 2012, 408–10). However, it must also be noted that the other international trading centres of the Viking Age, such as Hedeby or Kaupang, comprise a very limited number of graves with coin-pendants. Under such circumstances, the exceptional

[5] The grave and the grave goods are thoroughly described by Arbman (1943, 317–19).

concentration recorded at Birka should primarily be related to the local environment, and more particularly to local clothing fashions and burial customs. The fact that as many as thirty-nine coin-pendants were deposited in other graves from Uppland, the province where Birka is located, further points in that direction (see e.g. Arne 1934; Melin & Sigvallius 2001).

Birka grave 844 is a well-furnished grave (Fig. 7.5). It is not one of the richest in Birka, but several grave goods are indicative of a high social status, such as the fragment of gold band found at the head of the grave. Despite being an

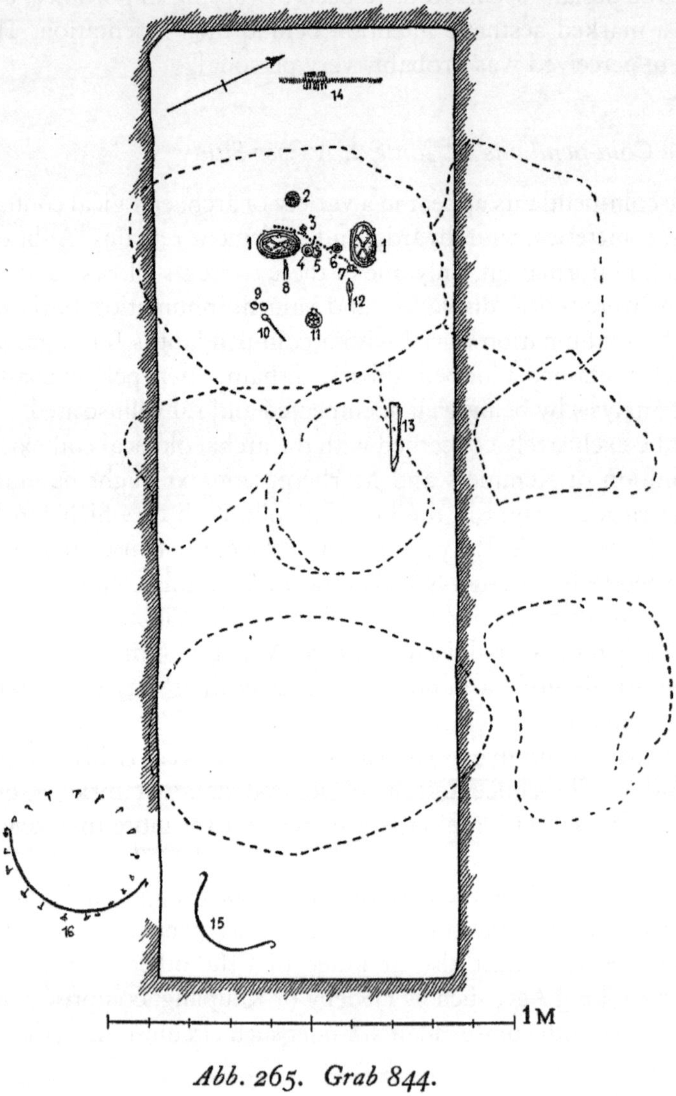

Fig. 7.5. Birka grave 844 (after Arbman 1943).

inhumation, the grave is typical of tenth-century eastern Scandinavia, with a mixture of local and foreign items. The most characteristic ones are probably the two bronze oval brooches, type P51b (Jansson 1985, 204). The Abbasid coin-pendant was found between these two brooches, together with twenty-nine beads and a set of pendants. All of them were presumably once strung together on a string. The row of ornaments included a four-sided mount adapted as a pendant, a fragment of a shield-shaped pendant, a coiled snake, and a Carolingian or Anglo-Saxon fastening adapted as pendant. It also included beads of rock crystal, carnelian, and glass paste. A circular pendant was found 10 cm above the row of beads. It was probably worn in isolation. A chair-pendant is believed to originate from the grave, but its original position is unknown. The two oval brooches were accompanied by a third bronze brooch, which was adapted from a circular pendant of Scandinavian manufacture. Between the circular brooch and the row of ornaments was a small collection of domestic implements: a pair of tweezers, a bronze needle, an ear-spoon, and two weights. A knife was found further away. The deposition of grave goods in grave 844, especially the two buckets found at the foot, is to be considered as a pre-Christian custom. The pagan identity of the deceased is supported by the interpretation of some of the pendants that she wore, such as the coiled snake or the miniature chair (see Gräslund 2005).

The coin-pendant found in grave 844 (Fig. 7.6) is made from an Abbasid dirham minted in Balkh, Afghanistan, in AH 194 (AD 809/10). To the edge of the dirham is attached a silver suspension loop with ribbed ornament. This loop is, as argued by Mark Blackburn, 'the standard type of mount used for coins in the Viking period' (2006, 187). It was placed so as to display geometrically the ornamental lines of the Kufic inscription. The writing on the obverse would have appeared upside-down, and the writing on the reverse perpendicularly. The coin-pendant is believed to have been gilded, but very few traces of this treatment are still visible today.

Fig. 7.6. Islamic coin-pendant from Birka grave 844.
Photo: author.

It is easy to imagine how rare coins with distinctive designs, for instance Carolingian, Byzantine, or early Scandinavian coins, could make a powerful impression on Scandinavians and be selected for suspension (Audy 2012, 411). Islamic dirhams, on the other hand, were easily available in the earlier part of the Viking Age. They were imported to Scandinavia by the hundreds of thousands before the last quarter of the tenth century. By wearing one of them, the owner of the coin-pendant from grave 844 was wearing the early Viking Age coin par excellence. Anyone in contact with this individual would have recognized at first glance that the object used as ornament was an Islamic dirham, a valuable and usually very pure silver coin associated with journeys to the East. The identification of the object 'coin' was made easier by the large flan and the sharp strike of the Abbasid dirham.

When the coin-pendant was deposited in grave 844, the coin from which it was made had been in circulation (within the Caliphate and/or within Scandinavia) for a long time, more than a century, perhaps even 150 years. While the dirham was minted in AD 809/10, the grave can be dated to sometime in the tenth century, probably after the first quarter, as suggested by the two oval brooches (Jansson 1985, 195–6) and the set of beads (see Callmer 1977). That the dirham was old at the time of burial fits a broader pattern of eighth- and ninth-century Islamic coins being deposited in tenth-century graves at Birka and suggests the local accumulation of dirhams at this nodal trading point (see Gustin 2011, 228–9). By being used over a long period of time, perhaps over several generations, the reused coin from Birka grave 844 accumulated histories. It became connected to many persons and events (see Gosden & Marshall 1999, 170). In this context, the coin-pendant presumably had a very personal meaning for its owner.

Even though very little remains of the possible gold layer that was once applied to the coin-pendant, it must be emphasized that the gilding covered one of the main qualities of the Abbasid dirham: its silver materiality. Islamic coins were brought to Scandinavia because they were made of good-quality silver. Covering this 'silverness' meant a significant change in the status of the object. The coin was no longer suitable to be exchanged in the silver-based economy of the Viking Age and it is notable that gilded silver artefacts rarely occur in hack-silver hoards (Hårdh 1996, 133). Gilding gave the coin an exclusively symbolic function. A similar phenomenon can be observed in eleventh-century Denmark, where gilding was used to make a clear distinction between official coin issues and nummular ornaments (Jensen 1995, 102). At the same time, the gold-like appearance of the coin made it enter into a different social sphere. It is generally accepted that gold and silver were used in different ways in Viking Age Scandinavia (e.g. Hårdh 1996, 132; Zachrisson 1998, 85). Gold held more of a prestigious function than an economic one (though see Kershaw, this volume). In this spirit, the gilded coin-pendants seem to occur in very special contexts, often characterized by their richness, such as the Hoen hoard

(Fuglesang & Wilson 2006), the Vårby hoard (Fig. 7.1), or Birka grave 750 (Arbman 1943, 267–72). By being gilded, the coin-pendant from Birka grave 844 was obviously attributed to a prestige role.

The pendants displayed together with the Abbasid dirham fall into two main groups: amulets and reused metalwork. The first group of pendants is well studied (e.g. Fuglesang 1989; Jensen 2010). It includes a wide range of miniatures meant to protect those who wore them, the most famous being the Thor's hammers and the miniature weapons. In grave 844, three pendants are usually viewed as belonging to this category: the miniature chair, the coiled-snake, and the miniature shield. The connection between coins and amulets is not surprising. Coins were—and still are—often credited with magical powers of some sort. This belief can be explained by the pictures that they bear, for example crosses and masks (cf. Gräslund 2005), but also by the properties of the object itself. In ancient societies, there was a tendency to invest precious metals with value in the spiritual realm (Veit 1982, 65). In the Viking Age, this was particularly true for gold, which was believed to have a mythical origin and some magical powers (Zachrisson 1998, 29).

The second category, which has received increasing attention in recent years, consists of small items of metalwork turned into pendants (Kleingärtner 2014; Aannestad 2015). This group reveals considerable diversity. It includes many different types of objects, usually foreign, such as vessel fragments, belt elements, or book-mounts. However, all these ornaments share two important features. They were not meant to be worn as pendants, but were converted in a second phase. In addition, they were mounted by using simple techniques, most often by riveting a loop to the piece of metal. In Birka grave 844, two pendants can be viewed as belonging to this category: the four-sided mount of Scandinavian manufacture and the Carolingian or Anglo-Saxon fastening. The symmetry between them and the reused Islamic dirham is striking. They all are recontextualized and repurposed objects. These pendants, which usually retain a strong foreign character, were probably used as a way to display one's international connections and involvement in exchange relationships. In this line, they have recently been interpreted as identity markers functioning on both a social and a cultural level (Aannestad 2015).

Necklaces similar to this one are known elsewhere from Birka and from a number of other places in Scandinavia. One was deposited, for instance, in Birka grave 632 (Arbman 1943, 210–13), and at least one in the Hoen hoard (Fuglesang & Wilson 2006). All these necklaces represent elaborate female costume assemblages and share the same pattern of composition, with a combination of amulets, local pendants, and reused metalwork (see Oras, Leimus, and Joosu, this volume). They often include one or several looped coins, as well as some rare Scandinavian pendants, such as coiled snakes or miniature chairs (see Gräslund 2005). The role of the coin-pendants in these assemblages is not quite clear, but they seem to have functioned on several levels: prestige, personal identity, collective identity, and supernatural beliefs. Interestingly, the results of this contextual analysis are comparable to those obtained by investigating the coins' qualities.

Coins as Meaningful Objects

The Viking Age coin-pendants have multiple related meanings. A foreign coin with a cross can, at the same time, be used as a symbol for Christianity, for international connections, for a privileged status, and for emotional attachment. All these meanings are not mutually exclusive, even if some of them probably took precedence over others in certain contexts. Despite this plurality, it is possible to maintain that the meaning of the coin-pendants was largely derived from the meanings and functions of coins in general. The production of these ornaments depended upon the ideas with which coins were themselves associated. That coins were foreign objects, that they were made of silver, that they had intricate life histories, that they conveyed ideas of richness and power, that they were decorated with meaningful symbols or inscriptions—all of this was to be infused into the pendants.

With this in mind, the coins circulating in the Viking Age should not be viewed as neutral pieces of silver, as is often the case. Numismatists and archaeologists tend to believe, because of the focus on weight economy, that coins have no—or very little—value beyond their metal content (Talvio 1990, 85). This implies that all types of valuables are interchangeable, that a coin can be replaced by any other coin or by any other silver artefact of the same weight. The medium does not matter. This traditional view overlooks an important fact. Coins were also socially and culturally significant. They were imbued with meaning (Kemmers & Myrberg 2011, 93). This aspect is essential for understanding the different social situations in which coins were involved, including trading activities.

During most of the Viking Age, there seems to be a certain continuity in the way coins were perceived. While they varied a lot as economic objects, navigating between the different and interlocking precious-metal economies (Williams 2007, 178–80), they remained rather stable as cultural, social, and symbolic objects. It was not until the eleventh century that some important changes occurred, especially in Denmark, as suggested by the introduction of elaborate forms of coin-jewellery and by the increasing production of coin-like ornaments. In all likelihood, these developments can be associated with the establishment of national coinages in Scandinavia. The fact that coins were henceforth issued locally and accepted at face value affected the way they were used and treated, but also the way they were perceived. Secondary treatment, in particular, became synonymous with damage and final demonetization. Nevertheless, the establishment of a coin-based economy did not cause a sudden break with the past. The Viking tradition of wearing coins as pendants was to continue without interruption until the twelfth century and the very end of the period. This continuity reflects the special significance and the special value given to coins in the Viking world.

ABBREVIATIONS

KMK: Kungl. Myntkabinettet, Stockholm
SHM: Statens Historiska Museet, Stockholm
UMF: Uppsala Universitets Museum för Nordiska Fornsaker

REFERENCES

Aannestad, H.L. 2015. 'Transformasjoner. Omforming og bruk av importerte gjenstander i vikingtid'. PhD thesis, Universitetet i Oslo.

Ambrosiani, B. 2001. 'The Birka Falcon'. In *Eastern Connections: Excavations in the Black Earth 1990–1995*, ed. B. Ambrosiani, 10–27. Stockholm: Birka Project Riksantikvarieämbetet.

Appadurai, A. 1986. 'Introduction: Commodities and the Politics of Value'. In *The Social Life of Things: Commodities in Cultural Perspective*, ed. A. Appadurai, 3–63. Cambridge: Cambridge University Press.

Arbman, H. 1943. *Birka—Untersuchungen und Studien. 1. Die Gräber: Text*. Stockholm: Kungl. Vitterhets Historie och Antikvitets Akademien.

Arne, T.J. 1934. *Das Bootgräberfeld von Tuna in Alsike, Uppland*. Stockholm: Kungl. Vitterhets Historie och Antikvitets Akademien.

Audy, F. 2011. 'Møntsmykker i vikingetiden i lyset af gravfundene fra Birka'. *Nordisk Numismatisk Unions Medlemsblad* 2011.3: 91–6.

Audy, F. 2012. 'Pour une étude méthodique des pendentifs monétaires: Le cas des sépultures de Birka (Suède)'. *Revue Numismatique* 169: 403–26.

Audy, F. 2015. 'When was the Loop Added? Dating the Transformation of Coins in the Viking Age'. In Talvio & Wijk (eds), 102–5.

Audy, F. 2016. 'How were Byzantine Coins used in Viking-Age Scandinavia?' In *Byzantium and the Viking World*, ed. F. Androshchuk, J. Shepard, & M. White, 141–68. Uppsala: Uppsala Universitet.

Blackburn, M. 2006. 'The Loops as a Guide to How and When the Coins were Acquired'. In Fuglesang & Wilson (eds), 181–99.

Callmer, J. 1977. *Trade Beads and Bead Trade in Scandinavia ca.800–1000* A.D. Bonn: Rudolf Habelt Verlag.

Coupland, S. 2011. 'Raiders, Traders, Worshippers and Settlers: The Continental Perspective'. In Graham-Campbell et al. (eds), 113–31.

Duczko, W. 1986. 'Valboskatten—Ett senvikingatida silverfynd från Gästrikland'. *Från Gästrikland* 1986: 7–40.

Fuglesang, S.H. 1989. 'Viking and Medieval Amulets in Scandinavia'. *Fornvännen* 84: 15–27.

Fuglesang, S.H. & D.M. Wilson (eds) 2006. *The Hoen Hoard: A Viking Gold Treasure of the Ninth Century*. Rome: Bardi Editore.

Garipzanov, I.H. 2005. 'Carolingian Coins in Ninth-Century Scandinavia: A Norwegian Perspective'. *Viking and Medieval Scandinavia* 1: 43–71.

Garipzanov, I.H. 2008. 'Carolingian Coins in Early Viking Age Scandinavia (ca.754–ca.900): Chronological Distribution and Regional Patterns'. *Nordisk Numismatisk Årsskrift* 2003–5: 65–92.

Gosden, C. & Y. Marshall 1999. 'The Cultural Biography of Objects'. *World Archaeology* 31.2: 169–78.

Graham-Campbell, J. 2011. *The Cuerdale Hoard and Related Viking-Age Silver and Gold, from Britain and Ireland, in The British Museum*, British Museum Research Publication 185. London: British Museum Press.

Graham-Campbell, J., S.M. Sindbæk, & G. Williams (eds) 2011. *Silver Economies: Monetisation and Society in Scandinavia, AD 800–1100*. Aarhus: Aarhus University Press.

Gräslund, A.-S. 2005. 'Symbolik för lycka och skydd—Vikingatida amuletthängen och deras rituella kontext'. In *Fra funn til samfunn. Jernalderstudier tilegnet Bergljot Solberg på 70-årsdagen*, ed. K.A. Bergsvik & A. Engevik, 377–92. Bergen: Arkeologisk institutt, Universitetet i Bergen.

Gustin, I. 2011. 'Coin Stock and Coin Circulation in Birka'. In Graham-Campbell et al. (eds), 227–44.

Hårdh, B. 1996. *Silver in the Viking Age: A Regional-Economic Study*. Stockholm: Almqvist & Wiksell International.

Horsnæs, H. 2015. 'Byzantine Coins from Viking Age Denmark'. In Talvio & Wijk (eds), 51–63.

Jansson, I. 1985. *Ovala Spännbucklor: En Studie av Vikingatida Standardsmycken med Utgångspunkt från Björkö-Fynden*. Uppsala: Uppsala Universitet.

Jensen, B. 2010. *Viking Age Amulets in Scandinavia and Western Europe*. Oxford: Archaeopress.

Jensen, J.S. (ed.) 1992. *Danmarks Middelalderlige Skattefund c.1050–c.1550*. Copenhagen: Det Kongelige Nordiske Oldskriftselskab.

Jensen, J.S. (ed.) 1995. *Tusindtallets Danske Mønter fra den Kongelige Mont- og Medaillesamling*. Copenhagen: Nationalmuseet.

Jonsson, E. 2009. 'Halskedjan i Linnaniemiskatten'. *Myntstudier* 2009.1: 1–16.

Jonsson, K. 1982. 'Myntfynden'. In *Tusen år på Kyrkudden. Leksands kyrka, arkeologi och byggnadshistoria*, ed. B. Dandanell, 159–64. Falun: Leksands församling.

Jonsson, K. 2015. 'Viking-Age Coins found in Sweden'. In Larsson et al. (eds), 51–7.

Joy, J. 2009. 'Reinvigorating Object Biography: Reproducing the Drama of Object Lives'. *World Archaeology* 41.4: 540–56.

Kelleher, R.M. 2013. 'Coins, Monetisation and Re-Use in Medieval England and Wales: New Interpretations Made Possible by the Portable Antiquities Scheme'. PhD dissertation, Durham University.

Kemmers, F. & N. Myrberg 2011. 'Rethinking Numismatics: The Archaeology of Coins'. *Archaeological Dialogues* 18.1: 87–108.

Keynes, S. & R. Naismith 2011. 'The Agnus Dei Pennies of King Æthelred the Unready'. *Anglo-Saxon England* 40: 175–223.

Kilger, C. 2008. 'Wholeness and Holiness: Counting, Weighing and Valuing Silver in the Early Viking Period'. In *Means of Exchange: Dealing with Silver in the Viking Age*, ed. D. Skre, 253–326. Aarhus: Aarhus University Press.

Kleingärtner, S. 2014. 'Reuse of Foreign Objects'. In Williams et al. (eds), 74–5.

Larsson, L., F. Ekengren, B. Helgesson, & B. Söderberg (eds) 2015. *Small Things Wide Horizons: Studies in Honour of Birgitta Hårdh*. Oxford: Archaeopress.

Malmer, B. 1966. *Nordiska mynt före år 1000*. Lund: Akademisk avhandling.

Melin, J. & B. Sigvallius 2001. *Excavations at Helgö. 14, Cemetery 118 and Building Group 7 and Cemetery 115*. Stockholm: Kungl. Vitterhets Historie och Antikvitets Akademien.

Moesgaard, J.C. 2004. 'Christiana Religio'. *Skalk* 2004.6: 12–17.

Nylén, E. & B. Schönbäck 1994. *Tuna i Badelunda: Guld, kvinnor, båtar, vol. 1*. Västerås: Västerås stad.

Price, N. 2014. 'Belief and Ritual'. In Williams et al. (eds), 162–95.

Ravdina, T.V. 1988. *Pogrebenija X–XI vv. s Monetami na territorii Drevnej Rusi: Katalog*. Moscow: Nauka.

Roslund, M. 2015. 'At the End of the Silver Flow: Islamic Dirhams in Sigtuna and the Shrinking Viking Network'. In Larsson et al. (eds), 43–8.

Schultzén, J. 2009. 'Devaluing the Mitqal: Inherent Trading Fees in the Metrics of Birka'. Master's thesis in Scientific Archaeology, Archaeological Research Laboratory, Department of Archaeology, Stockholm University.

Screen, E. 2014. 'Currency Conversion: Coins, Christianity and Norwegian Society in the Late Tenth and Eleventh Centuries'. In *Early Medieval Monetary History: Studies in Memory of Mark Blackburn*, ed. M. Allen, R. Naismith, & E. Screen, 349–76. Farnham: Ashgate.

Stenberger, M. 1958. *Die Schatzfunde Gotlands der Wikingerzeit. I. Text*. Stockholm: Kungl. Vitterhets Historie och Antikvitets Akademien.

Söderberg, A. 2011. 'Eyvind Skáldaspillir's Silver: Refining and Standards in Pre-Monetary Economies in the Light of Finds from Sigtuna and Gotland'. *Situne Dei* 2011: 5–34.

Talvio, T. 1990. 'Agnus Dei: Mynt och myntsmycken'. *Nordisk Numismatisk Unions Medlemsblad* 1990.4: 83–5.

Talvio, T. 2000. 'Islamic and Western Coins as Jewellery in Viking-Age Finland'. In *XII. Internationaler Numismatischer Kongreß. Akten—Proceedings—Actes, Berlin 1997*, ed. B. Kluge & B. Weisser, 983–5. Berlin: Staatliche Museen zu Berlin.

Talvio, T. & M. Wijk (eds) 2015. *Myntstudier. Festskrift till Kenneth Jonsson*. Stockholm: Svenska Numismatiska Föreningen.

Varenius, B. 1994. 'The Hedeby Coinage'. *Current Swedish Archaeology* 2: 185–93.

Veit, L. 1982. 'Amulett und Talisman'. In *Münzen in Brauch und Aberglauben: Schmuck und Dekor—Votiv und Amulett—Politische und Religiöse Selbstdarstellung*, ed. H. Maué & L. Veit, 65–74. Mainz am Rhein: P. von Zabern.

Williams, G. 2001. 'Coin Brooches of Edward the Confessor and William I'. *British Numismatic Journal* 71: 60–70.

Williams, G. 2006. 'The Circulation and Function of Coinage in Conversional-Period England, *c*. AD 580–675'. In *Coinage and History in the North Sea World, c.* AD

500–1200: Essays in Honour of Marion Archibald, ed. B. Cook & G. Williams, 145–92. Leiden and Boston: Brill.

Williams, G. 2007. 'Kingship, Christianity and Coinage: Monetary and Political Perspectives on Silver Economy in the Viking Age'. In *Silver Economy in the Viking Age*, ed. J. Graham-Campbell & G. Williams, 171–208. Walnut Creek: Left Coast Press.

Williams, G., P. Pentz, & M. Wemhoff (eds) 2014. *Vikings: Life and Legend*. London: The British Museum Press.

Zachrisson, T. 1998. *Gård, gräns, gravfält: Sammanhang kring ädelmetalldepåer och runstenar från vikingatid och tidig medeltid i Uppland och Gästrikland*. Stockholm Studies in Archaeology 15. Stockholm: Stockholms universitet.

8

A Viking Age Gold Hoard from Essu, Estonia

Context, Function, and Meaning

Ester Oras, Ivar Leimus, and Lauri Joosu

Introduction

The Essu gold hoard is an antiquarian Viking Age find discovered in the nineteenth century in north-east Estonia. It is the only prehistoric gold hoard in Estonia, now stored at the Estonian History Museum (Tallinn). The find initially consisted of six gold pendants: a dinar and five pendants with elaborate filigree and granulation decorations, although one of the latter has been lost over time. Gold items are not rare in the Viking world, but gold hoards are not numerous, the most famous being the Norwegian Hoen hoard (Fuglesang & Wilson 2006). Considering its unique nature—being the only prehistoric gold hoard in Estonia and an additional example of Viking Age gold hoards in northern Europe—the Essu hoard has gained limited international attention, being published only by local researchers as part of other scholarly work (Leimus 2006; Tamla & Varkki 2009).

The aim of this chapter is to introduce the Essu gold hoard to a wider audience and, in doing so, to provide insights into the use of gold during the 'Age of Silver' (see also Kershaw, this volume). There is very little information on the context and exact discovery of this antiquarian find, and, as such, our sources for its interpretation are limited. However, our recent Scanning Electron Microscopy-Energy Dispersive X-Ray Spectroscopy (SEM-EDS) analysis has cast new light on the production technology, alloy content, and use-wear of its contents, enabling a better understanding of how and where the pendants were produced and used. Based on this analysis and similar finds, we suggest that the pendants were manufactured within Scandinavia and originally formed part of an elaborate female necklace. We also give particular attention to the Arabic gold dinar and assess the wider evidence for dinars in northern Europe. This gold coin was originally produced as currency, but lost its monetary role as it was secondarily transformed into an ornament. Such treatment fits a wider Scandinavian pattern. It stands in sharp relief to the pronounced bullion role of the—much more numerous—silver dirhams, suggesting a fundamentally different treatment of gold and silver.

The Discovery and Contents of the Hoard

According to archive materials based on the description of the discovery by the finder, the Essu gold hoard was discovered in the third quarter of the nineteenth century during peat cutting some eight feet deep in a peat bog in Essu (Germ. Jessen) village, Haljala Parish, Lääne-Viru County, north-east Estonia (Fig. 8.1). The find was handed over to the Estonian Provincial Museum (currently Estonian History Museum) archaeology collections by Baron von Dellingshausen in 1864 (Hansen 1875, 16).

The hoard (Fig. 8.2; Table 8.1) comprised six gold pendants, one of which was lost around the turn of the twentieth century. The total weight of the five remaining pendants is 22.68 g. Three pendants depict a tree motif, while two further pendants (including the one now lost) have a geometrical ornament with entwined circles surrounding bowen knots.[1] The sixth pendant was formed of an

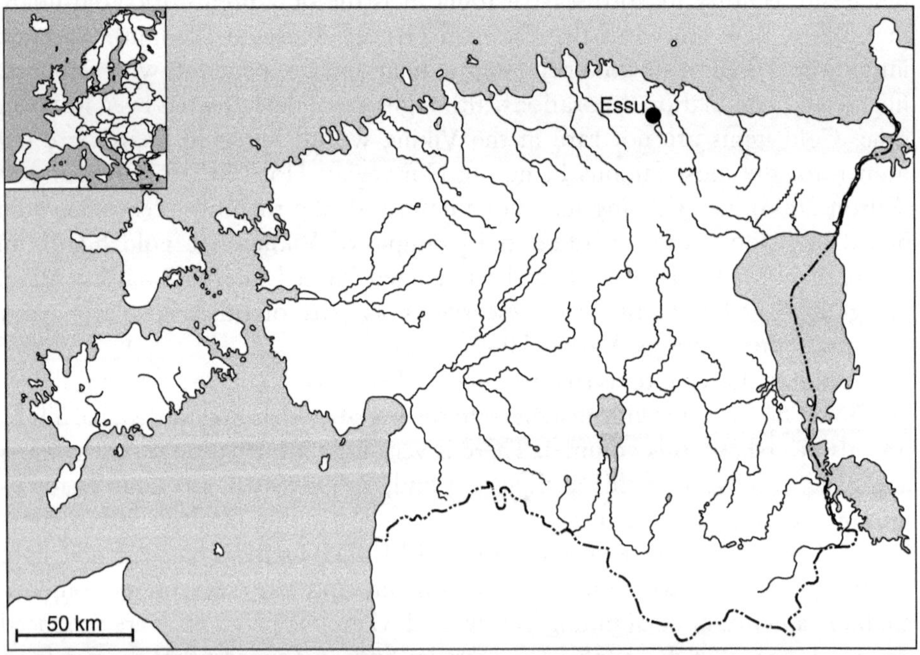

Fig. 8.1. Location map of the Essu gold hoard (E. Oras).

[1] The last depiction of the now lost pendant can be found on the pages of the catalogue of the Archaeology Congress held in Riga in 1896 (Katalog 1896, Taf. 27:4).

Fig. 8.2. The Essu gold hoard pendants (I. Leimus, E. Oras).

Table 8.1. Measurements of the pendants from the Essu hoard.

Pendant	Weight (g)	Diameter (mm)
1 (geometric ornament)	4.97	25
3 (tree ornament)	4.42	21.5
4 (tree ornament)	4.03	22
5 (tree ornament)	4.35	23
6 (dinar)	4.91	21.5

Arabic dinar, struck in AD 864/5. The dinar provides a *tpq* after which the artefacts must have been concealed. The hoard most likely belongs to the last quarter of the ninth century or to the early tenth century, although a slightly later date cannot be entirely excluded.

SEM-EDS Analysis: Technology, Alloys, and Use-wear

We carried out detailed SEM-EDS analysis of all the pendants, the aim being to determine their production technology alloy contents, and signs of wear, to reveal new insights into their provenance and function. Analyses and imaging were conducted at the geology laboratory at the University of Tartu using a variable pressure Zeiss EVO MA15 scanning electron microscope, equipped with an Oxford X-MAX energy dispersive detector system (EDS). Measured spectra were processed by Aztec software. Spectra were collected in high vacuum mode using 20 keV accelerating voltage and focused electron beam. Due to the surface contamination by various elements, only gold (Au), silver (Ag), and copper (Cu) normalized abundance were measured to obtain 'true' alloy composition. In addition, the presence of mercury (Hg) was checked, but proved absent in all samples.

Tree Decoration Pendants

Three pendants (Fig. 8.2 nos. 3–5) depict a plant ornament, the so-called world-tree, one of which is placed on a pendant upside down as if hanging from the loop. Other than that, these three pendants are very similar to each other both technologically and stylistically. The base of the pendants is made of flat gold foil which has been cut out in one piece as a circular body part with an additional oblong extension for a suspension loop. Extra small platforms have been left for decorative collared granules at the foot of the loop. The end of the back-bent loop is either triangular or oval. The suspension loops are decorated with S-shaped beaded bands, with either filed or impressed small decorative beads on top, on the front and back. The back of the suspension loop as well as all the filigree and granulation work seems to be fastened by chemical soldering (see Duczko 1985, 26–9). This allows for repeated soldering and must have been particularly necessary in the cases where granules are placed on top of filigree.

On the face of the pendants four different types of wires have been used (Fig. 8.3). The most elaborate is a beaded wire with an equator cut, which is utilized for all tree branches and around the pendants' edges. Two separate pieces of wire are used on the edges: one for the main body part, the other for a suspension loop. The latter starts on the front and travels all the way down the back of the loop, before returning to the front, where it ends. It first seemed that the same wire was used for edge decoration and for collars around the granules on the sides of suspension loops. However, the SEM-EDS analysis indicated that the alloy content of the collars is slightly different from other filigree wires with higher inclusion of gold (up to 89 per cent) and silver within the range of 10–13 per cent (other wires have gold around 79–84 per cent and silver around 14–17 per cent).

The tree branches are connected with pieces of grooved band. However, in one pendant the upper and lowermost branches are bound with beaded wire

Fig. 8.3. Selection of the SEM images of the tree-pendants. A—collared granule; B—beaded band on the suspension loop; C—tree branch with granule and two different connecting elements (beaded band (bottom) and beaded wire with small beads (top)); D—different size granules (E. Oras).

with smaller round beads. As with the collars noted above, their alloy was also slightly higher in gold and lower in silver compared to the rest of the filigree wires, indicating that the wires had different origins, and perhaps came from different manufacturers.

The granules are all perfectly round, although in slightly different sizes. If used as single granules, they are placed in the middle of coiled branches or as collared granules. Otherwise, they are placed in groups of three, resembling a bunch of grapes. In this case the groups are placed at the end of the tree branches or on top of the tree. Most of the granules have a very similar alloy content to the wires. There are also a couple of stylistic outliers. An additional granule, a fourth 'grape', is found at the tree-top on the pendant which depicts the tree upside down. It is slightly tilted off the central line and is most likely an accidental addition during granulation work. The second unusual detail is the use of two single granules at the foot of the tree on one pendant. Since in all the other cases granules are either surrounded by wire or placed in groups, this kind of decoration is unconventional. Despite those slight differences, all in all the pendants are produced with high craftsmanship skills and are very alike both technologically and stylistically. The stylistic similarity and techniques used suggest that they have been made by the same experienced jeweller.

The alloy content of the pendants is very similar for all three pendants (Fig. 8.4). With only slight fluctuations, the base, wires and granules include three main components: gold 80–84 per cent, silver 15–17 per cent and copper around 1.5 per cent. Only in one case does the copper content rise to 2.9 per cent. This is the highest measurement of copper in this pendant type and might be the result of slightly uneven distribution of different metal components in the alloy.

The use-wear of the tree-pendants indicates that they are all heavily worn (Fig. 8.5). The beads of the beaded wire and bands decorating the suspension loops are almost flattened out, especially on the main contact zones on top of, and at the back of, the loop. The edges and the back of the pendants' base show clear signs of wear. The wear on the sides of the loops varies: the one with a tree upside down is quite equally worn on both sides, whilst the other two are more worn and deformed at their right and left side respectively. This could indicate their position in an original necklace and directions of contact with possible other decorative elements such as beads or other pendants.

Parallels to this type of pendant are not numerous. There are no similar gold pendants known to the authors: all the parallels are either bronze or silver. Four tree-motif pendants, in silver or bronze, are known from Birka, Sweden (graves 119, 523, 791, 967) (Arbman 1940; 1943; Duczko 1985, 42). The silver filigree-granulation pendant from grave 791 has been gilded. All these pendants are from female graves with typical female accessories such as oval brooches. Besides Birka, another Scandinavian parallel to this pendant type is a silver example from Johannishus in Scania (Duczko 1985, 42). All these Swedish pendants date from the tenth to early twelth century (Duczko 1985, 42).

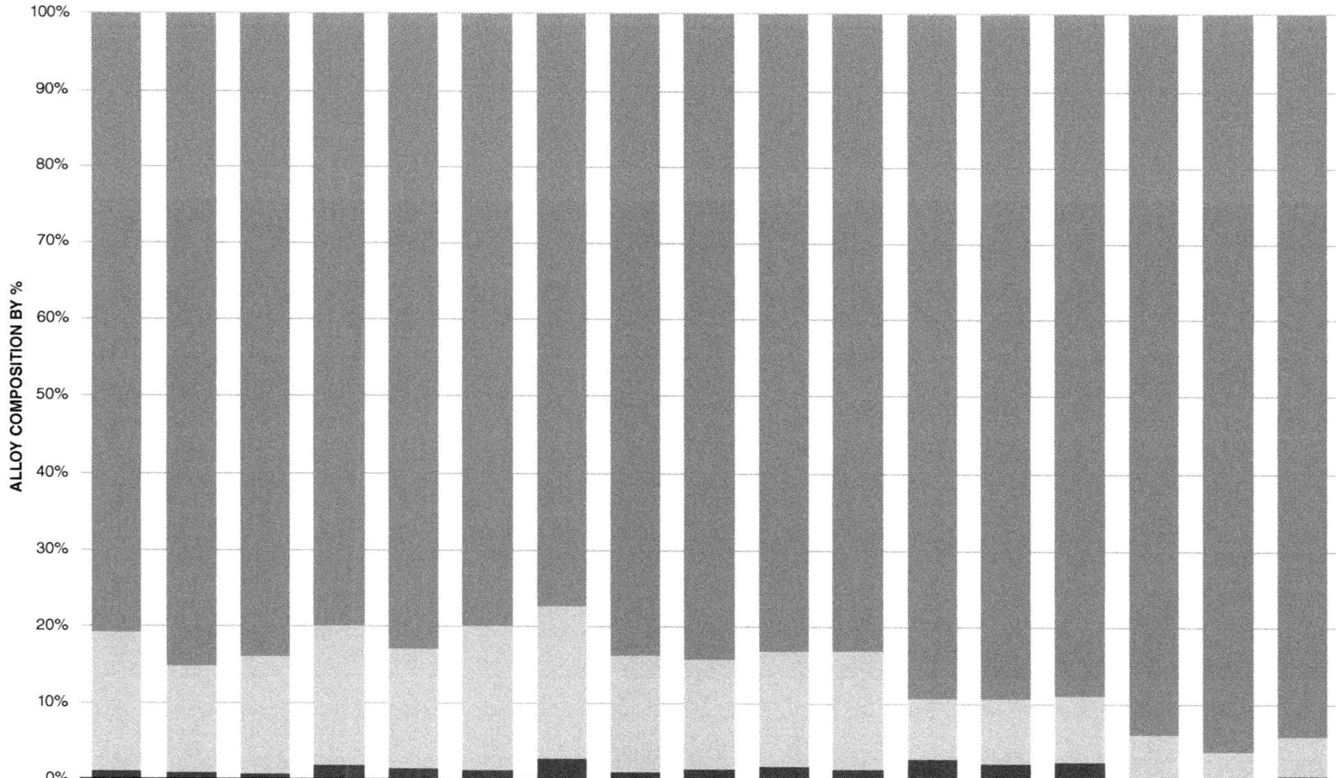

	Base Tree_P3	Filigree Tree_P3	Granule Tree_P3	Base Tree_P4	Filigree Tree_P4	Granule Tree_P4	Soldering Tree_P4	Base Tree_P5	Filigree Tree_P5	Granule Tree_P5	Soldering Tree_P5	Base Geom_P1	Filigree Geom_P1	Granule Geom_P1	Base Dinar_P6	Loop Dinar_P6	Rivet Dinar_P6
Au (%)	80.75	85.32	83.92	79.87	83.00	80.14	77.37	83.65	84.33	83.25	83.10	89.30	89.37	88.95	94.14	96.19	94.29
Ag (%)	18.25	13.90	15.42	18.30	15.49	18.52	19.74	15.23	14.13	14.91	15.41	7.84	8.31	8.67	5.86	3.64	5.00
Cu (%)	1.01	0.78	0.67	1.83	1.51	1.34	2.89	1.12	1.54	1.84	1.49	2.86	2.32	2.38	0.00	0.18	0.72

Fig. 8.4. Alloy content of the main elements of pendants (E. Oras).

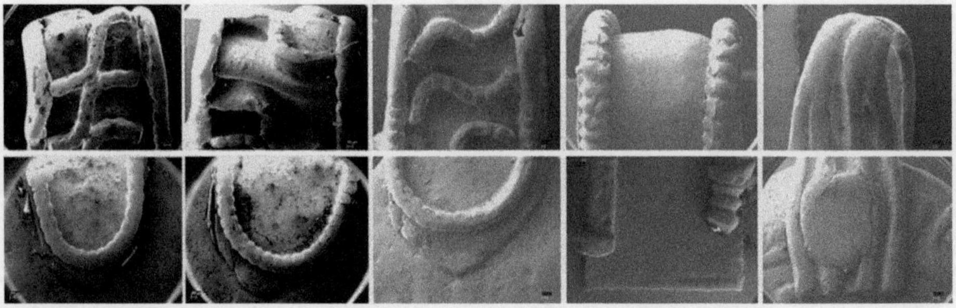

Fig. 8.5. SEM images reflecting different use-wear of the pendants (E. Oras).

Several similar pendants are known from Old Rus territory (Duczko 2004; Макаров 2012). Four are from the famous Gnëzdovo archaeological complex, including the 1867 hoard (*tpq* AD 953/4) and the (potentially female) graves nos. 105 and C 212, dating to the second half of the tenth century. At least one of the latter is a gilded bronze. Another similar, silver pendant has been found in a female burial from Timërevo, Russia, with a *tpq* AD 969/70. Similar silver pendants are known from the Chernigov and Vladimir burial mounds: in the case of the latter, the tree is also turned upside down. One bronze cast tree-pendant is known from Kiev.

All these Swedish and Rus territory pendants are from the later Viking period, i.e. mainly the second half of the tenth century AD. They are made of bronze or silver (sometimes gilded) and exemplify filigree and granulation, but also casting technology. Compared to the Essu pendants, they are stylistically simplified with less precision in details, giving the impression that the Essu pendants might be prototypes on which later pendants were based.

Geometric Decoration Pendant

Two larger pendants (one lost) depict geometric decoration comprising four entwined circles that surround slightly tilted bowen knots (Fig. 8.6). In the centre is a collared granule. Collared granules in groups of four are placed on the four sides of entwined circles, but two granules seem to have fallen out. There are also smaller plain granules on the two side group and bottom-most granulation decoration, whilst in the latter group a granule looks accidentally misplaced on top of the collared granule. A single collared granule is placed on the lower part of the suspension loop and, on the basis of an old picture of the lost pendant (Katalog 1896, Taf 27:4), there is an additional collared granule on top of its loop. The only difference between these two pendants seems to be this suspension loop decoration.

As with the tree-pendants, the base is made of flat gold foil cut out in one piece as a circular main part with an extension for a suspension loop, although, here,

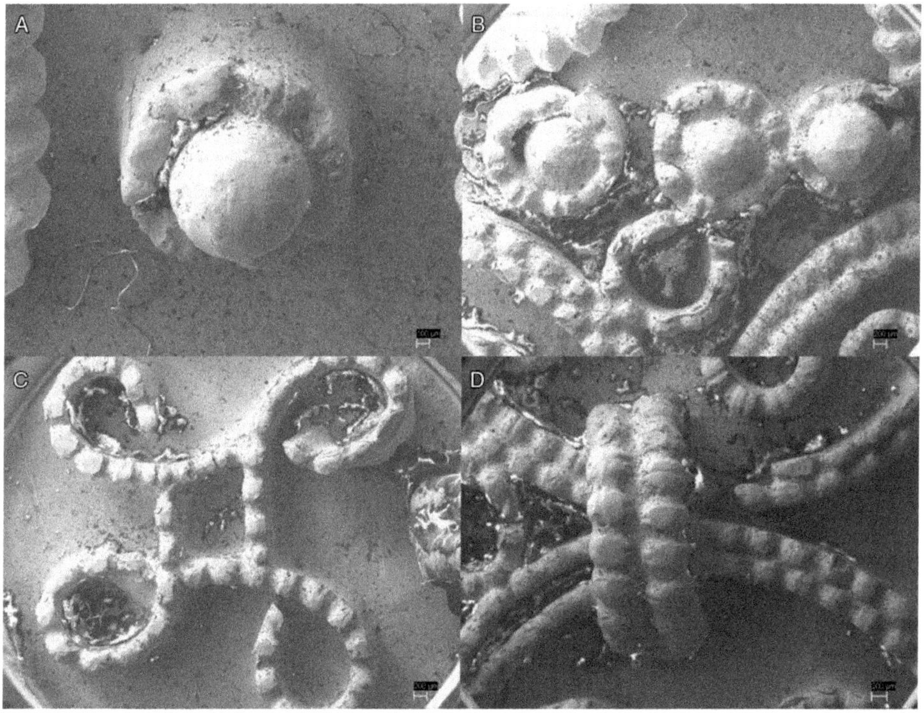

Fig. 8.6. Selection of the SEM images of the geometrical ornament pendant. A—collared granule on the suspension loop; B—group of collared granules at the top part of the pendant; C—bowen knot; D—double-beaded band circles and their connecting elements of beaded wire with small beads (E. Oras).

the end of the loop is straight. Most likely chemical soldering has been used for securing the filigree-granulation elements and the end of the suspension loop. However, in some instances, for instance at the top of the pendant, the collared beads appear to be more sunken into the solder and collars while the paired wires surrounding the bowen knots are sometimes melted together (see Fig. 8.6).

The use of decorative wires is different from the tree-pendants. The edge of the pendant and suspension loop are decorated with similar beaded wire (with equator cut), but here the edge decoration is in one piece: starting at one of the back corners of the loop following all the way around the main body part and ending in the other corner. The use of beaded band is elaborate: while, on the tree-pendants, this was only found as S-shaped decorations on the suspension loops, here it is employed for collaring the granules, creating bowen knots as well as circles surrounding the latter. The bowen knots are made of four separate, closely placed P-shaped wires and circles; surrounding the knots are two parallel beaded bands soldered together. Beaded wire with smaller beads (very similar to the one used for attaching the upper and lower branches of one tree-pendant) was used for connecting four double beaded band circles. As with the tree-pendants, all the granules are perfectly round, although in slightly different sizes.

The alloy content of the different elements of the extant pendant is very similar. Three main components (Fig. 8.4) are distinguished: gold with 88–9 per cent, silver with 8 per cent, and copper with up to 3 per cent, though usually around 2 per cent. Compared to the tree-pendants there is clearly a smaller amount of silver and higher content of copper in this pendant. The latter is possibly the reason why the overall colour of this piece is slightly more reddish and might also indicate different availability of silver at the point of manufacture.

The use-wear of the geometrical pendant is noteworthy (Fig. 8.5). It looks as if the pendant has barely been worn: there are clear and sharp cut marks visible at the edges and especially at the end of the suspension loop. The beads on the beaded wire look fresh and hardly worn down even on the upper part and back of the loop. Thus, this piece has a different life history to the tree-pendants.

There are few parallels to the geometrical ornament pendant and none of them overlaps with the Essu examples entirely. The Essu pendants are the only ones made of gold, the others are all silver. Stylistically closest is a pendant from the rich female burial from Aska, Sweden, dated to the second half of the tenth century (Jansson 1996, 41–2; Stenberger 1977, 437). The 'Aska lady' had several unique and imported jewellery items (e.g. small decorative gold pendants, a chair-shaped and a male head pendant), one of which is a geometrically decorated round silver pendant. It has four connected silver circles that surround three intertwined circles in the middle. Collared granules have been used as decorative elements at the sides of the larger circles; a single one is placed in the middle of the pendant. All these elements are very similar to the outline of the Essu example.

The second parallel is from the 1867 Gnëzdovo hoard with the *tpq* AD 953/4 (Duczko 2004, figs 46 no. 24 and 48b) with four connected circles surrounding wavy beaded band decorations. However, the specific decorative elements (loop decorations, use of granules, etc.) are still rather different from the Essu pendant. It is noteworthy that this pendant is the only example with strikingly similar S-shape decoration on the upper part of the suspension loop and collared granules at the side of the loop as we saw in the case of the Essu tree-pendants. A similar, fragmentary silver filigree pendant, with four circular fields, three of which are bound by overlying 'arms', is also known from a late tenth-century hoard from Øster Mose, Denmark, while a domed, cast silver parallel to this piece, with four circular fields each containing three or four pellets, comes from Manchester, England (Skovmand 1942, 61–5, fig. 12 (centre right); Kershaw 2013, 66–8, fig. 3.24).

These comparanda are again somewhat later than the late ninth-/early tenth-century date proposed for the Essu hoard. The elaborate decoration and manufacturing process for the Aska and Gnëzdovo pendants is very similar to the Essu pendants and no stylistic or production simplification over time is detected in the case of these two.

Dinar

The sixth pendant was made from a gold Arabic dinar. The coin was minted during the reign of the Abbasid caliph al-Mustaʿīn, in AH 250 (AD 864/5). The name of the mint (Table 8.2) is partly covered by the golden loop riveted to the coin. Only the beginning of the name of the mint, al, and the downward end tick can be seen, which suggest the name al-Shash (الشاش, present-day Tashkent in Uzbekistan) (al-Nakshabandī 2002, 137–9).

The loop is reeded, meaning that it is decorated with parallel ribs (for a discussion of this form of decoration, see Blackburn 2006, 181–99, type III Rr(f)). At first glance the loop seems to be worn considerably thinner at the top, but a closer survey suggests that it could have been deliberately hammered to a narrower, thicker shape, probably to give it strength.

The coin contains gold in the range of 93.1–95.3 per cent; the rest is silver (Fig. 8.4). This is in keeping with the alloys noted for other, roughly contemporary dinars minted in al-Shash (Table 8.3). The loop is purer still, containing 95.6–96.5 per cent gold, with less than 0.2 per cent copper besides the silver. The rivet attaching the loop is of somewhat different composition, containing besides gold (93.7–94.9 per cent) and silver (4.5–5.5 per cent) also a little copper (0.67–0.76 per cent). While it is possible that gold for the loop came from coins from the same region, the small copper content of the rivet suggests that the alloy had a different origin (for instance, in North Africa or Iraq, among other locations).

During the Viking Age, Arabic silver coins of the seventh to tenth centuries served as the main circulating and accumulating coin medium in Russia and the countries around the Baltic: Sweden, Denmark, East Prussia, Finland, Estonia, Latvia. The end of the eighth century witnessed the start of a massive influx of silver from the East to the region, which dominated silver stocks until the later tenth century. As a result, hundreds of thousands of dirhams have been discovered in northern and eastern Europe (Leimus 2006, 19 with references). Dirhams are rarer in western Europe, but still number in the low hundreds

Table 8.2. Inscription on the dinar.

Obv.	Rv.
لااللهالا	الله
الله وحد	محمد
لاشريك له	رسول
العباس بن	االله
امير المومنين	المستعين بالله

Table 8.3. Alloy content of two dinars minted in aš-Šaš in AH 251 and AH 253 (Gondonneau & Guerra 2002, 592, table 5).

Year	Gold	Silver	Copper
251	98.4	1.5	0.01
253	92.4	7.5	0.01

(e.g. Naismith records *c.*350 dirhams from Viking Age hoards in England: Naismith 2005).

Islamic gold coins of the same period provide a notably different picture (Duplessy 1956, 105). The total number of dinars recorded in Europe is less than 500, the majority of which—about 400 coins—belonged to a single hoard, discovered in the sixteenth century in San Lorenzo church, Venice; all but two coins are now lost. Only eighty-one accurately determined seventh- to tenth-century dinars from established find sites (together with imitations) are recorded in Europe. Both the temporal and geographic distribution of dinars found in Europe differs markedly from silver dirhams, indicating a fundamentally different function. Whereas most dirhams date to the tenth century, the majority of the dinars are quite early, minted by the Umayyads and the first Abbasids. More than three-quarters of the identified coins (sixty-four specimens) date from the end of the first century and second century AH. Pre-reform coins, minted before AH 77 (AD 696/7), are represented by a single specimen, while the rest cover the period AH 87–192 (*c.*AD 705–807) (Table 8.4).

Most of these early dinars come from a small number of hoards, where they frequently occur with numerous Byzantine solidi (e.g. from Venice and Reno, Italy; Petrovci, Croatia; and Anastasievka, southern Russia). Besides these, a handful have been found singly in France, England,[2] and Serbia. Only one Umayyad dinar, from AH 121 (AD 738/9), comes from northern Europe (Old Ladoga)[3] and one Abbasid dinar, from AH 159 (AD 775/6), with an uncertain find report may have been found in Poland. Hence, not only the temporal division of dinars but also their distribution area—focused in southern Europe—differs considerably from those of dirhams.

This pattern is not fortuitous. According to written sources, in Italy, particularly in Venice and its surroundings, Islamic gold coins called *mancus* were broadly used in the 770s–80s. From there, they spread further along trade routes, peaking in use around 800. The other contemporaneous route of the influx of dinars ran over the Pyrenees (McCormick 2001, 319–84). In southern Russia, relying upon the hoard of Anastasijevka (*tpq* 780), dinars also appeared

[2] To judge from the published description, a dinar from Eastbourne, Sussex, belongs to the first reform type, dated to AH 77–100 = AD 696–718 (*Numismatic Chronicle* 9 (1846–7), 85; compare: Broome 2006, 13–14). In the mid nineteenth century, Prof. Wilson attributed it, erroneously, to the reign of caliph Hišam ibn Abd-ul-Malik (AD 724–43). This inaccurate dating has been repeated in all subsequent publications.

[3] The remaining Umayyad dinars from Russia come from the south of Russia.

Table 8.4. Temporal division of dinars in European finds.

Hijri Year	Dynasty	Country	Find-spot
74?–77	Umayyad	France	Autun
77–100	Umayyad	England	Sussex, Eastbourne
87	Umayyad	Russia	Bashkiria, Levashovka grave field
89	Umayyad	Serbia	Futog
93	Umayyad	Russia	Krasnodar Krai, Anastasyevka
96	Umayyad	France	Grèzes
97	Umayyad	Italy	Venetia, church of San Lorenzo
91	Umayyad	France	Nord de Carcassonne
97	Umayyad	France	Eastern Pyrenees, Ruscino
97	Umayyad	France	Douzens
98	Umayyad	France	St Nazaire
100	Umayyad	Russia	Krasnodar Krai, Anastasyevka
106	Umayyad	Russia	Krasnodar Krai, Anastasyevka
112	Umayyad	Russia	Krasnodar Krai, Anastasyevka
113	Umayyad	Italy	Sicily, Palermo vicinity
114	Umayyad	Russia	Dagestan, Tarki
121	Umayyad	Russia	Staraja Ladoga
121	Umayyad	Russia	Chechnya, Grozny vicinity
121	Umayyad	Russia	Krasnodar Krai, Anastasyevka
121	Umayyad imitation	Russia	Krasnodar Krai, Anastasyevka
127	Umayyad	Russia	Rostov obl., Don river
136	Abbasid	Croatia	Petrovci
138	Abbasid	Russia	Chechnya
138	Abbasid	Serbia	Bulkeczi
138	Abbasid imitation	Ukraine	Crimea, Tepseni stronghold
138	Abbasid imitation	Italy	Bologna, Reno
143	Abbasid	Russia	Astrahan Obl., Ordõnski Bugor
143	Abbasid	Italy	Venetia, church of San Lorenzo
152	Abbasid	Norway	Hoen
152 or 155	Imitation	Sweden	Vadstena, Uppland
153	Abbasid	Italy	Bologna, Reno
154	Abbasid	Italy	Bologna, Reno
155	Abbasid	France	Eastern Pyrenees, Ruscino
157	Abbasid	England	Wickhampton, Norfolk
157	Abbasid	Italy	Bologna, Reno
159	Abbasid	Poland	Stara Rzeka-Retków
163	Abbasid	Croatia	Petrovci
164	Emirate of Cordoba	France	Chaunay
165	Abbasid	Croatia	Petrovci
165	Abbasid	Croatia	Petrovci
166	Abbasid	Italy	Bologna, Reno
166	Abbasid	Croatia	Petrovci
167	Abbasid	Croatia	Petrovci
167	Abbasid	Croatia	Petrovci
168	Abbasid	Croatia	Petrovci
168	Abbasid	Croatia	Petrovci
170	Abbasid	Italy	Bologna, Reno
172	Abbasid	Italy	Bologna, Reno
172	Abbasid	Croatia	Petrovci
173	Abbasid	Italy	Bologna, Reno
177	Abbasid	Italy	Bologna, Reno
178	Abbasid	Italy	Bologna, Reno

(continued)

Table 8.4. Continued

Hijri Year	Dynasty	Country	Find-spot
180	Abbasid	Norway	Hoen
181	Abbasid	Italy	Bologna, Reno
184	Abbasid	Italy	Bologna, Reno
185	Abbasid	Norway	Hoen
186	Abbasid	Norway	Hoen
186	Abbasid	Italy	Bologna, Reno
189	Abbasid	Norway	Hoen
189	Abbasid	Italy	Bologna, Reno
191	Abbasid	Italy	Bologna, Reno
192	Abbasid	Norway	Hoen
206	Abbasid	Norway	Hoen
223	Abbasid	Italy	Venetia, churh of San Tomà
234	Abbasid	Norway	Hoen
236	Aghlabid	Sardinia	Porto Torres
250	Abbasid	Estonia	Essu
258	Abbasid	Sweden	Kullsta, Uppland
267	Aghlabid	Sardinia	Porto Torres
270	Aghlabid	Sardinia	Porto Torres
274	Abbasid	Sweden	Kullsta, Uppland
289	Samanid	Russia	Uljanovsk Obl., Maina
295	Samanid	Sweden	Öland
312	Samanid	Poland	Gościejewice
320	Fatimid	Sweden	Köping, Västmanland
358	Fatimid	England	Wight island
364	Fatimid	Russia	Taman, Phanagoria stronghold
373	Samanid	Russia	Tatarstan, Staromataks
374	Imitation	Denmark	Bornholm

Sources: Brisholm 1986, 209–18; Carlsson & Jonsson 2012, 34–9; Duplessy 1956, 121–44; Ilisch 2004, 91–106; Linder Welin 1964, 5–25; McCormick 2001, 816–34; Moesgaard & Rispling 2002, 91–4; Naismith 2005, 193–222; Skaare 2006, 165–72, catalogue 262–75; Кулешов 2009, 59–61; Лебедев & Кожевин 2009, 63–4; Марков 1910; Slaski & Tabaczyński 1959, no. 33; pers. comm. Mateusz Bogucki; Parvérie 2014; 2015; Кулешов 2016, 93.

around the same time. None of these coins has a loop, i.e. they were not used as ornaments, suggesting that they were coins out of circulation. Geographically, only a number of dinars from the Norwegian Hoen hoard constitute an exception. However, this hoard dates to the late ninth century. It contains dinars accumulated over a long period, which were furnished with a loop and converted into ornaments (Blackburn 2006, 196–9).[4]

Gold coins from the third century AH occur in Europe in considerably smaller numbers: only eleven are known (Table 8.4). On the basis of information in written sources, the abrupt decrease coincides with the end of the use of *mancuses*

[4] The loops of the Hoen dinars (type III Sr(c)) need not all be of Scandinavian origin: this is indicated by an Umayyad dirham from AH 83 (AD 702), preserved in the Iraq museum, having a loop identical to them, although slightly shorter. The provenance of the coin is unknown, but we can hardly presume that it has come to Baghdad from North Europe (al-Nakṣhabandī 2006, 41, 114, plate 2:16).

in Italy by the 830s–40s. These were replaced by local silver coins, which became predominant by the mid ninth century AD (McCormick 2001, 329–30, 380, 383). The southernmost dinar is the Abbasid coin from AH 223 (= AD 837/8), found in the San Tomà church in Venice. The find area of dinars from the third century AH is quite different from the previous century, and now focuses on the Nordic countries. One dinar is known from Russia, from Volga-Bulgaria. Six of the coins have been minted by the order of Abbasid caliphs and two by the Samanid emir Ismáil ibn Ahmad. A separate phenomenon is the hoard of Porto Torres (Sardinia) with its three Aghlabid dinars evidently straight from North Africa (McCormick 2001, 356).

A particularly notable feature is that all dinars of this period found in the Nordic countries are mounted with a loop. Of these, the loops of Abbasid dinars are all, except one, riveted and reeded, belonging to Mark Blackburn's type IIIRr(f) (Blackburn 2006, fig. 6.3). The loops of many silver coins riveted in Scandinavia in the ninth–eleventh centuries were of the same type. The Vikings may have taken the technology of coin mounts with them when settling in foreign parts. For instance, the Byzantine gold coin from AD 912–13, discovered in a female burial from Gnëzdovo, is mounted with a loop of the same type (Eniosova & Pushkina 2013, 219). The loop of the Samanid dinar from Öland is also riveted, but smooth. The dinars from Volga-Bulgaria, Venice, and Sardinia have no loops: they have apparently been lost directly from monetary circulation. Here, a clear difference can be observed between the use of coins in the Nordic countries and elsewhere.

Finds of Islamic gold coins of the next, fourth, century AH in Europe are rarer still. Today we know about only five (or six) specimens (Table 8.4) (Кулешов 2016, 93 refers to four find locations in Russia but does not specify the find locations). None has a loop. One dinar found from the Tatarstan, Russia, and one from Poland, were minted by Samanids (some of them possibly by Sajids), but the specimens from Taman (Russia), England, and Sweden were minted by the Egyptian Fatimid dynasty. North African and Spanish provenances also characterize the Islamic dinars of the next couple of centuries, found in Europe (Brisholm 1986, 213, 216; Duplessy 1956, nos. 26–38; Naismith 2005, nos. 5–6; Кропоткин 1962, no. 176; Ingvardson 2015, 33).

Returning to the dinar from Essu, the general topography of the ninth-century finds as well as the typology of coin loops indicate that it belongs to the Scandinavian find group. Consequently, the coin likely reached Estonia via the Nordic countries, not directly from Russia or western Europe. In Scandinavia it was also mounted with a loop. As can be seen from the other Estonian Viking Age hoards of Parivere (*tpq* 952/3), Erra-Liiva (978), Kehra (978/9), and Paunküla (1009), the practice of mounting coins with loops appeared in Estonia considerably later, in the second half of the tenth century (Leimus 2007, nos. 12, 22, 23, 34). As a rule, in these cases these loops were smooth and mostly of bronze.

Discussion: Manufacturers and Origin of the Essu Pendants

The question of who made the Essu pendants and where is not easy to answer. Both pendant types are very similar within their group in terms of style and alloy content and exhibit well-developed crafting skills. However, between pendant groups the stylistic features, preferences in materials, and specific decorative elements are rather different. The difference in alloy content (especially the amount of silver) might hint at a different availability in, and preference for, raw materials in two production contexts. In stylistic terms, the geometrical pendants are clearly in favour of utilizing and experimenting with the beaded band, which is barely used in the case of tree-pendants (only as suspension loop decoration). The technology for decorating the edges of the pendants also differs between the two groups. The soldering is of higher quality for the tree-pendants with some faults detected on the geometrical pendant. The initial shape of the pendants' base also varies. These first choices in the manufacturing process reflect the initial ideas, previous technological experience, preferences, and habits of the craftsperson who produced the pendants. Since those initial decisions diverge and further choices regarding the materials and decorative techniques vary, we would argue that the pendants were made by different gold-work masters.

It cannot be excluded that more than one person was involved in making the final product of the specific type of pendant and that this might have taken place in different regions and even at different times. For instance, the small decorative element of the S-shaped beaded band on the suspension loops of the tree-pendants is missing from the main tree-ornament. Perhaps it was avoided, or just not available for whoever made them. Such small details could easily be added on the loop at a later stage, perhaps by someone who was keen on using this beaded band in abundance (as we see in the case of geometrical ornament). Furthermore, it could be that the craftspeople making the pendants were using some older 'raw material' or material of different origin for their final production. The reuse and redesign of, for instance, gold Carolingian jewellery or even liturgical items has been suggested for some items in the famous Hoen hoard (Westerman-Angerhausen 2006). In the case of the three identical tree-pendants it is also tempting to make a connection with, for example, trefoil brooches, which would give a perfect material basis for making a set of identical pendants. It is noteworthy that on many of the Scandinavian trefoil brooches plant motifs have been used, including on those found in Birka burials (Arbman 1940; 1943).

Where were the jewellers located? The parallel finds discussed above are found as often in hoards and burials in Scandinavia as in Old Rus territory. There are, furthermore, no direct gold parallels that could help to identify the production site of the Essu pendants. Pendants from the rich female grave from Gnëzdovo hill-fort exhibit different decorative elements, usually connected volutes in combination with collared granules (Duczko 2004, fig. 47a; Eniosova

2007, 176). Gold pendants from the Hoen hoard also show different motifs including volutes and geometrical four-part ornamentation which indicate both Carolingian and Scandinavian manufacturers with Carolingian counterparts as their prototype (Fuglesang 2006; 2013). In the technical execution of the tree-pendants and in the general ornamental lay-out of the pendant with geometric ornament, and its use of an elaborate beaded band, the Essu examples also somewhat resemble Anglo-Saxon gold jewellery, such as the rings in the recently discovered West Yorkshire hoard (Marzinzik 2014). They nonetheless remain without direct parallels.

Regarding the tree-pendants, it has been pointed out that Continental plant motifs were imitated by Scandinavian Viking jewellers, although there are very few examples of such locally produced ornaments (Duczko 1985, 42). Duczko notes that, in the case of Carolingian and Ottoman jewellery, the decorations using plant motifs have their 'branch' elements turned both up and down, whilst downward-directed branches are preferred in the Nordic style. He concludes that most of the ornaments with plant decoration are produced in Sweden or Swedish Viking environments in Rus territory. The use of the tree motif (or world-tree motif) in Scandinavia has also been linked to eastern art forms connected with Byzantine art (Rhodin et al. 2000) and Steppe people (Hedenstierna-Jonson 2012). In fact, nine belt mounts from the Swedish Vårby hoard depict strikingly similar tree motifs to those seen on the Essu pendants, with downward-directed and intertwined branches, and have been related to Magyar influences (Hedenstierna-Jonson 2012). Thus, it could be that the Essu tree-pendants were manufactured as local Scandinavian objects but with further elaborations of plant-decoration inspired by a mixing of eastern and western art motifs. However, there also remains a possibility that the tree-pendants are examples of redesigned jewellery initially serving a different function and/or produced in a different region (e.g. Carolingian Empire or Anglo-Saxon contexts), but shaped into pendants with some further decorative additions by the new owners—the Scandinavians.

Swedish Viking Age material provides several parallels for the Essu geometric pendant. From the Swedish Torsta find (deposited in the second half of the tenth century), there are silver pendants decorated with connected circles and granules on the sides of the suspension loop (Fuglesang & Wilson 2006, pl. 40B; Eilbracht 1999, pl. 7, cat. nos. 102–3). Similar decorations, such as bowen knots and binding 'arms', are found on filigree gold beads from Hallinge, Gotland (Fuglesang & Wilson 2006, pl. 41A–B). A silver pendant with collared granules at the sides of the suspension loop and one larger central collared granule is also known from the Gotlandic Fölhagen hoard (Stenberger 1977, fig. 304). All those Scandinavian stylistically similar works tend to have a mixture of different elements observed on the Essu pendants, used in different combinations and quantities. Besides Scandinavian influence, the principle of geometric four-part decoration also has parallels in western art styles from both the Carolingian and Anglo-Saxon worlds.

The pendant from the female Aska burial is closest to the Essu geometrical pendant: it has been interpreted as a Scandinavian product from the ninth or tenth century, which was inspired by western European jewellery (Jansson 1996, 41). The Gnëzdovo geometrical pendant is thought to have been Swedish-Danish in design, but in terms of decoration it is closer to Gotlandic tenth-century ornaments (Duczko 2004, 181). The Gnëzdovo gold pendants with volute decorations have been discussed within the framework of the Terslev and Hiddensee styles, produced in south-west Sweden and northern Germany and linked to specialized jewellers working for Danish nobility (Eniosova 2007, 176 with references). Thus, at least the known parallels, stylistic and technological elements seem to indicate a western (i.e. European or Scandinavian) source for the Essu geometrical pendants.

There are three further arguments in favour of a western origin for the hoard. First, it is worth remembering that the type of suspension loop on the Essu dinar is often used in Scandinavian coin pendants (see 'Dinar', above). Similar reeded loops are known from other ornamental pendants at Birka, Sweden (Duczko 1985) and Hoen, Norway (Blackburn 2006). This indicates that the coin has been turned into an ornament within Scandinavia. Second, although there are some gold ornaments in Rus territory and some signs of gold-working in, for example, Rjurikovo Gorodishe near Novgorod and Gnëzdovo, these are still very scarce finds and do not provide evidence for the larger-scale manufacture of gold jewellery (Duczko 2004, 200; Eniosova 2007). Larger sets of specialist gold-working kits are missing, and tiny fragments of gold, pieces of wires, granules, etc. have been seen as remains of local small-scale jewellery repair, rather than signs of local gold-ornament manufacture (Eniosova 2007). This also supports the idea that the Essu pendants were not produced in the Rus territory. Finally, the Essu pendants are earlier than all their parallels in the East. The Rus versions of these pendants are also often more stylized and simplified, some even cast, suggesting that they are chronologically later versions of Essu-type pendants.

All things considered, we conclude that the Essu pendants were manufactured in the western, rather than eastern, areas of the Viking world. On the basis of their style and technological execution, they were made by at least two different goldsmiths. There is a clear qualitative difference between the two pendant types. If the geometrical pendants show some slight technological faults and offsets in their decorative motifs, then the tree-pendants are examples of very high-quality, skilled, long-practised and strict motif-following craftsmanship. Based on fluctuations in alloy content, it seems that the filigree elements used on the tree-pendants come from at least two separate sources. This might hint at a very specialized production site with the selective use of decorative elements from different production events. It is possible that the decorated 'raw material' might have come from western Europe (Carolingian or Anglo-Saxon contexts) and that items originally serving a different jewellery function were reshaped into pendants with some further decorative additions by the Scandinavians. This would be supported by their very high-skilled level of technological execution for filigree and granulation. However, without any direct parallels it is also possible that the tree-pendants might be the products of some experienced craftsperson within Scandinavia, perhaps in southern Sweden, Denmark, or northern Germany, who might have been inspired by oriental and western art styles. This idea of production entirely within Scandinavia is supported by the fact that there are a few very similar, though later, examples of this pendant type in Swedish and Old Rus archaeological material which have not been found in western Europe. Thus, a Scandinavian origin should not be entirely excluded.

The Essu Hoard as a Female Assemblage?

The considerably different use-wear patterns exhibited by the pendants—the tree-pendants and dinar being heavily worn and the geometric pendant barely used—show that they did not form a collective set of ornaments at first. This also supports our argument that we are dealing with different manufacturers and places of origin for these six gold ornaments. The tree-pendants and a dinar must have been in contact with other artefacts (beads, pendants) and materials (textile) for many years if not decades. The use-wear markers on the suspension loop might be the result of being in contact with other elements of necklaces, for example glass beads, since this combination of precious-metal pendants and glass beads was widely distributed in Viking Age female ornament sets. Unfortunately, we have no further information about possible glass beads being found with the Essu pendants. The heavy wear on these four items hints that they must have been used as prestigious items for quite some period, perhaps beyond the lifetime of a single owner. The geometrical pendant(s), however, is a later addition. The fact that similar pendants in terms of style, material, and technique were later added to the 'old' set, suggests that there were certain established ideas of what jewellery types could be combined together in this specific (female) necklace type.

Notably, at least half of the similar pendants found in Scandinavia and Rus territory are related to women's jewellery in (presumably female) burials and hoards. The Hoen hoard has also been interpreted as a find with strong female connotations. The majority of its contents have been interpreted as pendants for an elaborate, multi-looped female necklace, such as are known from the 1867 Gnëzdovo hoard and from the female burial in grave 632 at Birka (Wilson 2006, 21). Thus, it is likely that such sets of gold pendants, sometimes in combination with coin-pendants, and often found together with glass beads, are a particular Viking Age female find group. C. Kilger has proposed that 'themed deposits' of female jewellery, often in gold or with gilding and often comprising coin-pendants and other necklace items as well as a central brooch, represent a special category of Viking Age hoard, distinct from the silver, and especially hack-silver, hoards of the tenth century (2008). Kilger suggests that such hoards reflect an older hoarding practice dating back to the Migration period, during which female items of gold bracteates, also combined with other parts of necklaces and gold fibula(e), were often deposited in ritual contexts (2008; for Migration-period gold deposits, and the question of gender, see Hines 1989; Arrhenius 1995; Gaimster 2001). Against this background it seems possible that Viking Age hoards of complete, gold jewellery had a special, gendered, connotation and sacrificial function, quite opposite to the 'male' realm of silver that could be hacked and deposited—usually in dry land, in the form of coins, bars, rings, etc. (see also Hårdh 1996, 132–4). While the Essu hoard appears to lack a central brooch, it shares several features in common with this distinctive group of hoards.[5] It is worth speculating that, as a deposit of gold, in particular gold pendants, it was part of a long-term depositional tradition of hoarding female costume sets in landscape contexts from which they were not meant to be retrieved.

Conclusions

The late ninth-/early tenth-century Essu gold hoard is a small treasure containing a unique set of golden pendants. The pendants were most likely manufactured in Scandinavia with some western Europe connotations, but share stylistic and technological as well as artefactual parallels with regions in both the east and west of the Viking world. With their elaborate and detailed decoration, the Essu pendants display the earliest, possibly a kind of prototype, pendant style of their kind, that was copied in Scandinavia and Russian territory in later decades.

The find-spot of the hoard, in the coastal region of north-east Estonia, is clearly situated on the Vikings' eastern route (the so-called *Austrvegr*) at an important midpoint on the seaways connecting Scandinavia with the north-west Russian territories. The hoard seems to be a material witness of Swedish Vikings heading to (or from) the Old Rus regions. Whether it was concealed by the Scandinavians themselves as a peaceful act at their stopping place, or perhaps acquired and hidden by locals as a result of possible pirate attack or peaceful trade contacts, remains unknown.

Although a small addition to the Viking Age gold finds, the Essu gold hoard follows the Viking Age pattern of precious and rare gold items being concealed in (probable) watery contexts, in that it was retrieved from a bog (see note 5). Perhaps similar cultural practices and ideas about how and where precious gold ought to be deposited are reflected here? There may also be a link between gold, high-status female adornments, and the concealment of these

[5] The discovery of the Essu hoard in a peat bog hints at its original deposition within a 'watery context'. Other gold hoards of female assemblages, including those from Kullsta, Sweden (from a flooded meadow area), and Hoen, Norway (also deposited in a peat bog), are likewise thought to derive from watery locations (Zachrisson 1998, 266–9, cat. no. 18; Mikkelsen 2006, 29, 37; see also Kershaw, this volume).

prestigious items into watery contexts where they are more difficult to reach and recover with possibly some ritual connotations. If this is the case, the Essu gold hoard is an important addition to this group of finds supporting the idea of a widespread cultural practice in the Viking world. Although the exact reasons for the concealment of this unique and beautiful ornament set remain open, the Essu gold hoard provides an excellent example of the cosmopolitan and constant betwixt and between nature of the Viking Age, and of the meeting and mixing of different people, identities, and material cultures.

ACKNOWLEDGEMENTS

This research was supported by the Estonian Ministry of Education and Research institutional research funding IUT20–7 'Estonia in Circum-Baltic Space: Archaeology of Economic, Social, and Cultural Processes', IUT20–34 'The Phanerozoic Journey of Baltica: Sedimentary, Geochemical and Biotic Signatures of Changing Environment—PalaeoBaltica', PUTJD64 'Feast in Afterlife: Multidisciplinary Study of Ritual Food in Conversion Period Cemetery at Kukruse, NE-Estonia', and the European Union through the European Regional Development Fund (Centre of Excellence CECT); IUT18–8 'The Making of Livonia: Actors, Institutions and Networks in the Medieval and Early Modern Baltic Sea Region'.

REFERENCES

al-Naḳshabandī, N.M. 2002. *The Islamic Dinar in the Iraq Museum. Umayyad & Abbasid Dinar*. 2nd edn. Damascus: Dar al-Watha iq.

al-Naḳshabandī, N.M. 2006. *Al-Dirham al-Umawī*. Damascus: Dar al-Watha iq.

Arbman, H. 1940. *Birka. Die Gräber: Tafeln*. Birka 1. Uppsala: Almqvist & Wiksell.

Arbman, H. 1943. *Birka. Die Gräber: Text*. Birka 1. Uppsala: Almqvist & Wiksell.

Arrhenius, B. 1995. 'Women and Gold: On the Role of Women in Society at the Time of the Great Migrations and their Relationship to the Production and Distribution of Ornaments'. In *Produksjon og Samfunn: Om Erverv, Spesialisering og Bosetning i Norden i 1. årtusen e.Kr.: Beretning Fra 2. Nordiske Jernaldersymposium På Granavolden Gjæstgiveri 7.–10. Mai 1992*, ed. H.G. Resi, 85–96. Oslo: Universitetets Oldsaksamling.

Blackburn, M. 2006. 'The Loops as a Guide to How and When the Coins Were Acquired'. In Fuglesang & Wilson (eds), 181–99.

Brisholm, K. 1986. 'An Archival Study on the Medieval Islamic Gold Coinage'. *Nordisk Numismatisk Unions Medlemsblad* 9: 209–18.

Broome, M. 2006. *A Handbook of Islamic Coins*. London: Spink.

Carlsson, A. & K. Jonsson 2012. 'Askahögen och Elias Brenners Guldmynt'. *Myntstudier* 2: 34–9.

Duczko, W. 1985. *The Filigree and Granulation Work of the Viking Period: An Analysis of the Material from Björkö. Birka V*. Stockholm: Almqvist & Wiksell.

Duczko, W. 2004. *Viking Rus: Studies on the Presence of Scandinavians in Eastern Europe*. Leiden: Brill.

Duplessy, J. 1956. 'La circulation des monnaies arabes en Europe Occidentale du VIIIe au XIIIe siècle'. *Revue Numismatique 5e série* 18: 101–63.

Eilbracht, H. 1999. *Filigran- und Granulationskunst im Wikingischen Norden: Untersuchungen zum Transfer Frühmittelalterlicher Gold- und Silberschmiedetechniken zwischen dem Kontinent und Nordeuropa*. Bonn: R. Habelt.

Eniosova, N. 2007. 'Viking Age Gold from Old Rus''. In *Cultural Interaction Between East and West: Archaeology, Artefacts and Human Contacts in Northern Europe*, ed. U. Fransson, M. Svedin, S. Bergerbrant, & F. Androshchuk, 175–80. Stockholm: Stockholms Universitet.

Eniosova, N. & T. Pushkina 2013. 'Finds of Byzantine Origin from the Early Urban Centre Gnëzdovo in the Light of the Contacts between Rus' and Constantinople (tenth–early eleventh centuries AD)'. In *From Goths to Varangians: Communication and Cultural Exchange Between the Baltic and the Black Sea*, ed. L. Bjerg, J.H. Lind, & S.M. Sindbaek, 213–55. Aarhus: Aarhus University Press.

Fuglesang, S.H. 2006. 'The Scandinavian Pendants'. In Fuglesang & Wilson (eds), 83–92.

Fuglesang, S.H. 2013. 'Copying and Creativity in Early Viking Ornament'. In *Early Medieval Art and Archaeology in the Northern World: Studies in Honour of James Graham-Campbell*, ed. A. Reynolds & L. Webster, 825–41. Leiden and Boston: Brill.

Fuglesang, S.H. & D.M. Wilson (eds) 2006. *The Hoen Hoard: A Viking Gold Treasure of the Ninth Century*. Rome: Bardi Editore.

Gaimster, M. 2001. 'Gold Bracteates and Necklaces: Political Ideas in the Sixth Century'. In *Roman Gold and the Development of the Early Germanic Kingdoms: Aspects of Technical, Socio-Political, Socio-Economic, Artistic and Intellectual Development, A.D. 1–550: Symposium in Stockholm, 14–16 November 1997*, ed. B. Magnus, 143–56. Stockholm: Almqvist & Wiksell.

Gondonneau, A. & M.F. Guerra 2002. 'The Circulation of Precious Metals in the Arab Empire: The Case of the Near and the Middle East'. *Archaeometry* 44.4: 573–99.

Hansen, G. von. 1875. *Die Sammlungen Inländischer Alterthümer und Anderer auf die Baltischen Provinzen Bezüglichen Gegenstände des Estländischen Provinzial-Museums*. Reval: Lindfors.

Hårdh, B. 1996. *Silver in the Viking Age: A Regional-Economic Study*. Acta archaeologica Lundensia. Series in 8° 25. Stockholm: Almquist & Wiksell International.

Hedenstierna-Jonson, C. 2012. 'Traces of Contacts: Magyar Material Culture in the Swedish Viking Age Context of Birka'. In *Die Archäologie der Frühen Ungarn: Chronologie, Technologie und Methodik: Internationaler Workshop des Archäologischen Instituts der Ungarischen Akademie der Wissenschaften und des Römisch-Germanischen Zentralmuseums Mainz in Budapest am 4. und 5. Dezember 2009*, ed. B. Tobias, 29–46. Mainz: Römisch-Germanisches Zentralmuseum.

Hines, J. 1989. 'Ritual Hoarding in Migration-Period Scandinavia: A Review of Recent Interpretations'. *Proceedings of the Prehistoric Society* 55: 193–205.

Ilisch, L. 2004. 'Die Imitativen Solidi Mancusi'. In *Fundamenta Historiae. Geschichte im Spiegel der Numismatik und ihrer Nachbarwissenschaften. Festschrift für Niklot*

Klüßendorf zum 60. Geburtstag am 10. Februar 2004, ed. R. Cunz, 91–106. Neustadt a.d. Aisch: Schmidt.

Ingvardson, G. 2015. '100 Viking Age Hoards of Bornholm'. In *Small Things, Wide Horizons: Studies in Honour of Birgitta Hårdh*, ed. L. Larsson, F. Ekengren, B. Helgesson, & B. Söderberg, 27–34. Oxford: Archaeopress.

Jansson, I. (ed.) 1996. *The Viking Heritage: A Dialogue Between Cultures = Nasledie Variagov: Dialog Kul'tur*. Stockholm: Statens Historiska Museum/Moscow: State Museums of the Moscow Kremlin.

Katalog der Ausstellung Zum X. Archäologischen Kongress in Riga 1896 (1896). Riga.

Kershaw, J. 2013. *Viking Identities: Scandinavian Jewellery in England*. Oxford: Oxford University Press.

Kilger, C. 2008. 'Kombinationer av Föremål. De Vikingatida Mittspännedepåerna'. In *Facets of Archaeology: Essays in Honour of Lotte Hedeager on Her 60th Birthday*, ed. K. Chilidis, J. Lund, & C. Prescott, 323–38. Oslo: Oslo Academic Press.

Кропоткин, В.В. 1962. *Клады византийских монет на территории СССР*. Moscow: Издательство Академии наук СССР.

Кулешов, В.С. 2009. 'О распространении золотых куфических монет VIII в. в Восточной Европе'. In *Тезисы докладов и сообщений XV Всероссийской нумизматической конференции, Ростов-на-Дону, 2009*, 59–61. Moscow.

Кулешов, В.С. 2016. 'Средиземноморье, Балканы и Восточная Европа: памятники монетного обращения еврейских общин (VIII–XIII века)'. In *Белградский сборник. К XXIII международному конгрессу византинистов, Белград, Сербия, 22–27 августа 2016 года. Труды Государственного Эрмитажа LXXX*, 85–104. Санкт-Петербург.

Лебедев В.П. & А.Е. Кожевин 2009. 'О находках золотых динаров династии Саманидов на памятниках Волжской Булгарии'. In *Тезисы докладов и сообщений XV Всероссийской нумизматической конференции, Ростов-на-Дону, 2009*, 63–4. Moscow.

Leimus, I. 2006. 'Viikingid—röövlid või kaupmehed?' *Tuna* 1: 17–29.

Leimus, I. 2007. *Sylloge of Islamic Coins. Estonian Public Collections*. Thesaurus Historiae 2. Tallinn: Estonian History Museum.

Linder Welin, U.S. 1964. 'Elias Brenners Arabiska Guldpenning och Andra Dinarer Funna i Sverige'. *Nordisk Numismatsk Årsskrift* 1964: 5–25.

McCormick, M. 2001. *Origins of the European Economy: Communications and Commerce*. Cambridge: Cambridge University Press.

Макаров, Н.А. (ed.) 2012. *Русь в IX–X Веках: Археологическая Панорама*. Moscow: Российская академия наук, институт археологии, Древности севера.

Марков, А. 1910. *Топография кладов восточных монет (сасанидских и куфических)*. Ст. Петербург.

Marzinzik, S. 2014. 'An Outstanding Hoard of Gold Objects Deposited in the Late Saxon Period'. *Medieval Archaeology* 58.1: 256–69.

Mikkelsen, E. 2006. 'The Find in its Context'. In Fuglesang & Wilson (eds), 29–53.

Moesgaard, J.C. & G. Rispling 2002. 'Guldefterligning af en Arabisk Mønt Fundet på Bornholm'. *Nordisk Numismatisk Unions Medlemsblad* 5–6: 91–4.

Naismith, R. 2005. 'Islamic Coins from Early Medieval England'. *Numismatic Chronicle* 165: 193–222.

Parvérie, M. 2014. 'Corpus des monnaies arabo-musulmanes des VIIIe et IXe siècles découvertes dans le Sud de la France'. *Revista Numismática OMNI*, Special Issue 1 05/2014: 79–100.

Parvérie, M. 2015. 'Updated Corpus of Arabic Coins found in France (04/01/15)', accessed via academia.edu on 30 January 2015.

Rhodin, L., L. Gren, & V. Lindblom 2000. 'Liljestenarna och Sveriges Kristnande från Bysans'. *Fornvännen* 95.3: 165–81.

Skaare, K. 2006. 'Numismatics'. In Fuglesang & Wilson (eds), 165–72.

Skovmand, R. 1942. 'De Danske Skattefund fra Vikingetiden og den Ældeste Middelalder indtil omrking 1150'. *Aarbøger for Nordisk Oldkyndighet og Historie* (1942): 1–245.

Slaski, J. & S. Tabaczyński 1959. *Polskie Skarby Wczesnośredniowieczne—Inwentarz. Wczesnośredniowieczne skarby srebrne z Wielkopolski*, Polskie Badania Archeologiczne 1. Warsaw/Wrocław.

Stenberger, M.K.H. 1977. *Vorgeschichte Schwedens*. Neumünster: K. Wachholtz.

Tamla, Ü. & H. Varkki 2009. 'Learning the Technologies of Making Beaded Wire'. *Estonian Journal of Archaeology* 13.1: 36–52. DOI: 10.3176/arch.2009.1.03.

Westerman-Angerhausen, H. 2006. 'The Carolingian Objects'. In Fuglesang & Wilson (eds), 103–18.

Wilson, D.M. 2006. 'Introduction and Summary'. In Fuglesang & Wilson (eds), 13–25.

Zachrisson, T. 1998. *Gård, Gräns, Gravfält: Sammanhang kring Ädelmetalldepåer och Runstenar från Vikingatid och Tidig Medeltid i Uppland och Gästrikland*. Stockholm Studies in Archaeology 15. Stockholm. Stockholms Universitet.

9

The Importance of Containers for the Deposition and Non-Retrieval of Silver Hoards

A Comparison between Gotland and Pomerania

Jacek Gruszczynski

Research into Viking Age hoards has a long and rich history beginning in the late nineteenth century and a whole array of views pertaining to the motives and interpretations of hoarding behaviour has been developed (Mogielnicka-Urban 1997, 17–20). Following R. Bradley (1987, 352) three major motives for the deposition of hoards can be distinguished:

- Political motives, where peaks in the deposition of hoards are interpreted as a direct result of social and political unrest and instability. This approach is exemplified by a statement by P. Grierson (1975, 132), that the 'most frequent cause of such permanent loss is warfare, since while in times of peace a prudent man may keep his money hidden, he will also be able to recover it at need'.[1] Such hoards, called *emergency hoards*, are deposits of precious objects and coins buried for protection in the face of impending disaster of whatever nature, and not retrieved as a direct result of the crisis. In the archaeological context, one would expect that such hoards would be buried within or in proximity to settlements, ideally associated with destruction horizons. However, they do not necessarily have to be buried on the spot, but can be found where the owner has taken refuge ('refugee hoard', Grierson 1975, 133).

[1] The discussion on the political aspects of hoarding was started by S. Bolin in his dissertation from 1926 where he stated that the number of hoards in a region reflects historical events that may lead to the deposition of hoards (1926, 197–203) and that the deposition is indicative of unrest/warfare rather than political and economic power and wealth (1926, 204–7).

- Economic motives, associated with trade and accumulation of wealth. One such interpretation perceives hoards as so-called *savings hoards*, accumulated over a long period of time and added to at intervals (Curta & Gandila 2013, 47). This means that they must have remained accessible to the saver so that withdrawals and additions could be made periodically (Casey 1986, 55). K. Odebäck (2009) interprets such hoards as family savings, transferred as inheritance with occasional new additions. M. Burström (1993) and S. Sindbæk (2011, 54–7) see them as associated with marriage and bridewealth. Alternatively, such hoards could be seen as wives' dowries or savings, particularly given that their women's labour and production would belong to the family into which they married (Sindbæk 2011, 60). The character of savings hoards is well summarized by J. Casey (1986, 53) who sees them as 'temporary immobilisations of coin put together with the intention of returning them to the currency pool sooner or later. The object of this exercise is not to create a hoard but to create future spending power.' One thing all these interpretations have in common is that, in the archaeological context, one would expect such hoards to be characterized by depositions in durable containers within domestic sites or even within houses themselves. The fact that they were never recovered is likely to reflect exceptional circumstances due to dramatic events rather than intentional non-retrieval.
- Ritual motives. It is generally accepted that ritual motives for hoard deposition are votive offerings seen as a fulfilment of a sort of a contract made between the worshipper and the gods, in line with the Roman religious formula *do ut des* meaning 'I give that you might give' (Bradley 1987, 361). The generally accepted criterion for interpreting hoards as *ritual deposits* is their deposition in places which would make their retrieval impossible. Therefore, marshes, bogs, springs, rivers—collectively described as the watery environment—are most often mentioned in the literature. One needs to also be aware that some of the ritual deposits could have been deposited in places which made them technically retrievable, but which could have been made intentionally irretrievable, for instance in being protected by oaths or spells (Mogielnicka-Urban 1997, 19). Examples of the magical protection of hoards are known from eastern European folklore and ethnography up to the early twentieth century (Макаров 1981, 262).

The issue is how to determine which hoard should be assigned to which interpretative category. The fact that the information on archaeological context is rarely available makes the task all the harder. Only a fraction (2 per cent) of all analysed Viking Age deposits have been investigated archaeologically, at varying levels of detail and scale. Most of the information on the archaeological context of hoards can only be gleaned from the circumstances of discovery, reported mainly in the nineteenth and early twentieth centuries. Could this imperfect data be of use in determining whether a particular hoard should be interpreted as unclaimed savings or a permanent ritual deposit? Might there be a 'hidden' category of information, which would allow such a distinction to be made?

Reasons for Hoard Deposition: The Importance of Containers

This chapter presents some of the preliminary results of research into the archaeological context of Viking Age silver hoards undertaken for a DPhil thesis started in October 2013,[2] the chief aim of which is to determine potential reasons for the deposition and non-retrieval of hoards.

The discussion is based on hoards[3] from two case-study areas: Pomerania (the southern shore of the Baltic sea area in modern-day northern Germany and Poland) and Gotland, which are some of the biggest clusters of hoards in the Baltic zone (Fig. 9.1). The dataset is a sample of Viking Age silver hoards from this region, which fulfil three criteria:

- they comprise coins, which provide fairly secure dating to *c.*800–1050;
- they were found in locations that can be determined with reasonable precision; and
- where the weight of silver is known or could be reconstructed statistically.

Overall, the dataset comprises 336 hoards from Gotland and 123 from Pomerania (Fig. 9.1).

My point of departure is a passage from the diary of Samuel Pepys, describing events of the Second Dutch War of 1667 (Pepys 1953). On the night of 12 June, on the news that the Dutch had broken the chain in the Medway, Pepys decided to send with his wife and father a part of his fortune in gold coins to place in safekeeping at his estate outside London. Only four months later, on 10 October, was he able to retrieve the hoard by digging at night to avoid attracting attention. Pepys describes the struggle to relocate the buried hoard in a most evocative way, and his trepidation and anger at the debacle is clear. Initially the hoard location could not be found and Pepys resulted to testing the ground with a spit. Once some coins had been located it transpired that the bags in which they had been deposited had rotted and split; coins became mixed with soil and had to be washed in pails of water, and some appeared to have been lost.

An important conclusion, which could be drawn from Pepys's experience, is that the inadequacy or indeed lack of a container would pose a serious problem

[2] Since the time of writing this chapter in 2015, the DPhil dissertation and research have been completed, and the final results will be published (Gruszczynski forthcoming). Although the hoard and other datasets relied upon in this chapter have since been enlarged and methodologies further refined, the conclusions presented here remain valid.

[3] Following W.A. von Brunn (1968, 236), I understand a hoard to mean at least two objects discovered in a single place and time as a form of material wealth which was disposed of for reasons known and important to the hoarder.

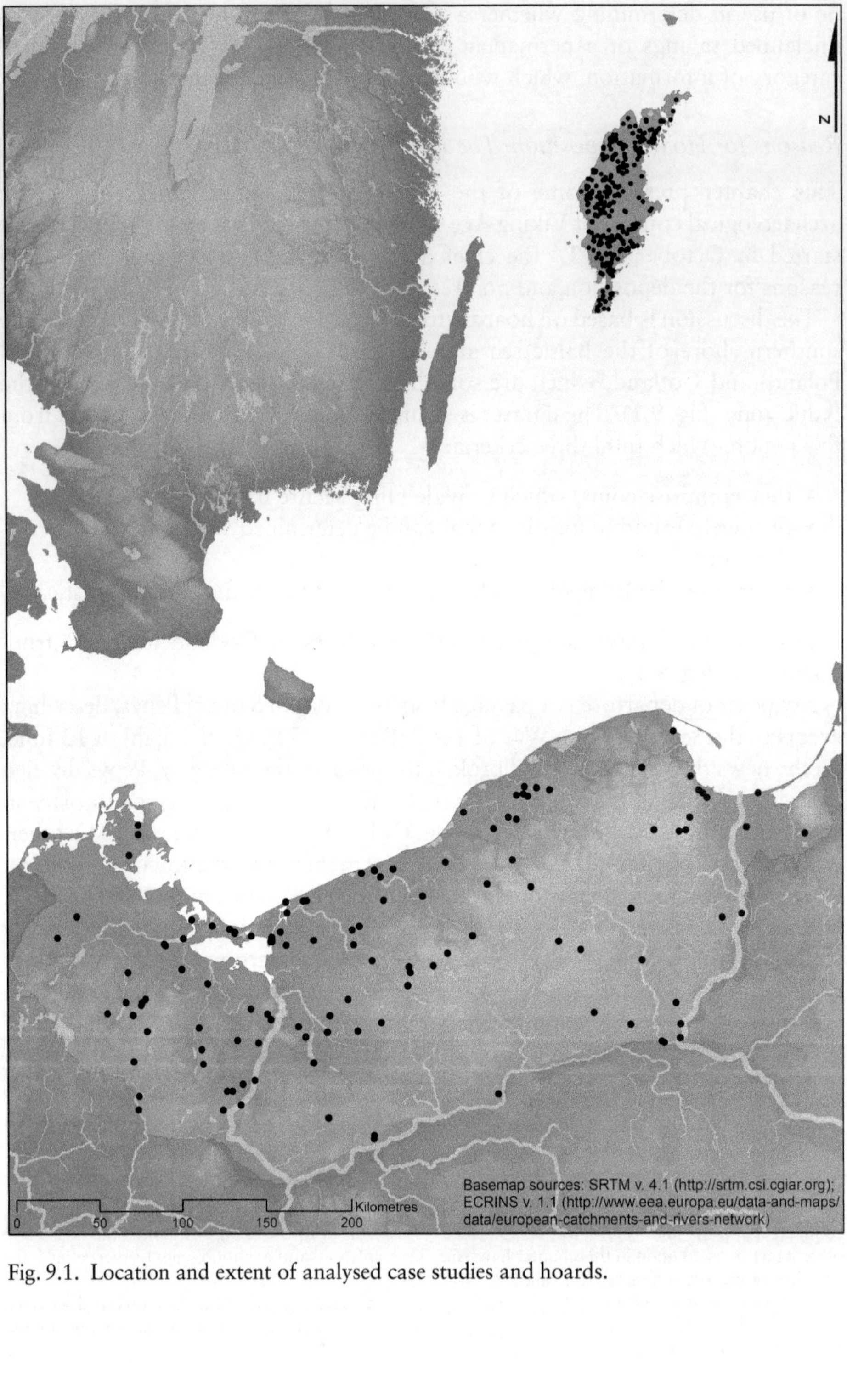

Fig. 9.1. Location and extent of analysed case studies and hoards.

for anyone who intended to retrieve their buried wealth. This issue is particularly poignant if we consider hoards in the context of the early medieval silver economy, where the commonly accepted commodity-money was silver bullion (Skre 2011, 77–82), conceivably buried for safety and accessed when needed. Furthermore, the deposition of a hoard in the face of danger was likely to be made using a container, although the choice of the material may be random. Consequently, hoard deposition without a container could be indicative of intentional irreversibility, akin to the deposition of hoards in watery environments, and may thus indicate ritual behaviour.

I would argue, therefore, that hoards buried with the aim of retrieval were placed in containers. Conversely, I assume that hoards deposited without receptacles are more likely to have been deposited without the aim of retrieval and should therefore be associated with ritual and symbolic practices.

The Preservation of Containers in the Archaeological Record

But there is a problem. Only *c.*19 per cent of Gotlandic hoards were deposited in containers, including organic and suspected organic containers (when, although no organic material was found, the coins and other objects were found in stacks, clumps, and so on) (Fig. 9.2). For a further 5 per cent of hoards there is sufficient

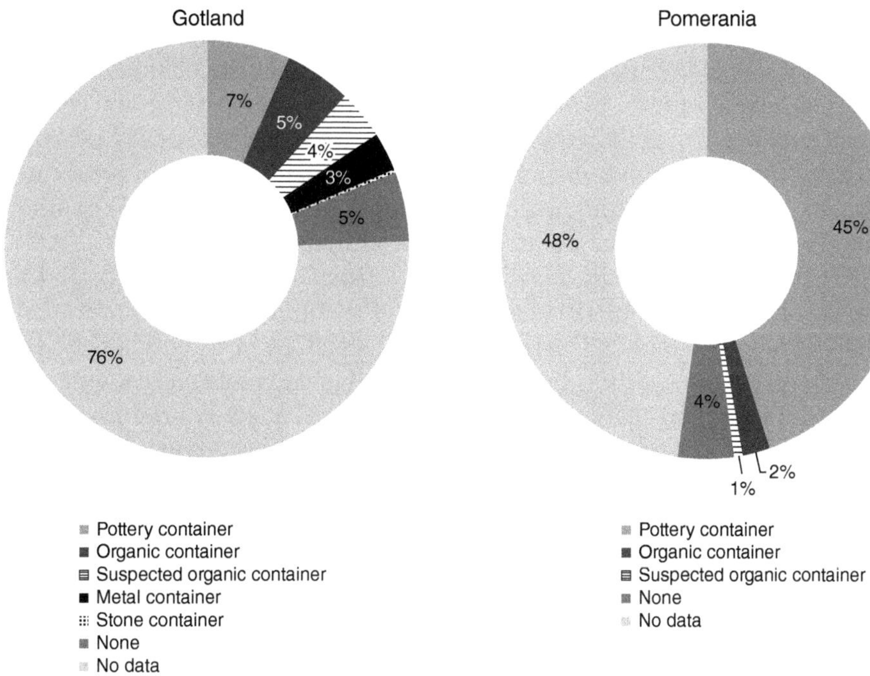

Fig. 9.2. Proportion of different container types on Gotland and in Pomerania.

information to establish that they were deposited without a container. Thus, for 76 per cent of hoards from Gotland, we do not know if containers were present or not. In Pomerania, 48 per cent of hoards have no data on the presence of a container. One could argue that such a lack of information stems from the poor recording of the circumstances of discovery. From the archaeological point of view there are two likely explanations for the absence of containers: such hoards were either deposited without a container to begin with, or the container was probably organic, but decomposed by the time of the discovery, and post-depositional processes disturbed the arrangement of artefacts.

Let us consider the latter possibility first. The preservation of organic material depends on a multitude of factors, but two of them are most crucial: the acidity of soil and the presence of anaerobic conditions. According to C. French (2003, 12) 'calcareous soil conditions favour the preservation of molluscs, bone and carbonized remains, and without the addition of water to exclude air, are detrimental to most other forms of organic environmental evidence. Acidic soil conditions usually destroy the molluscan and animal/human bone remains, but do allow the preservation of plant remains and pollen, although again the addition of water and the exclusion of air is the only way to ensure the preservation of organic remains in these circumstances.'

In other words, it could be expected that organic containers, particularly of leather or fabric, have the best chances of survival in relatively acidic and, most importantly, wet soil. These observations are confirmed by C. Sease (1992, table 1) and I. Good (2001, 211), who also indicate that linen and cellulosic fibres are best preserved in very rare (in the Baltic zone) alkaline conditions. Unfortunately, such data on soil conditions does not exist at the level of the find contexts of particular hoards. None of the accessible reports on archaeologically excavated hoard find-spots contained any information on soil acidity and water content.

However, some understanding of these two crucial aspects of soil conditions could be gleaned from the dataset of total available water content (TAWC) derived from the European Soil Database (Hiederer 2013a; 2013b), and the map of soil pH in Europe (Reuter et al. 2008) published at the European Soil Portal of the Joint Research Centre of the European Commission. These datasets cover the entire area of the European Union, but in a relatively low level of detail, with the pH available in 5 km and the TAWC in a 1 km resolution: they are thus not capable of reflecting local variations in soil chemistry at particular find-spots. The results of the following analysis are therefore approximations only capable of highlighting general trends, reflecting relative proportions rather than accurate values, and should be treated with caution.

The comparison of pH and TAWC in different categories of hoards with the overall mean of all deposits shows some interesting patterns (Table 9.1). Despite the inaccuracy of the data, the results seem to confirm French's and Sease's observations, as hoards found in organic containers were discovered in soils which, on average, are relatively more humid and acidic. However, out of ten

Table 9.1 Soil conditions by container type on Gotland and in Pomerania.

	Pomerania	Gotland
Container type	Mean pH	Mean pH
All finds	**5.731**	**5.071**
Organic	5.537	5.067
Suspected organic	5.862	5.091
Pottery	5.7	5.08
None	5.762	5.073
No data	5.764	5.071
	Pomerania	**Gotland**
Container type	Mean TAWC topsoil	Mean TAWC topsoil
All finds	**54.278**	**51.98**
Organic	58.935	53.964
Suspected organic	45.834	40.39
Pottery	54.78	55.751
None	54.136	52.634
No data	53.727	51.868

hoards found in waterlogged conditions, which would be most conducive to preservation of organic containers, only one was found in a receptacle (Norrgårda-Norrby II, Gotland, in remains of a wooden box). It seems, therefore, that despite favourable soil conditions, the presence of a container, particularly in the watery environment, was often determined by the intentions of a person making a deposit rather than soil conditions, a factor which cannot, however, be quantified by the dataset.

More interestingly, hoards in which a container was not recorded at the time of discovery, but for which the presence of a container is suspected from the arrangement of artefacts (in stacks, clumps, etc.), were discovered in less acidic and drier soils (Table 9.1). One needs to be aware, however, that only two examples of hoards found in suspected organic containers come from Pomerania: the corresponding values in Table 9.1 should thus be treated with caution. Nevertheless, from the archaeological point of view such hoards seem representative of circumstances where a container was in all likelihood present but has not survived due to low acidity and primarily the relative dryness of soil. This group of hoards could, therefore, be used as a benchmark for determining which deposits from the 'No data' category were deposited in similar or drier and less acidic conditions and therefore are likely to have been originally placed in organic containers that did not survive.

In terms of values obtained from the European soil datasets (cf. Table 9.1), those hoards for which we have no information about the presence or absence of a container, but which could have originally been contained, can be expected to have been deposited in soils with pH higher than 5.862 in Pomerania and 5.091

on Gotland (relatively low acidity), and TAWC lower than 45.834 in Pomerania and 40.390 in Gotland (relatively low humidity).

By applying the respective cut-off values to the 'No data' category, it transpires that only eight hoards in Pomerania and twelve in Gotland for which no data exists (*c.*12 per cent and 5 per cent respectively) are likely to have originally been in containers. Therefore, it would be mistaken to claim that that the majority of containerless hoards were originally placed in containers which simply did not survive.

This observation is confirmed by an analysis of the dates of hoard discoveries (Fig. 9.3). There is some indication that hoards deposited in containers were more often found in recent times, as one would expect if the lack of sufficient descriptions of the circumstances of discovery were to blame. But even in the last forty years, when the largest number of find-spots were discovered or investigated by archaeologists, the proportion of hoards found in containers is smaller than the peak in the late nineteenth-century Pomerania or early twentieth-century Gotland, when investigation of silver hoards was all but monopolized by numismatists whose attention was focused primarily on coins, not containers. Furthermore, even the earliest finds, if found in containers, were reported as such on Gotland and in Pomerania, for example the discovery of a hoard from

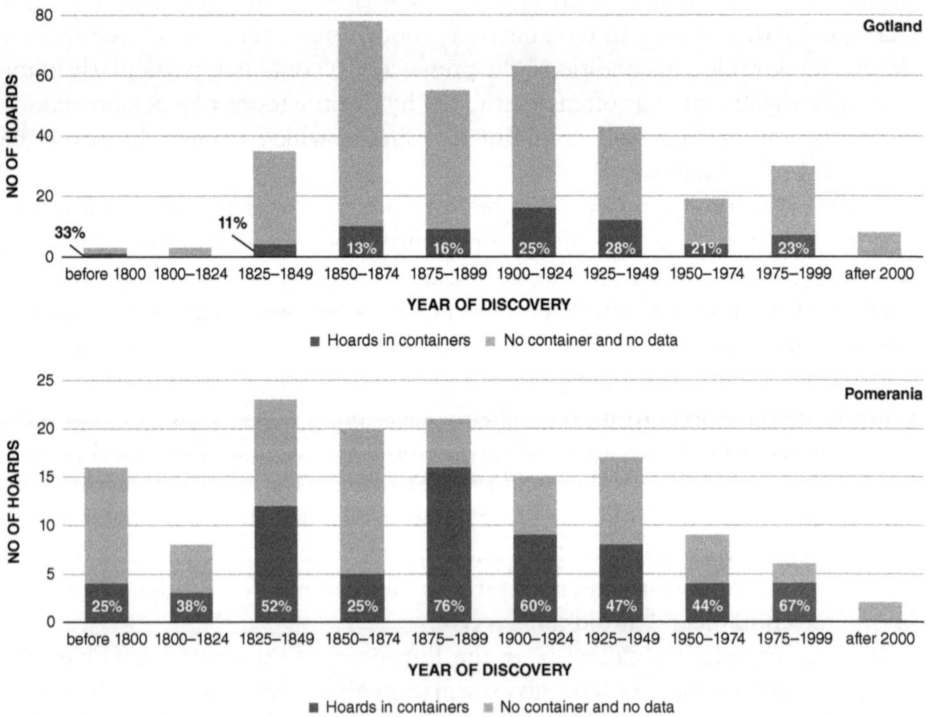

Fig. 9.3. Chronological structure of hoard discoveries.

Gdańsk made in 1591 or from the Havdhem vicarage in 1711. I believe that this indicates that regardless of when the discoveries were made, the information on an accompanying container or any special arrangement of artefacts was reported if present.

I would suggest, therefore, that the majority of deposits without explicit information on the presence or absence of a container, except those reclassified as a result of the soil conditions analysis, were in fact deposited without a receptacle and as such were deposited without the aim of retrieval. I am aware this is a simplification, but a necessary one in order to create a model which can help us understand the general trends of hoard deposition, particularly given that the exact archaeological context of Viking Age hoards is rarely known.

This hypothesis is reinforced by cross-referencing the type of deposition (in a container/without a container) with the weight of hoards (Fig. 9.4). The tipping point at which hoards are more often deposited in containers falls in Gotland at approximately 600 g and in Pomerania at 250 g, most likely reflecting the

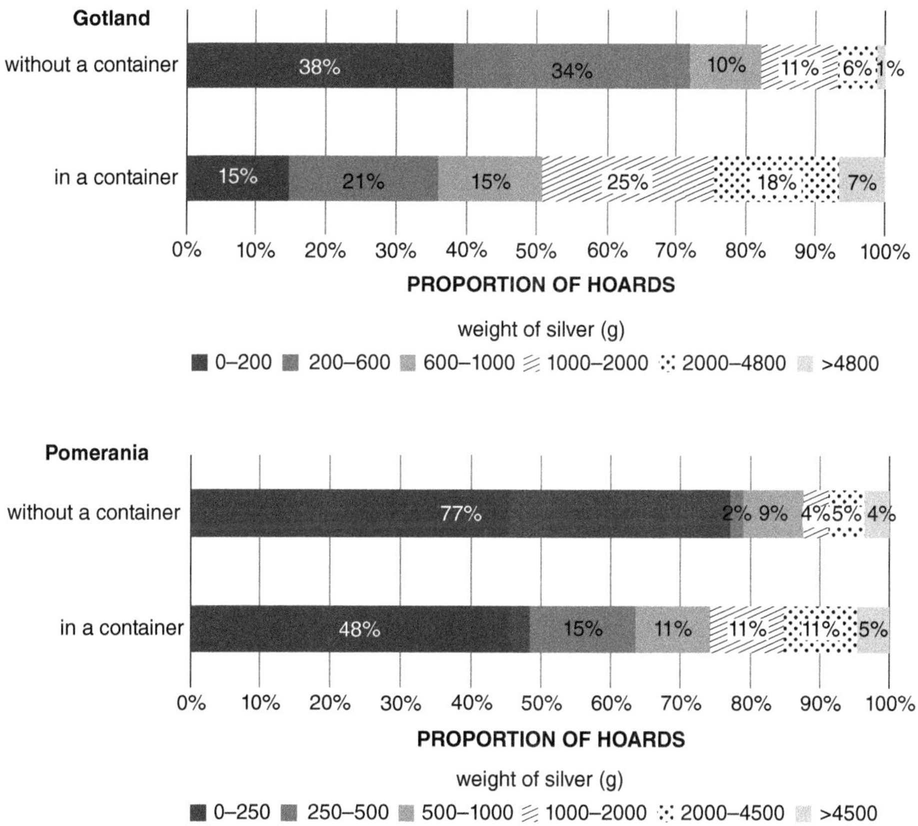

Fig. 9.4. Comparison of hoards with and without containers by weight of silver.

differences in the availability of silver in these areas. Smaller hoards are significantly more likely to be deposited without containers. Their interpretation deserves a separate discussion (Gruszczynski forthcoming), but if one was to apply the economic interpretation, one could argue that they might have been small volumes of 'petty cash' kept in sight within dwellings for regular expenses, and left behind for whatever reason. Archaeologically any traces of a container would be unlikely to survive. However, the only archaeologically investigated example of such a deposit known to me lies beyond the case-study areas, in Olhamra, Uppland, Sweden. A small hoard of Arabic coins was found in the corner of a presumed Viking Age building. However, the contemporaneity of the structure with the hoard is problematic as a radiocarbon sample from the structural remains provided a medieval date (Zachrisson 1998, 340–1). Even if the deposit was associated with earlier stages of the building, reused in the medieval period, the evidence for such containerless deposition elsewhere is scarce. In fact, 87 per cent of small containerless hoards in Gotland (168 deposits) and 93 per cent in Pomerania (41 deposits) were found beyond contemporary settlements or their immediate vicinity. I believe, therefore, it is more likely that they were personal possessions used in ritual or symbolic 'transactions', a fulfilment of a sort of a contract made between the worshipper and the gods or ancestors. This assumption may be confirmed by the fact that the deposition in a watery environment is dominated by small containerless hoards, which comprise 80 per cent (eight out of ten) of deposits found in such circumstances in both case-study areas.

Ritual Motives for the Deposition of Small Containerless Hoards

The symbolic aspect of such hoards, principally on Gotland, is particularly worth considering. M. Burström has noted (1993, 34–5) that the integrity of land and provision for its legal protection features heavily in at least twelve paragraphs in the Guta Lag ('The Law of the Gotlanders', a provincial law code probably dating from *c.*1220). Nowhere is this more categorical than paragraph 28, where statements such as 'no one may sell land unless pressing need arises' or 'land may never be bought out of the family' are used (Peel 2009, 41–2). Considering the importance of land to the Gotlanders and the widespread occurrence on the island of small unclaimed hoards of Viking Age date, I believe that the majority of small containerless hoards were symbolically associated with inherited landed property (allodial land),[4] and therefore with a settlement—but particularly with its field systems as an entity within the landscape as well as within the social and legal structures.

[4] The association of hoards with allodial land was T. Zachrisson's (1998, 218) conclusion for the average Viking Age hoards in Uppland and Gästrikland.

An example of such symbolic association comes from the Svarfdæla saga, written in the fourteenth century, but describing events dated to 875–980:

> Thorstein the Tumultuous now took control of the valley between mountain and fjord on the other side of the river. He went to the mountains and erected a boundary stake at the uppermost edge and broke a comb and threw the pieces on the ground. Afterwards he had silver buried in three places, a half mark in each place, and that strip of land is called Kamb. Thorstein named witnesses, made the valley his legal domicile, and gave it his name, calling it Svarfadardal. (Hreinsson 1997, 161–2)

This episode, referred to by scholars in the context of hoarding and boundaries (e.g. Eggers 1940, 30; Hatz 1974, 161; Zachrisson 1998, 199), indicates that the process of acquiring land involved not only staking one's claim to it by, literally, marking it out in the landscape, but also—and more importantly—by symbolically forging one's own personal bond with the land through an offering of a private possession. Here, the bond is subsequently reinforced by burying precious metal within the claimed area. Only then do the official legal proceedings ensue, almost as an afterthought. T. Zachrisson (1998, 199) believed that the deposition of personal objects and silver at the outskirts of newly taken land (which, with regard to the silver, is not made explicit by the text) was meant to bind Thorstein to his claims' boundaries, where his private possessions would act as symbolic guardians of the border zone in his stead.

I would like to take T. Zachrisson's interpretation a step further, and would emphasize the key importance of Thorstein's confirmation of his claim with hoarded silver. T. Zachrisson's study of the Eddic poetry and folklore legends suggests that, in the Viking Age, the precious metal one possessed was intimately associated with one's own self:

> it was a keeper and preserver of his happiness and well-being. By obtaining a treasure by force, one stole another person's well-being. Since happiness in older times was perceived as a limited resource, one not only stole the other person's treasure but also his or her well-being. This may be the reason why digging for treasure was considered to be a fatal act. (Zachrisson 1998, 221)

Therefore, by binding oneself to land through buried silver, one effectively added a potent new layer of protection for the prosperity of one's farm, as any seizure of land that had been claimed in such a way would be symbolically tantamount to an attempt on the owner's life.

This association may be confirmed by the preliminary results of my recent regression analysis,[5] which show a significant correlation between concentrations of hoards and sandy soils, wherever they are available (Gruszczynski forthcoming). In his recent work, G. Svedjemo (2014, 177) has shown that it was during the Viking Age that lighter and better-draining sandy soils

[5] Generalized linear model employing Poisson distribution.

began to be colonized on Gotland. Although the majority of hoards are still found on the traditionally used moraine soils, the regression analysis suggests that they had no statistically significant influence on hoard clustering, and the highest hoard concentrations tend to occur in connection with sandy soils (also influenced by other factors not discussed here). In my opinion, this could suggest that the most intensive hoarding in Viking Age Gotland, particularly the symbolic/ritual deposition (58 per cent of hoards were small and containerless), was focused on lands which were newly colonized at this time. This could well have intensified the need for symbolic behaviour described in the quoted saga—or to appease the *genius loci*.

Economic Motives for the Deposition of Large Hoards in Containers

On the other hand, large hoards discovered in containers are more likely to represent economic aspects of hoarding, which could be perceived as savings hoards. This suggestion seems to be confirmed by the fact that on Gotland, settlement finds are the most numerous group among savings deposits, even though only 12 per cent of the estimated 1,500 Viking Age settlements have been recorded (Östergren 1989, 248). Furthermore, of all hoards found in containers, large ones, i.e. potential savings hoards, are six times more likely to be found in settlements than smaller ones.

Interestingly, the Gotlandic 600 g cut-off point (after which hoards were more often deposited within containers) corresponds with three marks of weighed silver. According to laws codified in the Guta Lag, this was the standard amount payable in fines to the General Assembly, including serious crimes such as infanticide, heathen practices, wounding in a church, or killing a man at his home (Peel 2009, 198–214). This could suggest that many of the Gotlandic savings hoards acted as a 'portable but standardised medium for the payment of social obligations' (Bradley 1987, 358) such as compensations, dowries, and ransoms. It is not impossible that some of the Pomeranian hoards, with a lower cut-off point of 250 g, may connect to Slavic legal/weight systems, but there is no comparable evidence in the written sources to take this suggestion further.

Silver Investment in the Economic and Ritual Spheres

This division of hoards according to their depositional motives becomes even more telling when it is cross-referenced with the proportion of the total weight of silver within each case study, which I believe is crucial given the implications of weight economy in the Viking Age (Fig. 9.5). In terms of numbers of finds, Gotland is clearly dominated by ritual deposits, possibly linked to ancestral cult but also to the phenomenon of forging a symbolic bond with land, access to which was becoming ever more difficult thanks to stringent laws on the sale, inheritance, and division of family estate. Despite comprising 58 per cent of finds of hoards,

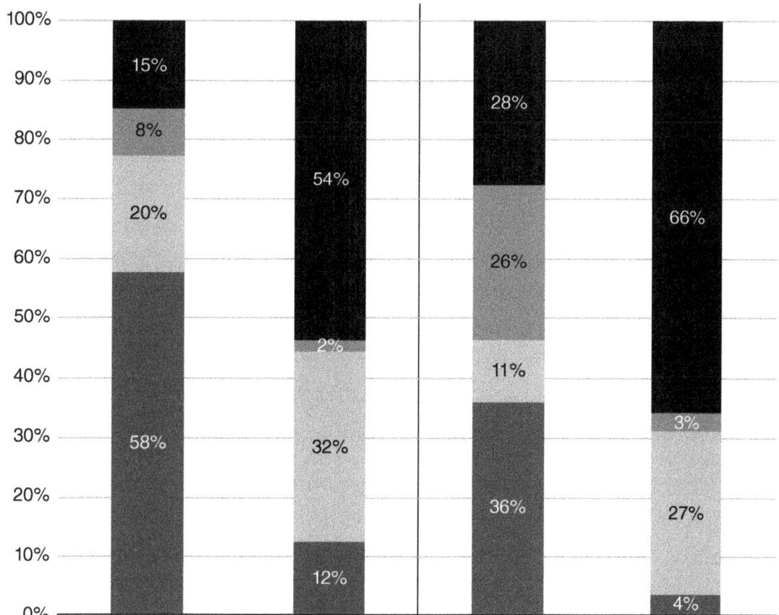

	Gotland no of hoards	Gotland weight of silver (kg)	Pomerania no of hoards	Pomerania weight of silver (kg)
large in container (savings)	50	173.35	34	61.08
small in container (emergency)	26	6.70	32	2.73
large no container (grey area)	66	102.75	13	25.31
small no container (ritual)	194	40.04	44	3.29

Fig. 9.5. Comparison of number of hoard finds and weight of silver.

ritual deposits on Gotland contained only 12 per cent of silver by weight. The level to which Pomeranian Slavs embraced the non-economic function of silver was much lower, with just 4 per cent of Pomeranian silver arguably being deposited without the aim of retrieval. Clearly, ritual deposits had only a marginal impact on the volume of silver in circulation in both regions. I also believe this statistic indirectly demonstrates the level of availability of silver in different regions by showing how much of it was allowed to 'trickle' into the sphere of 'sacrum': in Gotland at least 30 kg of silver was deliberately transferred from the economic to the ritual context, whereas in Slavic Pomerania it was just over 3 kg.

Furthermore, one would expect that the majority of hoards placed with the intention of retrieval were in all probability retrieved (Grierson 1975, 132). It is very interesting that despite all the differences between Pomerania and Gotland, the proportion of unclaimed savings by silver weight was similar. In Pomerania, such hoards contained 66 per cent of all silver by weight, and comprised 28 per cent of all deposits (Fig 9.5). In Gotland, the weight of silver in unclaimed savings hoards was 54 per cent but they comprised only 15 per cent of hoard finds. In other words, Pomeranian savings hoards contained proportionately only about one-eighth more silver than on Gotland, but it was deposited in nearly twice as many hoards. Even if we remove from this comparison the record-breaking silver hoard from Spillings, Gotland, weighing 67 kg, the volume of silver found in Pomeranian deposits would be proportionately just one-third more than on Gotland, but still deposited in twice as many hoards. This could mean that Gotlandic savings hoards were on average not necessarily larger (when Spillings is excluded), but were rather more likely to have been retrieved by their owner(s)—an observation which should be kept in mind in the context of a third group of deposits: small hoards which were nevertheless deposited in containers.

Small Hoards in Containers: Emergency Hoards?

The presence of a container seems to me a strong indicator that the deposit was meant to be retrieved. Small contained hoards might have been savings belonging to poorer members of the silver-owning society, or savings that were partially claimed, but not replenished again. But given the fact that, on Gotland, such hoards are so rare in general and on settlements in particular, I would be inclined to see them as haphazard collections of wealth hidden in the face of danger as emergency hoards. This interpretation can be reinforced by the situation in Pomerania. Here, I identified 8,291 contemporary open settlements and 459 strongholds.[6] Only fifteen hoards (11 per cent) were discovered within sites with evidence of early medieval occupation. However, none of those could be described as an ordinary open settlement, because they comprise emporia, strongholds, and suburban settlements surrounding strongholds. Of hoards found within such sites, only 17 per cent fall into the category of savings deposits, but 58 per cent could be interpreted as emergency hoards. Furthermore, small contained hoards comprise a significant proportion (56 per cent) of those Pomeranian hoards which can be associated with major episodes of destruction, remodelling of ramparts, and changes in settlement patterns, even despite a generally poor availability of exact scientific dating of Pomeranian sites. Overall, 86 per cent of all contained Pomeranian hoards were found outside any type of settlement. This could indicate that in Pomerania, to a much larger degree than on Gotland, the potential savings hoards which could be revisited relatively frequently and easily were, firstly, small and, secondly, extremely rare. If we were to interpret them as savings, they would more likely be long-term savings, which would not require

[6] The information on archaeological sites from the German part of Pomerania originates from the datasets kindly made available to me by Landesamt für Kultur und Denkmalpflege Mecklenburg-Vorpommern and by Brandenburgisches Landesamt für Denkmalpflege und Archäologisches Landesmuseum. The Polish Pomeranian data is derived from Ogolnópolski System Ewidencji Zabytków Archeologicznych 'e-Archeo' available online via the website of the National Heritage Borad of Poland: www.nid.pl.

regular access. But given the archaeological association of such hoards with dramatic events, it seems most likely that they were hidden in emergency situations.

Interestingly, the proportion of emergency hoards in Pomerania is over three times higher than on Gotland. Gotland is an island with a unique stability of settlement, where, according to D. Carlsson, the productive landscape remained relatively unchanged from the Roman Iron Age until the early eighteenth century (Carlsson 2009, 66). There is a lack of archaeological evidence for destruction horizons, and major political and social upheavals, and the silence of the contemporary written sources about any such events in Gotland should not be ignored. Of course, Viking Age weaponry is present in Gotlandic burials, but they do not automatically imply a martial society: 'it was the right to carry weapons that essentially signified and separated free men from unfree men, women and children' (Kjellström 2014, 237). Although later sagas do occasionally mention the island in the context of conflict (e.g. Monsen & Smith 1990, 132, 183, 424), the narrative never implies that Gotland was in a state of prolonged warfare or suffered invasion; it was rather used as a base for piratical attacks on the passing merchant shipping and subjected only to sporadic coastal raids. Furthermore, *Heimskringla* describes Gotlanders who deliberately avoid confrontation with St Olav by paying a tribute (Monsen & Smith 1990, 221), rather than endanger their lives and homes with an uncertain outcome of war.

In all probability, therefore, the Gotlandic savings hoards, so often associated with settlements or their immediate surroundings, were not retrieved only in exceptional circumstances, and deposition in emergency was extremely rare. If we take it as a rather well-attested benchmark for hoarding in a relatively stable rural and mercantile society, it becomes clear that nearly twice as high a proportion of unretrieved savings and four times as high a proportion of emergency hoards in Pomerania is hard to explain by just the odd calamity befalling the owners.

The political situation in Pomerania, as indicated by contemporary written sources, was decidedly unstable and dangerous. Numerous archaeological finds of weaponry and correlations between a number of hoard deposits with events of destruction and/or remodelling of defences of nearby strongholds seem to confirm it. Pomeranian hoards, as opposed to settlements, are also concentrated in marginal, sandy soils, which even today are generally under the cover of forests. A passage from the twelfth-century *Chronica Slavorum* by Helmold of Bosau implies a tendency among the Slavs to hide their valuables in secure places in the event of war:

> As soon as the tumult of war sounds, they hide corn cleaned from chaff, gold, silver, and all the valuables in pits, whilst their wives and children they hide safely in the fortresses and forests. For the gains of the enemy they leave nothing, but their dwellings, which they abandon without the slightest regret. (Book 2, Chapter 13, Popłoński 1862, 258)

Although it is often argued that in cases of attack there is no time to bury treasure, there is no reason why only immediate threats with no possibility of reacting should be considered (Wehner 2010, 263). Furthermore, it would make more sense to carry one's wealth to the place of refuge, away from settlements, which were the primary focus of aggression and plunder. Considering all these factors I believe that a significant proportion of Pomeranian deposits were most probably emergency hoards deposited in response to conflict and upheaval, and not retrieved as their direct result, just as the majority of unclaimed savings.

This leaves us with the final group of large hoards buried without containers. This is a truly problematic 'grey-area' where the interpretation needs to be based on a much closer individual scrutiny of the overall interpretative context. Depending on circumstances, such hoards could belong to either of the main interpretative groups. At the present stage of my research they are not suitable for using as general indicators of hoarding behaviour and I am still working on unlocking their meaning (cf. Gruszczynski forthcoming).

Conclusions

The main aim of this chapter has been to assess whether a hoard was deposited with the aim of retrieval (as savings revisited at intervals, or as emergency deposits buried in the face of danger and not subsequently retrieved) or made intentionally permanent as ritual or symbolic offerings, never to be visited again. The methodology presented, while still evolving, uses information about the presence or absence of a container and cross-references this with the weight of silver, supplemented by the archaeological and geoarchaeological data, and informed by written sources.

The results suggest that on Gotland, an island characterized by a remarkable social and political stability, the contained hoards are predominantly savings, unclaimed due to some calamity befalling the owner, but that the majority of finds are likely to be ritual or symbolic deposits. In politically insecure Pomerania the majority of deposits were in all probability buried and not retrieved as a result of conflict, while ritual deposition was far less common. This difference could tentatively be illustrated by a chronological breakdown of hoards in both areas (Fig. 9.6). On Gotland, hoard deposition is common and the rate of the process steady, almost habitual, with on average one hoard being buried each year, suggesting that hoarding was an expression of underlying social and symbolic practices. In contrast, Pomeranian hoards are deposited intermittently, peaking in tight chronological bands, some of which correspond with times of political unrest known from written sources,[7] indicating that a

[7] For instance, a peak in hoarding can be seen between 950 and 955. This correlates with Widukind's and Thietmar's descriptions of the year 955 as a time of exceptional uncertainty and upheaval caused by the Slav uprising synchronized with Hungarian raids, which culminated in a battle on the River Lech. Even if it is risky to associate major spikes in hoarding directly with military operations (Curta & Gandila 2013, 46), it would be not completely implausible to treat them as indirect indicators of times of unrest.

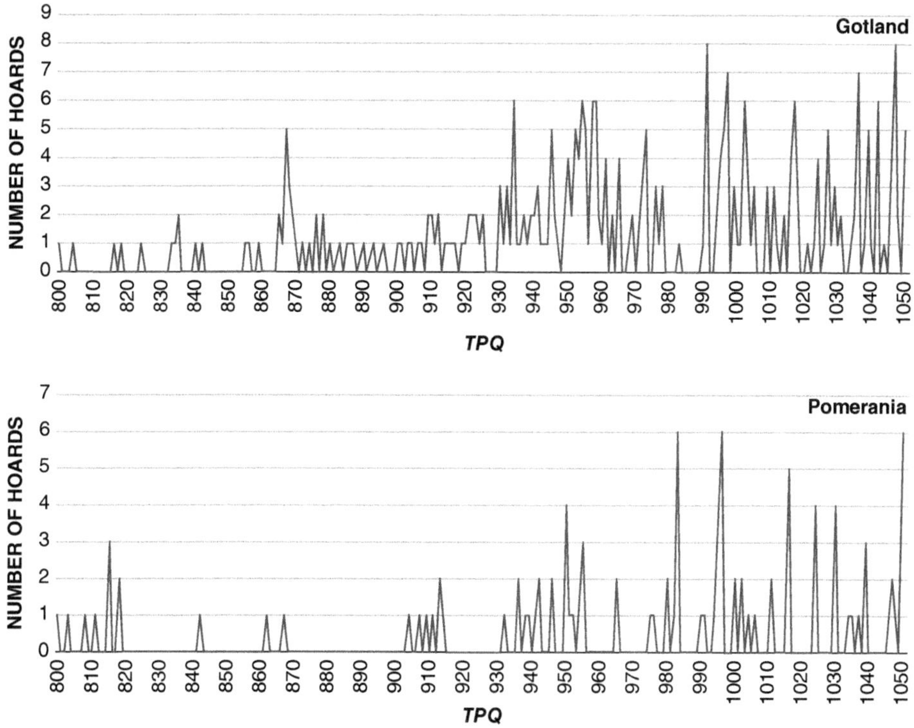

Fig. 9.6. Chronological breakdown of hoards by *tpq* (adjusted for peaks caused by the long chronology of dating Otto-Adelheid pennies).

large proportion of hoards were hidden as a response to times of uncertainty and crisis.

From this comparison Gotland, which boasts by far the largest number of hoards in Viking Age Europe, emerges as relatively stable in the turbulent Baltic zone. Perhaps so much silver was hoarded there, paradoxically, because it was comparatively safe? Gotland's stability could have secured economic conditions for an effectively uninterrupted flow of silver, which became so abundant that it found its way into the symbolic and ritual behaviour on a scale not seen elsewhere in Europe.

Clearly, the deposition and non-retrieval of Viking Age hoards cannot be explained by a single grand theory (see too Ingvardson, this volume). We should be aware that contemporary societies assigned to silver economic as well as symbolic and ritual value, and for them the distinction between material and immaterial was not as sharp as it is for us today. To paraphrase N. Price (2014, 167): they did not believe in the supernatural any more than they believed in a mountain—both were just there, equally relevant and real.

So maybe the fact that over 50 per cent of all hoards analysed here were small containerless deposits, implying that ritual deposition was common, should not be that surprising even in the context of silver economy. We need to remember that ritual hoards constituted only a fraction of the overall amount of silver in circulation, since the overwhelming majority of silver by weight was found in hoards deposited in containers, in all probability buried with the aim of retrieval. Clearly, therefore, the impact of the ritual practices on the economic sphere was minor; both mindsets did not have to compete for resources. In a way, the abundance of ritual deposits skews the picture of the hoarding habits in the Viking Age—we find such hoards more often because they were never meant to be retrieved, whilst a majority of the contained deposits were in all probability reclaimed by owners and we face only a small proportion of the original number.

REFERENCES

Bolin, S. 1926. *Fynden av Romerska Mynt i det Fria Germanien: Studier i Romersk och Äldre Germansk Historia*. Lund: C.W. Lindström.

Bradley, R. 1987. 'Stages of the Chronological Development of Hoards and Votive Deposits'. *Proceedings of the Prehistoric Society* 53: 351–62.

von Brunn, W.A. 1968. *Mitteldeutsche Hortfunde der Jüngeren Bronzezeit*, Römich-Germanishe Forschungen 29. Berlin: De Gruyter.

Burström, M. 1993. 'Silver as Bridewealth: An Interpretation of Viking Age Silver Hoards on Gotland, Sweden'. *Current Swedish Archaeology* 1: 33–7.

Carlsson, D. 2009. 'Owner Missing? The Hoard, the Farm and the Community'. In *The Spillings Hoard—Gotland's Role in Viking Age World Trade*, ed. A.M. Pettersson, 64–107. Visby: The Gotland Museum.

Casey, J. 1986. *Understanding Ancient Coins: An Introduction for Archaeologists and Historians*. London: Batsford.

Curta, F. & A. Gandila 2013. 'Hoards and Hoarding Patterns in the Early Byzantine Balkans'. *Dumbarton Oaks Papers* 65/66: 45–111.

Eggers, H.J. 1940. *Das Römische Einfuhrgut in Pommern*. Beiheft zum Erwerbungs- und forschungsbericht. Stettin: Pommersches Landesmuseum.

French, C.A.I. 2003. *Geoarchaeology in Action: Studies in Soil Micromorphology and Landscape Evolution*. London: Routledge.

Good, I. 2001. 'Archaeological Textiles: A Review of Current Research'. *Annual Review of Anthropology* 30: 209–26.

Graham-Campbell, J., S.M. Sindbæk, & G. Williams (eds) 2011. *Silver Economies, Monetisation and Society in Scandinavia, AD 800–1100*. Aarhus: Aarhus University Press.

Grierson, P. 1975. *Numismatics*. London, Oxford, and New York: Oxford University Press.

Gruszczynski, J. forthcoming. *Silver, Hoards and Containers: The Archaeological and Historical Context of Viking-Age Silver Coin Deposits in the Baltic* c. *800–1050*. London and New York: Routledge/Taylor & Francis Group.

Hatz, G. 1974. *Handel und Verkehr Zwischen dem Deutschen Reich und Schweden in der Späten Wikingerzeit. Die Deutschen Münzen des 10. und 11. Jahrhunderts in Schweden*. Stockholm: Almqvist & Wiksell.

Hiederer, R. 2013a. *Mapping Soil Properties for Europe—Spatial Representation of Soil Database Attributes*. Luxembourg: Publications Office of the European Union. DOI:10.2788/94128.

Hiederer, R. 2013b. *Mapping Soil Typologies—Spatial Decision Support Applied to European Soil Database*. Luxembourg: Publications Office of the European Union. DOI:10.2788/87286.

Hreinsson, V. (ed.) 1997. *The Complete Sagas of Icelanders, Including 49 Tales. Volume IV. The Saga of the People of Svarfadardal*, 149–92. Reykjavík: Leifur Eiríksson Pub.

Kjellström, A. 2014. 'Interpreting Violence: A Bioarchaeological Perspective of Violence from Medieval Central Sweden'. In *The Routledge Handbook of the Bioarchaeology of Human Conflict*, ed. C. Knüssel & M.J. Smith, 237–50. London and New York: Routledge/Taylor & Francis Group.

Макаров, Н.А. 1981. 'Магические обряды при сокрытии клада на Руси', *Советская Археология* 4: 261–4.

Mogielnicka-Urban, M. 1997. 'Uwagi w Sprawie Interpretacji Zbiorowych i Pojedynczych Znalezisk Przedmiotow Brazowych'. In *Beitrage zur Deutung der Bronzezeitlichen Hort- und Grabfunde in Mitteleuropa*, ed. W. Blajer, 17–32. Krakow: Oficyna Cracovia.

Monsen, E. & A.H. Smith 1990. *Heimskringla, or The Lives of the Norse Kings by Snorre Sturlason*. New York: Academic Press.

Odebäck, K. 2009. 'Familje- och Släkt-Skatter under Äldre Vikingatid'. *Myntstudier* 2009.2: 9–25.

Östergren, M. 1989. *Mellan Stengrund och Stenhus. Gotlands Vikingatida Silverskatter som Boplatsindikation*. Theses and Papers in Archaeology 2. Stockholm: Institute of Archaeology at the University of Stockholm.

Peel, C. 2009. *Guta Lag: The Law of the Gotlanders*. London: Viking Society for Northern Research.

Pepys, S. 1953. *The Diary of Samuel Pepys*, ed. M. Bright & J. Warrington. London: Dent.

Popłoński, J. 1862. *Helmolda Kronika Słowiańska z XII wieku*. Warsaw.

Price, N. 2014. 'Belief and Ritual'. In *Vikings: Life and Legend*, ed. G. Williams, P. Pentz, & M. Wemhoff, 162–201. London: The British Museum.

Reuter, H.I, L.R Lado, T. Hengl, & L. Montanarella 2008. 'Continental-Scale Digital Soil Mapping Using European Soil Profile Data: Soil pH'. In *SAGA—Seconds Out*, ed. J. Böhner, T. Blaschke, & L. Montanarella, 91–102. Hamburger Beiträge zur Physischen Geographie und Landschaftsökologie vol. 19. Hamburg: Univ. Inst. für Geographie.

Sease, C. 1992. *A Conservation Manual for the Field Archaeologist*. Los Angeles: Institute of Archaeology, University of California.

Sindbæk, S.M. 2011. 'Silver Economies and Social Ties: Long-Distance Interaction, Long-Term Investments—and Why the Viking Age Happened'. In Graham-Campbell, Sindbæk, & Williams (eds), 41–65.

Skre, D. 2011. 'Commodity Money, Silver and Coinage in the Viking-Age Scandinavia'. In Graham-Campbell, Sindbæk, & Williams (eds), 67–91.

Svedjemo, G. 2014. *Landscape Dynamics—Spatial Analysis of Villages and Farms on Gotland* AD *200–1700*. Occasional Papers in Archaeology 58. Uppsala: Uppsala Universitet.

Wehner, D. 2010. 'The Hinterland of the Early Trading Places Wolin and Menzlin: A Comparison'. In *Trade and Communication Networks of the First Millennium* AD *in the Northern Part of Central Europe: Central Places, Beach Markets, Landing Places and Trading Centres*, ed. B. Ludowici, H. Jöns, S. Kleingärtner, J. Scheschkewitz, & M. Hardt, 258–66. Hannover: Niedersächsisches Landesmuseum.

Zachrisson, T. 1998. *Gård, Gräns, Gravfält. Sammanhang kring Ädelmetalldepåer och Runstenar från Vikingatid och Tidigmedeltid i Uppland och Gästrikland*. Stockholm Studies in Archaeology 15. Stockholm: Stockholms Universitet.

10

From Local Supply to Long-Distance Trade Networks

Fingerprinting Early Medieval Silver

Guillaume Sarah

No large-scale official coinage was produced in the Scandinavian homelands prior to the late tenth century, and no major silver exploitation is known there. Instead, the Vikings acquired silver coins from western Europe and the Islamic world, preferentially preserving some coins in their original form, and melting down others into ingots, rings, and other forms of jewellery. The geographic origin of silver acquired by the Vikings, and the routes through which it diffused and circulated, are thus major questions of Viking Age archaeology. In this chapter, I present the use of the geochemical fingerprinting of silver as a contribution to the determination of the origin of the metal. My point of departure is analysis of early medieval coins where the aim is to determine the provenance of the precious metal they contain, but the methodology and approach outlined here are relevant for the future metallurgic analysis of Viking Age silver, whether coined or uncoined. I highlight recent work aiming to evaluate the diffusion of silver produced at the mine of Melle (Nouvelle-Aquitaine, France): a major source of silver coinage in the Frankish kingdoms, which the Vikings acquired through their raids in Aquitaine during the ninth century (Coupland 2011, 113–15).

The composition of ancient coins became a concern of historians and numismatists as early as when they started to be collected, studied, and classified. For a long time, the characterization of the alloy of ancient coins was limited to determining the amount of precious metal they contained, sometimes accompanied by the percentage of significant minor elements. This approach was useful for revealing the evolution of alloy fineness over time (a list of references can be found in Rehren & Pernicka 2008, 240–1), but distinguishing between different metal stocks and identifying the mines from which they originated lay beyond the interest and scope of most works. Furthermore, performing an analysis meant causing the destruction of the whole coin—or at least a significant part of it: a major limitation for an interpretation of the results on a wide scale since only a few objects were reluctantly sacrificed by institutions or collectors. As a consequence, prior to the mid twentieth century only a small number of analyses of ancient coins were performed and the aggregate results did not contribute significantly to the understanding of precious-metal circulation.

Things changed from the beginning of the second half of the twentieth century when new analytical methods aiming to sample material non-destructively were developed and applied to various archaeological artefacts. For more than sixty years now, spectroscopic and nuclear techniques in particular have been improved, supplemented in the 2000s by laser ablation ICP-MS (inductively coupled plasma mass spectrometry), making ancient coins characterization increasingly accurate, fast, and easy to perform. Given the presence of multiple elements, including small quantities of lead, within ancient minted 'silver', two approaches are of particular importance for linking coins and unminted silver items with their geological source: trace element and lead isotope analysis. The combination of these two types of analysis, although systematized in a few studies only so far (for instance, Merkel this volume), is likely to be extremely useful for determining the geological origin of the metal contained in ancient silver coins. In the most favourable cases, the analytical fingerprint may provide the geographic location of the origin of the silver contained in the coins or may distinguish between different stocks of precious metals, contributing to a better understanding of the networks and contacts of the coins' owners.

Silver Analysis for Provenance Studies

Ancient Silver Analysis: General Rules

In several parts of the ancient world, roughly during the same period in the first centuries of the Middle Ages, silver mines started to be exploited or saw their production rise significantly, whilst silver became the metal overwhelmingly minted to supply both small and large-scale transactions. Several mines or mining areas are known to us from texts, archaeology, numismatics, and prospection in relation to geology. A lot remains to be done to identify all the mines exploited during the early Middle Ages in Europe, northern Africa, the Near and Middle East and Central Asia, to understand the metallurgical processes involved in producing silver and to evaluate the diffusion of the precious metal obtained from the different types of sources available. However, our knowledge of these questions is constantly growing and it is not possible any more to study each aspect separately.

In numismatics, the expression 'silver coin' can be used to describe alloys covering a wide range of compositions, from 'pure' silver to billon of a very low silver fineness containing a majority of copper. For alloys with a high copper content, surface treatments such as blanching may have been applied to deliver a silvery appearance to the coin (Cope 1972; Arles et al. 2011). The combination of the initial bulk composition, production process, possible surface modifications, and burying condition of a coin may impact significantly on the results of metal analysis. Analysts have to face a sort of paradox in the sense that it is necessary to estimate an approximate composition and structure of an ancient coin before making its characterization. The visual appearance of the object can give clues but it should always be interpreted with caution. As a general rule, it is required to estimate the proportions of the major components of the coin, use this information to evaluate the thermodynamic characteristics of the alloy, and evaluate the possible changes that may have occurred to the coin after it was buried. These observations and interpretations should be taken into account when performing the analysis, and the protocol used has to be adapted to the specificities of both the coinage and the method available.

During the early Middle Ages, most silver coins contain a high percentage of precious metal, in the range of 90 per cent of silver or above. As a general rule, their diameter is 20 to 25 mm and they are particularly thin, around 1 mm and even sometimes less. Such coins were made from a hammered sheet of metal cut in squares to which a rounded shape was given before they were minted. While the working of silver sheet does not affect the chemical composition of the coin, the hammering and cleaning of the surface can entail a removal of copper for a very thin layer, which may in turn influence later corrosion processes (Arles et al. 2011). All those details need to be carefully studied for each coinage whose analysis is planned and need to be kept in mind when the analytical protocol is defined.

Ancient Coin Analysis: Elemental Composition

Concerning the analysis of ancient objects, non-destructivity should be respected in many cases. Several non-destructive or semi-non-destructive approaches have been developed, especially since the late 1950s. Nuclear methods (Kraay 1959; Thompson 1960) can be used for a bulk characterization of an object or sampling; surface methods, especially X-ray fluorescence (Hall 1960; Carter 1964) are widely used but should be applied with caution considering the heterogeneity in depth of some samples ('silver surface enrichment'; see below). More recently, a new approach, best described as 'minimally destructive', was developed for depth-profile analysis of ancient coins, using laser ablation ICP-MS to obtain concentration profiles for each element (Sarah et al. 2007; Sarah & Gratuze 2016).

Determining the composition of a coin may have several different meanings. The method used and the list of elements to measure should be adjusted both according to the specificities of the coinage studied and to the aim of the project. Obtaining the fineness of the alloy as it was considered by the ancient metallurgist can be the most important information in some cases, whereas in others the crucial point could be an accurate determination of as many trace elements as possible with low detection limits to help discriminate between metal stocks of different geographic origin. Moreover, all methods have their limitations, and these should be borne in mind constantly in order to avoid making mistakes in the interpretation of the results.

The most important thing to consider when analyses of ancient silver objects are performed is the phenomenon called 'silver surface enrichment' (Condamin & Picon 1972; Hall 1961). Due to several factors linked with the initial composition of the coin, its production process, its blanching (in some cases), and its burial conditions, an enriched silver surface layer of varying thickness can form. Crucially, this layer may not be representative of the whole object. This enrichment results from the depletion of oxidized copper at the surface. The thickness of this layer tends to increase with the bulk copper level but no general rule can be proposed due to the complexity of the physical and chemical reactions involved and the uncertainty we have about them for each specific case. However, silver surface enrichment is something to take into account whatever the method used, not only for those considering a thin surface analysis, but also for bulk methods as early medieval coins are generally very thin and the affected layer could be a significant part of the entire object. Nonetheless, this is a major concern mostly when the fineness of the alloys needs to be determined with good accuracy, so the problems related to silver surface enrichment will not be further developed in this study aiming to consider silver analysis for provenance purposes.

The use of elemental composition in order to discriminate between coins containing silver of different origins, and to further identify the deposit the metal originates from, relies on the study of trace elements. Thus, using a method which enables a determination of a wide range of elements with low detection limits is particularly important for such a purpose. In ancient times, silver derived in most of the cases from lead-rich ores such as galena (PbS) (for an overview of the whole process for different periods see Domergue 2008, 158–63; Tylecote 2002, 71–3, 89–92; Craddock 1995, 205–33). After it is extracted and separated from the barren rock surrounding it, the ore can be roasted and then smelted to obtain metallic lead, which contains many elements at very low levels, called 'impurities' or 'trace elements', susceptible of being specific to its origin. From a geochemical point of view, one of them is silver, although for the metallurgist it is the final product. After smelting, the silver-enriched lead is submitted to a process called cupellation. Heated in an oxidizing atmosphere, it is placed in a porous cupel typically made of pressed ashes; the liquid lead is progressively oxidized and the litharge, the product of this reaction, is slowly absorbed by the cupel or removed at the surface with a rod. Depending on the skills of the ancient metallurgist and the instructions given by the minting authority, the process could be stopped either when no lead was left, or when a significant percentage (typically 0.5–2 per cent) still remained, for cost savings to be made on fuel by stopping an expensive process before the complete removal of lead.

During the whole process, the trace elements present in the ore are not all affected equally by the metallurgical treatments (L'Héritier et al. 2015), so their concentration can remain at a level that still makes them distinguishable from other sources: they can thus be found in the silver finally obtained. If a series of coins is produced from a single source of silver and following the same technical process, they are expected to present all the same levels of trace elements, which may differ from those in another coinage made of metal from another mining area. Thus, the concentrations of trace elements such as gold and bismuth contained in ancient silver coins can be used as clues to separate series of objects made of precious metals from different origins. Their levels, as well as those of other minor and trace elements, can also give us clues to distinguish between silver stocks resulting from different production or recycling processes.

Ancient Coins Analysis: Lead Isotope Ratios

A second approach can be used to fingerprint ancient silver: lead isotope analysis. Here, it is the determination of the ratios between the different isotopes of lead contained in the silver coins which can be a valuable clue for identifying the sources of the precious metal they contain. Due to the advances in geochemical analytical methods since the 1980s, it is possible to determine with good accuracy the ratios between the different isotopes of lead in ancient silver from a negligible sampling (for general reviews of the use of lead isotope analysis for ancient metals and coins see Stos-Gale 1998; Rehren & Pernicka 2008; Villa 2009; Cattin et al. 2009).

Isotopes are variants of a chemical element. All isotopes of a given element have the same number of protons whereas they differ in their number of neutrons. In other words, different isotopes of an element have the same atomic number but their mass numbers are not the same. Some elements have one isotope only, whose isotopic abundance is 100 per cent, as for example ^{197}Au. Silver has two stable isotopes at the mass numbers 107 and 109; on Earth, their isotopic abundances are respectively 51.8 per cent and 48.2 per cent. Lead has four stable isotopes with the mass numbers 204, 206, 207, and 208. What is interesting for lead is that the last three of these isotopes represent the end of the radioactive decay chains of uranium and thorium whereas ^{204}Pb is a primordial isotope, which means that its particles have existed in their current form since before the Earth was formed. This means that the determination of the ratios between all three radiogenic isotopes and ^{204}Pb can be used to determine the age of the rock formations where they are found. The lead isotope ratios are not affected by the metallurgical processes used to produce silver from the ore, so the determination of lead isotope ratios can be used to link the silver contained in the coin—as it derives from an ore containing lead in majority—and the rock formation it comes from.

The use of lead isotope ratios to track the origin of silver appears to be extremely powerful at first sight. But like the use of trace elements, a campaign of analysis has to be undertaken under certain conditions only, and the results must be interpreted bearing in mind several possible limitations. Those limitations are linked with the possibility of remelting the silver from previous or foreign coinages, or from another source, to produce new coins. In a case when a series of coins is made of silver originating from a single specific mine and our historical knowledge is sufficient to suggest that a link may have existed between them, the lead isotope analysis can confirm a likely hypothesis or support the hypothesis of an unexpected provenance of the metal coined. In a case when coins made of silver from the same origin are melted down together to produce a new coinage, the fingerprint of each new coin remains unchanged and the use of lead isotope ratios is still relevant. However, there are many cases when limited meaning can be given to the values obtained from isotopic analysis: the most common case is the remelting of coins containing silver from various origins with different isotopic fingerprints. The coins resulting from this will present a new fingerprint; in the best case, so-called 'mixing lines' between end products can be defined, with the end products representing the metal of the different sources that were mixed (for 'mixing lines' see Merkel, this volume).

The same is true concerning the use of trace element contents. The bias with lead isotope analysis is that the mixing of metals from different origins can produce a new fingerprint which corresponds to an ore deposit or a mine having absolutely no link with the coinage under study, but identified by the analyst or geochemist in their database. Moreover, even when coins from a single origin are alloyed, lead can be added to make the metallurgical processes easier, in particular for cupellation during recycling and refining, and this lead can come from another source. Consequently, while the trace elements pattern may not be changed, the lead isotope ratios will no longer correspond to the original fingerprint. Thus, lead isotope determination and elemental analysis should be regarded as tools used in a multidisciplinary approach but not as methods which permit firm and direct links to be made between coins and ore deposits on the basis of data alone.

A Combined Approach for Silver Fingerprinting

The study of trace elements after elemental analysis and the comparison of lead isotope ratios appear to be two interesting ways to contribute to discriminating silver coins containing metal from different origins. In some cases, both approaches may give clues for identifying separate groups of coins on the basis of differences observed from one of those types of analysis, or even to identify the source of ore used to produce this silver. But even more promising is the combined use of trace element patterns and lead isotope ratios, which, together, provide unique geochemical information enabling the complete fingerprint of a coin.

The first thing to consider, as early as when a project including analysis of silver coins is planned, is the potential sources of silver supplying the mints: have silver mines been active in this territory and during the period of interest? If so, which particular mints are the most likely to have used their metal to produce coins? Which base metals were most commonly used in local coinage before the period in question? Do the fresh metal and coin production evaluations indicate that most of the coins are made of pre-existing currency that had been remelted? Where were the major places where trading took place with other kingdoms or areas, which could have directed the flow of 'foreign' goods and silver coins? And in this case, were there major silver mines known in the geographical areas trading with the considered territory? Clues are needed to answer those questions in order to locate the mints or areas which are most likely to yield a coinage made of silver of a specific origin, and thus where patterns in trace elements and lead isotope ratios are most likely to be revealed. In any case, the observation of differences in analytical results should always be considered with caution when they are to be interpreted: as it has already been stated, the discrimination based on the trace elements levels and lead isotope ratios should not be used alone. The meaning of the results can only be understood when they are compared with the coins' dating and origin, with the possible mines exploited at the time they were minted and with the knowledge of the historical, political, and economic context. As a consequence, elemental and isotopic analysis of archaeological silver must be performed in intense collaboration between specialists of materials sciences, numismatists, mining archaeologists, and historians in order to define a question to answer, a corpus of coins to select, and possible sources of metal for the silver of the coins or object.

Silver Provenancing in the Early Middle Ages: The Case of Melle

Melle: Geology, Archaeology, and Numismatics

The city of Melle (Deux-Sèvres, Nouvelle-Aquitaine, France) is located at the centre of a silver-rich galena deposit. During the early Middle Ages, from the fifth to tenth centuries, silver was produced in the Melle area. The study of radiocarbon datings from charcoal samples collected in the underground networks suggests that production peaked in the eighth and ninth centuries under the Carolingians (Téreygeol 2017; for a survey of the current knowledge about Melle see Téreygeol 2014). During this period, the name of Melle appears in several edicts or capitularies dealing with the kingdom's organization and especially coin minting. It is also borne by a wide number of coins, dating from the end of the seventh century to the twelfth century—which means that minting in the name of

Melle went on after the metal production ended—suggesting that at least part of the silver produced was coined locally.

The silver produced at Melle may also have been used for coinage at other minting places. If it is the case that 'fresh' silver from Melle has a specific fingerprint in trace elements or lead isotopes, the fingerprint may also be found in the coins bearing the names of other cities, more probably those located in neighbouring counties. According to current knowledge, Melle is the only mine in the Carolingian territory for which it can be stated that silver was produced on a large scale during the first centuries of the early Middle Ages. Nonetheless, it is estimated that its production was insufficient to fulfil the needs of all the mints under Carolingian control. As a consequence, a project aiming to identify the origin of the silver that fuelled the renascent economy in western Europe should focus on the coins from Melle alongside those from cities open to the arrival of foreign goods and coins, such as Dorestad, Quentovic, or Venice. Such methodology gives no certainty that one or several useful trace elements or interpretable differences in lead isotope ratios will emerge, but increases the probability of providing clues to answer historical questions. In the next sections, the emphasis is on the production of the mine of Melle and on the evaluation of the use of this silver at mints located in the same sub-kingdom of the Carolingian territory: the kingdom of Aquitaine.

Merovingian Silver Coins from the Area of Tours

The first example presented here is the silver Merovingian coinage of the area of Tours (*c.*AD 670–750) (Lafaurie 1963; Schiesser & Sarah 2017; Sarah & Schiesser 2013). As early as the late sixth and seventh centuries, Tours (Indre-et-Loire) was one of the most productive mints in the Merovingian kingdom. The coinage of the Tours area is of particular interest for a multidisciplinary investigation including silver analysis. Tours is located not far from Melle (*c.*160 km) and relationships between the counties of Touraine and Poitou are known from written sources. The chronology of silver coinage minted at Tours is also well established and spans a period from *c.*AD 670, when silver started to be minted, to the end of the Merovingian period eighty years later (Lafaurie 1988a; 1988b). The coinage of Tours is thus well suited to the study of the diffusion of the silver produced from the Melle mines in the Merovingian period.

Six main groups of Merovingian silver coins from Tours can be identified and classified chronologically. The focus in this study is on the last three, as they were found in a well-studied hoard (Schiesser & Sarah 2017) and they are the closest ones in time to the first Carolingian coins from Melle, which are both numerous and well identified. Those typological groups are designed as follows, in chronological order: facing busts, church name and moneyer, and circle of pearls and pentalpha. Although it can be stated that the last one of those coin types was not minted until the end of the Merovingian coinage around 750, our knowledge is insufficient to determine both when it started and when the other two were struck.

Here, and for the following results discussed, all elemental analyses were performed using laser ablation ICP-MS using concentration profiles (for which see Sarah & Gratuze 2016). Differences in trace elements correlated with the numismatic classification are observed for gold and zinc (Fig. 10.1). Each typological group seems to have its own fingerprint for those two elements: the facing busts type forms a very consistent group characterized by high gold (*c.*1 per cent), as well as high zinc (*c.*1,000 ppm) contents; the trend is similar for the church name type but the points are more scattered. The chronologically latest group, with a circle of pearls and a pentalpha, covers a wide area on Figure 10.1, but differs from the first two groups regarding its lower gold and zinc levels. This group instead displays a fingerprint in gold and zinc that is similar to early Carolingian coins in the name of Melle.[1]

The differences observed here in correlation with the typology should be interpreted carefully: they do not necessarily imply that each group of coins is

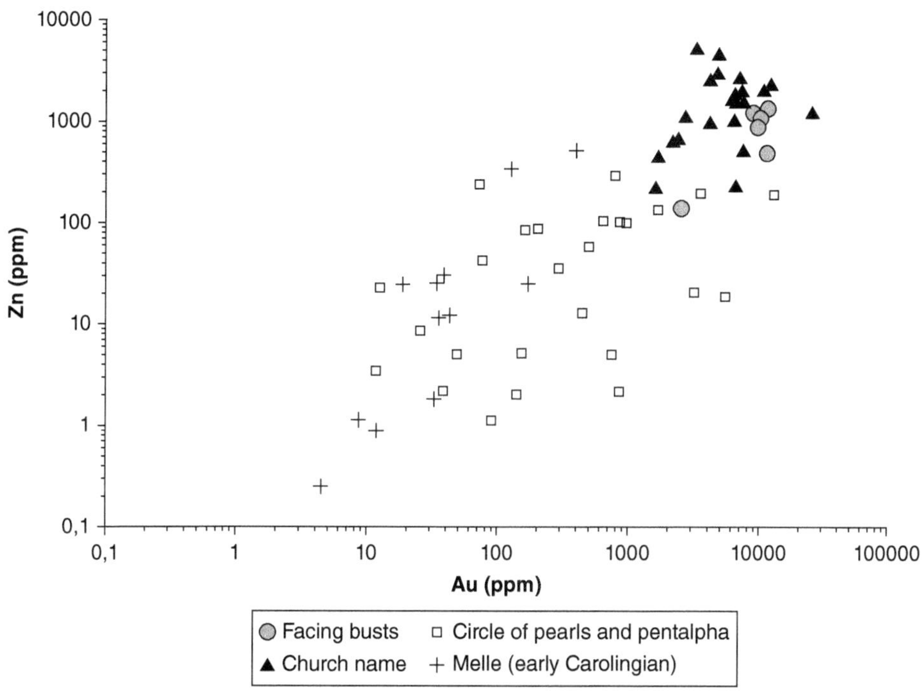

Fig. 10.1. Zinc content versus gold content for the Merovingian coins from Tours and early Carolingian issues from Melle (logarithmic scales).

[1] Although it is not the object of this study, it has to be noted that early Carolingian coins from Melle differ from contemporary issues from other mints regarding their low levels of trace elements, especially gold and zinc. See Sarah 2009.

made of silver of a different origin. More likely, they could suggest that the two groups with the higher contents in trace elements are made of recycled silver, possibly including Merovingian gold coins of the second third of the seventh century containing a majority of silver. This would explain the high levels of gold around 1 per cent. By contrast, the group characterized with lower values (circle of pearls and a pentalpha), closer to the coins of Melle, could have been made with silver more directly linked with the mine.

The lead isotope ratios, obtained via Thermal Ionization Mass Spectrometry (TIMS), have also been determined for some of the Merovingian silver coins from Tours. Referential data here is given by the samples of galena collected from multiple locations within the ancient mining network at Melle, not just a single mine. The results obtained for the three groups of Merovingian coins from Tours are presented in Figures 10.2 and 10.3. The interpretation for the facing busts type is far from clear as only three coins of this type could be analysed: two of them are close to the Melle area whereas the third one is not. For the two other groups, more lead isotope analyses were performed, enabling a better characterization. Coins of both types overlap in part with the lead isotope

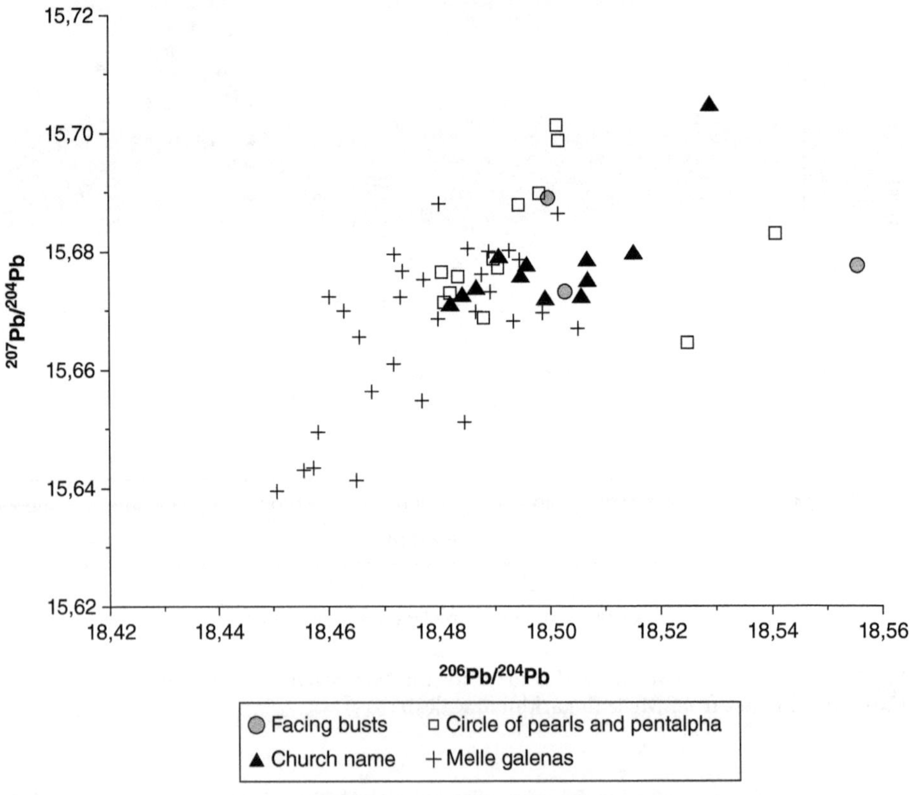

Fig. 10.2. Lead isotope ratios $^{207}Pb/^{204}Pb$ versus $^{206}Pb/^{204}Pb$ for the Merovingian coins from Tours and for samples of ore from Melle.

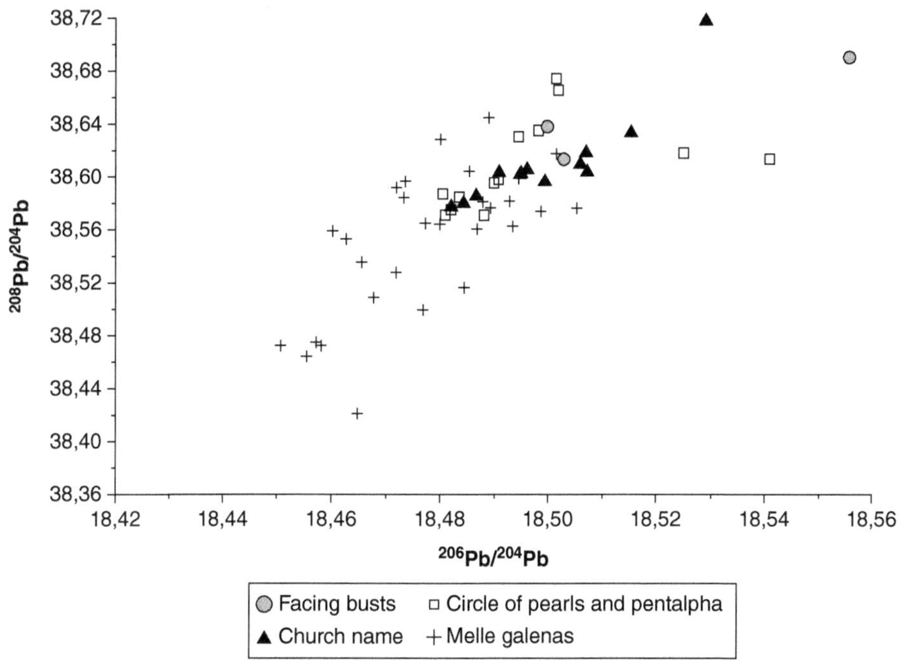

Fig. 10.3. Lead isotope ratios $^{208}Pb/^{204}Pb$ versus $^{206}Pb/^{204}Pb$ for the Merovingian coins from Tours and for samples of ore from Melle.

signature of the Melle ore, and in part with each other. One possibility is that each coin group partly contains silver from Melle, and partly silver from different (and differing) sources. However, the trace element results reveal a significant difference between the silver of Melle and that of the church name group, while the circle of pearls and a pentalpha group shows more overlap with Melle ore in terms of zinc and gold content. A possible interpretation of the apparent conflicting results for the church name type in particular could be the use of lead from Melle to refine silver from a different source used to produce this coinage: this would explain the similarity observed for lead isotope ratios but the inconsistency for the trace elements contents. The combined study of the two types of analysis performed is particularly interesting for the coins with a circle of pearls and a pentalpha, with both approaches revealing close correspondences with the Melle coins.

Carolingian Silver Coins from Toulouse

In this section I present the results obtained for the Carolingian coins from Toulouse in south-west France, located, like Melle, in the kingdom of Aquitaine. The aim of this project was both to confirm the numismatic classification of the coins of Toulouse from the late eighth century to the 870s bearing the name of a king Charles and to try to identify specific fingerprints for each period and evaluate their link with Melle (Sarah 2010; Geneviève & Sarah 2013; Sarah et al. 2016). The four classes for which the analytical results are presented are: coins of Charlemagne, minted at the end of the eighth century and the beginning of the ninth century; coins of Pippin II of Aquitaine and Charles the Bald found in large numbers in the Auzeville hoard (Haute-Garonne), dating from the 840s when troubles in the kingdom came from both internal confusion and Viking raids; and finally the coins of Charles the Bald minted after the important reform of the Edict of Pîtres (864), when a new coin type was introduced, providing a uniform type with a high and standardized silver content for all the mints of the kingdom.

Gold and bismuth are identified as the two trace elements that seem to define the silver of each period (Fig. 10.4). Coins of Charlemagne and those of Charles the Bald minted after 864 present both specific and distinct patterns. The coins of Pippin II of Aquitaine and of Charles the Bald dating from the 840s constitute a single and separate group, characterized by a high level in bismuth. The close correspondence of Pippin II's and Charles the Bald's coins, both struck in the name of Toulouse although bearing the names of two kings who ruled over this

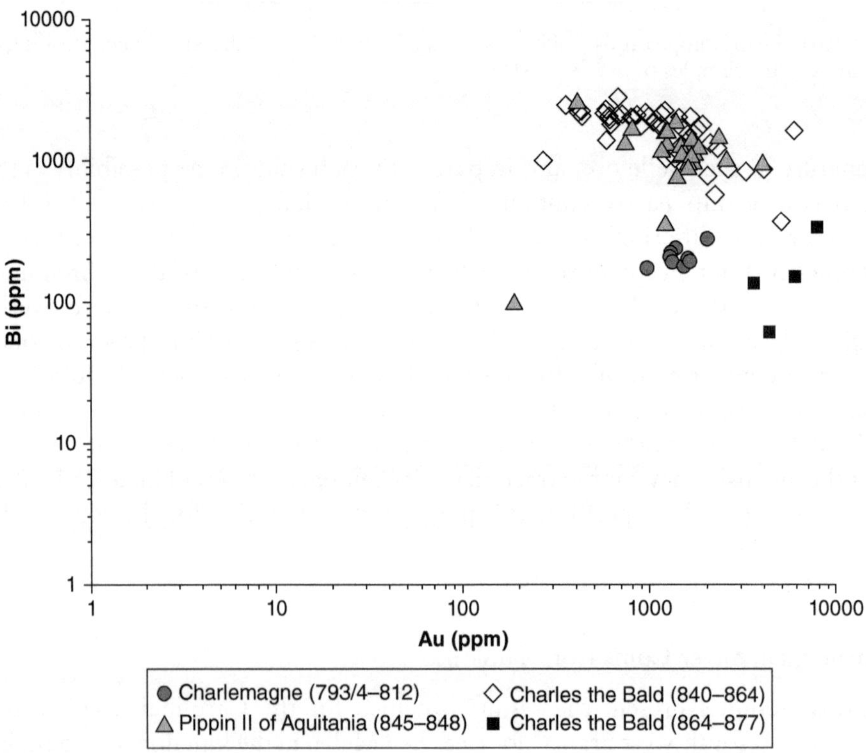

Fig. 10.4. Bismuth content versus gold content for Carolingian coins from Toulouse (logarithmic scales).

city alternatively during this period, suggests that there was continuity at this mint during the 840s and that the same stock of silver was used, possibly by the same moneyers and craftspeople. When compared to those obtained for Charlemagne and for Charles the Bald's later issues, the trace elements patterns suggest that the origin of the silver minted at Toulouse around 800, during the 840s, and after 864 was probably different. However, lead isotope analysis is required to assess whether the sources of silver can be identified, if Melle is involved, and for which period.

The lead isotopes ratios have also been determined via TIMS for a selection of Carolingian coins from Toulouse. Figures 10.5 and 10.6 show that the coins minted in Toulouse in the time of Charlemagne constitute a separate group from the other coins from the same mint but also from the Melle mine fingerprint. For the other groups of coins, minted after 840, some have a fingerprint corresponding to Melle, but only a few. For the more numerous groups, namely the coins of Charles the Bald before 864 and Pippin II of Aquitaine, the results are similar, as also observed for the trace elements patterns; part of those coins have a lead isotope fingerprint similar to Melle, whereas others tend to go to a direction

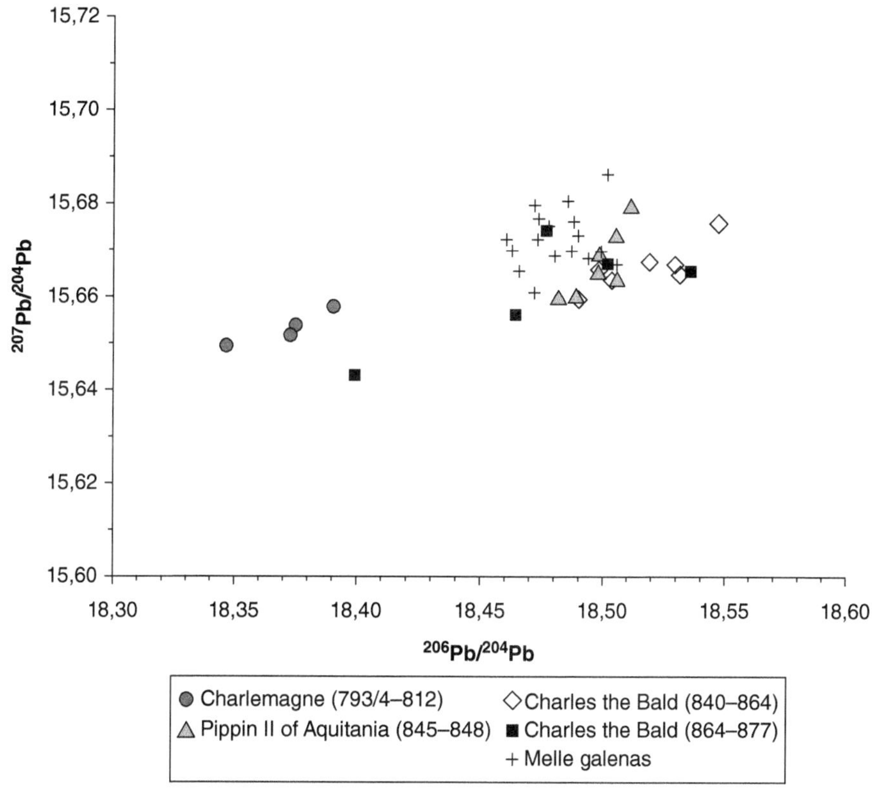

Fig. 10.5. Lead isotope ratios ^{207}Pb/^{204}Pb versus ^{206}Pb/^{204}Pb for Carolingian coins from Toulouse and for samples of ore from Melle.

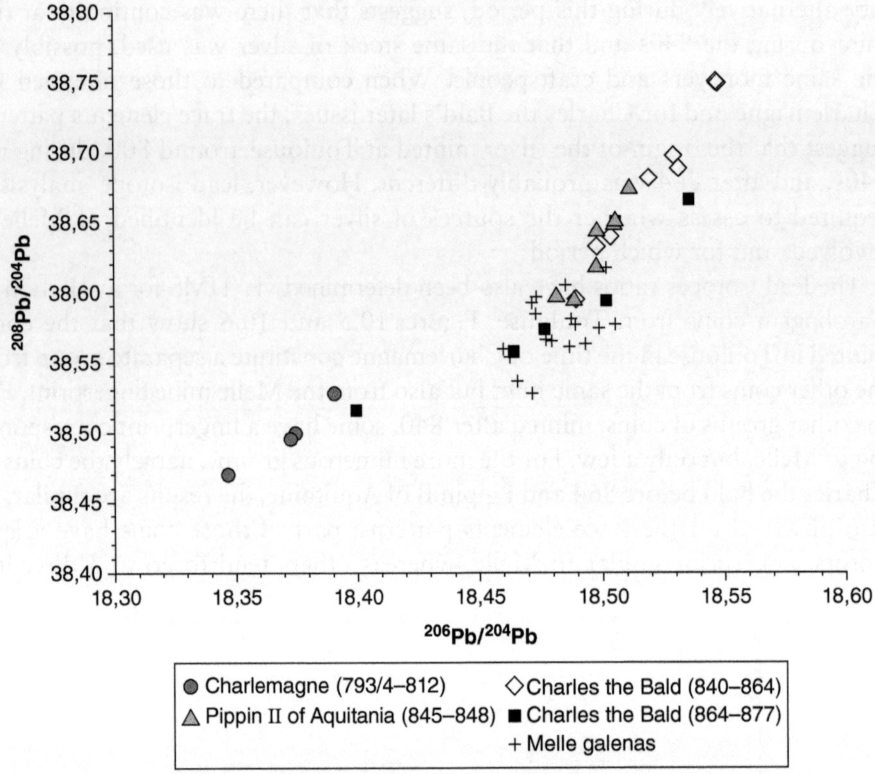

Fig. 10.6. Lead isotope ratios $^{208}Pb/^{204}Pb$ versus $^{206}Pb/^{204}Pb$ for the Merovingian coins from Tours and for samples of ore from Melle.

which is opposed to the fingerprint of the Charlemagne group. From those two figures, in addition to the trace elements patterns, it appears that silver from another source than Melle was coined in Toulouse during the 840s, as well as during the reign of Charlemagne, but so far they have not been identified.

Conclusion: Silver Circulation and Coin Analysis in a Broader View

From the point of view of the numismatist, the life of a coin starts when the dies are hammered and confer an official value and function to a rounded-shape piece of metal. The coin 'dies' in historical terms when it is lost or deposited not to be found until it is discovered by the modern archaeologist or by chance. The work of historians, archaeologists, and numismatists is to determine the place and time those two events took place and to try to reconstruct a plausible scenario for what happened in the meantime.

By contrast, the crucial information for the archaeometallurgist is to be found in what happened before the coin became the object given to us to study. The knowledge of the metallurgy of ancient alloys conservation is fundamental to carry out reliable analysis; but for provenance studies, the geochemistry, mineralogy, and technical processes involved are the most important aspects to understand. To be fruitful, projects aiming to determine the provenance of ancient silver require not only a large number of elemental and isotopic analysis but to identify and provide the keys to their interpretation. Those keys are built up by a long-term coordinated work aiming to gather different types of clues susceptible of contributing to solving a problem: this includes the study of official texts about coin minting or metal provisioning or the descriptions of travellers or geographers; archaeological surveys and excavations have to be carried out in relation to the geological and geochemical data available and to the numismatic and historical knowledge. In order to reach a broader view of silver circulation in the early Middle Ages, the current trend of close collaboration between research specialists from different areas ought to be continued and intensified.

REFERENCES

Arles, A., P. Piccardo, & F. Téreygeol 2011. 'Le procédé de blanchiment dans les ateliers monétaires français au XVIème siècle: approche archéométrique et expérimentale'. In *Craft Treatises and Handbooks: The Dissemination of Technical Knowledge in the Middle Ages*, ed. R. Córdoba, 123–46. Turnhout: Brepols.

Bompaire, M. & G. Sarah (eds) 2017. *Mine, métal, monnaie, Melle. Les voies de la quantification de l'histoire monétaire du haut Moyen Âge*. Genève: Droz.

Carter, G.F. 1964. 'Preparation of Ancient Coins for Accurate X-ray Fluorescence Analysis'. *Archaeometry* 7.1: 106–13.

Cattin, F., B. Guénette-Beck, M. Besse, & V. Serneels 2009. 'Lead Isotopes and Archaeometallurgy'. *Archaeological and Anthropological Sciences* 1.3: 137–48.

Condamin, J. & M. Picon 1972. 'Changes Suffered by Coins in the Course of Time and the Influence of These on the Results of Different Methods of Analysis'. In Hall & Metcalf (eds), 49–66.

Cope, L.H. 1972. 'Surface-Silvered Ancient Coins'. In Hall & Metcalf (eds), 261–78.

Coupland, S. 2011. 'Raiders, Traders, Worshippers and Settlers: The Continental Perspective'. In *Silver Economies: Monetisation and Society in Scandinavia,* AD *800–1100*, ed. J. Graham-Campbell, S. Sindbæk, & G. Williams, 113–31. Aarhus: Aarhus University Press.

Craddock, P.T. 1995. *Early Metal Mining and Production*. Edinburgh: Edinburgh University Press.

Domergue, C. 2008. *Les mines antiques: la production des métaux aux époques grecque et romaine*. Paris: Picard.

Geneviève, V. & G. Sarah 2013. 'Le médaillier carolingien du Musée Paul Dupuy à Toulouse (Haute-Garonne)'. *Mémoires de la Société Archéologique du Midi de la France* LXXII: 15–62.

Hall, E.T. 1960. 'X-ray Fluorescent Analysis Applied to Archaeology'. *Archaeometry* 3.1: 29–35.

Hall, E.T. 1961. 'Surface-Enrichment of Buried Metals'. *Archaeometry* 4: 62–6.

Hall, E.T. & D.M. Metcalf (eds) 1972. *Methods of Chemical and Metallurgical Investigation of Ancient Coinage*. London: Royal Numismatic Society.

Kraay, C.M. 1959. 'Gold and Silver Traces in Early Greek Silver: II'. *Archaeometry* 2: 1–16.

L'Héritier, M., S. Baron, L. Cassayre, & F. Téreygeol 2015. 'Bismuth Behaviour during Ancient Processes of Silver-Lead Production'. *Journal of Archaeological Science* 57 (May): 56–68.

Lafaurie, J. 1963. 'Trésor de deniers mérovingiens trouvé à Savonnières (Indre-et-Loire)'. *Revue Numismatique* 6.5: 65–81.

Lafaurie, J. 1988a. 'Un nouveau denier de Childéric II frappé à Tours'. *Bulletin de la Société Française de Numismatique* 43.7: 421–6.

Lafaurie, J. 1988b. 'À propos des deniers de Tours à la titulature de Childéric II'. *Bulletin de la Société Française de Numismatique* 43.9: 462–4.

Rehren, T. & E. Pernicka 2008. 'Coins, Artefacts and Isotopes—Archaeometallurgy and Archaeometry'. *Archaeometry* 50.2: 232–48.

Sarah, G. 2009. 'Analyses élémentaires de monnaies de Charlemagne et de Louis le Pieux du Cabinet des Médailles: le cas de Melle'. In *Numismatique et archéologie en Poitou-Charentes, Actes du Colloque de Niort, 7–8 décembre 2007*, ed. A. Clairand & D. Hollard, 63–83. Niort: Musée Bernard d'Agesci.

Sarah, G. 2010. 'Charlemagne, Charles the Bald and the Karolus Monogram Coinage: A Multi-Disciplinary Study'. *Numismatic Chronicle* 170: 227–86.

Sarah, G., V. Geneviève, & C. Guerrot 2016. 'Le trésor carolingien découvert à Auzeville (Haute-Garonne) en 1878. Étude des monnayages toulousains de Charles le Chauve et de Pépin II d'Aquitaine'. *Revue Numismatique* 173: 417–98.

Sarah, G. & B. Gratuze 2016. 'LA-ICP-MS Analysis of Ancient Silver Coins Using Concentration Profiles'. In *Recent Advances in Laser Ablation ICP-MS for Archaeology*, ed. L. Dussubieux, M. Golitko, & B. Gratuze, 73–87. Berlin and Heidelberg: Springer.

Sarah, G., B. Gratuze, & J.-N. Barrandon 2007. 'Application of Laser Ablation Inductively Coupled Plasma Mass Spectrometry (LA-ICP-MS) for the Investigation of Ancient Silver Coins'. *Journal of Analytical Atomic Spectrometry* 22.9: 1163–7.

Sarah, G. & Ph. Schiesser 2013. 'Les "grands deniers" de Tours, ou un exemple local de l'apparition du monnayage d'argent mérovingien'. *Revue Numismatique* 170: 355–82.

Schiesser, Ph. & G. Sarah 2017. 'Analyses et typologie des deniers mérovingiens présents dans le trésor de Savonnières'. In Bompaire & Sarah (eds), 209–58.

Stos-Gale, Z.A. 1998. 'Lead Isotope Analysis of Coins—A Review'. In *Metallurgy in Numismatics 4*, ed. W.A. Oddy & M.R. Cowell, 348–66. London: Royal Numismatic Society.

Téreygeol, F. 2014. *Du monde franc aux califats omeyyade et abbasside: extraction et produits des mines d'argent de Melle et de Jabali*. Begleitband zur Ausstellung 'Silberpfade zwischen Orient und Okzident' im Deutschen Bergbau-Museum Bochum 28.02.14–28.09.14. Bochum: Deutsches Bergbau Museum.

Téreygeol, F. 2017. 'La quantification de la production argentifère: Melle, un cas d'école?'. In Bompaire & Sarah (eds), 39–53.

Thompson, M. 1960. 'Gold and Copper Traces in Late Athenian Silver'. *Archaeometry* 3.1: 10–15.

Tylecote, R.F. 2002. *A History of Metallurgy*. 2nd edn. London: Maney.

Villa, I.M. 2009. 'Lead Isotopic Measurements in Archeological Objects'. *Archaeological and Anthropological Sciences* 1.3: 149–53.

11

Provenancing Viking Age Silver

Methodological and Theoretical Considerations and a Case Study

Stephen Merkel

The relationship between archaeometry and the other disciplines of archaeology and history has not always been easy. The methods of analytical chemistry and geoscience have been applied to archaeological materials like silver, but difficulty often arises when interpreting the results and deciding how to integrate them into the body of archaeological and historical knowledge. The archaeometric analysis of Viking silver has been pursued since the 1970s, and has significantly enhanced our knowledge of metallurgy and trade in the Viking world (Merkel 2016; Ilisch et al. 2003; Steuer et al. 2002; Metcalf & Northover 1988; McKerrel & Stevenson 1972). Nevertheless, not all the results obtained are as clear or as easily interpreted as one would hope.

One of the key questions concerning Viking silver of the ninth and tenth centuries is its source: was it plundered from western Europe, as a number of historical accounts suggest, or was it brought to Scandinavia via the eastern trade routes, as the plentiful finds of Kufic dirhams indicate? This leads to the questions whether and how silver from the Islamic world can be differentiated from silver stemming from European sources. Tracking the movements of metals in the Viking Age is anything but a simple task. The numismatic evidence shows that the networks supplying silver to Scandinavia stretched from western Europe to Central Asia, and the networks were complex and chronologically dynamic. Silver coins and hack-silver were widely traded, recycled, melted down, and minted or made into jewellery or ingots. Moreover, the resolution of many analytical methods themselves has added to the ambiguity, masking elemental patterns and relationships. For this reason, analyses must be continually renewed using the most sensitive instrumentation. However, the data obtained, regardless of how accurate or precise, is of little value if the broader archaeological and historical context is not considered.

An integrated approach that takes into account archaeology, numismatics, archaeometallurgy, and mining history is the only way forward in provenancing Viking Age silver. State-of-the-art methods, such as laser ablation inductively coupled plasma mass spectrometry (LA-ICP-MS), provide a level of sensitivity in elemental compositions rarely obtained before and are capable of measuring the lead isotope ratios in silver objects, a seldom investigated variable of great potential in exploring questions of provenance and recycling. This chapter looks at silver provenancing in two parts. Beginning with the theory, it considers the characterization of regional and chronological differences in Viking Age silver and critically evaluates two analytical methods commonly used in provenancing: trace element and lead isotope analysis. These methods are then applied in a case study concentrating on the silver bar ingots, hack-silver, and the early tenth-century Malmer KG7 coinage from Hedeby to explore their possible connection to sources of silver in Volga Bulgaria and the Islamic East.

Understanding the Alloy

In order to discover the usefulness of elemental and lead isotope analysis in answering questions concerning the trade of silver and metallurgical technologies, the behaviour of the elements and isotopes over the lifespan of the object, in the broadest possible sense, must be taken into consideration; however, one must also be critical of the methods used for analysis and how they may influence the results. Experimental archaeology has greatly contributed to our understanding of the behaviour of the minor and trace elements during the refining of silver, a process known as cupellation. Cupellation is defined as the process of separating lead and other impurities from precious metals like gold and silver by heating the alloy to oxidize the lead and other impurities to form litharge while the precious metals remain metallic. It can be assumed that nearly all silver produced in the Middle Ages derived from argentiferous lead that was smelted from silver ores of various forms; therefore, medieval silver went through the cupellation process.

Three studies (McKerrel & Stevenson 1972; Pernicka & Bachmann 1983; L'Héritier et al. 2015) have shown how the elements divide during the cupellation process. Gold survives completely while bismuth resists oxidation until the very end of the process at which time silver begins to oxidize. The removal of bismuth from silver is technically possible but would likely have been uneconomical, imparting high losses of silver during cupellation. As shown by L'Héritier et al. (2015), the amount of bismuth in the original argentiferous lead used to produce the silver may be traced using the bismuth to lead (Bi/Pb) ratio, and this ratio may be used for provenancing silver. Most other trace elements, including zinc, tin, arsenic, antimony, and mercury, readily oxidize and almost entirely enter the litharge or are vaporized. Amounts of copper contained in the ore may be present in the silver, but are typically under 2 per cent. Gold and bismuth levels and/or Bi/Pb ratios are important because they are some of the few characteristics that may stem from the original ore from which the silver was extracted: they may therefore be useful in provenancing. Even when the cupellation process is carefully carried out, a small portion of lead remains in the silver, which is important for lead isotope analysis. When present, elements such as zinc, tin, arsenic, antimony, and mercury primarily enter the silver during steps after the last cupellation, possibly by alloying with copper-alloys or as unintentional contamination.

Gold and bismuth are the standard elements used in provenancing silver. Though one could argue that recycling fire-gilded silver may artificially increase the gold content, one must contemplate what impact the recycling of gilt ornaments could have had in relation to the enormous scale of medieval silver minting. In the twelfth century, Theophilus the Presbyter even mentions that gilding was carefully scraped from silver so as not to lose the precious gold during recycling (Hawthorne & Smith 1979, 147). Bismuth is partially affected by oxidation during cupellation and its ratio to silver is not static (in contrast to gold), which limits its suitability in provenance studies. However, an advantage of significant levels of bismuth in silver is that it is unlikely to have entered the system as an impurity other than being in the original ore or from mixing with bismuth-bearing silver. Although bismuth is often found as a trace element in copper, the amounts of bismuth in the silver are often at such a scale that any contribution from alloying would be irrelevant. For example, a silver artefact has 6,000 ppm (parts per million) of bismuth and 8 per cent copper (by weight). If the bismuth entered the silver with the copper, the original copper-alloy would have almost 7 per cent bismuth, a level yet to be found in any medieval copper. As part of an ongoing study of copper-alloy objects from Hedeby and Schleswig, very few of the ninety-two objects analysed by ICP-MS had more than 0.1 per cent bismuth and the highest concentration was 0.13 per cent: far from the percentage range needed to influence the bismuth content in the silver. Moreover, the silver with the highest bismuth contents tends to have the lowest levels of copper, exemplified by the silver from the region of Panjhir (Cowell & Lowick 1988; Ilisch et al. 2003, 84–5; Merkel 2016, 92).

Characterization of Elemental Compositions

As more studies of Viking Age silver are carried out, it is becoming increasingly evident that the composition of silver objects has geographical and chronological dimensions. There is a close relationship between numismatics and the emergences of silver provenancing studies. In the Anglo-Saxon realm, McKerrel and Stevenson's (1972) seminal work identified some of the major differences between the Anglo-Saxon coinages and dirhams primarily of Samanid mints. No relationship was found between the Anglo-Saxon coinage and the Samanid dirhams, but importantly it showed the peculiarity and time-sensitivity of the alloys. The major differences are that the Samanid dirhams typically contain higher levels of bismuth with lower gold contents than the contemporary Anglo-Saxon alloys and were alloyed with pure copper rather than the brass or bronze commonly used in Anglo-Saxon England. The authors discovered that the compositions of the Anglo-Saxon coinage change over the course of the tenth century. They go as far as to suggest that non-minted silver could possibly be dated based on the compositional trends of the coinage (McKerrel & Stevenson 1972, 201).

The compositions of the Anglo-Saxon coinages were more thoroughly investigated in a series of articles by Metcalf and Northover (1985; 1986; 1989; 2002) and confirm the trends identified by McKerrel and Stevenson. Summarized briefly, the alloys of the Anglo-Saxon coinages of the early ninth century contain variable amounts of gold, which tends to increase towards the end of the ninth century to contents between 0.5 and 1.0 per cent. The gold content gradually declines in the second half of the tenth century to levels between 0.3 to 1.0 per cent, and further declines in the eleventh century to 0.15 to 0.5 per cent. The zinc and tin contents also evolve during this period. The coins of the ninth century prior to AD 840 are often alloyed with small amounts of brass or brass copper mixtures, but between 840 and the end of the ninth century, brass and increasingly bronze were used to debase the coinages. In the tenth century, the zinc contents gradually subside, but remain present, and increase again in the late tenth and eleventh centuries, indicating the use of new brass in alloying.

As Guillaume Sarah (2010; this volume) has shown with Carolingian coinage, there seems to be a chronological dimension to the silver coin compositions to such an extent that coins unable to be attributed to a ruler through numismatic methods can often be differentiated by their elemental composition. Notably, there is a contemporaneous debasement of the silver coinages in the Carolingian Empire and Anglo-Saxon England with brass during the reign of Charles the Bald (AD 823–77). This not only represents an economic link, but may also indicate shared sources of silver and/or brass.

Turning to the Islamic world, the published analyses show that dirham compositions are chronologically and geographically dependent. Kufic dirhams began to replace the Sassanian silver-based coinage in the seventh century. Initially, the early Islamic dirhams and pre-Islamic coinage seem similar with high gold contents (*c.*1 per cent), but in the eighth century, the gold contents of dirhams are no longer consistent and range from high (1 per cent) to low gold contents (<0.1 per cent) (Gordus 1972). This trend can be seen in repeated analyses from mints all over the Islamic world (Gondonneau & Guerra 2002, 583; Ilisch et al. 2003). It has been suggested that there was a shift in the extractive metallurgy of silver in the Islamic world during the eighth and ninth centuries and new types of silver ores were being mined (Meyers 2003, 278). Based on the work of Ilisch et al. (2003), Abbasid mints of the ninth century produced high-quality silver dirhams with low to moderate gold and bismuth contents. As established by Ilisch et al., the average contents of 450 ninth-century

Abbasid dirhams are 0.16 per cent gold and 0.26 per cent bismuth. Gold and bismuth contents seem to vary regionally. Above average gold contents can be found in Isfahan, Baghdad, Bukhara, and Samarkand; the highest bismuth contents are in Transoxania and the lowest in Baghdad.

There are some dramatic changes at the turn of the tenth century. Most strikingly, the bismuth contents in the coinage of the Samanids increase significantly, to above 1 per cent on average at the major mints of Central Asia (Merkel 2016, 73 table 5.2). The bismuth contents found in the dirhams of Central Asia and northern Afghanistan in all likelihood originate from the silver sources in the Shash-Ilak region and Panjhir, which were intensively mined under the Samanids (Negmatov 1998, 89). Interestingly, beginning between AD 898 and 919 (AH 285–300), an increase in bismuth contents is detectable in the dirhams of Baghdad, Nishapur, Isfahan, and Balkh (see analyses of Ilisch et al. 2003). Although the Samanids did not have to pay tribute directly to the Abbasid Caliphate, the intensity of dirham minting between the two regions seems to be linked (Lowick 1975, 122–3), and the increase in bismuth contents may be a further hint that Samanid silver was recycled by the Abbasids.

The Use of Lead Isotope Analysis

Though one can show similarities in silver objects with the gold and bismuth contents and suggest relationships, it is difficult to build a firm argument with trace elements alone. Lead isotope analysis is a well-established method for provenancing metals such as copper, lead, and silver, and there is substantial literature on the subject (for example Gale & Stos-Gale 2000; Gale 2009; Pollard 2009; Pernicka 2014). It is a powerful technique that, in ideal situations, can be used to link ore to production debris to final products. It can also be used to exclude metal sources and to help understand recycling. The lead isotope ratios found in copper, lead, and silver objects have embedded geological information, though in many cases the true meaning of this data is obscured by the various processes (such as refining and recycling) that could have been or were carried out, which can significantly limit its interpretation. A second major problem with lead isotope analysis is that there can be extensive overlap of geologically similar ore deposits, which would produce metals that are indistinguishable with this method alone. Despite the difficulties in unlocking the true meaning of lead isotope ratios and in identifying the precise source of the metal through overlap or lack of reference data, lead isotope ratios can still be used to provide more variables that may be helpful in defining differences and similarities. One can liken trace elements to a two-dimensional image, and trace elements together with lead isotope analysis to a three-dimensional image.

The relationship between the metallurgy of lead and silver is intertwined, but not always directly. Two principles are particularly important in the provenancing of Viking Age silver: the mixing principle and the refining principle. Firstly, when silver with differing lead isotope ratios are mixed, the resulting silver will have lead isotope ratios that are the average of all the silver pieces mixed together. In theory, this means that recycled silver will have a smaller variation of lead isotope ratios than the individual silver objects from which it is recycled. If, for example, silver from two geochemically distinct sources with differing lead isotope ratios were to be mixed they would graphically plot on a line between the two sources—the 'mixing line' (Pernicka et al. 1984, 592–6; Gale & Stos-Gale 2000, 532–3). In order to argue for mixing, objects must fall on a line (or within a polygon for multiple sources) outlined by the potential raw materials/sources; the elemental compositions must also support the possibility of mixing.

The second principle is that when silver is refined by cupellation, the lead isotope ratios will be altered to reflect the lead used in refining. Refining could occur anytime and practically anywhere between when the silver was produced and when it was fashioned into its final form. Initially, the refining principle may seem like a major interpretational barrier, but the usefulness of the mixing principle should not be underestimated. The isotope ratios of lead originating in the British Isles, for example, are distinctly different from the isotope ratios of lead found in the Samanid dirhams of Transoxania and Khorasan (compare Merkel et al. 2013 and Rohl 1996). When the lead isotope ratios of the silver are different enough from the lead mined and used in Europe, then an argument can be made that the silver was not refined in Europe, nor could the silver have entirely originated there. In theory, this can help to differentiate silver that may have been refined in Europe from recycled silver of more distant origins.

Mining, Minting, and Recycling

Mints may be linked to nearby silver mines, or mints can be supplied with silver acquired by commerce or taxation, which can derive from multiple sources. The question of whether mints were supplied with newly produced silver or recycled silver is of great interest. The purity and homogeneity of trace elements may be one indication of a link between minting and mining in regions where suitable silver sources may have existed; examples could be Panjhir in Afghanistan, Carolingian Melle (see Sarah, this volume), or the Ottonian Harz Mountains and the Otto-Adelheid-Pfennig. However, this situation seems to be rare; many prolific mints are not located near ore deposits, like Abbasid Baghdad or Carolingian Dorestad, and must have relied on silver carried over larger distances. In cases like these, the silver probably does not reflect single sources but mixtures of the silver circulating at that time in that region.

The kingdom of Volga Bulgaria, in the middle of modern-day Russia, is a particularly interesting example of silver mixing as it was located on one of the major arteries supplying dirhams to northern Europe (Noonan 2001). The Volga Bulgars had an important role as intermediaries to the Rus, the Khazars, and Muslim traders on this lucrative trade route. Whereas the wider Islamic world contained numerous mints with various kinds of silver, the silver recycled in Volga Bulgaria and Khazaria might better reflect the average compositions of dirhams in circulation than the individual mints in the Abbasid Caliphate and Samanid Empire. When silver is recycled, it is homogenized and the resulting compositions will reflect less extreme values than its components. The large-neck rings known as Permian spiral rings (Fig. 11.1) elucidate this point. These rings were likely produced in Russia, possibly in Volga Bulgaria, and were made in units as large as 400 grams (Hårdh 2007), which would equate to more than one hundred dirhams. The dirhams used to make a single ring may have been struck at ten or more mints and have various elemental and lead isotope compositions, but when melted together, their compositions are homogenized and averaged. Though this may sound abstract, it is simple; for example, if two pieces of silver of the same weight but very different compositions are melted together the composition of the final silver will be precisely in the middle between the two. The compositions of the Volga-Bulgar dirham imitations in relation to the Malmer KG7 half-bracteates struck at Hedeby and hack-silver fragments found at Hedeby will be discussed in the case study below, but first it is necessary to discuss some issues concerning analytical methods and data comparability.

Fig. 11.1. Permian spiral ring terminal found during metal-detecting, Hb 2003–788.

Methods of Analysis and Data Comparability

Two questions that arise with any type of elemental or lead isotope analysis are: can the results be trusted and can they be compared to other published data? Numerous methods have been used in the past to analyse silver objects: atomic absorption spectrometry (AAS), X-ray fluorescence (XRF), scanning electron microscopy with energy dispersive spectroscopy (SEM-EDS), neutron activation analysis (NAA), inductively-coupled-plasma mass spectrometry (ICP-MS), to name a few. Some methods are bulk analyses requiring small amounts of material, while others can be used to analyse the objects in situ with little to no damage to the object.

Non-destructive surfaces analyses relying on X-ray spectra, namely XRF, portable XRF (pXRF), SEM-EDS, electroprobe microanalysis (EPMA), and particle-induced X-ray emission (PIXE), are often used to analyse precious metals for a number of practical reasons, but the data obtained must be treated with care. In the literature, some researchers have polished portions of the silver objects so as to remove the corrosion or corrosion-impacted layer, but others have analysed the surface of objects in various states of preservation. The natural corrosion of silver alloys, the intentional treatments used in the production of the object, and the conservation/cleaning treatments applied all impact the surface composition and will be reflected in non-destructive surface analyses (see Mortimer 1986; Beck et al. 2004; Arles 2009, 461–502).

Mass spectrometry is highly sensitive and has been used to obtain elemental compositions and lead isotope ratios, but it requires small amounts of sample material, which has limited its application to the study of precious metals. Mass spectrometry by laser ablation, though technically destructive, requires such small amounts of sample material that the damage to the object is not visible to the eye. The laser produces a crater approximately 40–100 μm wide and can blast through the upper layers of corrosion and contamination to get more representative compositions of the interior of the object; however, particularly deep penetration of corrosion may still impact the elemental composition.

Comparing the two types of instruments, ICP-MS is calibrated using external standards and offers much higher precision and accuracy than the pXRF, but the pXRF is more versatile for its ease of transport and the range of materials that can be analysed with little preparation. To investigate the analytical differences of laser ablation ICP-MS and pXRF, a small study was carried out; fourteen cleaned and conserved Viking Age coins were analysed with both methods. Nano-second laser ablation inductively coupled plasma quadrupole mass spectrometry (ns-LA-ICP-QMS) was used at the Leibniz University in Hanover (Merkel 2016) and results were compared to the non-destructive pXRF Thermo Scientific NITON XL3t Analyzer from the Deutsches Bergbau-Museum, Bochum (Table 11.1).

Table 11.1. Comparison of compositions of select coins obtained by portable XRF and laser ablation mass spectrometry.

Find number	Type	Method	Ag	Cu	Au	Bi	Zn	Sn	Pb	Fe
Hb 2011/14424	Denar Frisian Imitation	pXRF	93.2	1.3	<0.04	<0.01	**5.1**	<0.1	0.3	<0.1
	S COLONIA	ns-LA-ICP-QMS	98.2	1.8	<0.01	0.01	**<0.01**	<0.01	0.2	<0.01
Hb 2004/10439	Denar Frisian Imitation	pXRF	97.9	1.3	<0.04	<0.01	**0.4**	<0.1	0.2	0.2
	S COLONIA	ns-LA-ICP-QMS	98.4	1.6	<0.01	<0.01	**<0.01**	<0.01	0.1	<0.01
Hb 2003/4174	Denar Archb. Pilgrim	pXRF	96.3	1.7	**0.30**	0.1	**1.0**	<0.1	0.4	0.1
	Cologne	ns-LA-ICP-QMS	97.7	2.1	**0.10**	0.07	**0.04**	0.1	0.3	<0.01
Hb 2003/3795	Denar Otto III.	pXRF	95.4	2.4	**0.26**	0.05	**1.1**	–	0.5	0.1
	Cologne	ns-LA-ICP-QMS	97.9	1.9	**0.10**	0.04	**0.1**	0.04	0.3	<0.01
Hb 2005/11490	Sachsenpfennig	pXRF	97.8	1.6	0.08	0.04	**0.1**	<0.1	0.4	<0.1
		ns-LA-ICP-QMS	98.8	1.2	0.02	0.03	**<0.01**	0.01	0.2	<0.01
Hb 2003/3205	Sachsenpfennig	pXRF	95.0	1.9	<0.04	<0.01	**2.7**	–	0.2	0.1
		ns-LA-ICP-QMS	98.7	1.3	0.02	0.01	**<0.01**	<0.01	0.1	0.1
Hb 2003/2499	Miliaresion Basil II.	pXRF	93.1	2.2	**0.59**	0.05	**3.0**	<0.1	0.7	0.2
		ns-LA-ICP-QMS	96.9	2.9	**0.18**	0.03	**<0.01**	<0.01	0.5	<0.01
Hb 2005/11816	Penny Æthelred II.	pXRF	95.4	2.4	**0.78**	0.05	**0.7**	<0.1	0.5	<0.1
	Second Hand	ns-LA-ICP-QMS	97.3	2.2	**0.31**	0.04	**0.2**	0.1	0.4	<0.01
Hb 2005/11299	Penny Æthelred II.	pXRF	95.7	2.2	**0.96**	0.05	0.3	<0.1	0.6	<0.1
	Long Cross	ns-LA-ICP-QMS	96.9	2.6	**0.36**	0.03	0.1	0.02	0.4	<0.01
Hb 2007/14334	Penny Cnut	pXRF	95.7	2.7	**0.34**	0.12	0.3	<0.1	0.6	0.2
	Quatrefoil	ns-LA-ICP-QMS	96.8	2.8	**0.13**	0.08	0.2	0.05	0.4	<0.01
Hb 2003/4191	Gift-Dirham al-Mu'tamid	pXRF	97.8	0.3	**0.65**	<0.01	**0.8**	<0.1	0.4	<0.1
	Samarra (Abbasid)	ns-LA-ICP-QMS	99.0	0.6	**0.25**	0.001	**0.1**	<0.01	0.3	0.2
Hb 2004/9671	Dirham al-Mu'tamid	pXRF	94.5	0.05	<0.04	1.16	<0.02	<0.1	0.4	**3.7**
	Panjhir (Abbasid)	ns-LA-ICP-QMS	98.7	0.1	<0.01	1.18	<0.01	<0.01	0.4	**0.4**
Hb 2004/8792	Dirham Nasr ibn Ahmad	pXRF	96.7	**0.8**	0.08	**0.62**	**0.7**	<0.1	0.8	0.1
	Samarkand (Samanid)	ns-LA-ICP-QMS	95.6	**4.0**	0.07	0.31	**0.02**	<0.01	0.9	0.2
KSD 598.814	Denar Svend Estridsen	pXRF	**57.1**	**32.9**	<0.04	0.03	**7.2**	<0.1	**2.0**	0.1
	Viborg	ns-LA-ICP-QMS	**78.8**	**17.2**	0.09	0.01	**3.9**	0.1	**0.8**	<0.01

The results (Table 11.1) indicate that, when gold is present in the coin above 0.1 per cent, the pXRF gave regularly higher values, but bismuth contents are more consistent between the two instruments. Zinc is consistently higher in the pXRF results, and, in some cases, is highly exaggerated and unreliable. The reason behind these high zinc values has yet to be investigated; some possibilities might be contamination from galvanized surfaces or spectral peak overlap. The debased coin of Sven Estridsen shows a large disparity, but the relative proportions of copper, zinc, and lead seem consistent. The difference in composition may reflect the heterogeneous distribution of segregated brass and silver-rich phases because the laser only collects material from a point of the sample while the pXRF analyses a broader region. More points could be ablated and the results averaged together to better capture the composition of heterogeneous alloys.

Table 11.2 presents the results of two hack-silver objects analysed by seven different machines in four laboratories, and enables a comparison between different instruments and techniques. There is variation in the major elemental compositions between the quantitative methods, but the trace elemental compositions are relatively close among the three ICP-MS regardless of whether samples were taken by laser ablation or by solution (dissolved bulk samples representing 10 mg of drillings or clippings). The pXRF results vary only slightly from the quantitative methods and this may be due to the fact that a corrosion-free cut surface was measured. The scanning electron microscope was found to be unsuitable for measuring the concentration of elements at or below 1 per cent. Lead isotope analyses by multicollector ICP-MS performed in Frankfurt am Main by liquid solution and in Hannover by laser ablation showed minimal differences (for methods see Merkel 2014). The variation between the laboratories is within the analytical error.

Thus, there is some variability in the data produced with the different methods and the results can be different if corroded surfaces are measured by surface-analysing techniques like pXRF. The ICP-MS results in the present comparison show good comparability in the trace elements whether by laser or by bulk liquid solution analysis. The pXRF was able to detect similar quantities of many of the important trace elements, but while the results were highly reliable when targeting cut surfaces, they were found to be unreliable for several elements on corroded surfaces. This goes to show that destructive analysis is clearly superior, but to confirm interlaboratory and intermethod comparability it is important to compare the results of the same object or to use certified reference materials.

Case Study: Hack-silver, Dirham Imitations, and the Malmer KG7

In this case study, the Malmer KG7 coinage minted at Hedeby around the first two decades of the tenth century (Malmer 2007; Wiechmann 2007) is compared to hack-silver and bar ingots found at Hedeby and contemporary coinages from

Table 11.2. Two fragments of hack-silver from Hedeby analysed by various instruments and methods to demonstrate the data comparability. Quantitative mass spectrometry was carried out by laser ablation in Hanover by Robert Lehmann and in Orleans by Guillaume Sarah and by liquid solution by Michael Bode at the DBM Bochum. The lead isotope ratios were determined by laser ablation in Hanover by Robert Lehmann and by liquid solution by Sabine Klein in Frankfurt am Main. The pXRF represents averages of two analyses and the SEM-EDS is of three areas averaged and normalized to 100%. The '–' means below the limit of detection when not otherwise specified and 'n.m.' means not measured. All analyses except those from Orleans are presented in Merkel (2016).

Object	Method	Lab	Ag %	Au %	Cu %	Zn %	Sn %	Sb %	Hg %	Bi %	Pb %	As ppm	Co ppm	Ni ppm	Fe %	Sum %
a	LA-ICP-QMS	Hanover	96.7	0.42	2.8	0.05	0.02	0.001	0.001	0.016	0.49	5	0.3	2	<0.4	100.5
a	HR-ICP-MS	Bochum	91.0	0.35	4.2	0.03	0.01	<0.001	<0.001	0.014	0.52	17	0.1	2	0.01	95.8
a	LA-ICP-QMS	Orleans	95.8	0.39	3.3	0.03	0.01	<0.001	n.m.	0.013	0.46	14	n.m.	3	n.m.	100.0
a	pXRF	Bochum	94.1	0.54	2.7	0.07	–	–	–	0.030	0.43	–	–	–	0.31	97.9
a	SEM-EDS	Bochum	95.0	–	3.1	–	–	–	–	–	–	–	–	–	–	100
b	LA-ICP-QMS	Hanover	96.1	0.17	3.4	0.35	0.024	0.005	0.001	0.063	0.94	37	1	3	<0.4	101.0
b	HR-ICP-MS	Bochum	90.2	0.20	6.8	0.44	0.023	0.008	<0.001	0.066	1.18	285	1	15	0.01	98.7
b	LA-ICP-QMS	Orleans	91.8	0.21	6.3	0.53	0.024	0.004	n.m.	0.066	1.08	302	n.m.	11	n.m.	100.0
b	pXRF	Bochum	91.4	0.21	6.0	0.45	–	–	–	0.080	1.30	–	–	–	0.15	99.5
b	SEM-EDS	Bochum	94.3	–	3.4	0.40	–	–	–	–	–	–	–	–	–	100.

Object	Lab	$^{206}Pb/^{204}Pb$	2σ	$^{207}Pb/^{204}Pb$	2σ	$^{208}Pb/^{204}Pb$	2σ	$^{207}Pb/^{206}Pb$	2σ	$^{208}Pb/^{206}Pb$	2σ
a	Frankfurt/Main	18.452	0.004	15.639	0.004	38.48	0.02	0.8475	0.0001	2.0855	0.0004
a	Hannover	18.457	0.017	15.643	0.016	38.49	0.04	0.8475	0.0004	2.0855	0.0011
b	Frankfurt/Main	18.533	0.006	15.660	0.006	38.65	0.01	0.8449	0.0001	2.0854	0.0003
b	Hannover	18.535	0.004	15.662	0.004	38.66	0.01	0.8449	0.0001	2.0856	0.0003

the West and East in an attempt to discover the source of silver. Heiko Steuer was the first to analyse Malmer KG7s with the same goal (2003). Using XRF, Steuer found that the KG7s were most similar to the Volga-Bulgar dirham imitations and Anglo-Saxon coinage (Steuer et al. 2002, 153). However, he did not analyse Anglo-Saxon coinages contemporary to the Malmer KG7, but late Anglo-Saxon coinages minted more than fifty years after the KG7. From published analyses, truly contemporary coins, namely the Carolingian and the Viking coinage of East Anglia and York from the Cuerdale hoard (deposited *c.*AD 905–10) (Metcalf & Northover 1988) and the Wessex coinage of Edward the Elder (McKerrel & Stevenson 1972, 205), tend to have higher gold contents than the KG7s measured by Steuer. This may be a reason to doubt a connection. However, the Volga-Bulgar dirham imitations do seem to fit well with the chronology.

A study of hack-silver and coinage found at Hedeby and some nearby hoards in Schleswig-Holstein was carried out between 2011 and 2014. A total of 187 silver objects of the ninth to eleventh centuries were analysed by mass spectrometry to determine elemental compositions and lead isotope ratios (Merkel 2016). It was quickly realized that the data obtained was not random and that there were relationships between certain types of objects. Two groups of non-minted silver consisting of wires, bars, jewellery fragments, and ingots were identified based on gold and bismuth contents; a distinction was also reflected in the lead isotope ratios (Table 11.3). One group has moderate to high gold contents and low bismuth, while the other group has moderate gold contents with high bismuth.

The first group contains all of the silver ingots (Wiechmann 1996, Ingot Type 1), one ribbed bar (Wiechmann 1996, Ingot Type 3), an arm-ring fragment with stamped decoration, various wires and bars, a terminal of a Permian spiral ring (Fig. 11.1), and a fragment of a silver strap fitting of oriental (Volga-Bulgar) style (Fig. 11.2). Complete ingots of the Wiechmann Type 1 tend to appear in hoards of the late ninth to first half of the tenth century and have their greatest concentration in southern Scandinavia with Hedeby as a possible production centre (Wiechmann 1996, 65–7). The one complete ingot analysed was probably weight-adjusted (73.66 grams = *c.*3 øre of *c.*24.6 g – see Brøgger 1921, 85). The ribbed bar may have an eastern Scandinavian origin where complete ribbed bar ingots tend to be found, often rolled into spirals to be worn as arm-rings (Wiechmann 1996, 68). Two objects likely to be of eastern origin, the Permian spiral ring terminal and the Volga-Bulgar style strap fitting, also have similar gold and bismuth contents and lead isotope ratios. The Permian ring terminal is cast and welded to the end of the ring, and with a weight of 50 grams, it may have belonged to the largest type rings originating in Russia (see Hårdh 2007). The oriental style belt mount/harness fitting was most likely cast and has negative relief on the reverse side with one broken stud visible. It is more difficult to place, despite the eastern style; such strap fittings could have been manufactured

Table 11.3. Analysed hack-silver and ingots from Hedeby (Merkel 2016). All but one object were measured by liquid solution mass spectrometry in Bochum and Frankfurt am Main, the oriental fitting was analysed by laser ablation in Hanover. Two hack-silver fragments were measured with all methods to insure inter-laboratory comparability.

Find number	Type	Weight	Total %	Ag %	Cu %	Au ppm	Bi ppm	Zn ppm	Sn ppm	Pb ppm	$^{206}Pb/^{204}Pb$	2σ	$^{207}Pb/^{204}Pb$	2σ	$^{208}Pb/^{204}Pb$	2σ	^{207}Pb	2σ	$^{208}Pb/^{206}Pb$	2σ
Group 1																				
Hb 2003–217	Ingot	73.66g	93.1	84.7	6.8	4140	1600	2370	2840	8500	18.503	0.014	15.643	0.011	38.61	0.03	0.8454	0.0002	2.0865	0.0002
Hb 2003–609	Ribed Bar	3.06g	91.9	85.6	6.0	7160	110	310	1280	1300	18.451	0.014	15.649	0.011	38.50	0.03	0.8481	0.0002	2.0866	0.0003
Hb 2003–1064	Arm-Ring Frag.	1.15g	95.1	91.4	2.8	2580	10	830	3	6900	18.572	0.012	15.656	0.009	38.69	0.02	0.8429	0.0001	2.0830	0.0002
Hb 2003–3456	Bar Frag.	4.22g	96.9	90.9	5.8	8700	130	120	60	2200	18.371	0.006	15.622	0.006	38.34	0.02	0.8503	0.0001	2.0869	0.0002
Hb 2003–3834	Two Twisted Wires	1.95g	95.8	91.0	4.2	3530	140	330	110	5200	18.452	0.004	15.639	0.004	38.48	0.02	0.8475	0.0001	2.0855	0.0004
Hb 2004–6119	Bar Frag.	4.57g	97.7	90.0	6.7	4160	550	640	690	8300	18.534	0.009	15.655	0.008	38.65	0.02	0.8446	0.0001	2.0852	0.0002
Hb 2004–8163	Ingot Frag.	6.23g	96.7	87.3	7.2	5030	960	810	8610	11,900	18.572	0.004	15.658	0.004	38.66	0.01	0.8431	0.0001	2.0816	0.0002
Hb 2004–10611	Ingot Frag.	2.42g	99.0	88.2	8.0	2640	1000	1260	7230	18,500	18.588	0.003	15.656	0.004	38.66	0.01	0.8422	0.0001	2.0796	0.0002
Hb 2006–12467	Twisted Wire	9.45g	98.7	90.2	6.8	2020	660	4440	230	11,800	18.533	0.006	15.660	0.006	38.65	0.01	0.8449	0.0001	2.0854	0.0003
Hb 2006–12587	Ingot Frag.	11.82g	98.7	91.6	5.8	2030	2430	200	2330	9100	18.697	0.004	15.685	0.004	38.89	0.01	0.8389	0.0001	2.0801	0.0002
LA 48, Fd.Nr. 8476	Bar/Wire	4.82g	97.6	91.3	5.3	2930	520	1210	330	7300	18.525	0.011	15.644	0.009	38.60	0.02	0.8444	0.0001	2.0835	0.0002
Hb 2003–788	Permian Spiral Ring	50.67g	94.4	86.6	6.5	3550	780	2910	1310	8400	18.574	0.008	15.660	0.008	38.68	0.02	0.8431	0.0001	2.0823	0.0002
LA 48, Fd.Nr. 7755	Oriental Fitting	0.68g	100.4	97.1	2.4	4100	210	750	950	3300	18.600	0.006	15.670	0.006	38.68	0.02	0.8424	0.0002	2.0818	0.0004
Group 2																				
Hb 2003–2788	Wire	4.08g	98.1	92.1	5.1	1600	4540	660	85	3800	18.296	0.005	15.637	0.003	38.49	0.01	0.8546	0.0001	2.1037	0.0002
Hb 2004–8540	Wire	3.63g	98.3	89.3	7.5	2620	6340	110	40	8900	18.234	0.004	15.623	0.004	38.46	0.01	0.8567	0.0001	2.1094	0.0002
Hb 2004–11071	Arm-Ring Frag.	2.21g	98.6	91.7	5.2	1730	6630	1240	360	8000	18.261	0.008	15.631	0.007	38.52	0.02	0.8560	0.0001	2.1091	0.0003
Hb 2004–12396	Bar Frag.	5.75g	93.4	85.8	6.0	2570	4410	2330	1460	7600	18.363	0.030	15.634	0.026	38.55	0.06	0.8513	0.0003	2.0990	0.0004
Hb 2007–13926	Wire	4.07g	98.1	89.7	6.7	2370	5530	1140	630	9600	18.323	0.003	15.639	0.003	38.60	0.01	0.8535	0.0001	2.1067	0.0002

Fig. 11.2. Oriental, or Volga-Bulgar, style silver belt mount or harness fitting found at Hedeby, LA 48, Fd.Nr. 7755.

anywhere between Volga Bulgaria and the western Baltic (Volker Hilberg, pers. comm., May 2015).

A major difference between the two hack-silver (non-minted silver) groups is that the second group has double the bismuth contents of the first group (Table 11.3). In addition to the differing bismuth contents, the lead isotope ratios show higher $^{208}Pb/^{206}Pb$ and $^{207}Pb/^{206}Pb$ values clearly indicating differing origins of the lead in the silver. The high bismuth group consists of wire fragments and part of an arm-ring with stamped decoration. Few of these objects are diagnostic and none are easily dated. When we compare these objects to the Malmer KG7 coins, however, it is apparent that the first group of hack-silver is more similar (Figs 11.3 and 11.4). The Malmer KG7s are made of an alloy that has direct parallels in both the trace elemental composition and the range of lead isotope ratios to the first group of hack-silver, including the Permian spiral ring and the oriental fitting, but a portion of the Volga-Bulgar dirham imitations also are similar. The Volga-Bulgar dirhams have a range of bismuth contents, but the coins with less than 0.3 per cent bismuth are most similar to the Malmer KG7 coins in both elemental composition and lead isotope ratios; these low bismuth dirham imitations are plotted in Figure 11.4. The only official dirham that fits with both the elemental and lead isotope composition of the KG7 is a Saffarid dirham minted in Shiraz between AD 878 and 884. Another dirham from Iran minted in al-Muhammadiya around AD 794–803 has similar lead isotope ratios, but has significantly less gold and bismuth. Two mid-ninth-century dirhams from Iraq are low in bismuth and have low to moderate gold contents, but their lead isotope ratios seem more similar to deposits in the Taurus Mountains published by Yener et al. (1991) and are not similar to the two Iranian dirhams, which have lead isotope ratios that fall in line with the range of Sassanian drachma from the published literature (see Stos-Gale 2001, 65).

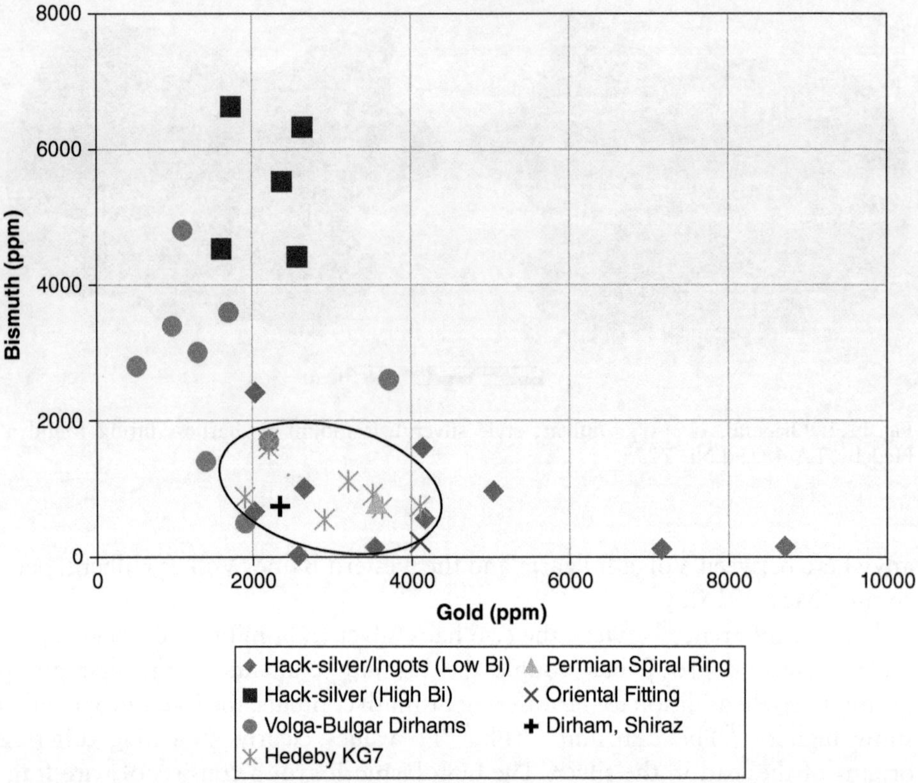

Fig. 11.3. Comparison of gold and bismuth contents of select finds measured by single collector ICP-MS and ns-LA-ICP-MS. The ellipse encloses the range of compositions of the Malmer KG7 Hedeby coins.

Of all the silver analysed, the only silver found that may be related to the Malmer KG7 are of eastern origin or are hack-silver fragments and ingots. The low bismuth content of the KG7 indicates that it is unrelated to the Samanid silver of Central Asia and Afghanistan, which regularly has significant amounts of this element. Despite the fact that Samanid silver entered circulation in the Baltic quickly in the early tenth century (Blackburn 2008, 41), it does not appear to have been a source for southern Scandinavian coinage in the first decades of the tenth century. Western silver dating to the turn of the tenth century is rare at Hedeby. An Anglo-Saxon silver strap end of the Trewhiddle style found at Füsing (Dobat 2010, cat. no. 1310), a site about 7 kilometres from Hedeby, is roughly dated to AD 850–925. The composition based on pXRF results is slightly debased, with a brass-bronze mixture common in Anglo-Saxon alloys of the second half of the ninth century and the lead isotope ratios of this object measured by laser ablation are consistent with lead ore from Derbyshire and the Mendips (see Rohl 1996) and do not match the Malmer KG7. The KG7 lead isotope ratios are dissimilar to all of the major lead and silver deposits in the

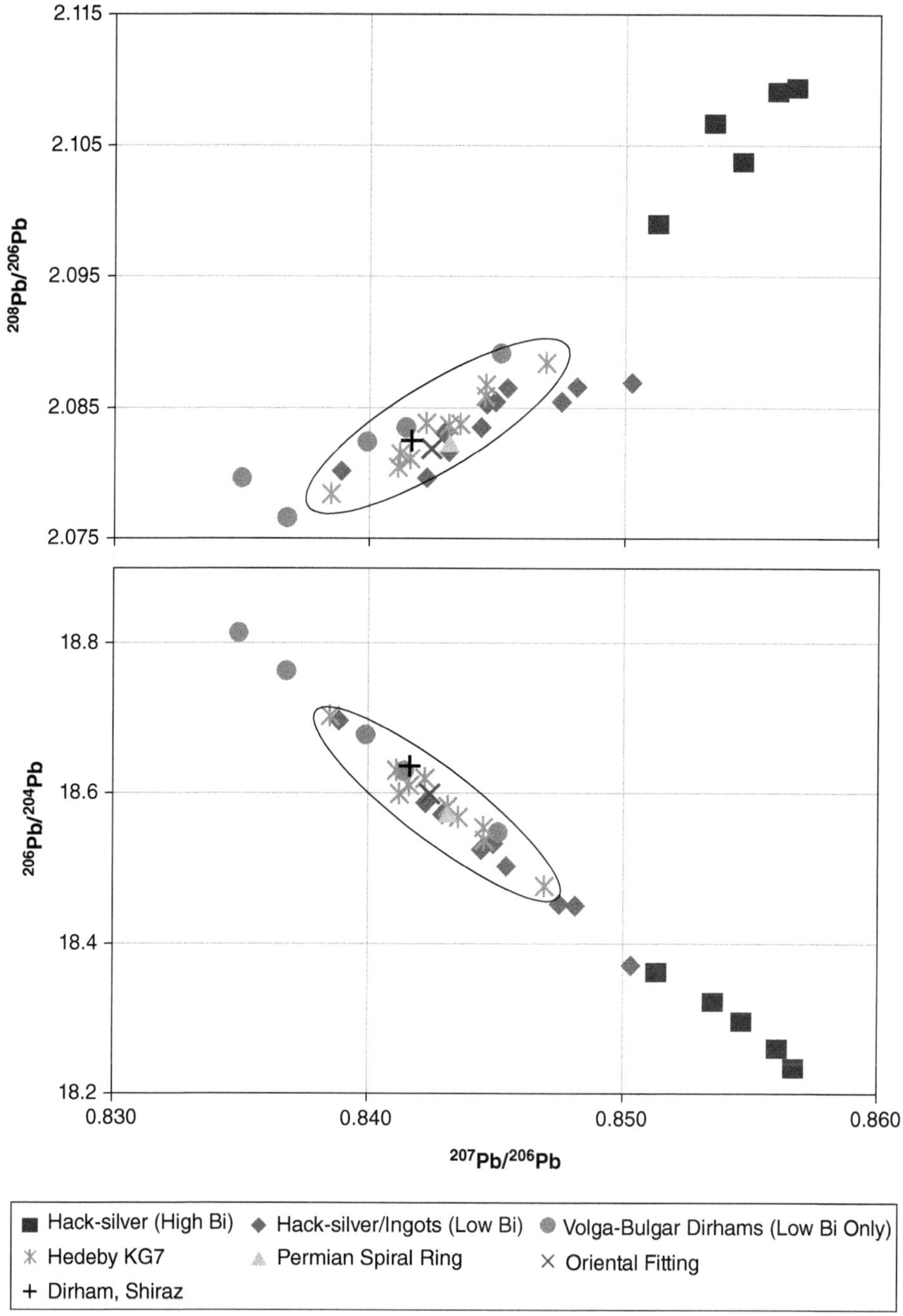

Fig. 11.4. Lead isotope diagram of select objects compared to the Malmer KG7 Hedeby coins (encircled). The lead isotope ratios were measured by multi-collector ICP-MS and by femtosecond LA-ICP-MCMS. Analytical error of two standard deviations is smaller than the symbol.

Rhenish Massif, the Harz, and the British Isles, as well as the Carolingian mine of Melle (see Lehmann 2011; Rohl 1996; Téreygeol et al. 2005). Therefore, it appears that the silver used for the KG7 was not refined with lead originating from any of these sources. When interpreting the alloy and lead isotope ratios of the KG7 and the Volga-Bulgar dirham imitations, it should be made clear that these are most likely mixtures of silver from several origins, whether it is the recycling of hack-silver at Hedeby or the recycling of Kufic dirhams in Bulgar, respectively. The range of compositions and isotope ratios should therefore be smaller than the range of the silver objects recycled, although there are parallels between the lead isotope ratios of the KG7 and Sassanian silver that possibly originates in Iran. Theoretically, the right mixture of silver from various regions could also produce lead isotope ratios similar to Sassanian silver and the KG7. We should not fully exclude the possibility that silver from western Europe formed at least a minor part of this mixture. Presently, however, the data available does not support the option that the KG7 silver is on a mixing line with western European sources. To sum up, the KG7 appears to be made from a stock of silver of primarily eastern origin (perhaps with ties to Iran) that entered the Baltic region in the late ninth century and clearly predates the widespread use of Samanid silver in the tenth century.

Conclusions

Silver of the Viking Age was constantly in motion. Underlying patterns in silver compositions and lead isotope ratios have been and are continually being identified, allowing for the linkage and differentiation of objects and coinages, and can be useful in reconstructing the movement of silver. Compositions seem to be highly time sensitive, but there also appears to be a delay from when new silver types begin to emerge to when they dominate the silver stock. If Samanid silver did begin to be traded in the Baltic area shortly after AD 900, as Blackburn suggests (2008, 41), then it does not seem to have made much of an impact on the silver stock used to make the Malmer KG7 at Hedeby. Instead, it seems that an older stock was used, perhaps that used by Volga-Bulgaria, Russia, and the Baltic region just before the large-scale import of Samanid silver. The origins of this silver are not entirely clear; it may stem from late ninth-century Iranian silver or it may be a more complex mixture stemming primarily from the Islamic East.

The various analytical methods used to study silver each have their benefits and disadvantages. The methods do not always produce comparable or reliable results and this is particularly the case for non-destructive surface analyses. The ability to take samples destructively is almost essential for provenance studies, and the growing use of high-resolution mass spectrometry and development of certified silver standards emulating archaeological alloys, such as the MBH Analytical 133x AGA1–3 (Thomas Birch, pers. comm. June 2016), together with interlaboratory collaboration will be responsible for great advancements in the production of dependable and comparable analytical data.

There is certainly much more work to do to increase the amount and improve the quality of available data, which is required to produce a statistically valid and representative basis. Careful data selection for comparison is also necessary to filter out the 'noise' of the vast amounts of data on various ore deposits and compositions of objects, some of which may not be archaeologically relevant or produced with less sensitive analytical methods. Some of the most important factors to consider include the evidence/chronology of mining and evidence of export from potentially silver-producing regions, evidence of contact in the material culture, extent and quality of the ore geology/metal characterization, and the metallurgical technologies in common use. Despite this, there remains great potential in the approaches discussed in this chapter for advancing the understanding of the movement of silver in the Viking Age.

ACKNOWLEDGEMENTS

I gratefully acknowledge the work of Lutz Ilisch and Volker Hilberg for the identification of coins and artefacts from Hedeby. Additionally, I would like to thank Robert Lehmann and Daniel Fellenger of the Leibniz Universität Hannover, Michael Bode of the Deutsches Bergbau-Museum Bochum, Sabine Klein of the Goethe-Universität Frankfurt am Main, and Guillaume Sarah of the French National Centre for Scientific Research in Orleans for their analytical work. Lastly, I would like to thank the anonymous reviewer and Jane Kershaw for helpful comments that have improved the quality of this chapter.

REFERENCES

Arles, A. 2009. 'Entre monnayage officiel et faux-monnayage. La fabrication de la monnaie au marteau en France (XIII–XVII siècles)'. Doctoral thesis, Université d'Orléans https://tel.archives-ouvertes.fr/tel-00418642v1.

Beck, L., S. Bosonnet, S. Réveillon, D. Eliot, & F. Pilon 2004. 'Silver Surface Enrichment of Silver-Copper-alloys: A Limitation for the Analysis of Ancient Silver Coins by Surface Techniques'. *Nuclear Instruments and Methods in Physics Research B* 226: 153–62.

Blackburn, M. 2008. 'The Coin-Finds'. In *Means of Exchange: Dealing with Silver in the Viking Age*, ed. D. Skre, 29–74. Kaupang Excavation Project Publication Series, Volume 2. Aarhus: Aarhus University Press.

Brøgger, A.W. 1921. 'Ertog og Øre: Den Gamle Norske Vegt'. *Videnskapsselskapets skrifter. II, Historiks-foliosofisk klasse, Vol. 3*. Kristiania: Dybwad.

Cowell, M.R. & N.M. Lowick 1988. 'Silver from the Panjhīr Mines'. In *Metallurgy in Numismatics, Vol. 2*, ed. W. A. Oddy, 65–74. London: Royal Numismatic Society.

Dobat, A.S. 2010. 'Füsing: Ein Frühmittelalterlicher Zentralplatz im Umfeld von Haithabu/Schleswig'. In *Studien zu Haithabu und Füsing*, ed. C. von Carnap-Bornheim, 129–256. Neumünster: Wachholtz.

Gale, N.H. 2009. 'A Response to the Paper of A.M. Pollard: What a Long, Strange Trip it's Been: Lead Isotopes and Archaeology'. In Shortland, Freestone, & Rehren (eds), 191–6.

Gale, N.H. & Z. Stos-Gale 2000. 'Lead Isotope Analysis Applied to Provenance Studies'. In *Modern Analytical Methods in Art and Archaeology*, ed. E. Ciliberto & G. Spoto, 503–84. New York: Wiley.

Gondonneau, A. & M.F. Guerra 2002. 'The Circulation of Precious Metals in the Arab Empire: The Case of the Near and the Middle East'. *Archaeometry* 44.4: 573–99.

Gordus, A.A. 1972. 'Neutron Activation Analysis of Coins and Coin Streaks'. In *Methods of Chemical and Metallurgical Investigations of Ancient Coinage*, ed. E.T. Hall & D.M. Metcalf, 127–48. London: Royal Numismatic Society.

Graham-Campbell, J. & G. Williams (eds) 2007. *Silver Economy in the Viking Age*. Walnut Creek: Left Coast Press.

Hårdh, B. 2007. 'Oriental–Scandinavian Contacts on the Volga, as Manifested by Silver Rings and Weight Systems'. In Graham-Campbell & Williams (eds), 135–48.

Hawthorne, J.G. & C.S. Smith 1979. *Theophilus on the Diverse Arts: The Foremost Medieval Treatise on Painting, Glassmaking and Metalwork*. New York: Dover Publications.

Ilisch, L., S. Lorenz, W.B. Stern, & H. Steuer 2003. *Dirham und Rappenpfennig. Mittelalterliche Münzprägung in Bergbauregionen. Zeitschrift für Archäologie des Mittelalters, Beiheft* 17. Bonn: Rudolf Habelt.

L'Héritier, M., S. Baron, L. Cassayre, & F. Téreygeol 2015. 'Bismuth Behaviour During Ancient Process of Silver-Lead Production'. *Journal of Archaeological Science* 57 (May): 56–68.

Lehmann, R. 2011. 'Archäometallurgie von Mittelalterlichen Deutschen Silberbarren und Münzen'. Doctoral thesis, Leibniz Universität Hannover. http://edok01.tib.uni-hannover.de/edoks/e01dh11/646461346.pdf.

Lowick, N.M. 1975. 'An Early Tenth Century Hoard from Isfahan'. *Numismatic Chronicle* 7: 110–54.

Malmer, B. 2007. 'South Scandinavian Coinage in the Ninth Century'. In Graham-Campbell & Williams (eds), 13–28.

McKerrel, H. & R.B.K. Stevenson 1972. 'Some Analyses of Anglo-Saxon and Associated Oriental Silver Coinage'. In *Methods of Chemical and Metallurgical Investigation of Ancient Coinage*, ed. E.T. Hall and D.M. Metcalf, 195–209. London: Royal Numismatic Society.

Merkel, S. 2016. *Silver and the Silver Economy at Hedeby*. Rahden: Marie Leidorf.

Merkel, S., L. Sverchkov, A. Hauptmann, V. Hilberg, M. Bode, & R. Lehmann 2013. 'Analysis of Slag, Ore and Silver from the Tashkent and Samarkand Areas: Medieval Silver Production and the Coinage of Samanid Central Asia'. In *Archäometrie und Denkmalpflege 2013, Metalla*, Sonderheft 6, ed. A. Hauptmann, O. Mecking, & M. Prange, 62–6. Bochum: Deutsches Bergbau Museum.

Metcalf, D.M. & P. Northover 1985. 'Debasement of the Coinage in Southern England in the Age of King Alfred'. *Numismatic Chronicle* 145: 150–76.

Metcalf, D.M. & P. Northover 1986. 'Interpreting the Alloy of the Later Anglo-Saxon Coinage'. *British Numismatic Journal* 56: 35–63.

Metcalf, D.M. & P. Northover 1988. 'Carolingian and Viking Coins from the Cuerdale Hoard: An Interpretation and Comparison of their Metal Contents'. *Numismatic Chronicle* 148: 97–116.

Metcalf, D.M. & P. Northover 1989. 'Coinage Alloys from the Time of Offa and Charlemagne to *c.* 864'. *Numismatic Chronicle* 149: 101–20.

Metcalf, D.M. & P. Northover 2002. 'Sporadic Debasement in English Coinage, *c.* 1009–1052'. *Numismatic Chronicle* 162: 217–36.

Meyers, P. 2003. 'Production of Silver in Antiquity: Ore Types Identified Based Upon Elemental Compositions of Ancient Silver Artifacts'. In *Patterns and Process: A Festschrift in Honor of D. Edward V. Sayre*, ed. L. van Zelst, 271–88. Suitland, Md.: Smithsonian.

Mortimer, C. 1986. 'Early Use of Brass in Silver Alloys'. *Oxford Journal of Archaeology* 5.2: 233–42.

Negmatov, N.N. 1998. 'The Samanid State'. In *History of Civilizations of Central Asia: The Age of Achievement:* A.D. *750 to the End of the Fifteenth Century. Vol. 4*, ed. M.S. Asimov & C.E. Bosworth, 83–101. Paris: UNESCO.

Noonan, T. 2001. 'Volga Bulghāria's Tenth-Century Trade with Sāmānid Central Asia'. *Archivum Eurasiae Medii Aevi* 11: 140–218.

Pernicka, E. 2014. 'Provenance Determination of Archaeological Metal Objects'. In *Archaeometallurgy in Global Perspective: Methods and Syntheses*, ed. B.W. Roberts & C.P. Thornton, 239–68. Heidelberg: Springer.

Pernicka, E. & H.-G. Bachmann 1983. 'Archäometallurgische Untersuchungen zur Antiken Silbergewinnung in Laurion: III. Das Verhalten einiger Spurenelemente beim Abtreiben des Bleis'. *Erzmetall* 36.12: 592–7.

Pernicka, E., T.C. Seeliger, G.A. Wagner, F. Begemann, S. Schmitt-Strecker, C. Eibner, O. Oztunali, & I. Baranyi 1984. 'Archäometallurgische Untersuchungen in Nordwestanatolien'. *Jahrbuch des Römisch-Germanischen Zentralmuseums* 31: 533–99.

Pollard, A.M. 2009. 'What a Long, Strange Trip it's Been: Lead Isotopes and Archaeology'. In Shortland, Freestone, & Rehren (eds), 181–9.

Rohl, B.M. 1996. 'Lead Isotope Data from the Isotrace Laboratory, Oxford: Archaeometry Data Base 2, Galena from Britain and Ireland'. *Archaeometry* 38.1: 165–80.

Sarah, G. 2010. 'Charlemagne, Charles the Bald and the Karolus Monogram Coinage: A Multi-Disciplinary Study'. *Numismatic Chronicle* 170: 227–86.

Shortland, A.J., I.C. Freestone, & T. Rehren (eds) 2009. *From Mine to Microscope: Advances in the Study of Ancient Technology*. Oxford: Oxbow.

Steuer, H. 2003. 'Schatzfunde mit Münzen und/oder Hacksilber aus dem Ostseeraum'. In Ilisch et al. (eds), 127–49.

Steuer, H., W.B. Stern, & G. Goldenberg 2002. 'Der Wechsel von der Münzgeld- zur Gewichtsgeldwirtschaft in Haithabu um 900 und die Herkunft des Münzsilbers im 9. und 10. Jahrhundert'. In *Haithabu und die Frühe Stadtentwicklung im Nördlichen Europa*, ed. M. Müller-Wille, C. Radtke, & K. Brandt, 133–67. Neumünster: Wachholtz.

Stos-Gale, Z.A. 2001. 'The Impact of the Natural Sciences on Studies of Hacksilber and Early Silver Coinages'. In *Hacksilber to Coinage: New Insights into the Monetary*

History of the Near East and Greece, ed. M.S. Balmuth, 53–76. New York: American Numismatic Society.

Téreygeol, F., S. Hoelzl, & P. Horn 2005. 'Journee archéologique de Melle—Le monnayage de Melle au haut moyen âge: état de la recherche'. *Association des Archéologues de Poitou-Charentes, Bulletin de Liaison et d'Information* 34: 49–56.

Wiechmann, R. 1996. *Edelmetalldepots der Wikingerzeit in Schleswig-Holstein. Vom 'Ringbrecher' zur Münzwirtschaft. Offa Bücher* 77. Neumünster: Wachholtz.

Wiechmann, R. 2007. 'Haithabu und sein Hinterland—ein Lokaler Numimatischer Raum? Münzen und Münzfunde aus Haithabu (bis zum Jahr 2002)'. In *Das Archäologische Fundmaterial VIII. Ausgrabungen in Haithabu*, Vol. 36, ed. K. Schietzel, 182–278. Neumünster: Wachholtz.

Yener, K.A., E.V. Sayre, E.C. Joel, H. Özbal, I.L. Barnes, & R.H. Brill 1991. 'Stable Lead Isotope Studies of Central Taurus Ore Sources and Related Artifacts from Eastern Mediterranean Chalcolithic and Bronze Age Sites'. *Journal of Archaeological Science* 18: 541–77.

12

Gold as a Means of Exchange in Scandinavian England (*c.*AD 850–1050)

Jane Kershaw

It is widely accepted that gold and silver were used in different ways in Scandinavia and the Scandinavian territories during the Viking Age (*c.*AD 800–1100). Whereas silver had a fluid and versatile role, as a means of display, wealth storage and medium of payment, gold, it is conventionally argued, functioned mainly as prestige jewellery, to be gifted, worn in public demonstrations of wealth and power, and, sometimes, sacrificed (Hårdh 1996; Graham-Campbell 2011a). In this chapter, I offer a different perspective, highlighting archaeological evidence for the potentially monetary use of gold in Scandinavian England from the late ninth to early eleventh century. In doing so, I aim to further understanding of the diverse material forms 'money' could take in this period, to provide a more rounded and accurate view of Viking Age exchange.

There are two compelling reasons why the monetary role of gold in particular deserves new investigation. First, the late Mark Blackburn demonstrated that gold was more available in northern Europe in the ninth century than in the centuries immediately before or after, and it is worthwhile to consider whether this increased availability encouraged a shift in the standing and function of gold from ornament to means of exchange (2007, 78–9). Second, an expanding corpus of reported metal-detector finds from areas of Scandinavian settlement in England has brought to light fresh data requiring interpretation. Using this new data, and approaching existing material from a novel perspective, I argue that Scandinavian settlers in England practised a bi-metallic bullion economy incorporating a limited amount of gold alongside silver, particularly during the ninth century. I aim to demonstrate a monetary role for gold in commercial transactions, in which the primary aim was to exchange material goods, as distinct from what might be termed social transactions, in which payments were made primarily to transform social relationships and smooth social tensions (e.g. fines, bridewealth, gifts to followers) (Williams 2011, 350–1; Graeber 2012). The monetary use of gold in commercial contexts is suggested by the presence of hack-gold, gold ingots, and, less certainly, complete items of jewellery that are tested and, often, weight-adjusted. Such finds occupy the opposite end of the spectrum to finely fragmented hack-silver and hint at the existence of, and need for, high-value bullion exchange. This material is introduced here for the first time, following a brief review of the current evidence for the monetary use of gold during the Viking Age in the wider Scandinavian world.

The Scandinavian Background

Whereas gold dominated precious-metal deposits in Migration-period Scandinavia, the Viking Age was a 'Silver Age'. Across Scandinavia and the Scandinavian territories, gold was scarce in comparison to the vast silver wealth known from Viking-period finds (Blackburn 2007, 75). But the memory of gold lived on: in Old Norse sources, gold, unlike silver, is endowed with mythical power and symbolic meaning. In his *Prose Edda*, Snorri Sturluson poetically describes the origins of gold as Freyja's tears, Sif's hair, and Ægir's fire. Silver has no such mythological associations (Zachrisson 1998, 30). The desire to acquire gold often drives the narrative of Old Norse stories. Gold objects are named, they are given and received as a way of building social relationships and political alliances; they may also be cursed (Hedeager 2011, 144–5). As the 'fire of the hawk's ground (arm)', gold arm-rings had a special status in ritualized gift-giving, their weight providing an important index to their value (Zachrisson 1998, 29).

There are several indications in the archaeological record that gold functioned differently to silver, and possessed little or no monetary role. Within Scandinavia gold and silver rarely appear in hoards together. Birgitta Hårdh has remarked on the tendency for gold items to be deposited either 'singly or together with other gold objects' (1996, 132), a pattern confirmed by several regional analyses of Viking Age precious-metal deposits (Hårdh 1976, 31; Zachrisson 1998, 85; Stenberger 1933, 79; Rundkvist 2011, 158–64; Wideen 1955, 278–9; Munksgaard 1962, 109). Separate deposits of gold and silver are also characteristic in overseas Viking territories (Graham-Campbell 1976, Appendix C; 1995, 1). A compelling example is provided by two late ninth-/early tenth-century hoards from Hare Island on Lough Ree in the River Shannon, Co. Westmeath, Ireland. Deposited only a few metres apart, the (now lost) hoards are monometallic, one consisting entirely of gold and the other exclusively of silver. James Graham-Campbell has proposed that the two were nonetheless deposited at the same time, implying the deliberate separation of metals prior to deposition (1974, 272; see Sheehan, this volume).

Gold was, of course, much rarer than silver, and much more valuable, at around ten to twelve times its worth (Steuer 2004, 116, note 1). It was, therefore, far less convenient than silver as a medium of exchange, with even small pieces of gold worth substantial sums. Despite gold's high value, which—if used as currency—might be expected to result in its fragmentation into smaller units, gold items are usually complete. In both bullion hoards and at Scandinavian trade sites, items of hack-gold (deliberately cut pieces from gold ornaments and ingots) are rare, though numbers are increasing (see below). The same is true of gilded silver objects, including Carolingian imports, a pattern that suggests that the primary function of gold was one of display and ornamentation (Hårdh 1996, 133). Moreover, gold items usually take the form of wearable ornaments, especially arm- and finger-rings (Zachrisson 1998, 86). Gold ingots, which might, like their silver counterparts, serve as a non-ornamental store of wealth and a ready source of hack-gold, are extremely rare. The handful of examples that are known are complete and appear to relate to gold-working (cf. examples from Avaldsnes, Norway, and Gnezdovo, Russia: AMS sf60812; Eniosova 2007, 177–8, fig. 10; a cut gold ingot is known from Hedeby, but is also linked to a workshop: Armbruster 2002, 132, Abb. 22.1–2).

Finally, deposits of gold were frequently sited in or near watery places, such as rivers, marshes and bogs, or beaches (Zachrisson 1998, 117–18). Within Scandinavia, 'more gold than silver objects are reported to have been found in water or on the shore or beach of a lake', despite the fact that silver is much more common (Hårdh 1996, 134). This is the case, for instance, with the largest surviving, and most famous, gold hoard from Hoen, Buskerud, Norway, which was wrapped in a cloth and deposited in a peat bog during the late ninth century (Mikkelsen 2006, 29, 37). A similar association has been noted for Viking Age gold deposits from Scotland, while in Ireland all but one Viking Age gold hoard has a connection with water or a watery place (Graham-Campbell 1995, 60, 164; Graham-Campbell & Sheehan 2009, 81; see too Oras, Leimus, and Joosu, this volume). The implication is that such deposits, being awkward if not impossible to retrieve, were made without the intention of recovery, potentially for votive reasons.[1] The cumulative evidence thus suggests that gold served first and foremost as 'gifts and marks of honour and . . . suitable objects of sacrifice' (Hårdh 1996, 134).

Despite these broad trends, there are hints that gold could occasionally function as a means of payment, as well as ornament. In the Viking period, as in the centuries before, both gold and silver rings could be weight-adjusted (Brøgger 1921, 29–41; Fonnesbech-Sandberg 1988; Lundström 1973, but see Hårdh 1996, 142). Indeed, all eight (more or less) complete Viking Age gold neck-rings known from Scandinavia are weight-adjusted, to a unit of around

[1] This interpretation certainly finds support in the case of a gold ingot hoard, deposited in Cullen bog, Co. Tipperary, Ireland. This bog is referred to in antiquarian accounts as the 'Golden Bog', because of the large number of gold and bronze antiquities discovered within it (Wallace 1938). Many date from the Bronze Age, suggesting that this expanse of still water served as a long-standing focus for ritual metalwork deposition. It is nonetheless salutary to note that a second Viking Age hoard, composed entirely of silver, is also recorded from the same location (Graham-Campbell & Sheehan 2009, 80).

100 grams (Graham-Campbell 2006) (Table 12.1). Weight analysis of sixty complete hoarded gold arm-rings from Norway, Denmark, and Sweden reveals that such items were also frequently, although not uniformly, manufactured to a weight based on the same 25 g unit, particularly its multiples: 50 and 100 g (Fig. 12.1). Alignment with these weights is not exact, and there is a diffuse distribution of weights between 50 and 100 g, but the evident grouping at 50, 100, and, to a lesser extent, 200 g, suggests that there was often an attempt to correlate gold arm-rings with set weight standards, even if that standard was not always precisely realized. The manufacture of such weight-adjusted jewellery clearly involved the weighing of gold. Unn Pedersen has suggested lead and copper weights with gold inlays, as recorded at Kaupang, Norway, and Birka, Sweden, may have been instrumental in this regard (2008, 168).

There is little doubt that complete, weight-adjusted rings served as a form of high-denomination currency in what might be termed social transactions: for

Table 12.1. Complete gold neck-rings from Scandinavia.

Location	Find context and date	Weight (g)
Vester Vedsted, Jutland, Denmark	Hoard, 914/43	196
Vester Vedsted, Jutland, Denmark	Hoard, 914/43	103.5
Tissø, Zealand, Denmark	Single find, tenth century	1830 (c.2 kg originally)
Fjälkestad, Skåne, Sweden	Single find	173.7
Hiddensee, Rügen, Germany	Hoard, late tenth century	152.8
Hoen, Buskerud, Norway	Hoard, late ninth century	408
Hoen, Buskerud, Norway	Hoard, late ninth century	1105
Hæstad, Vester-Agder, Norway	Hoard, tenth century	213.85

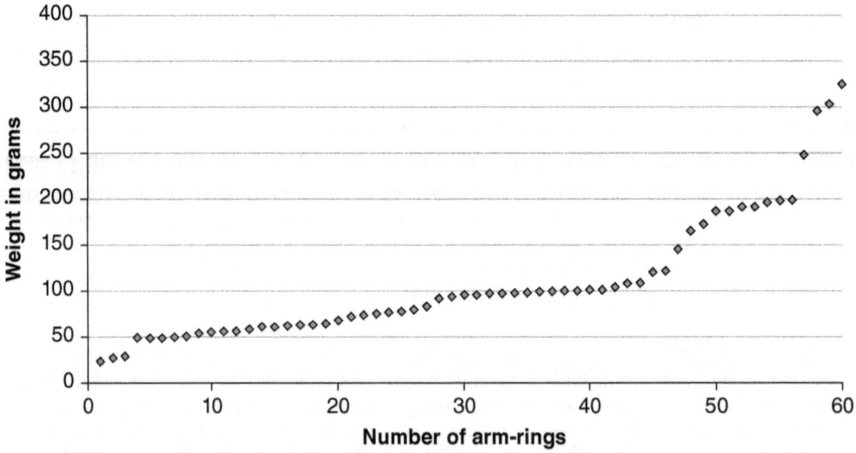

Fig. 12.1. The weight distribution of sixty hoarded gold arm-rings from Denmark, Norway, and Sweden (data from Skovmand 1942; Grieg 1929; Hårdh 1976 and Munksgaard 1962).

payments 'primarily in support of the social relationship between the parties to the transaction, rather than exclusively for any directly economic purpose' (Williams 2011, 350). These could encapsulate payments for fines, including compensation payments for murder, which the Icelandic and medieval Norwegian law codes indicate were settled in rings, gifts bestowed on followers or poets, also described in documentary sources in ring form, as well as bridal wealth and other marriage payments (Gaimster 1991; Kilger 2008, 315–16; Ager 2011; Sindbæk 2011). Documentary references to 'oath-rings' made to a certain weight, upon which pledges were sworn in public meetings, also imply a ritualistic and legal role for wearable gold or silver arm-rings (Graham-Campbell 2007, 217–18; 2011c, 111).

In certain contexts, complete gold rings may have served as currency for use in commercial exchange, a category that encapsulates payments for goods and services, including rents, taxes, and wages (Williams 2011, 351). Eniosova views a group of twenty-one plain, penannular, weight-adjusted gold arm-rings from Scandinavian contexts in southern Rus as a form of currency (2007). Her interpretation is supported by the presence of testing marks on the rings, as well as their uniform appearance and occasionally fragmented state. The suggestion is that, in the southern Rus, gold rings facilitated trade with Byzantium, where gold served as the basis for local currency. In the Scandinavian countries, complete, weight-adjusted gold rings occasionally occur in predominantly silver bullion hoards (that is, hoards with a substantial hack-silver component), raising the possibility that they too had a direct commercial currency role, presumably for high-value transactions involving goods such as land, livestock, or other bulk purchases. Thus, seven weight-adjusted gold neck- and arm-rings along with two weight-adjusted cut rods, appear alongside various items of hack-silver and ten silver dirhams in the Danish hoard from Vester Vedsted, Ribe (*tpq* 914/43) (Skovmand 1942, 71–4). A further example can be found in the seven complete, weight-adjusted gold arm-rings, found with other gold and silver objects, hack-silver, and dirhams, in a hoard from Erikstorp, Östergötland, Sweden (*tpq* 956) (SHM 5671).

However, in general it seems clear that complete gold ornaments were not used primarily for commercial purposes, but, as with many other widely employed social currencies (beads, shells, feathers), as a means of adornment (Graeber 2012). Tellingly, testing by means of 'nicking' the ring to expose plated forgeries and/or to test gold content by means of a resistance test, is not a common feature of gold rings from Scandinavia (unlike those from England, discussed below), although in the absence of a comprehensive survey, the frequency of nicking on gold remains unknown. A notable exception is provided by at least two of the seven weight-adjusted twisted-rod arm-rings from the mixed silver/gold hoard from Erikstorp, Sweden (SHM 5671). Also rare is the fragmentation of gold rings into smaller units more convenient for exchange. And while Scandinavian gold rings usually possess a simple construction, they are ornamental, often composed of pairs of twisted or plaited rods, with variously constructed terminals and, occasionally, stamped decoration. These features suggest that such items were primarily intended to be worn: it was only in exceptional circumstances that complete gold jewellery circulated as currency in commercial settings.

Firmer evidence for the monetary use of gold alongside silver is found in the small corpus of hack-gold from Scandinavia. The deliberate fragmentation of ingots and ornaments into small units of hack-metal is one of the hallmarks of a metal-weight economy, with most scholars accepting a direct relationship between the degree of fragmentation and the intensity with which the metal circulated in transactions (Hårdh 1996). Hack-gold is rare in bullion hoards from the Viking Age, but there are notable exceptions in which hack-gold appears together with hack-silver. The tenth-century Danish hoard from Oster Mose, Viskum, contains two cut pieces of gold, one from a twisted-rod ring and one from a plain rod, along with both complete and hack-silver items (Skovmand 1942, 61–3, fig. 12). A large tenth-century Danish hoard (*tpq* 932) discovered between 1994 and 1997 in Ramløse, Zealand, is characterized by very finely fragmented silver. It also contains fifteen gold items, including four items of hack-gold, mainly cut pieces of twisted gold rods derived from arm-rings, and an incomplete and flattened gold 'pendant ring' (Pedersen & Grønnegaard 2012; NMC I 7785/95). A late Viking Age hoard from Vanneberga, Skåne, Sweden (*tpq* 1056), contains two cut pieces of twisted gold rod and two thin, linked rods of gold alongside two thin silver-wire rings and many silver coins (SHM 1373) (Fig. 12.2). That these gold items passed hands in commercial exchange is suggested by the fact that one of the cut gold rods is nicked. Even more unusually, a cut gold ingot is contained in a hack-silver hoard from Lilla Valla, Gotland (*tpq* 1048) (SHM 3099).[2]

The discovery of hack-gold within bullion hoards of Viking Age date implies that, in these instances, gold fulfilled a currency role alongside silver. Recognizing the monetary use of hack-gold at settlement sites is more problematic, since most potentially relevant items are detector-finds and derive from plough layers at sites with long lifespans. It can also be unclear whether the gold relates to exchange or metalworking. Thus, thirty-five pieces of gold are recorded from Uppåkra, Skåne, including items of hack-gold that could date to the Viking Age. Hårdh, however, connects all of the evidence with metalworking (2010, 291). Multiple fragments of cut gold rod and ingot are known from the Baltic island of Bornholm, including the enormously rich multi-period area of Sorte Muld

[2] A gold hoard containing six and a half finger-rings (one unfinished), two ingot fragments, and a section of cut rod is on record from the Hebrides, Scotland. It has been interpreted as 'the stock-in-trade of a goldsmith' and has a low occurrence of nicking, with contender 'nicks' on the rod section only (Graham-Campbell 1995, 55, cat. no. 25, pl. 50a). Nonetheless, a partial bullion function for the contents cannot be ruled out.

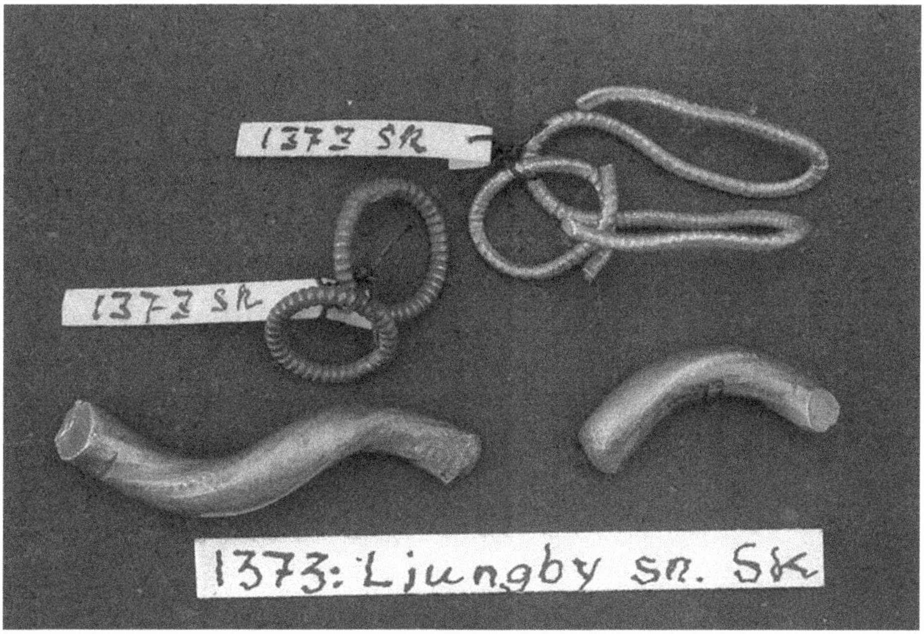

Fig. 12.2. Hack-gold contained in the Vanneberga, Skåne hoard.
Photo: Ulf Bruxe, the Swedish History Museum.

(Thorsen 2009). Many pieces are likely to date to the Migration period, but some fragments, such as a cut gold ring found together with a pierced dirham and cut German silver coin in Klinten Syd, Vestemarie, are candidates for Viking Age pieces and could relate to exchange (NMC 37007). Without greater contextualization and chronological resolution, however, the precise function of such pieces cannot be proved.

The Monetary Use of Gold in Viking Age England

In Scandinavian England, the evidence for the monetary use of gold in commercial settings is more substantial. Recent research has demonstrated that the Scandinavians maintained a thriving bullion economy in England, despite also issuing official coin (Kershaw 2017). That this bullion economy involved occasional payments in gold, alongside silver, is suggested by three sources of evidence: hack-gold, gold ingots, and, less certainly, complete gold ornaments that have also been tested.

Hack-gold

In England hack-gold derived from Scandinavian forms of ornament and ingot occurs at settlement and single finds, as well as in a single hoard, suggesting that gold fulfilled a limited role in exchange alongside silver. It is notable that most assemblages containing hack-gold date to the late ninth century, and are associated directly with the military activities of the *micel here* (Great Army). The majority of the evidence for hack-gold comes from Torksey, Lincolnshire, the documented location of a Viking military camp in AD 872/3 and a site that has seen extensive metal-detecting over the last three decades. Torksey has yielded extensive evidence of silver bullion use, including fragmented dirhams, regulated, copper-alloy weights (both cubo-octahedrals and oblate-spheroids), silver ingots, and ingot- and ornament-derived hack-silver (Blackburn 2011). The corpus of hack-gold from the site is also significant. In 2011, Mark Blackburn was aware of thirteen items, including multiple cut pieces from gold ingots and rods, two of which appear to derive from arm-rings, a cut piece of a Frisian gold solidus, and a cut quarter of gold solidus of Louis the Pious (2011, 233). Subsequent metal-detecting at the site has yielded five further finds: two further cut gold ingots (Fig. 12.3a) (PAS 'Find-ID' DENO-938F91; SWYOR-8A8324), a square piece of gold with distinctive punched circles, cut from the bezel of a finger-ring (Fig. 12.3b) (BM 2007,8035.1), a bent and cut section of faceted gold rod (SWYOR-C74077), and a rectangular fragment of otherwise

(a)

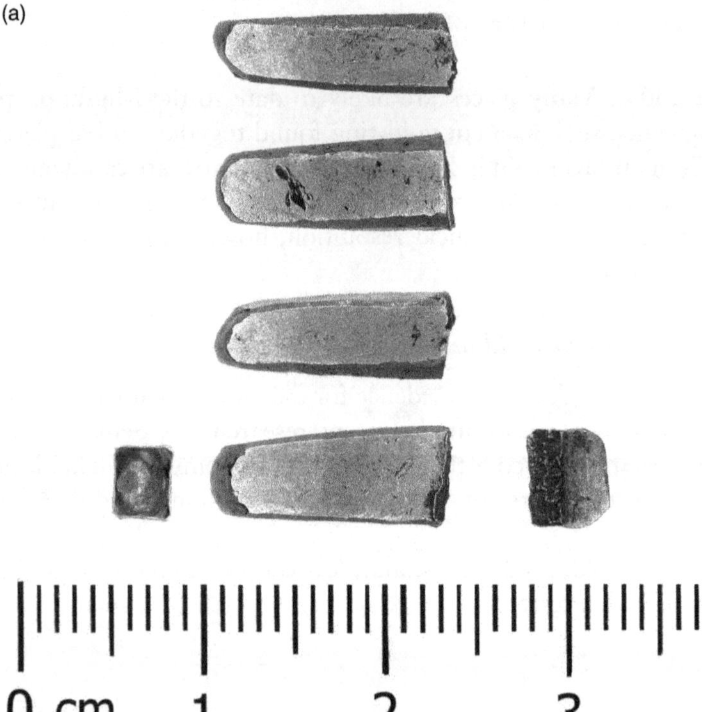

Fig. 12.3(a). A cut gold ingot from Torksey, Lincolnshire.
Photo: Portable Antiquities Scheme.

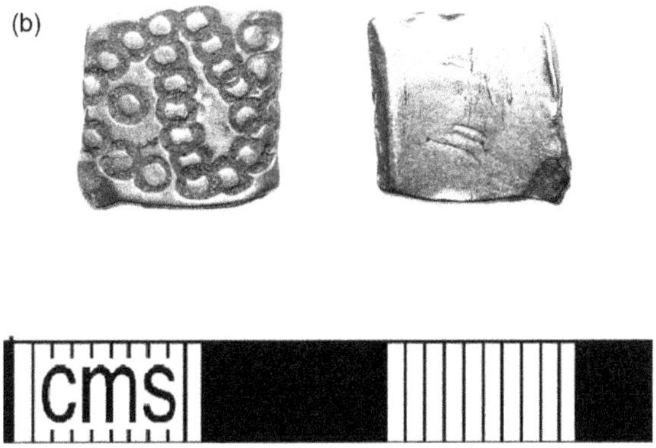

Fig. 12.3(b). A cut piece from a gold finger-ring from Torksey, Lincolnshire.
Photo: Portable Antiquities Scheme.

unidentifiable gold (SWYOR-DCD80F). The comparable camp site known as 'A Riverine Site Near York' (ARSNY), currently dated on the basis of coin evidence to the mid-to-late 870s, has yielded two equivalent items of hack-gold, both cut fragments of round-sectioned rod, weighing 2.49 g and 0.86 g respectively, in addition to multiple finds of hack-silver, dirhams, and cubo-octahedral weights relating to a silver bullion economy (Williams 2014, figs 2–3; forthcoming). None of the hack-gold is nicked, but the items are such small pieces that evidence for such treatment is unlikely to survive.

It is possible that some or even all of the items were intended for melting down, rather than for use as currency, as gold-working is attested at Torksey (Blackburn 2011, 241). However, Torksey has also yielded three pieces of *fake* hack-gold, comprising an ingot and two rods with copper cores and gilded surfaces (weights: 3.87 g, 2.84 g, not recorded), as well as a lead sheet struck with dies for imitative Louis the Pious solidi, which Blackburn interprets as a trial piece for the production either of imitative solidi (in gold) or plated base-metal copies thereof (Blackburn 2011, 234, 242). Such counterfeit gold cannot have been intended for metalworking, and points to a role for gold in trade at Torksey.

An economic role for hack-gold is also supported by the recent (2015) discovery of a hoard of Scandinavian character from near Watlington, Oxfordshire. The hoard contained characteristically Scandinavian silver items in both complete and fragmentary forms and Anglo-Saxon and Carolingian coins, and is thus typical of a Viking bullion assemblage. Also included was a small cut piece of twisted gold rod (Williams & Naylor 2016, 11–12, fig. 23). Coins contained within the hoard include issues of Alfred the Great and his contemporary Ceolwulf II of Mercia, and suggest a date of deposition in *c.*879–80. This evidence, combined with the hoard's unusual location, in south Oxfordshire, has encouraged the view that the hoard was deposited shortly following Alfred's defeat of the Great Army at Edington, Wiltshire, in 878, perhaps during the army's move from Cirencester to East Anglia in 879 (Williams & Naylor 2016, 29–30). It can thus be interpreted within the same context of Viking military activity as the finds from Torksey and ARSNY detailed above.

In many ways evidence for the use of high-value currency by the Viking Great Army is unexpected. An interesting feature of silver bullion at both Torksey and ARSNY is its high degree of fragmentation. Not a single complete dirham is recorded at either site. The average weight of the ninety-three fragmentary dirhams known from Torksey in 2011 was just 0.44 g and that of the fourteen dirhams from ARSNY just 0.40 g: less than a sixth of a complete coin (weighing *c.*3 g) (Blackburn 2011, 230; Williams forthcoming). Given such low weights, one might expect bullion use at these sites to have been orientated towards low-value exchange of an everyday nature.[3] The finds of hack-gold occupy the opposite end of the currency spectrum, but it is worth noting that both the new and the older finds of hack-gold are very small pieces, all weighing less than 5 g (the weights of the more recent discoveries from Torksey are 0.74, 0.8, 1.13, 2, and 2.9 g). Such a high degree of fragmentation supports the view that gold was used intensively for trading at the site, in what appears to have been a flexible and versatile metal-weight economy, capable of accommodating exchange at a range of scales (Blackburn 2011, 233–4, table 1).

Additional single finds of hack-gold from England are presumed to be Scandinavian losses of the late ninth and early tenth centuries (Blackburn 2007, 75). The current corpus is not large, but includes a cut piece from a gold broad-band arm-ring, from West Wratting, Cambridgeshire (weighing 11.37 g), and three cut gold finger-rings: from Aldborough and Pocklington, Yorkshire, and Fransham, Norfolk (weights: 1, 2.61, and 1.27 g respectively) (Blackburn 2007, Appendix C9, 92–3; PAS 'Find-ID' NCL-BE0716; YORYM-6056B7; NMS-D7AC68). All may be dated on typological grounds to the late ninth or tenth century. In addition, there is a single gold ingot fragment, from Springthorpe, Lincolnshire, which is cut at both ends and nicked: a treatment highly suggestive of its use in financial transactions (see below, 'Test Marks on Gold') (Blackburn 2007, Appendix C4, 90, where it is mistakenly described as having no nicks). A number of other fragmentary gold ingots of characteristic Viking Age form have been recorded from England, but these are broken, rather than deliberately cut, and their status as hack-gold thus remains uncertain. All these finds are within the Danelaw region, and can be presumed to have formed part of the same economic sphere as hack-silver.

[3] In this context, it is worth speculating that the many brass stycas and copper-alloy ingots known from both Torksey and from ARSNY may have functioned as a base-metal bullion currency within a trimetallic metal-weight economy (Williams 2011, 353–4; forthcoming).

Gold Ingots

Given the potential for gold ingots to be transformed into hack-gold, it is worth highlighting the presence of ten complete gold ingots of characteristic Viking Age form from England (Table 12.2). Precise dating of these single finds is impossible, and it is cautioned that Bronze Age gold ingots have a similar appearance to those identified here as 'Viking' (cf. the gold ingot and bar fragments contained in the Late Bronze Age gold hoard from Fittleworth, West Sussex, now in the British Museum: BM 1996,0902 (Graham-Campbell 2011b, 84)). Nonetheless, several gold ingots, including a particularly fine example excavated from an unstratified context at the Millennium Library site in Norwich, have signs of transverse hammering, a feature encountered on some Viking Age silver ingots, but not on gold ingots securely dated to the Bronze Age (Blackburn 2007, C1, 89). This feature, together with the ingots' characteristic Scandinavian form (cigar shape, rounded ends, and regular oval, D-shaped or sub-rectangular sections) and their exclusively Danelaw distribution, makes it appropriate to view these ingots as Viking Age unless proved otherwise (following Graham-Campbell 2002, 57).

In the Scandinavian bullion economy silver ingots served multiple functions: as a first stage in the production of some forms of jewellery; a store of wealth suitable for cutting up when needed as currency; and a form of 'money in large units', which could be traded whole in commercial transactions (as demonstrated by the fact that complete ingots are often nicked). The hammering carried out on several of the complete gold ingots from England could suggest that some items were being prepared for fashioning into jewellery (cf. the broad-band arm-ring from West Wratting, Cambridgeshire, with fine transverse hammering, transformed into bullion). Indeed, the variable gold content of the ingots, ranging from 42 per cent to 91 per cent, is consistent with the range encountered in Viking Age gold jewellery, whereas we might expect gold ingots intended for use in commercial transactions to have a consistently high gold fineness

Table 12.2. Complete gold ingots from England. Here and in subsequent tables, hyphen indicates unknown.

Location	Weight	Gold fineness	Hammered	Nicked
Linton, Cambs.	3.31 g	–		
West Dereham, Norfolk	58.26 g	79%		
Fenstanton, Cambs.	38.57 g	77%		
Norwich, Norfolk	7.06 g	85%	x	
South Leverton, Notts.	8.13 g	89–91%	x	
Polesworth, War.	8.35 g	44–8%		
Southburn, Yorks.	18.16 g	81–4%	x	
Belton with Browston, Norfolk	12.28 g	–		
Norwell, Notts.	–	–		x
Beadlam, Yorks.	10.5 g	42%	x	x

(Eniosova 2009, table 1). However, my recent XRF analysis of three items of hack-gold from Torksey—two cut gold ingots and one cut gold rod—also revealed only moderate gold contents (69.09 per cent, 76.87 per cent, and 74.85 per cent respectively), the bulk of the remaining metal being silver. It is possible that the relative scarcity of gold made people more willing to accept debased gold in transactions of a commercial nature.

Gold ingots may have passed hands in commercial environments as complete objects. This is suggested by the fact that two complete gold ingots, from Norwell, Nottinghamshire (Fig. 12.4), and Beadlam, North Yorkshire, are nicked (PAS 'Find-ID' LIN-152759; YORYM-7706AD). Interestingly, both ingots are pale gold in colour, with the latter being composed of just 42 per cent gold, 47 per cent silver, and 11 per cent copper, and thus more accurately described as a silver-gold alloy (the ingot from Nottinghamshire has not yet been analysed). These items may have aroused suspicion because of their pale colour, but assuming that they circulated subsequent to testing, and were not discarded (in which case we might expect them to have been melted down), it would appear that debased gold ingots could circulate legitimately in what were presumably commercial settings (see below for a discussion of the function of nicking).

Fig. 12.4. A complete, nicked gold ingot from Norwell, Nottinghamshire.
Photo: Portable Antiquities Scheme.

Complete Gold Ornaments: Nicking and Weight Adjustment

While complete ingots had no obvious display function, wearable gold ornaments were prominent visual symbols of wealth and status. It is as display pieces that such ornaments have usually been interpreted, but there are hints that their role was more complex, and could on occasion encompass both display and bullion functions. This might be suggested for complete gold ornaments contained in predominantly silver bullion hoards that are weight-adjusted and/or have evidence for nicking. One example is a narrow-band gold arm-ring, weighing 46.7 g, from the Vale of York hoard (*tpq c.*927) (Ager 2011, 127, fig. 9). The arm-ring is complete, with no nicks, but its apparent weight adjustment to a 50 g unit, alongside its find context, suggests that it could have functioned as both wearable jewellery and an item of tradable bullion. Other objects from the hoard include both hack-silver and whole objects, including a gilded Carolingian silver vessel, in addition to 617 late ninth- and early tenth-century coins, suggesting a dual display/currency purpose for the assemblage as a whole (Ager & Williams 2011). The Halton Moor hoard, deposited *c.*1025, also contained a gilt silver cup, along with a weight-adjusted and heavily nicked silver neck-ring and six gold foil discs. Only two of the gold foils survive, but one has a contender test mark (Graham-Campbell 2011b, 239, cat. no. 4:3).[4] Conversely, the gold-inlays and rings that adorn an Anglo-Saxon iron sword pommel and hilt recently found along with mainly complete silver items in a late ninth- or early tenth-century hoard from Bedale, Yorkshire, form part of a prestige weapon, and seem more likely to have related exclusively to the 'display economy' (PAS 'Find-ID' YORYM-CEE620; Graham-Campbell 2011a).

Evidence for weight adjustment can also be found in the corpus of single finds of complete gold finger- and arm-rings from England. In addition to the gold arm-ring contained in the Vale of York hoard, six more or less complete Viking Age gold arm-rings are recorded singly. These discoveries date from the nineteenth century onwards and are relatively well known, but what has thus far escaped comment is the fact that several of the arm-rings show evidence for weight adjustment, to the same standard as gold rings from Scandinavia. A weight unit based on 25g, and its multiples of 50 and 100g, is manifest in five of the seven rings (Table 12.3).

Of particular interest is the unusual composite gold arm-ring 'assemblage' weighing 52.9 g from Shotton Hall, near Sunderland, County Durham (Graham-Campbell 2011b, 242, cat. no. 6). This piece, which 'defies exact classification' (Graham-Campbell 2011b, 91), is formed of a pair of twisted rods crudely linked

[4] One certain nick is also carried on one of two gold finger-rings of Scandinavian type contained in another eleventh-century mixed gold and silver hoard, from Soberton, Hampshire (Graham-Campbell 2011b, 243, cat. no. 7:3). The hoard post-dates Viking activity in England, but it is likely that the ring acquired its nick in Scandinavian hands, sometime before its eventual deposition.

Table 12.3. Complete gold arm-rings from England.

Location	Find context	Construction	Weight (g)	Nicks	Gold fineness	Association with water
Brightlingsea, Essex	Single find	twisted-rod	49.15	2	–	X
Eastbourne, Sussex	Single find	plaited-rod	82.3	*c.*12	–	X
Goodrington, Devon	Single find	twisted-rod	114.9	2	99%	X
Shotton Hall, Durham	Single find	twisted- and plain-rod	52.9	6	95–8%	
Wendover Dean, Bucks.	Single find	twisted-rod	144.2	*c.*4	–	
near York, Yorks.	Single find	twisted-rod	324.6	1	95%	–
Vale of York, Yorks.	Hoard (*tpq* 927)	band	46.7	0	94–7%	

Fig. 12.5. A gold arm-ring 'assemblage' from Shotton Hall, Durham (© Trustees of the British Museum).

via a short, looped rod to a cut piece from a plain annular arm-ring, which is bent back on itself so as to form a ring shape (Fig. 12.5). Notably, the twisted and plain rods have different alloy compositions, suggesting that two rings were not manufactured together, but were joined at a later stage (ibid., 102, 242). It is worth speculating that the unusual 'assemblage' was so formed for the purpose of achieving a weight of *c.* 50 grams.

As discussed above, weight adjustment does not, in itself, indicate that an item was intended for use in commercial transactions. But the case for the monetary status of the Shotton Hall 'assemblage' is strengthened by the fact that the ring(s) carries six nicks, across both the twisted and plain rods. Such test marks are rare on gold arm-rings within Scandinavia, but are a recurring feature on those from England: with the exception of the Vale of York ring, all have evidence for nicking, with the number of nicks per artefact ranging from one to *c.*twelve (Table 12.3). Nicking is also encountered on complete gold finger-rings of Viking Age date. From a total corpus of fifty-six complete gold finger-rings

Table 12.4. Nicked gold finger-rings from England.

Find location	Find context	Ring type	Nicks	Association with water	Gold fineness
Balmer, East Sussex	Single find	twisted-rod	2		–
Ivychurch, Kent	Single find	single-rod	1	X	94–6%
near Lewes/Ringmer, East Sussex	Single find	plaited-rod	1		–
Saddleworth, Yorks.	Single find	coiled-rod	2 + *c*.24	X	–
near Thaxted, Essex	Single find	single-rod	6		–
West Bergholt, Essex	Single find	twisted-rod	5		–
Weston Turville, Bucks.	Single find	twisted-rod	3	X	–
Fishergate, York	Single find	single-rod	10?		–
Eastling, Kent	Single find	single-rod	2+	X	–
Boston Spa, Yorks.	Single find	twisted-rod	1	–	–
Soberton, Hants	Hoard (*tpq* *c*.1068)	plaited-rod	1		–

from England (the forty-two examples listed by Graham-Campbell in 2011, in addition to more recent discoveries), I have identified nicking on eleven examples, although the status of nicking on fifteen rings that are now lost or otherwise unavailable for study is uncertain (Graham-Campbell 2011b, 160) (Table 12.4). Interestingly, nicked gold finger-rings span the late ninth to the eleventh centuries. Thus, a gold coiled-rod finger-ring from Saddleworth, Yorkshire, with two substantial nicks as well as over twenty smaller test marks is dated on typological grounds to the late ninth or tenth century (Graham-Campbell 2011b, cat. no. 30, 107). By contrast, the ring from Fishergate, York, with at least ten nicks, is dated to the eleventh century by its use of Scandinavian Ringerike-style decoration.[5] Overall, however, the concentration of nicked gold finger-rings in southern England, outside the Danelaw settlement region of the late ninth and early tenth centuries, points to a late date for the finger-ring corpus as a whole.

Test Marks on Gold

How are we to understand nicking on gold? It is customary to interpret nicks on non-numismatic silver, as with 'pecks' on coinage, as being applied in commercial environments, the aim being to expose plated forgeries as well as heavily alloyed precious-metal artefacts/coins, and thus guard against fraud during transactions (Malmer 2000). In this context, the number of test marks acts as a guide to the degree of circulation: the greater the number of test marks, the greater the number of transactions. It is possible, however, that an item

[5] The Fishergate ring has previously been published as belonging to the early ninth century (Tweddle, Moulden, & Logan 1999, 284, no. 170, 285, figs 104–5).

acquired multiple nicks or pecks on a single occasion. James Graham-Campbell has suggested that nicks on ingots were often made in pairs, on opposite sides and from opposite angles, and has proposed that clusters of similar-looking nicks (of similar depth and length) were probably made on a single occasion (2011b, 79). Items may have also acquired multiple nicks if they looked suspicious, or passed through the hands of an unusually distrusting individual (Archibald 2011, 56).

Some scholars have questioned this interpretation, however, suggesting that nicking/pecking was a social convention, akin to shaking hands or signing a contract (Kilger 2006). Others have proposed that it was ritually motivated by a desire to 'clear evil power from the metal' (Bogucki 2011, 145; Duczko 2002). Proponents of these views argue that the existence of heavily nicked objects, such as a silver neck-ring terminal from Sanda, Dalarna, Sweden, with 101 nicks (Duczko 2002, 204), defies economic rationale since it implies the fresh testing of objects that had already been repeatedly validated.

Yet the economic case for nicking is strong. Were test marks applied simply for routine social or ritual purposes, irrespective of the need to check the quality of the silver, we would expect surviving silver to encompass a range of alloy compositions. Yet wide-ranging analyses show that this is not the case: Viking Age silver consistently reveals a high silver content, typically over 90 per cent, suggesting that debased silver was routinely removed from circulation (Kruse & Tate 1992, tables 1–2; Arrhenius, Linder Welin, & Tapper 1972–3, 153–4; Ilisch et al. 2003, 138–49). Moreover, in her study of pecking on coins contained in the Cuerdale hoard, Marion Archibald noted that it was usually 'coins of abnormal appearance' (for instance, with blundered inscriptions) that were selected for pecking. Viking copies of English coins were more likely to be pecked than their English prototypes, as were rare coin issues (Archibald 1990, 21–2). Indeed, Archibald has demonstrated that the phenomenon of pecking arose in England out of the need to distinguish 'bad' silver coins from 'good', in response to the move from debased to fine silver coinage during the late ninth century (Archibald 2011). A rise in the practice of pecking silver in late tenth-century Scandinavia has also been causally linked to a contemporaneous increase in circulation of English and German coins of variable silver content (Williams 2011, 356). All these features suggest that test marks were applied principally for the purpose of testing the quality of the metal.[6] Here, it is worth noting that there are sound economic reasons for subjecting heavily nicked objects to further testing. Blanching an object in an acid solution enabled copper to be leached and could superficially enrich the surface of silver alloys (Beck et al.

[6] The old Icelandic laws, Grágás, state that nobody was required to accept silver as payment without being able to assess its fineness. Specifically, law 245 states that 'white silver . . . should stand the test of a nick and be more of silver than not' (Gullbekk 2011, 179, note 3, 184). However, see Ingvardson (this volume) for the suggestion that metalsmiths could have also nicked silver to test its purity.

2004). Since even extensively nicked objects could be blanched, it was necessary to carry out new tests to reveal the core of the metal upon each transaction. Indeed, heavily nicked objects may have been specially selected for further testing, having clearly aroused the suspicion of previous silver handlers.

Given the symbolic value of gold, as well as its higher status in the 'display economy', it is possible that nicking on gold, especially on complete gold objects, should be considered separately from that on silver. This may be the case for late Viking Age objects in England in particular, since by the late tenth century a coin-based economy was well established in southern and eastern England, and silver bullion use had ceased. Perhaps the donor of a gold ring tested it in order to demonstrate the quality of his/her gift. Alternatively, the receiver may have wanted to check its metal content before formally acquiring it in a social transaction. With the possible exception of one of the nicks on the Shotton Hall ring(s), none of the nicks encountered on the gold rings from England were so deep as to prevent the object functioning as jewellery.[7] It is certainly possible, for instance, that the massive gold arm-ring from 'near York', with one discreet nick near the terminal, was a display piece that had been gifted and tested (in public/in secret) by its donor/new owner. Such a hypothetical scenario highlights the possibility that objects could flow between different economic spheres.

It is also relevant to note that several of the nicked gold arm- and finger-rings from England were deposited in water or wetland contexts, without the intention of recovery. We may speculate that such deposition was carried out as a ritualized performance, which could have involved nicking (Lund 2008). The arm-ring from near Eastbourne was 'dragged up in a gill-net... from a seabed in the English Channel... about 7km off the coast of Eastbourne', while that from Goodrington, Devon, was found on the shore at Tor Bay. The coiled-rod finger-ring from Saddleworth was found 'in the river bed at the foot of Chew Valley', while the two finger-rings from Kent were both metal-detected on the historically boggy land of the Romney Marsh (Graham-Campbell 2011b, cat. nos. 18, 19, and 30). Other nicked gold rings were 'ploughed up' on dry land and have been interpreted as casual losses (Graham-Campbell 2011b, 153).

However, the nicking of complete gold rings is not widely encountered within Scandinavia, suggesting that the testing of complete rings was not part of a broader Scandinavian cultural practice. The presence of multiple test marks on the rings (cf. the finger-rings from Saddleworth and Fishergate) is also not easily explained by a donor/owner simply wanting to test its content, unless the ring changed ownership multiple times and was tested by each new wearer. Here, it is worth recalling that fake hack-gold (gilded copper-alloy) was in circulation in Viking contexts, as the finds from Torksey described above demonstrate. Multiple nicking may have therefore been required to guard against replating

[7] I am grateful to James Graham-Campbell for this insight.

through mercury gilding, since this would have had the effect of improving the surface appearance of previously tested artefacts, much in the same way as blanching on silver objects. Moreover, there is no reason why a ring which had at some point passed hands in a commercial environment could not subsequently have been deposited without the intention of recovery. Indeed, nicked and/or hacked silver is also occasionally found in wetland contexts, suggesting that assemblages with a clear bullion character could also be deposited permanently.[8] The depositional contexts of Viking Age silver hoards from England are poorly understood, but fragmented broad-band arm-rings form part of a silver bullion hoard from Cushalogurt, Co. Mayo, Ireland, discovered on a small peninsula, six yards from the shoreline of Clew Bay (Graham-Campbell & Sheehan 2009, 81). A votive context of deposition has also been suggested for the Ballacamaish hoard, found in 'a marl pit' on the Isle of Man, with a silver bullion content comprising a nicked silver arm-ring and two deliberately hacked (but unnicked) neck-rings (Graham-Campbell 2011b, 157, cat. no. 12).[9] The nicking encountered on three single gold ingots (two complete and one fragmentary) described above, as likewise on a hammered gold ingot from 'Co. Cork', Ireland, also supports an economic rationale for nicking on gold, as does the presence of nicks on the rare instances of hack-gold from bullion hoards within Scandinavia, discussed above (Cahill 2006, 263–4; Graham-Campbell 2011b, 84).

The cumulative evidence thus suggests that, in general, nicking on gold, as on silver, is best interpreted within an economic framework. The function of nicking on complete late Viking Age objects is admittedly less clear given the lack of contemporary silver bullion use. It is possible that nicking was carried out simply to test the content of a ring that was given as part of a social transaction. Alternatively, the practice of nicking may have been reintroduced in the later tenth century by incoming settlers or visitors from Scandinavia, where bullion use and nicking on silver continued well into the eleventh century.

Discussion

The material reviewed here enables a number of observations on the nature of exchange in Viking Age England. The first is that the use of gold as a transactional medium appears to have been more extensive in England than in Scandinavia. This is suggested by the greater presence of hack-gold and gold ingots in

[8] From the thirteenth-century *Egil's Saga*, we read that Egil's father, Skallagrim, deposited a chest of silver as well as a bronze cauldron 'in Krumskelda Marsh with a great slab of stone on top', although the nature of the silver contents (whole ornaments or hacked pieces?) are not elucidated (Scudder 2000, 108). For a discussion, see Graham-Campbell 2011c, 108–11.

[9] A complete silver rod arm-ring of Scandinavian type was lost or deposited with two Anglo-Saxon coins in the River Thames near Deptford, London, around 935. It has one nick, but its associated coins and findspot in southern England are not suggestive of Viking activity (Graham-Campbell 1986).

England and more extensive evidence for the testing of complete gold objects, a treatment that, I have argued, is likely to be indicative of currency use. In particular, it seems clear that the Viking 'Great Army' operated a gold bullion economy in England during the 870s, albeit on a limited scale. There is, at present, little evidence to suggest that an equivalent gold currency was in use within Scandinavia at the same time, although that may change if hack-gold from settlement sites can be better elucidated.

It is possible that heightened access to gold during this period encouraged its use as a means of exchange. Mark Blackburn has demonstrated that gold was widely available among elite circles in Late Anglo-Saxon England (2007). He has described the ninth century as a period of 'revival' in the use of gold coin and metalwork, with gold survivals from this century being more common than those of the eighth or tenth, both in England and on the Continent (2007, 78–9). One source of gold newly available to the members of the 'Great Army' was, of course, ransom payments, details of which are known principally through documentary sources. Thus, in 872, immediately prior to the occupation of Torksey, the bishop of Worcester sold land for '20 mancuses of tested gold' to meet a ransom payment (Whitelock 1979, no. 94; on the *mancus*, see Blackburn 2007, 57–9). Famously, an inscription contained in the Gospel Book known as the *Codex Aureus* describes how an Anglo-Saxon Ealdorman and his wife paid 'pure money, that was with pure gold' in order to recover the book from the clutches of a Viking army (Whitelock 1979, no. 98). In this context, it is perhaps not surprising that the largest extant gold hoard from Scandinavia, from Hoen, Norway, containing a selection of gold acquired through trade or, more probably, raids in northern and western Europe, dates to the late ninth century (Fuglesang & Wilson 2006).[10] No doubt such newly acquired wealth fuelled gold currency use within the Viking camps and contributed towards reserves from which ingots and rings were produced during the later ninth and early tenth centuries.

The reign of Æthelred II (978–1013/1014–16) also saw a surge in ransom payments to pay off Viking attackers, providing a renewed source of gold to Scandinavians active in England during the late tenth and early eleventh centuries (Naismith 2012, 293). In 994, for instance, the archbishop of Canterbury hastily sold off land to the bishop of Dorchester for £90 of silver and 200 mancuses of gold, in order to deflect an imminent attack on Canterbury Cathedral. Æthelred himself raised £200 of gold and silver from the sale of land to Abbot Leofric 'when tribute to the Danes was needed' in 1005. Whether such gold payments took the form of gold coin, weighed bullion, or ornament is an

[10] Frankish sources record that 685 lb of gold were extracted via loot and ransom payments by Vikings on the Continent, while Arab sources describe how, in 861, a Viking force ransomed a local regent in Pamplona, Spain, for 70,000 gold pieces. Not all the money was received, however (Price 2008, 466). Given that Viking forces who raided the Continent were also active in England, it is possible that such gold ended up in the Danelaw.

open question—in contrast to the many documentary references to gold payments (both ransom and more generally), actual survivals of contemporary Anglo-Saxon gold coins and objects are extremely rare (Blackburn 2007; Naismith 2012, 308–13). Whatever the case, such acquisitions presumably enabled the contemporary fashion for Scandinavian gold rings, including several of the finger-rings discussed here.

Scandinavian settlers in England appear to have had a requirement for high-value currency that gold bullion fulfilled. Indeed, the material reviewed here suggests that the wealth involved in gold bullion payments could be extremely large. While the evidence from Torksey and ARSNY points to the use of light pieces of hack-gold in (relatively) small-scale payments, perhaps even suggesting the use of gold alongside silver in the same transactions, the circulation of complete, tested gold rings and ingots is indicative of very substantial sums of wealth passing hands in Scandinavian contexts. The complete, nicked, gold arm-ring from Wendover Dean, Buckinghamshire, weighs almost 150 g. Assuming a gold-to-silver value ratio of 10–12 to 1, its value is equivalent to between *c.*500 and 600 silver dirhams. The value of the (untested) gold ingot from West Dereham, Norfolk, weighing close to 60 g, has been estimated at 420 silver pennies, although this is perhaps an overestimate, given that the gold content of the ingot is only 79 per cent (Pestell 2013, 249).

Given that the Scandinavian bullion economy in England also made use of light cubo-octahedral weights (weighing under 4 grams) and extremely fragmented dirhams (often weighing less than 1 gram), it is perhaps surprising to find evidence for high-value payments at the extreme opposite end of the scale. Indeed, recent studies have drawn attention to the potentially monetary use of copper-alloy within the Scandinavian bullion economy, suggesting a need to make low-value payments of a day-to-day nature (Sindbæk 2001; Williams 2011, 354; Pestell 2013, 249–50). But the key feature of the bullion economy was versatility, and I have argued elsewhere that the bulk of silver bullion payments in England were in fact geared towards medium-to-high value payments (the small-value payments at Torksey and ARSNY thus being unrepresentative). This is evident in the weight range of single finds of oblate-spheroid weights, which cluster between 20 and 40 g, as well as that of complete but tested silver ingots, most of which weigh between 10 and 20 g and thus possess a weight well suited to the use of oblate-spheroid weights (Kershaw 2017). A number of recently discovered silver hoards from England also contain very heavy silver ingots and rings, well in excess of 50 g. An elaborate silver neck-collar contained in the Bedale, Yorkshire, hoard weighs 546.4 g (PAS Find-ID YORYM-CEE620). Broadly speaking, it is worth the equivalent of a gold arm-ring weighing *c.*50 g, three of which are known from England. Clearly, gold was a much more rare and valuable transactional medium than silver, but seen against a background of substantial silver use it represents a natural extension of bullion resources in a flexible and multi-metallic metal-weight system.

ABBREVIATIONS

AMS: Arkeologisk Museum Stavanger
BM: British Museum
NMC: Nationalmuseum, Copenhagen
PAS: Portable Antiquities Scheme
SHM: Statens Historiska Museet, Stockholm

REFERENCES

Abramson, T. (ed.) 2011. *Studies in Early Medieval Coinage: New Perspectives.* Woodbridge: Boydell & Brewer.

Ager, B. 2011. 'A Preliminary Note on the Artefacts from the Vale of York Viking Hoard'. In Abramson (ed.), 121–34.

Ager, B. & G. Williams 2011. 'The Vale of York Viking Hoard: Preliminary Catalogue'. In Abramson (ed.), 135–45.

Archibald, M.M. 1990. 'Pecking and Bending: The Evidence of British Finds, Including Cuerdale'. In *Sigtuna Papers, Proceedings of the Sigtuna Symposium on Viking-Age Coinage 1–4 June 1989,* ed. K. Jonsson & B. Malmer, 11–24. Stockholm: Kungl. Vitterhets Historie och Antikvitets Akademien and London: Spink.

Archibald, M.M. 2011. 'Testing'. In Graham-Campbell 2011b, 51–64.

Armbruster, B. 2002. 'Goldschmiede in Haithabu—Ein Beitrag zum Frümittelalterlichen Metallhandwerk'. In *Das Archäologische Fundmaterial VII. Berichte über die Ausgrabungen in Haithabu,* Bericht 34, ed. K. Schietzel, 87–201. Neumünster: Wachholtz Verlag.

Arrhenius, B., U. Linder Welin, & L. Tapper 1972–3. 'Arabiskt Silver och Nordiska Vikingasmycken'. *Tor* 15: 151–60.

Beck, L., S. Bosonnet, S. Réveillon, D. Eliot, & F. Pilon 2004. 'Silver Surface Enrichment of Silver-Copper Alloys: A Limitation for the Analysis of Ancient Silver Coins by Surface Techniques'. *Nuclear Instruments and Methods in Physics Research B* 226: 153–62.

Blackburn, M. 2007. 'Gold in England During the "Age of Silver" (Eighth–Eleventh Centuries)'. In Graham-Campbell & Williams (eds), 55–98.

Blackburn, M.A.S. 2011. 'The Viking Winter Camp at Torksey, 872–3'. In *Viking Coinage and Currency in the British Isles,* ed. M. Blackburn, 221–64. London: Spink/British Numismatic Society.

Bogucki, M. 2011. 'The Use of Money in the Slavic Lands from the Ninth to Eleventh Century: The Archaeological/Numismatic Evidence'. In Graham-Campbell, Sindbæk, & Williams (eds), 133–52.

Brøgger, A.W. 1921. *Ertog og Øre. Den Gamle Norske Vegt.* Kristiania.

Cahill, M. 2006. 'John Windele's Golden Legacy—Prehistoric and Later Gold Ornaments from Co. Cork and Co. Waterford'. *Proceedings of the Royal Irish Academy* 106c: 219–337.

Duczko, W. 2002. 'Test or Magic? Pecks on the Viking-Age Silver'. In *Moneta Mediaevalis. Studia Numizmatyczne i Historyczne Ofiarowane Profesorowi Stanisławowi*

Suchodolskiemu w 65. Rocznicę Urodzin, ed. B. Paszkiewicz, 193–208. Warsaw: DiG: Instytut Archeologii i Etnologii, Polskiej Akademii Nauk.

Eniosova, N. 2007. 'Viking Age Gold from Old Rus". In *Cultural Interaction Between East and West: Archaeology, Artefacts and Human Contacts in Northern Europe*, ed. U. Fransson, M. Svendin, S. Bergerbrant, & F. Androschuck, 175–80. Stockholm: Stockholm University.

Eniosova, N. 2009. 'A Unique 10th Century AD Gold-Plated Brooch from South-East Russia: Technical and Stylistic Authentication'. *ArchéoSciences, Revue d'Archéométrie* 33: 375–80.

Fonnesbech-Sandberg, E. 1988. 'Vægtsystemer i Ældre Germansk Jernalder'. *Aarbøger for Nordisk Oldkyndighed og Historie* 1987: 139–60.

Fuglesang, S.H. & D.M. Wilson 2006. *The Hoen Hoard: A Viking Gold Treasure of the Ninth Century*. Rome: Bardi Editore.

Gaimster, M. 1991. 'Money and Media in Viking Age Scandinavia'. In *Social Approaches to Viking Studies*, ed. R. Samson, 113–22. Glasgow: Cruithne Press.

Graeber, D. 2012. 'On Social Currencies and Human Economies: Some Thoughts on the Violence of Equivalence'. *Social Anthropology* 20.4: 411–28.

Graham-Campbell, J. 1974. 'A Viking-Age Gold Hoard from Ireland'. *The Antiquaries Journal* 54: 269–72.

Graham-Campbell, J. 1976. 'The Viking-Age Silver Hoards of Ireland'. In *Proceedings of the Seventh Viking Congress, Dublin, 15–21 August 1973*, ed. B. Almqvist & D. Greene, 31–74. Dublin: Royal Irish Academy.

Graham-Campbell, J. 1986. 'The Re-Provenancing of a Viking-Age Hoard to the Thames, near Deptford (S.E. London)'. *British Numismatic Journal* 56: 186–7.

Graham-Campbell, J. 1995. *The Viking-Age Gold and Silver of Scotland (A.D. 850–1100)*. Edinburgh: National Museums of Scotland.

Graham-Campbell, J. 2002. 'The Dual Economy of the Danelaw: The Howard Linecar Memorial Lecture 2001'. *British Numismatic Journal* 71: 51–61.

Graham-Campbell, J. 2006. 'The Rings'. In Fuglesang & Wilson (eds), 73–81.

Graham-Campbell, J. 2007. 'Reflections on "Silver Economy in the Viking Age"'. In Graham-Campbell & Williams (eds), 215–23.

Graham-Campbell, J. 2011a. '"Silver Economies" and the Ninth-Century Background'. In Graham-Campbell, Sindbæk, & Williams (eds), 29–39.

Graham-Campbell, J. 2011b. *The Cuerdale Hoard and Related Viking-Age Silver and Gold, from Britain and Ireland, in the British Museum*. London: British Museum Press.

Graham-Campbell, J. 2011c. '"The Serpent's Bed": Gold and Silver in Viking-Age Iceland—and Beyond'. In Sigmundsson et al. (eds), 103–31.

Graham-Campbell, J. & J. Sheehan 2009. 'Viking-Age Gold and Silver from Irish Crannogs and Other Watery Places'. *Journal of Irish Archaeology* 18: 77–93.

Graham-Campbell, J., S.M. Sindbæk, & G. Williams (eds) 2011. *Silver Economies, Monetisation and Society in Scandinavia, AD 800–1100*. Aarhus: Aarhus University Press.

Graham-Campbell, J. & G. Williams (eds) 2007. *Silver Economy in the Viking Age*. Walnut Creek: Left Coast Press.

Grieg, S. 1929. 'Vikingetidens skattefund', *Universitetets Oldsaksamlings Skrifter* 2: 177–311.

Gullbekk, S.H. 2011. 'Money and Its Use in the Saga Society: Silver, Coins and Commodity Money'. In Sigmundsson et al. (eds), 176–88.

Hårdh, B. 1976. *Wikingerzeitliche Depotfunde aus Südschweden: Katalog und Tafeln*. Bonn: Rudolf Habelt.

Hårdh, B. 1996. *Silver in the Viking Age: A Regional-Economic Study*. Stockholm: Almqvist & Wiksell International.

Hårdh, B. 2010. 'Viking Age Uppåkra'. In *Från Romartida Skalpeller till Senvikingatida Urnesspännen. Nya Materialstudier från Uppåkra (Uppåkrastudier 11)*, ed. B. Hårdh, 247–316. Lund: Almqvist & Wiksell.

Hedeager, L. 2011. *Iron Age Myth and Materiality: An Archaeology of Scandinavia, AD 400–1000*. London: Routledge.

Ilisch, L.S., W.B. Stern, & H. Steuer (eds) 2003. *Dirham und Rappenpfennig. Mittelalterliche Münzprägung in Bergbauregionen*, Zeitschrift für Archäologie des Mittelalters, Beiheft 17. Bonn: Dr. Rudolf Habelt.

Kershaw, J. 2017. 'An Early-Medieval "Dual-Currency Economy": Bullion and Coin in the Danelaw'. *Antiquity* 91: 173–90.

Kilger, C. 2006. 'Silver Handling Traditions during the Viking Age: Some Observations and Thoughts on the Phenomenon of Bending and Pecking'. In *Coinage and History in the North-Sea World, c. AD 500–1250: Essays in Honour of Marion Archibald*, ed. B. Cook & G. Williams, 449–65. Leiden: Brill.

Kilger, C. 2008. 'Wholeness and Holiness: Counting, Weighing and Valuing Silver in the Early Viking Period'. In Skre (ed.), 253–325.

Kruse, S.E. & J. Tate 1992. 'XRF Analysis of Viking Age Silver Ingots'. *Proceedings of the Society of Antiquaries of Scotland* 122: 295–328.

Lund, J. 2008. 'Banks, Borders and Bodies of Water in a Viking Age Mentality'. *Journal of Wetland Archaeology* 8: 51–70.

Lundström, L. 1973. 'Silverringar som Pengar under Vikingatiden'. *Numismatiska Meddelanden* XXXI: 11–33.

Malmer, B. 2000. 'Om registrering av cirkulationspår på mynt från Vikingatiden'. *Nordisk Numismatisk Unions Medlemsblad* 2: 23–7.

Mikkelsen, E. 2006. 'The Find in its Context'. In Fuglesang & Wilson (eds), 29–53.

Munksgaard, E. 1962. 'Skattefundet fra Duesminde'. *Aarbøger for Nordisk Oldkyndighed og Historie* 1962: 94–112.

Naismith, R. 2012. 'Payments for Land and Privilege in Anglo-Saxon England'. *Anglo-Saxon England* 41: 277–342.

Pedersen, J.-A. & T. Grønnegaard 2012. *Ramløse-Skatten. En Vikinge-Stormands Nedgravede Bank af Hård Valuta?* Gilleleje: Gilleleje Museum.

Pedersen, U. 2008. 'Weights and Balances'. In Skre (ed.), 119–78.

Pestell, T. 2013. 'Imports or Immigrants? Reassessing Scandinavian Metalwork in Late Anglo-Saxon East Anglia'. In *East Anglia and its North Sea World in the Middle Ages*, ed. D. Bates & R. Liddiard, 230–55. Woodbridge: Boydell Press.

Price, N. 2008. 'The Vikings in Spain, North Africa and the Mediterranean'. In *The Viking World*, ed. S. Brink, with N. Price, 462–9. London and New York: Routledge.

Rundkvist, M. 2011. *Mead-Halls of the Eastern Geats: Elite Settlements and Political Geography AD 375–1000 in Östergötland, Sweden*. Stockholm: Kungl. Vitterhets Historie och Antikvitets Akademien Handlingar.

Scudder, B. 2000. 'Egil's Saga' (trans.). In *The Sagas of the Icelanders: A Selection*, 3–184. London and New York: Penguin Books/Viking Penguin.

Sigmundsson, S., A. Holt, G. Siguurðsson, G. Ólafsson, & O. Vésteinsson (eds) 2011. *Viking Settlements and Viking Society, Papers from the Proceedings of the Sixteenth Viking Congress, Reykjavik and Reykholt, 16–23 August, 2009*. Reykjavik: Hið Íslenzka Fornleifafélag & University of Iceland.

Sindbæk, S.M. 2001. 'An Object of Exchange: Brass Bars and the Routinization of Viking Age Long-Distance Exchange in the Baltic Area'. *Offa* 58: 49–60.

Sindbæk, S.M. 2011. 'Silver Economies and Social Ties: Long-Distance Interaction, Long-Term Investments—and Why the Viking Age Happened'. In Graham-Campbell, Sindbæk, & Williams (eds), 41–65.

Skovmand, R. 1942. 'De Danske Skattefund fra Vikingetiden og den Ældeste Middelalder indtil omrking 1150'. *Aarbøger for Nordisk Oldkyndighet og Historie* (1942): 1–245.

Skre, D. (ed.) 2008. *Means of Exchange: Dealing with Silver in the Viking Age*. Kaupang Excavation Project Publication Series 2. Aarhus: Aarhus University Press.

Stenberger, M. 1933. *Öland under Äldre Järnåldern. En Bebyggelsehistorisk Undersökning*. Stockholm: Akademiens Förlag.

Steuer, H. 2004. 'Minting, Silver Routes and Mining in Europe: Economic Expansion and Technical Innovation'. In *The World in the Year 1000*, ed. J. Heitzmann & W. Schenkluhn, 105–17. Lanham, New York, and Oxford: University Press of America.

Thorsen, K. 2009. 'Weights, Ingots and Scrap Metal'. In *Sorte Muld: Wealth, Power and Religion at an Iron Age Central Settlement on Bornholm*, ed. C. Adamsen, U.L. Hansen, F.O. Nielsen, & M. Watt, 111–13. Rønne: Bornholms Museum.

Tweddle, D., J. Moulden, & E. Logan 1999. *Anglian York: A Survey of the Evidence*. The Archaeology of York 7/2. York: Council for British Archaeology.

Wallace, J.N.A. 1938. 'The Golden Bog of Cullen'. *North Munster Antiquarian Journal* 1: 89–109.

Whitelock, D. 1979. *English Historical Documents I. c.500–1042*. 2nd edn. London: Eyre Methuen.

Wideen, H. 1955. *Västsvenska Vikingatidsstudier. Arkeologiska Källor till Vänerområdets Kulturhistoria under Yngre Järnålder och Äldsta Medeltid*. Göteborg: Göteborgs Arkeologiska Museum.

Williams, G. 2011. 'Silver Economies, Monetisation and Society: An Overview'. In Graham-Campbell, Sindbæk, & Williams (eds), 337–72.

Williams, G. 2014. 'Viking Camps in England and Ireland'. In *Vikings: Life and Legend*, ed. G. Williams, P. Pentz, & M. Wemhoff, 120–1. London: British Museum.

Williams, G. (ed.) forthcoming. *A Riverine Site Near York: A Possible Viking Camp?* British Museum Research Publications.

Williams, G. & J. Naylor 2016. *King Alfred's Coins: The Watlington Viking Hoard*. Oxford: Ashmolean Museum.

Zachrisson, T. 1998. *Gård, Gräns, Gravfält: Sammanhang kring Ädelmetalldepåer och Runstenar från Vikingatid och Tidig Medeltid i Uppland och Gästrikland*. Stockholm Studies in Archaeology 15. Stockholm: Stockholms Universitet.

13

Vaðmál and Cloth Currency in Viking and Medieval Iceland

Michèle Hayeur Smith

In Viking Age Scandinavia, textiles and textile production were critically intertwined with all aspects of life, death, and fate (Heide 2006; Bek-Pedersen 2008, 175; Hayeur Smith forthcoming). In Iceland specifically, textiles wove their way into all aspects of human existence and were used for many utilitarian purposes: as clothing, household implements, sails for ships, and tents (Hayeur Smith 2014, 731). However, they were also used as a legal mode of payment within a complex commodity-money system, the roots of which most likely came to Iceland from Norway along with other cultural traits. In this chapter, I present the results of recent and ongoing research conducted on Icelandic archaeological textile collections, reviewing late Viking Age and medieval data to pinpoint and identify the beginnings of *vaðmál*'s standardized production as currency in Iceland. I further explore what characterized *vaðmál* as currency both legally and as an item of material culture, and why cloth became so highly valued in Iceland. I begin, however, by considering the origins of *vaðmál*. In exploring the use of textiles as legal currencies in Norwegian commodity-money systems of the late Viking Age and early medieval periods, I aim to reveal the degree to which medieval Icelanders' use of cloth currency can be contextualized within continental Scandinavian practices.

Background: Cloth Currency—Vaðmál

The Icelandic commodity-money system, as understood through medieval and post-medieval Icelandic law codes (Dennis et al. 1980; 2002; Jónsson 2004; Bernharðsson et al. 2005; Schulman 2010) was based on stable, legally negotiated exchange rates for the value of different goods relative to other products. Thus, values for domestic commodities such as cattle, butter, sheep, foodstuffs, and manufactured goods, including cloth, as well as hack-silver and coins, were established through exchange rates initially based upon standardized weights of refined silver. Dagfinn Skre and Svein Harald Gullbekk describe the structure and details of the Norwegian commodity system through reference to both linguistic and legal sources (Skre 2011; Gullbekk 2011). This reveals sufficient similarities to the Icelandic commodity-money system, as described in the medieval Icelandic law codes, that there can be little doubt of their close developmental relationships.

However, towards the end of the Viking Age the commodity-money systems of Iceland and Norway evolved and diverged. In Iceland, cloth gained tremendous importance within the currency system, possibly due to a combination of population increase, stabilization of the Icelandic pastoral economy, and declining access to sources of silver (Gelsinger 1981, 34). While regulated barter still formed the basis for this economic system, it is clear from the legal texts that formalized and standardized units of cloth emerged and gained such importance that homespun woollen fabric became a legal form of currency throughout the medieval period. While its value was still measured, in theory, against silver, this cloth—*vaðmál* or *vöruvaðmál*—was eventually legally regulated as an exchange good in and of itself. It is ubiquitous as a measure and medium of exchange in Icelandic legal texts, sales accounts, church inventories, and farm registers into the seventeenth century (e.g. Lárusson 1967; Hayeur Smith 2014, 731).

Standards for the production and trade of cloth were legally defined in Iceland's successive law codes: *Grágás* (1117–1271) (Dennis et al. 1980; 2002), *Járnsíða* (1271–81), *Jónsbók* (after 1281), and *Búalög* (twelfth–nineteenth centuries). To be used legally as currency, cloth had to be woven in a particular manner and in specific lengths and widths, as evaluated by regional authorities. The name of this cloth currency, *vaðmál*, integrates the Old Norse root words 'váð' (stuff/cloth) and 'mál' (a measure) to mean 'cloth measured to a standard' (Cleasby et al. 1957, 673, 683).[1]

While *vaðmál* was also used as an exchange good in mainland Scandinavia (Einzig 1966), literary and legal descriptions of the Icelandic commodity-exchange system suggest that it played a more central role as a currency there than in the mainland systems. In Iceland, the role of cloth as a currency during the early medieval period is well documented. Its production was heavily regulated, as is evident from legal provisions in *Grágás* and later law codes that enumerated its physical characteristics. Its role as a commodity is also well

[1] In continental Scandinavia and other parts of northern Europe, the term *vaðmál* appears to represent a less specific range of legally defined cloth types than in Iceland and, in some areas, may have encompassed tabby weaves as well. Hoffman suggests that the definition varied according to region, in places referring simply to twills and coarse homespun tabbies (plain weave), while Gelsinger notes that in Germany and around the southern Baltic region the term 'watmal' was synonymous with rough cloth used for the poor, regardless of its formal definition in Iceland (Hoffman 1974; Gelsinger 1981, 253–4). Today it is a term that is sometimes misused to refer to any type of textile recovered archaeologically regardless of weave or time frame. The true meaning of the term *vaðmál* should be limited to the use of cloth currency during the medieval period when it was made according to very strict criteria that will be discussed below.

documented from medieval exchange lists, contracts, and property assessments that used its value relative to other goods to facilitate transactions. However, the degree to which it was actually produced or used as a currency, rather than serving as a theoretical standard for the exchange of other products, has remained unclear, because the historical sources (in the absence of material evidence) can be read either way (Þórláksson 1988; 1991; Hoffman 1974) and the material evidence for such a currency—the Icelandic archaeological textile corpus—has been largely ignored.

The Origins of Icelandic Cloth Currency in Norway

Hoffman (1974, 195, 218–19), Gelsinger (1981) and Þorláksson (pers. comm.) have all argued that the use of cloth as currency in Iceland had its roots in Norway. This is not surprising. Notwithstanding mitochondrial DNA evidence for a significant Celtic female contribution to Iceland's Viking Age population (Helgason et al. 2001), most settlers were of Norwegian descent, and brought with them a Norwegian cultural background. Among these cultural traits, they brought the warp-weighted loom and Norwegian weaving traditions (Hoffman 1974). Iceland also seems to have incorporated some weaving elements from the British Isles, including a shift in spin direction quite early on in the settlement period (see Hayeur Smith 2015).

In the early years of the settlement (AD 870–930), goods were measured against agreed values of silver, considerable amounts of which are thought to have circulated in Iceland during the tenth century as the result of Viking raids and trading (Gelsinger 1981, 34; for information on Icelandic silver see Graham-Campbell 2011). Eventually, however, these raids ceased and population increased along with exchange and trade. Gelsinger argues that, in this context, Icelandic silver supplies were no longer adequate to support local needs and silver was mixed with foreign coins and alloys creating a new currency called 'bleikt silfir' and worth half the value of pure silver (1981). Silver coinage was never produced within Iceland, but *vaðmál* was valued in terms of silver and was used as a parallel currency. Gelsinger argued that its production was 'the most important industry during the Commonwealth period and possibly during the settlement as well' (1981, 35).

Silver and coins were critically important within the Norwegian economic system of the Viking Age. However, as in Iceland, this was not an economy based solely on coinage, but rather on a more complex system including various commodities used as media of payment, equated with silver (Skre 2011, 74). According to Skre, economic transactions could be paid using weights of silver or with other items such as cows, cloth, butter, grain, etc., whose value in silver was known and agreed upon, such that all were interchangeable at regular rates in Viking Age Norwegian transactions (2011, 74). By the medieval period, when the law codes were written down, this, too, was true of Iceland. Similar values were ascribed to the weights of silver, whether pure or impure, and parallel units of measure were established following the Norwegian model. In Iceland, the unit of weight and value with the highest mass was a *vætt*, followed by the *fjórðung*, *mörk*, *eyrir/aurar*, *örtugar*, and *penningar* (Gelsinger 1981, 33). The Icelandic *mörk* was equal to 217 grams (1981, 33), comparable to the Norwegian *mark* of 214 grams (Skre 2011, 73). In both systems, values were comparable: in Iceland one *eyrir* of silver was equivalent to three *örtugar*, while in Norway one *ora* was equivalent to three *ertogs*. In both places one *eyrir/ora* of silver was equal in value to six ells of *vaðmál* during the late Viking Age and early medieval period (one legal ell = 49.2 cm) (Larson 1935, 421–2; Dennis et al. 2002, 155).

In establishing *vaðmál* as a regulated currency, Iceland's legal system mirrored that of Norway. According to the thirteenth-century *Íslendingabók*, a Norwegian settler named Úlfjótur was sent from Iceland back to Norway to draft a law code modelled on the legal system of the Gulathing: the legislative assembly for a western coastal Norwegian province (Dennis et al. 1980). The Gulathing law contains some of Norway's earliest recorded laws and in its current form is thought to date to 1150, roughly contemporary with *Grágás*, its Icelandic equivalent (1117–1271) (Dennis et al. 1980; 2002; Larson 1935, 26). Both of these written law codes are assumed to contain legal provisions considerably older than the dates at which the formerly orally transmitted laws were written down. The Gulathing law provides several instances in which cloth is mentioned as a form of payment, for instance for shipbuilding or the consecration of a church, or legal compensation, including for killing the king's bailiff at the Thing (Larson 1935, 333). *Vaðmál* does not dominate the Gulathing law code, as it does in *Grágás*, and appears less frequently as a form of payment than silver or cows; however, it has clear legal standing, importance, and value as a form of commodity-currency. In the Gulathing law, no distinctions were made between the values of linen and *vaðmál*, as there were in *Grágás*, where one ell of linen was worth four ells of Icelandic *vaðmál* (Gelsinger 1981). Instead, cloth in all of its forms possessed the legal equivalent of one *ora* in silver to six ells of cloth. The specific guidelines that regulated the ell/*öln*/*ölnir* as a unit of measure for cloth will be discussed in more depth below, but for the moment it is sufficient to suggest that the Icelandic model was heavily based on the Norwegian one and that cloth currency in Norway was important enough that its roles and values were described in the Gulathing law.

Vaðmál: *An Archaeological Approach*

Archaeological evidence for textile production and circulation has not, until recently, been central to dialogues about currency in the Viking Age, which have focused almost exclusively on the circulation of precious metals (Gullbekk 2011). This is largely because textiles, as organic products, are rarely preserved in the archaeological record in quantities sufficient to assess the degree to which they were produced according to standards or were ubiquitously circulated. As Skre notes, 'the scant remains of a woollen dress in a grave carry no mark of once having formed parts of payment for grain, as they might actually have been'. He stresses further that 'when found during excavations, the money function of ... cloth remains a potential', warning that 'to disregard that potential, and to take the artefactual evident only at face value, must be characterized as overly empirical' (Skre 2011, 76).

However, where large numbers of textile fragments are found both at individual sites and from many sites across a large area, possibilities arise for moving beyond the individual object that cannot easily be evaluated for its role in a currency system (as Skre suggests) and for looking, instead, for features that may point to a monetary function for cloth: patterns of standardization in the production of cloth types; ubiquity in the distribution of such standardized products; and changes through time marking transformations in the use of such products. Where, as in Iceland, such archaeological evidence is not only abundant but can also be compared with standards for currency cloth recorded in medieval and post-medieval legal texts, material evidence for this legally regulated product are quite exceptional. However, until recently the potential use of Iceland's archaeologically recovered textile assemblages for resolving the questions of whether cloth was actually produced as a currency (rather than just being a theoretical standard), and when that production of cloth as currency began and ended, has not been realized.

While mainland Scandinavian textiles have been the topic of numerous detailed and invaluable scholarly works (among others Andersson Strand 2003a; 2003b; 2011; Andersson Strand et al. 2010; Bender Jørgensen 1986; 1992; 2003; Christensen & Nockert 2006; Geijer 1938; Hägg 1974; 1984a; 1984b; 1986; 1991; Hagen 1994; Kjellberg 1979; 1982; Kjellberg & Hoffmann 1991), Icelandic textiles have seen less intense study. Nana Damsholt (1984) assembled historical records about women's roles in the production of *vaðmál*, but never examined the material evidence. The late Else Guðjónsson, faced with a diverse range of ethnographic, historical, and archaeological textiles, focused her work largely on embroideries, tapestries, ethnographic items of clothing, and finer items of cloth, rather than examining the discarded fragments of uniformly coloured, brown, simply woven cloth periodically recovered from the middens of Norse farms (1962; 1965; 1970; 1973; 1980; 1990; 1992; 1994; 1998a; 1998b). More recently, Hrefna Róbertsdóttir (2008) used a combination of historical records and archived textile samples to explore early modern Icelandic textile production, primarily during the eighteenth century. Individual fragments and textile objects from a few site-specific collections have also been analysed by Guðjónsson (1962), Marta Hoffman (1974), and Penelope Walton Rogers (2012).

However, a vast corpus of at least 6,000–10,000 textile fragments from excavations around Iceland, dating from the Viking Age to the early modern period and curated by the National Museum of Iceland and at a number of smaller repositories, remained largely untouched until recently (Hayeur Smith 2012; 2013; 2014; 2015). Unassuming and difficult to process or clean, these scraps and pieces of cloth accumulated without much notice over the course of a century of excavations. However, when considered as a group, this remarkable textile corpus includes fragments from sites of differing ages, scales, socio-economic ranks, and functions and from all parts of Iceland. Together, they form a representative cross-section of contexts within which cloth would have been made, used, and discarded.

The textiles discussed here include 110 Viking Age and 1,206 medieval items. The complete Icelandic textile assemblage comes largely from archaeological excavations in farm sites where midden layers representing accumulations of household waste alternated with dense blankets of silt and clay from the demolition of turf-walled structures to form 'farm mounds' up to 3.5 metres deep. They thus provide information on domestic production and consumption, and exclude ecclesiastic fineries, tapestries, and embroideries that were sufficiently fine and valuable to be preserved and guarded by the churches. Preservation conditions suitable for textile preservation are frequently found within the damp midden layers sealed by demolition horizons. As with other material culture recovered from such settings, these objects give information on textiles that were made and used at these sites. Comparisons among such sites provide insights into the ubiquity or divergence of consumption and production patterns across the island. In addition to these, burials from the Viking Age through the early modern period have provided additional information through preserved fabrics and pseudomorphs (mineralized textiles in contact with copper-alloy or iron objects) shedding light on cloth worn by the deceased or used as shrouds. Burials are a particularly rich source for Viking Age textiles (see note 5).

Microscopic analysis of these vast collections has revealed that *vaðmál* was made from the end of the Viking Age into the early post-medieval period with such degrees of standardization and ubiquity that one can only conclude cloth truly had become a unit of measure, a type of 'legal cloth currency' produced and circulated among households of all ranks across the island.

*Identifying 'Legal Cloth'/*Vaðmál *in Iceland's Archaeological Record*

Documenting exchange systems based on the production and circulation of organic products can be difficult archaeologically due to poor preservation (Gullbekk 2011, 102) and the potential transformation of these commodities into other products before being discarded (Skre 2011). In Iceland, for example, many pieces of cloth collected from midden deposits show evidence of stitching, repatching, and wear that suggest a high degree of recycling and the importance of cloth as a household commodity. However, the standardized nature of their production suggests most were made initially to serve as currency before they were 'consumed' by being transformed into useful products. It is to the issues of standardization and changes in Icelandic textile production over time that we now turn.

Iceland's archaeological textile collections have been recovered from a wide range of sites that include ecclesiastic centres, harbours, wealthy farms, smaller farms, and burials (Table 13.1). Identifying *legal cloth* within these assemblages presented a critical first task before assessing its ubiquity, origins, and chronological development. Icelandic historical documents and post-medieval textile collections indicate that Icelandic *vaðmál* was a 2/2 twill, but while these sources describe the length and breadth of complete panels of legal *vaðmál* (Hoffman 1974; Gelsinger 1981; Þórláksson 1991) archaeological specimens are inevitably fragmentary. Thus, the identification of *vaðmál* as a standardized commodity-currency in the archaeological record also entails an assessment of changes through time in weaving, expressed as a reduction in the range of variability for basic features of the cloth, especially its warp and weft counts, its spin directions, and its surface finishes.

One would expect some degree of standardization in cloth used as a legally regulated form of currency in order for buyers and sellers to assess the suitability of goods provided in exchanges. Gelsinger argued that standardization was necessary for *vaðmál* to serve as a unit of exchange (1981, 35). Standardization is a key factor in the emergence of any currency beyond the barter system, providing a 'universal yardstick' by which to evaluate objects (Maurer 2006), while currency itself comes to symbolize and measure the social value of other objects (Harris 1995; Saul 2004).[2]

Identifying the production and use of cloth as a commodity-currency in the archaeological record requires looking for temporally consistent and regionally ubiquitous shifts in the range and variety of the textiles produced, used, and consumed at archaeological sites. Specifically, one should expect to see a shift from the production and use, at the household level, of a wide range of weaves and qualities of textiles, each produced to meet different needs (clothing, packing, bedding, etc), to the focused production and circulation of one or more specific types of fabric characterized by a restricted and recognizable range of qualities that reflect the axes along which its production was standardized and measured. Prior to the promotion of this specific

[2] In textile analyses, the term 'standardization' is often used to refer to the quality, consistency, and uniformity of fabrics in industrial or quasi-industrial production, whether to satisfy customer demands, improve the fabric's physical qualities, or maintain a 'brand' for commercial purposes (Geijer 1938; Bender Jørgensen 1986). However, a more accurate term for this is 'uniform production', rather than 'standardized production', as it refers to efforts to maintain consistency in production rather than the production of cloth to regulated standards for the use as a legal unit of exchange. Here, 'standardization', for the production of legal currency, is defined as production made according to legally defined uniform or consistent standards—creating a product that was socially integrated as a regulated exchange product and that was ubiquitously accepted and produced to those standards throughout the areas where it was understood to be legal tender.

Table 13.1. List of sites featured with numbers of textiles. For the Viking Age, numbers include both mineralized and non-mineralized textiles. 'Periods' reflect the temporal span over which textiles were preserved at the site, not necessarily the full temporal range of the cultural deposits present there.

Site name	Site type	County and region	Periods	Number
Búaland	Burial	Skaftafellsýsla (S)	1780	2
Skálholt	Elite residence	Árnessýsla (S)	1600–1900	2000 +
Gilsbakki	Elite residence	Mýrasýsla (W)	1450–1900	124
Möðruvellir	Elite residence, monastery	Eyjafjarðarsýsla (N)	1450(?)–1850	103
Skriðuklaustur	Monastery	Múlasýsla (N)	1400–1500	2
Kúabot	Mid-ranked farm	Skaftafellsýsla (W)	1400–1500	6
Bergþórshvöll	Mid-ranked farm	Rangárvallasýsla (S)	1350–1900	169 +
Vík	Mid-ranked farm	Skagafjörðursýsla (N)	1300–1500	1
Meðalheimur	Small farm	Skagafjörðursýsla (N)	1300–1700	50
Stóraborg	Mid-ranked farm	Rangárvallasýsla (S)	1200–1900	754–1000 +
Gásir	Harbour	Eyjafjarðarsýssla (N)	1200–1500	79
Reykholt	Elite residence	Borgarfjarðarsýsla (W)	1050–1900	705
Alþingisreitur	Harbour	Reykjavik (SW)	Late Viking–1600	161
Bessastaðir	Elite residence	Gullbringusýsla (SW)	Viking Age–1900	102 (1 VA)
Þórisá, Eyrartigur	Burial	Múlasýsla (S)	Viking Age	17
Ketilstaðir	Burial	Múlasýsla (N)	Viking Age	16
Reykjasel	Burial	Múlasýsla (N)	Viking Age	12
Hofstadir	Farm	Mývatnssveit (N)	Viking Age and 18th century	17
Kaldarhöfði	Burial	Árnessýsla (S)	Viking Age	9
Granagil	Burial	Skaftafellssýsla (W)	Viking Age	8
Dalvík Brimnes	Burial	Eyjafjarðarsýsla (N)	Viking Age	8
Vestdalur	Burial	Seyðisfjörður	Viking Age	5
Daðastaðir	Burial	Þingeyjarsýsla (N)	Viking Age	3
Syðri Hofdalir	Burial	Skagafjarðarsýsla (N)	Viking Age	2
Silastaðir	Burial	Eyjafjarðarsýsla (N)	Viking Age	2
Selfos	Burial	Árnessýsla (S)	Viking Age	2
Hrísar	Burial	Eyjafjarðarsýsla (N)	Viking Age	2
Gamla Berjanes	Burial	Rangárvallasýsla (S)	Viking Age	2
Snæhvammur	Burial	Múlasýsla (N)	Viking Age	1
Berufjórður	Burial	Barðastrandarsýsla (NW)	Viking Age	1
Austarihóll	Burial	Skagafjarðarsýsla (N)	Viking Age	1
Glumbær	Burial	Þingeyjarsýsla (S)	Viking Age	1
Heynes	Farm	Borgarfjarðarsýsla (W)	Viking Age	1
Kalastaðir	Burial	Borgarfjarðarsýsla (W)	Viking Age	1
Skógar í Flokadal	Burial	Borgarfjarðarsýsla (W)	Viking Age	1
Litlu Nupar	Burial	Þingeyjarsýsla (S)	Viking Age	1
Hrisheimar	Burial	Mývatnssveit (N)	Viking Age	1
Hábaer	Burial	Rangárvallasýsla (S)	Viking Age	1

standardized product, one might expect to see it as one among a wide range of textile types that were already being produced within the corpus of fabrics known from the region, with its relative frequency within the textile assemblages of different sites reflecting the needs and decisions of the households that once occupied them. Some sites might produce a lot of that fabric type and others very little.

With the promotion of cloth to a commodity-currency, one would expect to see a nearly simultaneous adoption and circulation of that fabric type, and increasing standardization in its physical structure and appearance across all regions in which it was used or accepted as currency, as individual households began to 'make money' for exchange or acquired it for payments and transactions. Standardization of production, ubiquity across the archaeological record, and a rapid adoption of the standardized form should, therefore, be hallmarks of the appearance and adoption of standardized cloth currency in much the same way that standardization of size and mass, metal quality, and decorative elements signal the appearance of coins used as legally accepted currencies.

Thread counts reflecting how finely or coarsely a textile is woven are useful data points for tracking changes in textile production strategies, assemblage variability, cloth standardization, industrialization, and more (Hayeur Smith 2012; 2014). This is particularly so in the Icelandic case, where close parallels exist between the physical cloth and technical descriptions and regulations of cloth currency provided in historic texts.[3] They may also be important attributes for identifying legal cloth. At Gásir and Möðruvellir—two medieval sites with clear links to mercantile trade—the textile assemblages are dominated by 2/2 twills with tightly constrained, overlapping thread-count distributions: six to twelve threads/cm on the warp and four to eight threads/cm on the weft (Fig. 13.1). Given these sites' documented roles in commercial activity and tithe/tribute consolidation, legal cloth currency would be expected to dominate their assemblages and, therefore, the thread-count boundaries at these sites were examined to identify contextually reasonable *archaeological* signatures for *vaðmál*. Although these signatures were generated independently from medieval historical sources, they are consistent with Hoffman's (1974) and Þórláksson's (1991) inferences about *vaðmál* thread counts, based on later medieval and post-medieval texts (see below). Having established archaeological parameters for the identification of legal cloth currency, we are now in a position to ask: how widespread and significant was *vaðmál* production in Viking Age and medieval Iceland?

[3] Thread counts are one of many methods used in textile analysis. To quote Andersson Strand et al.: 'a textile is not simply a binary system of spun, twisted, or spliced fibres, but first and foremost a result of complex interactions between resources, technology and society' (2010, 150). Thus, following preliminary basic visual analysis, a combination of analytical techniques is added to supplement information on the use, wear, and function of textiles. These can include SEM analyses, fibre and dye analysis, as well as molecular analyses such as aDNA and strontium.

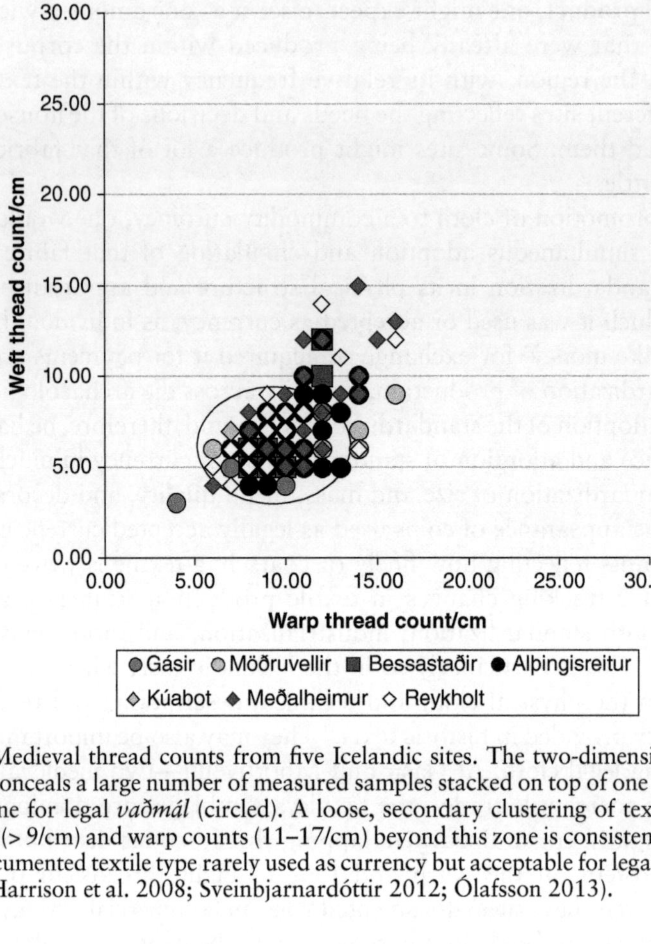

Fig. 13.1. Medieval thread counts from five Icelandic sites. The two-dimensional nature of this graph conceals a large number of measured samples stacked on top of one another within the core zone for legal *vaðmál* (circled). A loose, secondary clustering of textiles with both higher weft (> 9/cm) and warp counts (11–17/cm) beyond this zone is consistent with *smávöð*, another documented textile type rarely used as currency but acceptable for legal payments and tithes (see Harrison et al. 2008; Sveinbjarnardóttir 2012; Ólafsson 2013).

Viking Age Icelandic Textiles and the Origins of Vaðmál *as Cloth Currency*

The narrow and concentrated range of thread counts seen in the medieval Icelandic assemblages (Fig. 13.1) contrasts markedly with the roughly even distribution of thread-count combinations seen in Viking Age assemblages (Fig. 13.3). Viking Age textiles recovered from Icelandic archaeological contexts (unlike medieval textiles, Viking Age textiles come largely from burials; for exact numbers see note 5) are quite diverse, with plain weaves, panama weaves, simple and patterned twills, tablet weaves, and pile weaves all represented, along with evidence for colourful patterning, dying, or decorative additions.[4] Importantly, this diversity is true of textiles from both burial and settlement contexts, even

[4] These assemblages have been examined at the National Museum of Iceland from 2010 to the present. Data has been systematically collected on fibre types, thread counts, spin direction and tension, weave structure, wear, surface treatment, and evidence of use as textile objects. Many pieces have been subsampled for AMS dating, dye analysis, and fibre identification.

though textiles from settlements are far fewer.[5] The diversity in Viking Age weaves contrasts remarkably with medieval textiles that consist of 2/2 twill predominantly and fewer tabbies. Within the Icelandic Viking Age corpus, 40 per cent of all textiles analysed from burials (total number: fifty-nine fragments) tested positive for indigotin, implying they were dyed blue, with the majority of these coming from female burials.[6] Blue dye was also identified at Viking Age Birka (Walton Rogers 1988, 19), and Icelandic sagas suggest that blue was a colour associated with death (Wolf 2007, 71).

Bender Jørgensen (1992, 40) determined that early Viking Age textiles in Norway were overwhelmingly spun in a very specific manner—z/z (Fig. 13.2).

Fig. 13.2. Viking Age z/z spun tabby weaves from the grave of Eyrartigur in Eastern Iceland, magnification x 200.

[5] The total number of fragments from Viking Age Iceland is 110; 102 of these are from burials and include mineralized, pseudomorphic, and non-mineralized textiles.

[6] Actual (non-mineralized) textiles account for fifty-nine objects, twenty-three of which tested positive for indigotin. It is difficult to assess the sex of each burial containing textiles as some textiles come from locations with multiple burials or grave fields excavated 100 years ago when little attention was paid to the provenance of artefacts (Hayeur Smith 2004). In other cases, the burials have not been properly sexed due to the devastating effects of erosion on the Icelandic landscape, when the only thing that remains are teeth or very badly preserved bone. Thus, the numbers here are a rough estimate, with seven possible male burials containing textiles, ten possible female, and an additional seven that are unknown.

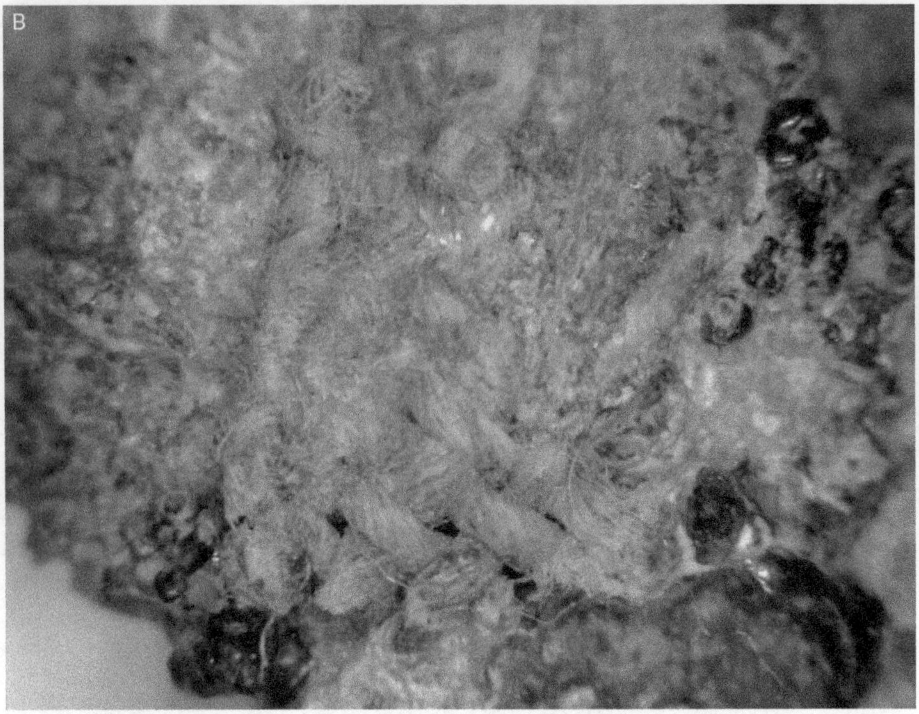

Fig. 13.2. Continued.

The z/z spin structure is also commonly found in Icelandic Viking Age textiles. However, early in Iceland's settlement period (AD 870–930), a new spin direction was introduced—z/s—producing considerable heterogeneity in the composition of the island's Viking Age woven products.[7] Similarly, counts of warp threads range over a broad span of four to twenty-five threads per centimetre, while weft thread counts range from at least four to fifteen (Fig. 13.3). The presence of multiple, loose clusters within this distribution, as well as the breadth of the distribution itself, suggests that a wide range of cloth types differing in quality, coarseness, and probably use, were produced at the household level to meet farms' needs for clothing, storage, and transport media, and so on. When variability in spin directions, in finishes (colour, etc.), and in site-level assemblage composition are added to this, it seems clear that while cloth may have

[7] The terms z-spin and/or s-spin refer to whether yarn was spun clockwise or counter-clockwise, respectively. Spin direction is technologically neutral—either direction produces usable yarn—yet choices to spin one way or the other often remain constant across large geographic regions. Some scholars regard these decisions as cultural markers passed from experienced to inexperienced cloth makers across generations (Minar 2001; Bender Jørgensen 1992, 13).

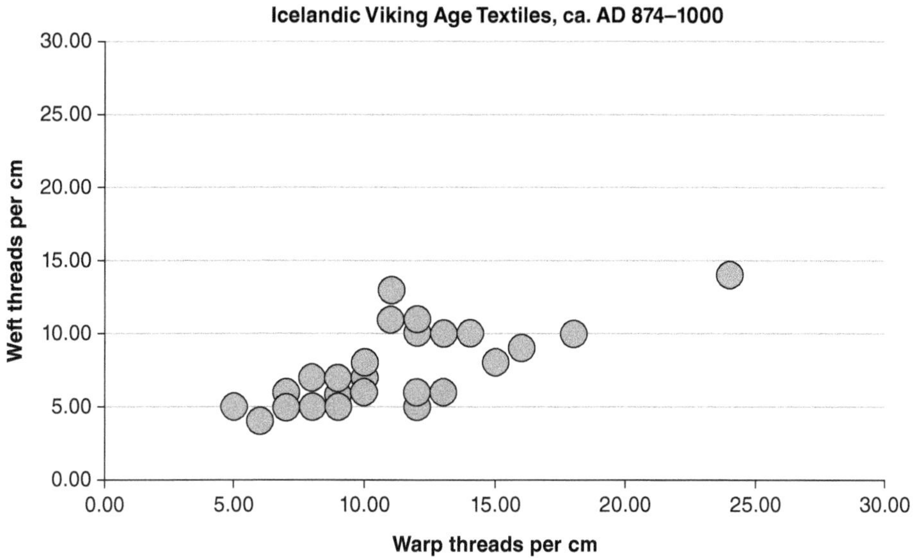

Fig. 13.3. Thread counts for Viking Age textiles in Iceland AD 874–1000 (The total number of Viking Age textiles from Iceland is 110. Only those well-preserved textiles from which thread counts could be made are included here.).

been exchanged locally through sales or gifts, there is little evidence yet that any Viking Age Icelandic textiles were standardized to the degree expected for legal currency.

Early Medieval Icelandic Cloth: From Commodity to Legal Currency

During the medieval period (1050–1550), changes in spin direction, weave types, and thread counts provide a clear indication that, in Iceland, cloth had become more than just a base material for producing other objects. It had become, instead, a standardized legal unit of currency produced on a quasi-industrial scale.

At every medieval site analysed to date, 2/2 twills vastly outnumber all other textiles, with the majority of these mirroring the narrowly constrained thread-count distributions (four to fifteen warp threads/cm; four to eight weft threads/cm) recorded at Gásir and Möðruvellir (Fig. 13.1). Furthermore, the directions in which warp and weft threads were spun—z/s—are similarly consistent across assemblages of medieval legal cloth. The constrained nature of these distributions is especially evident when they are compared with textile assemblages from earlier Icelandic Viking Age sites, where thread counts ranged from four to twenty-five warp and four to fifteen weft threads per centimetre (Fig. 13.3), and where a greater diversity in spinning directions is apparent. Similarly, in the post-medieval period, assemblages regularly return to this broader range of thread counts, and beyond (four to twenty-four warp and weft threads per cm)

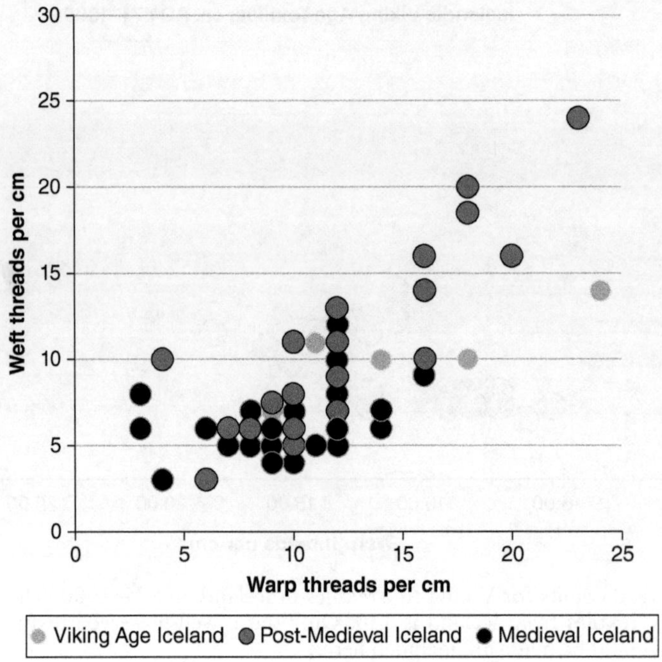

Fig. 13.4. Icelandic, Viking Age, medieval, and post-medieval thread counts. A smaller subset of medieval textiles than in Fig. 13.2 are displayed in this graph.

(Fig. 13.4). These broader thread-count ranges from the Viking Age and the post-medieval period contrast with the tightly constrained pattern seen from *c.*1050–1600 and are what would be expected of production for domestic/household use, where the broader ranges signal the production and consumption of a diverse assemblage of cloth, including coarser and finer textiles employed in a similarly broad range of uses. In contrast, medieval Icelandic textile production appears to have been remarkably constrained and standardized.

In Scandinavia, as elsewhere, the standardization of currencies (silver or otherwise) developed as inter-regional trade intensified and conflicts or confusion over exchange rates increased (Skre 2011). In Iceland, the period during which this standardized pattern of textile production emerges correlates with both legal and literary evidence for intensified trade with mainland Europe through Scandinavia and the British Isles (Gelsinger 1981). The impact of this trade on the Icelandic economy can be gauged, in part, from these standardized assemblages' ubiquity. Not only does standardized *vaðmál* dominate textile assemblages from every medieval site examined so far, but evidence for the *production* of cloth has also been recovered at virtually every site of this period (Hayeur Smith 2014; 2015).

There are no indications in historical, archaeological, or ethnographic sources that specialist tools were required to produce *vaðmál*, as distinct from other types of cloth. However, the tools of cloth production—loom weights and spindle whorls, supplemented, where organic preservation is poor, by examples of rovings (unspun bundles of wool), spun threads, tablet-woven starting border scraps, and off-cuts of cloth from the warp-weighted loom—have been found on virtually every medieval farm excavated in Iceland. At farms of this period, where both organic and inorganic evidence of textile production have been found (such as Alþingisreitur, Stóraborg, Bergþórshvoll, Möðruvellir, and others), standardized 2/2 twills with the characteristics of *vaðmál* described above are the only or the dominant type of textile recovered archaeologically. In sum, the evidence for textile production on farms is ubiquitous and the type of cloth found on these farms, where preserved, is *vaðmál*. Interestingly, this appears to characterize farms at all levels of the socio-economic hierarchy, from elite sites such as Reykholt (Sveinbjarnadóttir 2012), to smaller sites such as Meðalheimur, suggesting that the production of cloth currency was not a prerogative of elite farms alone. Historical records and sagas similarly record the payment of debts in cloth by smaller farms and its use in legal and commercial transactions by farms at all levels within the hierarchy, supporting the archaeological evidence that *vaðmál* was produced in the home, on nearly all farms that had sufficient labour (women) and resources (wool) to sustain it. In essence, it appears that, during the medieval period, Icelanders were weaving money in abundance.

To summarize the results of my analysis of the Icelandic textile corpus, the adoption of uniform and tightly constrained thread-count ranges, the reduction seen in the variability of spin directions at sites all across Iceland at the end of the Viking Age, and the reduction in weave types all suggest levels of standardization similar to those apparent in other monetary systems (Maurer 2006; Gullbekk 2011), while the dominance of *vaðmál* in medieval textile assemblages from the full range of site types of this period implies that its production was decentralized and household-based.

At which point in Icelandic history did this cloth currency become so standardized that nearly all other types of weave disappeared? Dating this transition archaeologically is complicated by the limited number of excavated Icelandic sites with organic preservation from the period 1050–1200. Nevertheless, direct AMS dates on *vaðmál* from the sites described here suggest a clear temporal sequence (Fig. 13.5). While twills do occur in the Viking Age, such as at the site of Hofstaðir in north-eastern Iceland (Lucas et al. 2009), most of them do not have thread counts that fall consistently within the ranges discussed above. Furthermore, within these sites they are present as minor elements within a far more variable and evenly divided textile assemblage that implies production for diverse uses rather than a focus on making standardized products for exchange.

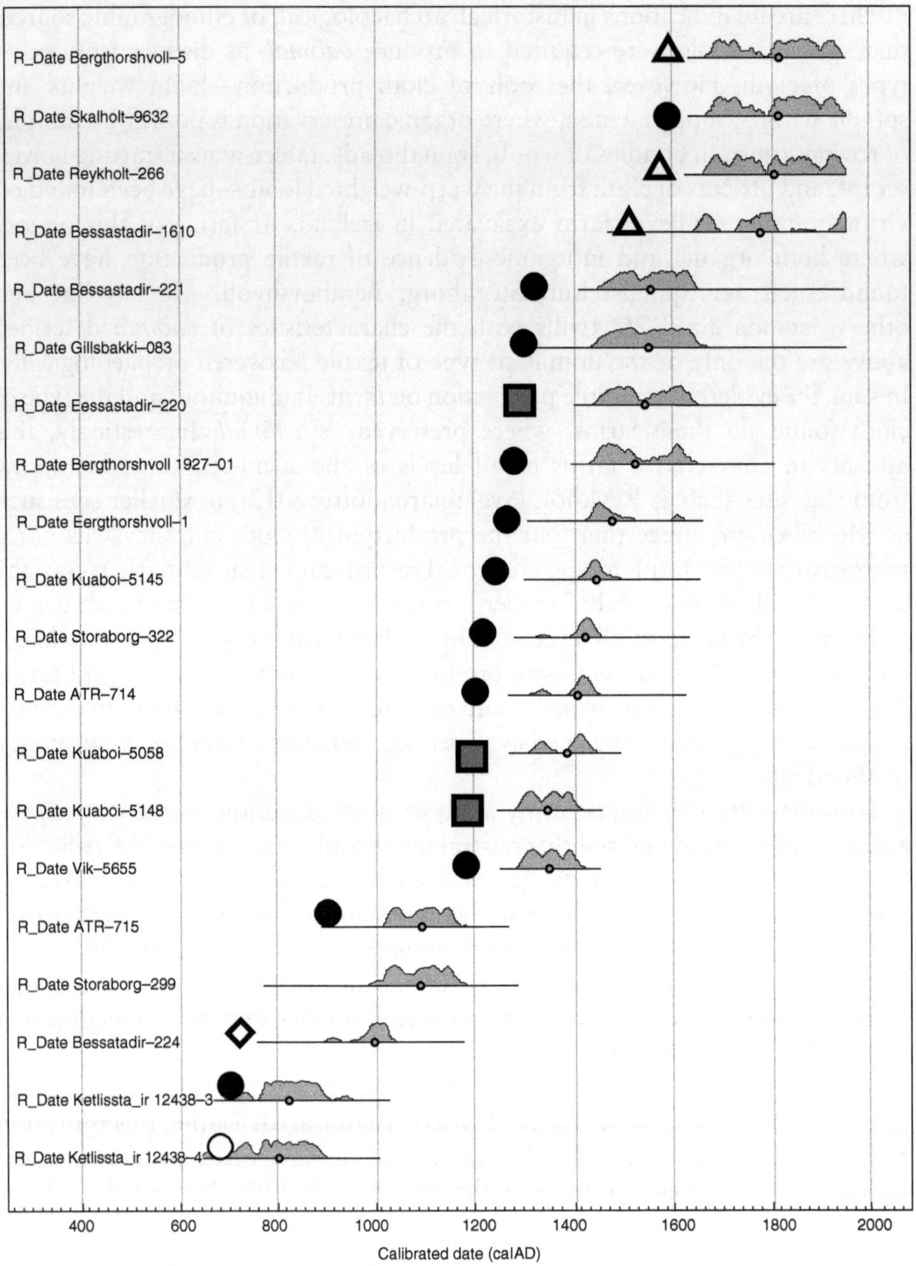

Fig. 13.5. Direct AMS dates on Icelandic textiles run through the *Rags to Riches* and *Weaving Islands of Cloth* projects. Black circles identify *vaðmál* (2/2 twill z/s spun yarns); white circles identify 2/2 twills with z/z spun yarns; open triangles are plied-wool 2/2 twills; grey squares represent plain weaves; the open diamond is a Viking Age basket weave; and Stóraborg-299 was an unspun wool fragment. *Vaðmál* dominates dated assemblages from the eleventh century until the sixteenth/seventeenth centuries.

For example, only one fragment from Hofstaðir and one from Ketilstaðir fit the criteria of later legal cloth. The former is a z/s-spun, 2/2 twill with a thread count of twelve warp yarns to seven wefts, though no AMS dates have been run on this piece. The Ketilstaðir fragment, from a Viking Age woman's burial, would also fall within the legal guidelines of cloth currency. This object (12438–3), part of an apron strap, is a z/s, 2/2 twill with a thread count of nine warp threads to seven wefts. AMS dating of the fragment produced a calibrated age at two standard deviations (95.4 per cent probability) of calAD 716–940 (Beta-380903; 1200±30 bp), with an 87.8 per cent internal probability that the age of this sample falls within the interval calAD 765–895. This is a very early date for Iceland and would, in the absence of other evidence on cloth production, be a very early date for the emergence of standardized legal cloth. However, this fragment and a small number of others of similar type represent just a small percentage within the full range of Viking Age weaves.

While these examples are infrequent, they suggest that the type of cloth that became legally regulated *vaðmál* had its origins in the Viking Age and was being produced before it dominated the textile assemblages of the medieval period. The earliest known example of *vaðmál* that fully exhibits all of the characteristics listed above for legal cloth comes from a deeply buried wet site (Alþingisreitur) in the centre of Reykjavík (Garðarsdóttir 2010). This fragment (ATR 2008-32–715) produced a calibrated AMS date of calAD 1020–1160 (Beta-339967, 2 sigma) with intercepts at 1040, 1110, and 1120 and highest internal probabilities at calAD 1082–1125. Eight further dates on cloth meeting the descriptive characteristics of *vaðmál* and from assemblages dominated by this form of cloth were obtained from the sites of Vík, Reykjavík (Alþingisreitur), Stóraborg, Kúabot, Bergþórshvoll, Bessastaðir, and Gilsbakki. These dates document *vaðmál*'s production through the sixteenth century and suggest that while woollen cloth may have declined as an item of international trade by 1300, as some have suggested (e.g. Gelsinger 1981), to be replaced by dried fish or *skreid*, it continued to be used in Iceland and circulated as a medium of exchange until the sixteenth century.

Although more dated and analysed samples are needed from the eleventh and twelfth centuries to establish precisely when z/s-spun, 2/2 twills became legal cloth, the degree of standardization seen within the data from medieval Iceland suggests that during the late eleventh or early twelfth century, this 2/2 twill with four to fifteen warp threads and four to eight weft threads was promoted for use both as a legal currency and as a commercial product. This twill dominates all Icelandic site assemblages after *c.*1100 and, given the date from Alþingisreitur, combined with the age at which the earliest portions of *Grágás* containing references were written (*c.*1117) (Dennis et al. 1980, 9–13), one may reasonably conclude that this currency acquired its official standardized status roughly between 1080 and 1150, and from that point onwards was produced on farms of all types across Iceland until the late sixteenth century, or even later (Þórláksson 1991).

The Legalities of Cloth Currency

Emerging archaeological data for the appearance of *vaðmál* as a standardized and ubiquitously circulated commodity-currency in Iceland fits with the earliest historical documents for its regulation in Iceland. As noted above, the earliest regulations addressing cloth currency are found in the law code *Grágás*, the oldest portions of which were written in 1117 and remained Iceland's law until 1271 (Dennis et al. 1980; 2002). According to *Grágás*, panels of *vaðmál* two ells in width and six ells in length were considered legal as currency. This unit, the *eyrir* (pl. *aurar*)—equivalent to one ounce of silver, became the basic unit of measurement for all types of exchange in Iceland (Dennis et al. 1980, 246).

The quality and standardization of woven cloth were critical for its use as currency. *Grágás* describes methods for evaluating legal cloth on a twenty-ell piece:

> A new law. Homespun shall not be so slack at the selvage that it makes a difference of more than one ell in a twenty-ell piece. If the difference is greater, it is to be measured along the middle. Homespun is to be double the forearm broad and it is lawfully offered if the breadth amounts to that, measured with fingers extended and it is of good quality. The parties to a deal shall take two lawful viewers to view trade goods offered as payment should it be slack in the selvage or narrow. (Dennis et al. 2002, 350)

The twenty-ell unit is mentioned in another passage of *Grágás* under the heading 'lawful measures', which describes using the '*stika*' to measure legal cloth. This measuring tool, one-tenth of the twenty-ell unit in length (thus, roughly 100 cm long), was marked on the wall of the church at Þingvöllr, where the Althing met, around 1200. Both this twenty-ell mark on the wall of the church at the national assembly and individual *stikur* held elsewhere in the country were materialized legal mechanisms to standardize units of cloth measure (Gelsinger 1981; Dennis et al. 2002). Information on the quality required for cloth to be legally used as currency is less clearly specified in the earliest medieval sources; yet regulations clearly existed regarding the widths, warp thread counts, cloth weight, and values for a number of specific types of cloth currency that were named *gjaldavoð* (*vaðmál* suitable for legal payments), *klæðavoð* (cloth suitable for clothing), *vöruvoð* (marketable cloth or common *vaðmál*), and *smávoð* (finer-quality cloth). Hoffman felt these guidelines were frequently inconsistent, but concluded that all of the forms of legal cloth fell within a production range of four to fourteen warp threads per centimetre (1974, 213–14). Þorláksson, however, identified guidelines for legal cloth production from later medieval and post-medieval sources (*c.*1300 and 1613–40) that suggest clarifications. These sources stated that *gjaldavoð* was to have nine to ten warp threads per cm, *klæðavoð* eleven warp threads per cm, and *smávoð* eleven to fourteen warp threads per cm (Þorláksson 1991). The finest and most valuable of these, *smávoð* and *pragðarvoð*, had the highest thread counts. Although rarely used in domestic trade, these could be used in legal contexts—for example to pay tithes to the church (Østergård 2004, 62–3). These different qualities of *vaðmál* are listed in the later sources such as *Búalög* but it is unclear whether these were in use during the later Viking Age, whether they were established at the outset of using *vaðmál* as a commodity-currency, or whether these divisions emerged over the course of the medieval period when the use of cloth as an exchange medium and trade good gained momentum.

Legal Cloth and Gender Relationships

The study of medieval legal documents, together with anthropological studies of textile work in ancient communities, suggests that cloth was often produced by women, and it is widely accepted that, in Iceland, textile production was exclusively women's work (Hayeur Smith 2014; 2015; Róbertsdóttir 2008). Strong sexual taboos surrounded textile work in both Viking Age Scandinavia and Iceland (see Bek-Pedersen 2007; 2008; Hayeur Smith forthcoming), while legal texts are also explicit that women were not considered legally equal to men, nor always permitted a public voice (Jochens 1995; Hayeur Smith 2004; Norrman 2008). Women in Scandinavia, including Iceland, were the keepers of the home, while men were normally more active participants in the world outside (Norrman 2008). Yet women had critical economic roles. Among other things, women produced *vaðmál* and other textiles from wool that they gathered, carded, washed, and spun (Meulengracht Sørensen 1983). While men were responsible for other aspects pertaining to sheep husbandry, establishing trade relationships, and setting legal guidelines, women made cloth that conformed to legal regulations and established standards. How did relations between the sexes play out regarding the production and distribution of cloth currency in a society without urban centres and in which cloth was quite likely produced on every farm for both household and legal use?

It has been argued that gender roles were more balanced in the pre-Christian world of the Viking Age, when more personal power was bestowed on women through rights to marry, own property, and to divorce, than they were during the Middle Ages (Jesch 1991; Gräslund 1995; 1999; 2001a; 2001b). Weaving provided a means of expression that was uniquely female and perhaps associated with strong female deities linked to concepts of birth, life, and death (Heide 2006; Bek-Pedersen 2007; 2008; Hayeur Smith 2012). The silence of historical sources on women's roles in the regulation and distribution of cloth currency obscures their involvement in this important activity, but an illustration in *Heynesbók*, a fifteenth-century manuscript of the *Jónsbók* law code (GKS 3269b 4to.), suggests that women in Iceland were not excluded from its public distribution. In this image, a woman is depicted conversing with a man who carries a measuring stick to verify the dimensions of the *vaðmál* she is presenting to him. She asks, 'Ert þú konungs umboðsmaður' ('Are you the king's steward?'), to which he answers, 'Já, já' ('yes, yes'). It is not clear whether she is assisting him or whether the illustration points to the necessity of identifying who had the king's authority to validate goods in exchange after Iceland became a colonial dependency. In either case, the artist's choice of a woman as a participant in the legal action is significant.

Iceland's medieval sources provide little evidence of women's resistance to male domination of the economic interactions that set values for cloth currency. Each gender appears to have understood its complementary role in this economic system. At the same time, making *vaðmál* was making money and this may have provided women with a source of power that was socially understood, as the weavers knew best the differences between good- and poor-quality *vaðmál*. This seeming symbiosis may stem from the small size of the Icelandic colony, the harsh nature of the North Atlantic environment, and the need for collaboration between the sexes to guarantee survival. This is not to say that resistance did not exist, but it may have been subtle and reflected in the values and symbolic associations connected to the making of cloth (Hayeur Smith 2013).

Why Cloth?

The discussion of cloth currency in Iceland brings us to the final question: why cloth? While legal sources and archaeological data both indicate that cloth was used in Norway and Iceland as a means of exchange, why was it chosen as a form of commodity-money in the first place and what lay behind its value and worth?

Skre (2011) argues that commodities that are given the value of currency also have utilitarian value. This differentiates a commodity-money system from a purely monetary system based on abstract representations of value (Skre 2011, 70). In Viking Age Scandinavia, coinage and silver were introduced and used as methods of payment alongside other commodities for nearly one millennium. In this system, different commodity-money media functioned not only as units of account and media of payment, but also as commodities with inherent utilitarian value (Skre 2011, 71).

In late Viking Age and early medieval Iceland, textiles served all of these functions: they could be kept and stored for future use; used to pay taxes, tithes, and other financial obligations; or consumed and transformed into household items. They were transportable, malleable, and catered to basic human needs for shelter and protection (Schneider & Weiner 1989, 2). When transformed into clothing, textiles also behaved, at some level—to use Terence Turner's apt expression—as a 'social skin', a second skin that protects our nudity, creating a barrier between our biological person and our social one and providing information about the 'social self'—our social rank, status, gender, and cultural affiliation (Eicher & Roach-Higgins 1992, 12; Turner 1993, 15). Through these diverse concepts and the predominant roles women held in cloth production in many cultures, textiles and textile work have frequently become associated with concepts of birth, death, and fate (Schneider & Weiner 1989, 21).

Bek-Pedersen notes that the apocryphal Book of James, when describing the Annunciation, depicts Mary spinning when the Angel comes to her, and argues that the making of thread was a symbol for the making of a child (Bek-Pedersen 2008, 180). She describes a similar motif in a Norse context: in *Orkneyinga Saga*, Earl Sigurðr of Orkney consults his mother about the fate of an upcoming battle, to which she responds negatively, adding:

> 'I would have kept you for a long time in my wool basket, if I knew that you would live forever, but it is fate which rules life and not where a man comes from; better to die with dignity than to live with shame.' (Bek-Pedersen 2008, 180)

For Bek-Pedersen, keeping someone inside the wool basket suggested ideas of enduring life and protection from death, and of the basket as a symbolic womb with the unspun wool that has not yet been transformed into textile symbolizing a person-to-be, or their fate (2008, 179–80).

The Norse concept of birth, fate, and death being entangled with textiles and weaving in general is graphically presented in the poem 'Darraðarljóð', near the end of *Njál's Saga*. This poem recounts a vision of twelve valkyries weaving the web of fate by using human entrails for the warp and weft, and using the heads of warriors as the weights for their warp-weighted loom. At the end of the scene they take the cloth from the loom and cut it up into twelve fragments and depart. Following this vision, a series of tragic events takes place, as the valkyries had created a 'second skin' from human flesh and, by destroying it, sealed the fates of men and nations in the process.

One may wonder what this has to do with cloth used as a commodity for exchange. I argue that these concepts reflect deeply held understandings about cloth in the Viking Age that may have contributed to its valuation by endowing it with more than just utilitarian value, as a product that also evoked a symbolic system deeply rooted in mythology and belief, female agency and power (Hayeur Smith forthcoming). Schneider and Weiner suggest that, in many cultural contexts, textiles became metaphors for society itself and social relations, while arguing that it is a convincing analogue for the regenerative and degenerative processes of life and death (1989, 3).

In Viking Age Iceland and Norway, textiles acquired value not only for their utilitarian uses but also from these many deeply rooted metaphors. But regardless of their symbolic or metaphoric representations, in both Iceland and Norway textiles gained sufficient importance that they were given a formalized and legal value on a par with silver. When it came to actual economic transactions, did everyone in Iceland routinely pay their debts in cloth from the eleventh century onwards? Probably not, as the commodity-money system was as fluid as it was in Norway and gave people opportunities to choose from diverse media depending on what they had available. Yet legal obligations and the standard exchange values of those diverse commodities used ells of *vaðmál* as the official unit of measure. *Grágás* frequently lists *vaðmál* as the official unit of measure, and equivalents are provided for its worth in relation to silver and other commodities. In 1281, when *Jónsbók* was handed down from the Norwegian crown as Iceland's new law of the land in a novel colonial context, *vaðmál* was not as frequently mentioned by name as a commodity, but the standard unit of measure remained the 'one ounce unit' that was still equivalent to six ells of *vaðmál*.

The difference between the two sources is that in *Grágás* it seems to have been important not only to reiterate that cloth was acceptable as a medium of exchange but also to provide legal guidance on how to assess its qualities. However, by the time *Jónsbók* was written, it appears that the transition from silver to cloth as the basic unit of account had been formalized and naturalized to the degree that, I argue, it was no longer necessary to justify its value or describe its appearance anymore, since cloth had become a means to economic ends that were understood by all.

Conclusion

When the early Norse settlers arrived in Iceland, they brought with them economic and cultural traditions from Norway, within which weaving, its products, and its symbolic meaning were already important. Cloth was sufficiently important to have been given legal equivalents in Norway's Gulathing law, on which Iceland's early laws were framed, and may have been used in exchange within a broader commodity-money system in early Viking Age Iceland. By the end of the Viking Age, quite likely due to declining quantities of silver, textiles were promoted to the status of a basic unit of measure and value. Through a novel combination of Norwegian and Celtic textile traditions, a specific type of cloth, *vaðmál*, with a clearly recognizable physical structure—a 2/2 twill spun with z/s yarns and with a thread-count range of four to fifteen warp yarns per centimetre—became legally regulated in Icelandic law codes from the eleventh to sixteenth centuries as cloth currency. While *vaðmál* is archaeologically visible as a form of textile that had its origins within the diverse weaving repertoire of Viking Age women, only in the late eleventh century did it dominate Icelandic textile production, with levels of standardization that bespeak legal regulation and a level of ubiquity that implies it was made in virtually every household and circulated far and wide. It acquired some of its value from the very nature of textiles themselves as means of protection that were malleable and easily transportable. But some of its worth must have come from less obvious origins, trickling down from deeply rooted beliefs that connected textiles to mythological themes of life, birth, death, and fate.

ACKNOWLEDGEMENTS

Funding for these analyses was provided by the National Science Foundation, Arctic Social Sciences, Polar Programs, awards nos. 1023167 (2010–12) and 1302898 (2013–16). I would like to thank the following institutions: Haffenreffer

Museum of Anthropology, the National Museum of Iceland, Fornleifastofnun Íslands, and the following individuals: Freyja Hliðkvist Ómarsdóttir, Lilja Árnadóttir, Ármann Guðmundsson, Guðrún Alda Gísladóttir, Howell Magnus Roberts, Ramona Harrison, and Guðrún Sveinbjarnardóttir, Vala Garðarsdóttir, Guðmundur Ólafsson, Mjöll Snæsdóttir, Gavin Lucas, and special thanks to my husband Kevin P. Smith, for his constructive comments and help proofreading and editing this paper.

REFERENCES

Andersson Strand, E. 2003a. *Tools for Textile Production from Birka and Hedeby: Excavations in the Black Earth, 1990–1995*. Birka Studies, vol. 8. Stockholm: Birka Project for Riksantikvarieämbetet.

Andersson Strand, E. 2003b. 'Textile Production in Scandinavia during the Viking Age'. In *Textilien aus Archäologie und Geschichte. Festschrift für Klaus Tidow*, ed. L. Bender Jørgensen, J. Banck-Burgess, & A. Rast-Eicher, 46–61. Neumünster: Wachholtz Verlag.

Andersson Strand, E. 2011. 'Tools and Textiles: Production and Organization in Birka and Hedeby'. In Sigmundsson et al. (eds), 1–17.

Andersson Strand, E., K.M. Frei, M. Gleba, U. Mannering, M.-L. Nosch, & I. Skals 2010. 'Old Textiles—New Possibilities'. *European Journal of Archaeology* 13.2: 149–73.

Bek-Pedersen, K. 2007. 'Are the Spinning *Nornir* just a Yarn?' *Viking and Medieval Scandinavia* 3: 1–10.

Bek-Pedersen, K. 2008. 'Weaving Swords and Rolling Heads: A Peculiar Space in Old Norse Tradition'. In *Space and Time in Europe: East and West, Past and Present*, ed. M. Mencej, 167–80. Ljubljana: Univerza v Ljubljani, Filozofska fakulteta.

Bender Jørgensen, E. 1986. 'Northern European Textile Production and Trade in the 1st Millennium AD: A Research Project'. *Journal of Danish Archaeology* 3: 124–34.

Bender Jørgensen, E. 1992. *North European Textiles until* AD *1000*. Aarhus: Aarhus University Press.

Bender Jørgensen, E. 2003. 'Scandinavia AD 400–1000'. In *The Cambridge History of Western Textiles I*, ed. D. Jenkins, 132–8. Cambridge: Cambridge University Press.

Bernharðsson, H., M.L. Magnússon, & M. Jónsson 2005. *Járnsíða og Kristniréttur Árna Þorlákssonar*. Reykjavík: Sögufélag.

Christensen, A.M. & M. Nockert 2006. *Osebergfunnet bind IV Tekstilene*. Oslo: University of Oslo.

Cleasby, R., G. Vigfusson, & W. Craigie 1957. *An Icelandic–English Dictionary*. 2nd edn. Oxford: Clarendon Press.

Damsholt, N. 1984. 'The Role of the Icelandic Women in the Sagas and in the Production of Homespun Cloth'. *Scandinavian Journal of History* 9: 75–90.

Dennis, A., P. Foote, & R. Perkins 1980. *Laws of Early Iceland, Grágás I*. Winnipeg: University of Manitoba Press.

Dennis, A., P. Foote, & R. Perkins 2002. *Laws of Early Iceland, Grágás II*. Winnipeg: University of Manitoba Press.

Eicher, J.B. & M.E. Roach-Higgins 1992. 'Definition and Classification of Dress: Implications for Analysis of Gender Roles'. In *Dress and Gender: Making and Meaning in Cultural Contexts,* ed. R. Barnes & J.B. Eicher, 1–28. New York and Oxford: Berg.

Einzig, P. 1966. *Primitive Money in its Ethnological, Historical, and Economic Aspects.* Oxford: Pergamon Press.

Garðarsdóttir, V. 2010. Alþingisreiturinn, Bindi 1 og 2, Unpublished Excavation Report. Reykjavík.

Geijer, A. 1938. *Birka III Die Textilfunde aus den Gräbern.* Uppsala: Almqvist & Wiksell.

Gelsinger, B. 1981. *Icelandic Enterprise: Commerce and Economy in the Middle Ages.* Columbia: University of South Carolina Press.

Graham-Campbell, J. 2011. '"The Serpent's Bed": Gold and Silver in Viking-Age Iceland and Beyond'. In Sigmundsson et al. (eds), 103–31.

Graham-Campbell, J., S.M. Sindbæk, & G. Williams (eds) 2011. *Silver Economies, Monetisation, and Society in Scandinavia* AD *800–1100.* Aarhus: Aarhus University Press.

Gräslund, A.-S. 1995. 'The Christianization of Central Sweden from a Female Perspective'. In *Rom und Byzanz im Norden, Mission und Glaubenswechsel im Ostseeraum Während des 8.–14. Jahrhunderts, Band I,* ed. M. Müller-Wille, 313–28. Mainz: Akademie der Wissenschaften und der Litteratur.

Gräslund, A.-S. 1999. 'Is there Evidence of Powerful Women in Late Iron Age Svealand?' In *Völker an Nordun Ostsee und die Franken Akten des 48. Sachsensymposiums in Mannheim vom 7. Bis 11. September 1997,* ed. U. Von Freeden, U. Kock, & A. Wieczorek, 91–8. Bonn: Dr. Rudolf Habelt GmbH.

Gräslund, A.-S. 2001a. 'Kvinnan Satt Där, Snodde Sin Slända... Några Reflektioner om Fynd av Sländtrissor i Birka'. In *Vi Får Tacka Lamm,* ed. B. Magnus, 73–8. Stockholm: Statens Historiska Museum.

Gräslund, A.-S. 2001b. 'The Position of Iron Age Scandinavian Women: Evidence from Graves and Rune Stones'. In *Gender and the Archaeology of Death,* ed. B. Arnold & N. Wicker, 91–8. Walnut Creek: Alta Mira Press.

Guðjónsson, E. 1962. 'Forn Röggvarvefnaður'. *Árbók hins Íslenzka Fornleifafélags* 1962: 12–71.

Guðjónsson, E. 1965. 'Um Skinnsaum'. *Árbók hins Íslenzka Fornleifafélags* 1964: 69–87.

Guðjónsson, E. 1970. *The National Costume of Women in Iceland.* Reykjavik: Litbrá.

Guðjónsson, E. 1973. 'Íslenzk Útsaumsheiti og Útsaumsgerdir á Miðöldum'. *Árbók hins Íslenzka Fornleifafélags* 1972: 131–50.

Guðjónsson, E. 1980. 'Note on Medieval Icelandic Shaggy Pile Weaving'. *Bulletin de Liaison du Centre International d'Études des Textiles Anciens.* Lyon: CIETA.

Guðjónsson, E. 1990. 'Some Aspects of the Icelandic Warp Weighted Loom, Vefstaður'. *Textile History* 21.2: 165–79.

Guðjónsson, E. 1992. 'Um Rokka, Einkum med tilliti til Skotrokka'. *Árbók hins Íslenzka Fornleifafélags* 1992: 11–52.

Guðjónsson, E. 1994. 'Um Vefstóla og Vefara á Íslandi á 18. og 19. Öld'. *Árbók hins Íslenzka Fornleifafélags* 1993: 5–50.

Guðjónsson, E. 1998a. 'Um Vefstóla á Íslandi á 18. öld. Nokkrar Athugasemdir'. *Árbók hins Íslenzka Fornleifafélags* 1996–7: 129–40.

Guðjónsson, E. 1998b. 'Kljásteinavefstaðir á Íslandi og á Grænlandi'. *Árbók hins Íslenzka Fornleifafélags* 1996–7: 95–120.

Gullbekk, S.H. 2011. 'Norway: Commodity Money, Silver and Coins'. In Graham-Campbell, Sindbæk, & Williams (eds), 93–111.

Hagen, K.G. 1994. *Profesjonalisme og Urbanisering*. Universitetets Oldsakssamling Skrifter. Ny rekke nr. 16. Oslo: Universitetets Oldsakssamling.

Hägg, I. 1974. *Kvinnodräkten i Birka. Livplaggens Rekonstruktion på Grundval av det Arkeologiska Materialet*. Uppsala: Institutionen for Arkeologi.

Hägg, I. 1984a. 'Birkas Orientaliska Praktplagg'. *Fornvännen* 78: 204–33.

Hägg, I. 1984b. *Die Textilfunde aus dem Hafen von Haithabu*. Berichte über die Ausgrabungen in Haithabu 20. Neumünster: K. Wachholtz.

Hägg, I. 1986. 'Die Tracht'. In *Systematische Analysen der Gräberfunde*. Birka II: 2, ed. G. Arwidsson, 51–72. Stockholm: Kungl. Vitterhets, Historie och Antikvitets Akademien & Almqvist and Wiksell International.

Hägg, I. 1991. *Textilfunde aus der Siedlung und aus den Gräbern von Haithabu. Beschreibung und Gliederung*. Berichte über die Ausgrabungen in Haithabu 29. Neumünster: K. Wachholtz.

Harris, M. 1995. *Cultural Anthropology*. 4th edn. New York: HarperCollins.

Harrison, R., H. Roberts, & W.P. Adderley 2008. 'Gásir in Eyjafjörður: International Exchange and Local Economy in Medieval Iceland'. *Journal of the North Atlantic* 1: 99–119.

Hayeur Smith, M. 2004. *Draupnir's Sweat and Mardöll's Tears: An Archaeology of Jewellery, Gender and Identity in Viking Age Iceland*. BAR Int. Series 1276. Oxford: Archaeopress.

Hayeur Smith, M. 2012. 'Some in Rags, Some in Jags and Some in Silken Gowns: Textiles from Iceland's Early Modern Period'. *International Journal of Historic Archaeology* 16.3: 509–28. DOI: 10.1007/s10761-012-0190-1.

Hayeur Smith, M. 2013. 'Textiles from the 1988 Bessastaðir Excavation'. In Ólafsson (ed.), 105–9.

Hayeur Smith, M. 2014. 'Thorir's Bargain: Gender, Vaðmál and the Law'. *World Archaeology* 45.5: 730–46.

Hayeur Smith, M. 2015. 'Weaving Wealth: Cloth and Trade in Viking Age and Medieval Iceland'. In *Textiles and the Medieval Economy: Production, Trade and Consumption of Textiles, 8th–16th Centuries*, ed. A. Huang & C. Jahnke, 23–40. Oxford: Oxbow.

Hayeur Smith, M. forthcoming. 'The Heddle-Rods are Blood-Soaked Spears: Life, Death, Fate, and Female Embodiment through Weaving in Viking Age and Medieval Iceland'. In *The Archaeology of Fear*, ed. C. Wolf & K.P. Smith. New York: Routledge.

Heide, E. 2006. 'Spinning Seiðr'. In *Old Norse Religion in Long-Term Perspectives: Origins, Changes and Interactions: An International Conference in Lund Sweden, June 3–7, 2004*, ed. A. Andren, K. Jennbert, & C. Raudvere, 164–70. Lund: Nordic Academic Press.

Helgason, A., E. Hickey, S. Goodacre, V. Bosnes, K. Stefánsson, R. Ward, & B. Sykes 2001. 'mtDNA and the Islands of the North Atlantic: Estimating the Proportions of Norse and Gaelic Ancestry'. *American Journal of Human Genetics* 68: 723–37.

Hoffman, M. 1974. *The Warp-Weighted Loom: Studies in the History and Technology of an Ancient Implement*. Oslo: Hestholms Boktrykkeri.

Jesch, J. 1991. *Women in the Viking Age*. Woodbridge: Boydell.

Jochens, J. 1995. *Women in Old Norse Society*. Ithaca: Cornell University Press.

Jónsson, M. 2004. *Jónsbók, Lögbók Íslendinga*. Reykjavík: Háskólaútgáfan.

Kjellberg, A. 1979. 'Tekstilmaterialet fra "Oslogate 7"'. In *De Arkeologiske Utgravninger in Gamlebyen, Oslo* 2, ed. E. Schia & P.B. Molaug, 83–105. Oslo: Universitetsforlag.

Kjellberg, A. 1982. 'Medieval Textiles from the Excavations in the Old Town of Oslo'. In *Texilesymposium Neümunster: Archäologishe Textilien,* ed. L. Bender Jørgensen & K. Tidow, 136–50. Neümunster: Textilmusuem.

Kjellberg, A. & M. Hoffmann 1991. 'Tekstiler'. In *De Arkeologiske Utgravninger i Gamlebyen, Oslo* 8, ed. E. Schia & P.B. Molaug, 3–80. Oslo: Riksantikvaren/ Universitetets Oldsakssamling.

Larson, L.M. (trans.) 1935. *The Earliest Norwegian Laws: Being the Gulathing Law and the Frostathing Law*. New York: Columbia University Press.

Lárusson, B. 1967. *The Old Icelandic Land Registers*. Lund: C.W.K. Gleerup.

Lucas, G., C. Batey, G. Gudmundsson, I.T. Lawson, T.H. McGovern, & I.A. Simpson 2009. *Hofstaðir: Excavation of a Viking Age Feasting Hall in North-Eastern Iceland.* Reykjavík: Institute of Archaeology.

Maurer, B. 2006. 'The Anthropology of Money'. *Annual Review of Anthropology* 35: 15–36.

Meulengracht Sørensen, P. 1983. *The Unmanly Man: Concepts of Sexual Defamation in Early Northern Society*. Odense: Odense University Press.

Minar, C.J. 2001. 'Motor Skills and the Learning Process: The Conservation of Cordage Final Twist Direction in Communities of Practice'. *Journal of Anthropological Research* 57.4: 381–405.

Norrmann, L. 2008. *Viking Women: The Narrative Voice in Woven Tapestries*. New York: Cambria Press.

Ólafsson, G. 2013. *Bessastaðarannsókn 1988*. Reykjavík: Skýrslur Þjóðminjasafn Íslands.

Østergård, E. 2004. *Woven Into the Earth: Textiles from Norse Greenland*. Aarhus: Aarhus University Press.

Róbertsdóttir, H. 2008. *Wool and Society: Manufacturing Policy, Economic Thought and Local Production in 18th-century Iceland*. Göteborg and Stockholm: Makadam förlag.

Saul, M. 2004. 'Money in Colonial Transition: Cowries and Francs in West Africa'. *American Anthropologist*, New Series 106.1: 71–84.

Schneider, J. & A.B. Weiner 1989. 'Introduction'. In *Cloth and the Human Experience*, ed. A.B. Weiner & J. Schneider, 1–29. Washington: Smithsonian Institution Press.

Schulman, J.K. (trans.) 2010. *Jónsbók: The Laws of Later Iceland: The Icelandic Text according to MS AM 351 fol. Skálholtsbók eldri.* Saarbrucken: AQ-Verlag.

Sigmundsson, S., A. Holt, G. Siguurðsson, G. Ólafsson, & O. Vésteinsson (eds) 2011. *Viking Settlements and Viking Society: Papers from the Proceedings of the Sixteenth Viking Congress, Reykjavik and Reykholt, 16–23 August, 2009.* Reykjavik: Hið Íslenzka Fornleifafélag and University of Iceland.

Skre, D. 2011. 'Commodity Money, Silver and Coinage in Viking-Age Scandinavia'. In Graham-Campbell, Sindbæk, & Williams (eds), 67–92.

Sveinbjarnardóttir, G. (ed.) 2012. *Reykholt: Archaeological Investigations at a High Status Farm in Western Iceland*. Reykjavík: National Museum of Iceland.

Þórláksson, H. 1988. 'Gráfeldir á Gullöld og Vodaverk Kvenna'. *Ný Saga* 2: 40–53.

Þórláksson, H. 1991. *Vaðmál og Verðlag: Vaðmál í Útanlandsviðskiptum og Búskap Íslendinga á 13. og 14. Öld*. Reykjavík: Háskóli Íslands.

Turner, T.S. 1993. 'The Social Skin'. In *Reading the Social Body*, ed. C.B. Burroughs & J.D. Ehrenreich, 15–39. Iowa City: University of Iowa Press.

Walton Rogers, P. 1988. 'Dyes in the Viking Age: A Summary of Recent Work'. *Dyes in History and Archaeology* 7: 14–20.

Walton Rogers, P. 2012. 'Textiles, Wool and Hair'. In Sveinbjarnardóttir (ed.), 196–217.

Wolf, K. 2007. 'The Colour Blue in Old Norse-Icelandic Literature'. In *Scripta Islandica, Isländska Sällskapets Årsbok, 57–2006*, ed. R.A.H. Williams, M. MacLeod, E. Mundal, G. Nordal, R. Palm, H. Palsson, & D. Sävborg, 55–78. Uppsala: Swedish Science Press.

14

Tracing the Late Viking Age and Medieval Butter Economy

The View from Quoygrew, Orkney

Aaron J. Critch, Jennifer F. Harland, and James H. Barrett

Around the turn of the first and second millennia, increasing trade in bulk staple goods altered the social and economic traditions of northern European society (Barrett 2015). For archaeologists and historians, these shifts in trade and production are an important area of investigation, typically driven by excavated and archival evidence regarding commodities such as grain products, fish, beer, wine, hides, and cloth (e.g. Berggren et al. 2002; Cameron 1998; Hayeur Smith 2015). Still, for certain products, their organic nature and limited documentation make their histories more ephemeral than others. Butter was one of Norway's staple export goods in the medieval period, albeit less important than dried fish, fish oil, hides and timber products (Nedkvitne 1976; 2014). In documentary sources, it appears in both qualitative narrative accounts (e.g. Sephton 1994, 129, 178) and in quantitative toll records regarding the cargoes of ships bound from Norway to England (Rigby 2005; Nedkvitne 2014). Further records describe butter as a medium of payment—that is, as 'commodity-money', with socially defined and maintained rates for exchange or for payment of taxes, rents, and tithes (e.g. Anderson 1981; Thomson 1996; 2008, 130, 208–9; Challinor 2004; Skre 2011). Yet archaeologically, it seldom leaves any trace. Was butter truly a significant economic driver in the medieval northern world? If so, then why? Furthermore, how might intensified production and circulation as commodity-money have impacted subsistence strategies at the local level, and can we recognize relevant changes in the archaeological record?

From the archaeologist's perspective, these questions face obvious challenges. Archaeological examples of butter finds are known, normally from bog deposits, but they are exceptional (e.g. Earwood 1991). As a result, zooarchaeological and other bioarchaeological evidence from excavated farm sites offer the best alternative: as such data helps us to elucidate the strategies employed in raising dairy animals, one can identify sites that probably produced high quantities of butter and place them within their historical and economic context. The site of Quoygrew in Orkney (Fig. 14.1), a settlement of farmers and fishers occupied from the Viking Age until the twentieth century, provides one such opportunity, given the direct (sometimes monopolistic) trade link between the kingdom of Norway and the earldom of Orkney (Barrett 2012a). Quoygrew's rich ecofactual evidence for economic intensification (including dairying) from the eleventh to

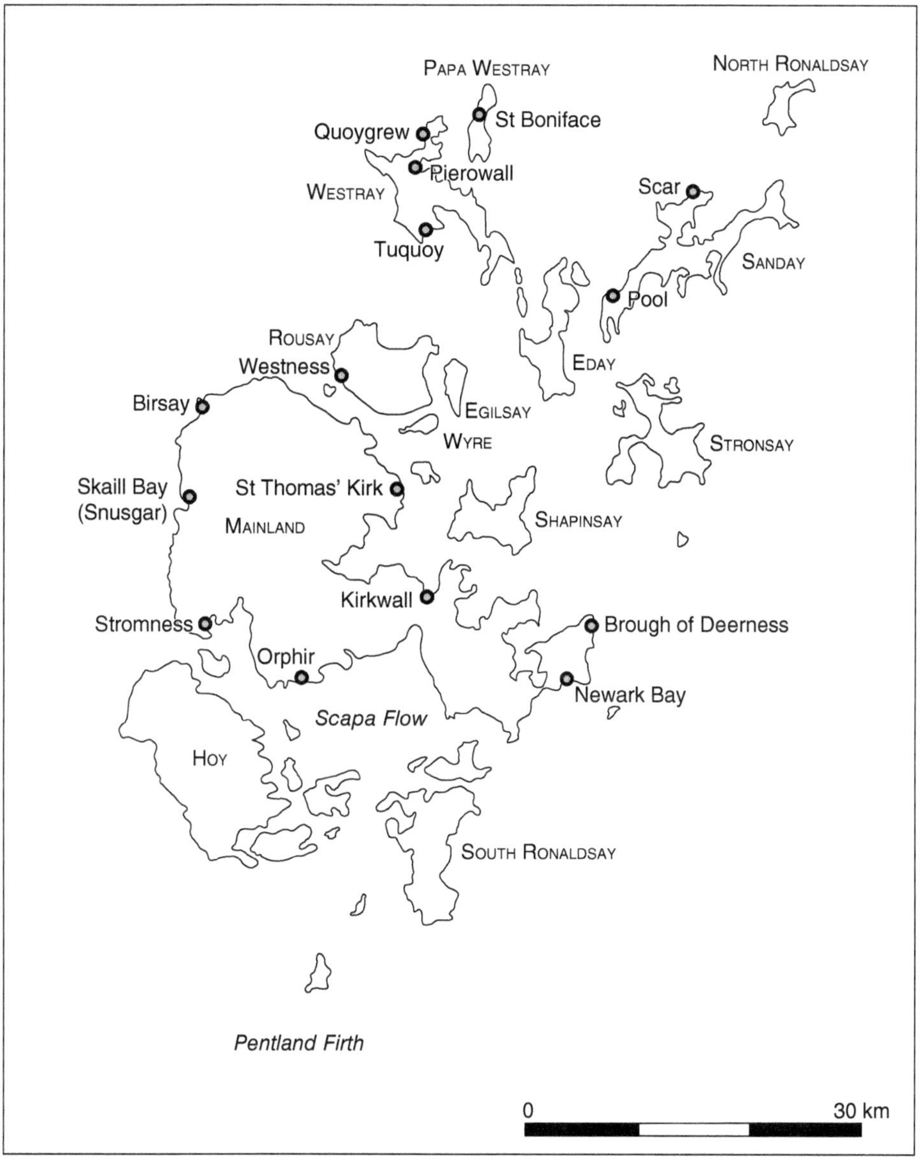

Fig. 14.1. Quoygrew in its local context (map by Dora Kemp).

thirteenth centuries, the trade connections implied by its artefact assemblage, and its evolving status within the Orcadian landscape hint at an intensive dairying site for which surplus butter production required to meet a growing demand for butter tax, or *skat*, would have been logical, necessary, and perhaps profitable.

Butter in Subsistence and Trade

Easily preserved and high in energy, butter is ideally suited to the northern diet, offering a dependable food source in a region where short growing seasons and crop failure were not unknown (Challinor 2004 and references therein). It is made by churning milk, which serves to separate and consolidate a water-in-fat emulsion of *c.*80 per cent fat. This mixture retains milk's fat-soluble vitamins, as well as *c.*0.5 per cent casein (the main protein in dairy) and *c.*0.2 per cent cholesterol. In the case of cows' milk butter, the result is a product with an energy value about thirteen times that of bovine wholemilk. Furthermore, the reduction in microbial activity resulting from salting and storage allows butter to remain preserved for an extended period. Converting milk to butter, particularly ahead of winter, would simply have been shrewd store management.

Beyond its nutritional uses, butter had other purposes that would have made it valuable. If made purely from cows' milk, butter could be an element of the high-status diet enjoyed by noblemen, from the pre-Viking period in Ireland to the Middle Ages in England and Scandinavia (Magnus 1555/1996; Woolgar 2006; McCormick 2008). With regards to church restrictions on meat consumption, it conveniently fell into a grey area, likely playing an important role in meeting energy and protein needs (Woolgar 2006). Post-medieval Scottish ethnography describes home medicinal remedies that include butter as an ingredient, and ascribe to them a Norse origin (Magnus 1555/1996; Martin 1716/1981; Fenton 1976). Even so-called 'corrupt' or 'grease butter', degraded from tainted wooden churns, or from the oily mixture of cows' and ewes' milk, had market potential; in the post-medieval period (and perhaps before) it was used as a lubricant (Anderson 1992). Butter has also been a key component of northern seafaring rations through time, be it for medieval Icelandic inshore fishermen (Vésteinsson 2016), the Tudor navy (Black 1990), or long-range post-medieval fishing expeditions to Newfoundland (Candow 2009).

Given its multipurpose nature, one can imagine that northerners were reluctant to let their butter supply flow out of the region through the market, especially during conflict, famine, or plague. On multiple occasions, northern rulers attempted to curb its export. In fact, one such anecdote perhaps indicates movement of butter from Orkney to Norway, and beyond: a speech against drunkenness given by the Norwegian king Sverre Sigurdsson (1184–1202) to a Bergen assembly in 1186, known from a near-contemporary source:

> We desire to thank the Englishmen who have come here, bringing wheat and honey, flour and cloth. We desire also to thank those who have brought here linen or flax, wax or

> caldrons. We desire next to make mention of those who have come here from the Orkneys, Shetland, the Færeys or Iceland; all those who have brought here such things as make this land the richer, and we cannot do without. But there are Germans who have come here in great numbers, with large ships, intending to carry away butter and dried fish, of which the exportation much impoverishes the land; and they bring wine instead... From that purchase much evil and no good has arisen. (Sephton 1994, 129–30)

Similarly, the Norwegian king Håkon Magnusson (1299–1319) ruled in 1316 during the Great Famine that 'nobody should take... dried fish or butter, except those who bring in malt, flour, and other cereal products' (quoted in Urbanczyk 1992, 141, author's translation). Evidently, butter was exported in large enough quantities that officials felt compelled to control the market and to guarantee that locals were the primary benefactors of its production.

Careful regulation of butter export is best understood in relation to an increasingly commercial European network. As trade expanded in the North Sea region during the eleventh and twelfth centuries, Norwegians found they could easily obtain grain, alcoholic beverages (first wine and later beer), cloth, and other products from England, Germany, and the Low Countries (Nedkvitne 2014; Nielssen 2016). Central to new trade was the foundation, in the eleventh century, of Bergen (Hansen 2015), corresponding chronologically with the emergence of English ports such as King's Lynn (Carus-Wilson 1962–3; Nedkvitne 2016) and of the (later Hanseatic) centre at Lübeck (Nedkvitne 2014). Driving Norway's long-range trade relations was, of course, stockfish—that is, cod dried in the open Arctic air without salt. The fishery had long been a part of traditional northern subsistence (Perdikaris 1999; Wickler & Narmo 2014; Hufthammer 2016). Stockfish was durable, easy to transfer, and in increasingly high demand among town-dwellers of England and the Continent as the Middle Ages progressed (e.g. Nielssen 2009; Barrett et al. 2011). Increasing specialization in commercial fishing translated to demand for imported grain products (Nedkvitne 2014; Nielssen 2016). In the Norse colonies of the North Atlantic, grain production could rarely help meet Norwegian demand. Even Orkney, the most agriculturally rich of them, had its own shortages (Barrett 2007). However, they could provide goods sought elsewhere in Europe, thus enabling the purchase of grain.

Foreign merchants flocked to Bergen, together with producers from Arctic Norway and the islands of the North Atlantic. Norwegian rulers sought to formalize this monopoly on northern routes. From 1294, royal economic policy barred foreign merchants from sailing to Norwegian territories beyond Bergen in order to regulate access and maintain ultimate control of resources (DN vol. 23). Bergen's prosperous place as the epicentre of North Atlantic trade was thus solidified, but for the modern scholar its official status as a hub partly masks the root of trade—particularly those who fished, spun wool, and made butter in the colonies of the Norse North Atlantic (Barrett 2012a).

Paying Butter Skat *at Quoygrew, Orkney*

Within this market context, butter production, already essential to the seasonal round, offered one option for Norway to meet its import needs. But how might this drive have altered subsistence strategies at a farm like Quoygrew? To place Quoygrew within its historical and landscape context, it is a site on the northwest coast of Westray, an island in Orkney, founded in the tenth century and continuously occupied until the mid twentieth century. It was part of a substantial multifocal settlement during the Viking Age and Middle Ages that, collectively, was likely the nucleus of a substantial *bý* farm now known as Trenabie, in turn the core of the large Rackwick township, valued at about thirty-five pennylands (with one pennyland roughly the size of a small farm), a substantial sum in the local land-assessment system. Its occupants were likely tenants of either the bishopric or earldom of Orkney at least from the twelfth century and perhaps before. Quoygrew's surroundings would have made it an attractive place to settle: a convenient landing place, a rocky foreshore providing shellfish and seaweed, extensive fields for cultivation, wet meadows for fodder, and access to peat and turf for building and fuel. It also maintained an important connection to the ritual landscape, through a nearby Neolithic cairn, a pagan Viking Age cemetery to the south, and, later, the parish church in nearby Pierowall (Barrett et al. 2012).

As at many such farms in the Scandinavian north, butter production at Quoygrew was more than convenient—under *butter skat*, it was mandatory. *Butter skat* was a system whereby farmers paid tax to the earldom, initially on cows and later land, in butter (Challinor 2004, 165; Thomson 2008, 208–9). The origins for such a system within the region are uncertain; however, the earliest known evidence of its existence comes from Trøndelag, Norway, where in the eleventh century each *bóndi* was required to give a 'spann' of butter and a *reykmaelir*—a 'maelir' of malt—per hearth (Thomson 1996). The best-documented system of *butter skat* during the period is that of Orkney. Based on late-medieval and post-medieval sources, *butter skat* was paid there in 'spanns', divisible into five 'lispunds', each of *c.*30–2 lb, or perhaps the total annual product of a single pre-modern cow (Challinor 2004, 166).

These units represent no small values. Carl Challinor (2004, 166–7) has considered the details, determining that in order to produce one lispund of butter, a cow would have had to yield about four pints of milk per day for five months. However, with the need to 'dry off' cows in anticipation of winter, the decrease in fat content over the course of a lactation cycle, and the rearing of calves, the cattle dairying window shrinks from five to two months, making a yield of ten pints per day necessary for a lispund. With such pressure, sheep may have helped to close any gaps. Eight ewes, at a rate of only one pint per day, could also provide a lispund in fifty days.

Orkney's earliest surviving rental—that is, an account and schedule of rent payments charged to each of a landowner's tenants—from 1492 helps shed light on the development of *butter skat* in the medieval period. Residents of the island Sanday testified that in 'auld tymes', *skat* was one spann per ten cows (Thomson 1996, xii). This rate is significant when looking further back in time. A bishop in Caithness attempted to exact this rate as tithe in 1222, doubling the customary amount. He was met with more than resistance. *Orkneyinga Saga* describes the dramatic outcome (see also Crawford 2013, 268–9):

> It was ancient custom that the Bishop should receive a spann of butter for every twenty cows . . . Bishop Adam wished to increase the impost, and demanded a spann of every fifteen cows; and when that was obtained, he demanded it of twelve; and when this too was conceded, he demanded it of ten. But this was thought by all men most unreasonable . . . the Bishop went out to make an arrangement with them; but when he was seen by the more wicked ones, who were most furious, they seized the Bishop, brought him into a small house, and set fire to it, and the house burnt so quickly that those who wished to save the Bishop could not do anything. (Anderson 1981, 200–1)

Butter skat eventually evolved from a charge on cows to a more consistent basis in land. In Orkney, land was valued in ouncelands consisting of eighteen pennylands. The introduction of the pennyland system has been variously dated to the eleventh and twelfth centuries (see Williams 2004; Thomson 2008, 61–2, 206–19). Under land assessment, *butter skat* was six spanns per ounceland, or one spann for every three pennylands (Thomson 2008, 209). Whatever the intricacies of the system of pennyland, it is clear that, through this levy, butter was accumulating in the hands of the elite—earls, bishops, and landowners, who presumably required it to meet the demands of an emerging export market.

While butter seems to have been a medium for the payment of taxes, it is also possible that it served a broader role, as a form of commodity-money for wider purchases. Epstein (2009, 91) notes that, in the more isolated areas of Norway and the North Atlantic islands, it would likely have been necessary to import grain, fine cloth, and (in the treeless islands) timber to satisfy demand during this period. Such items could have been purchased with payments-in-kind in a commodity-money system, in which the chosen monetary media (here, butter), in addition to serving as a unit of account and medium of payment, also possessed a utilitarian value (unlike silver coins) (Skre 2011, 70–1). Skre (2011) and Gullbekk (2011) note that a commodity-money system would have established stable exchange rates for regularly traded goods. In medieval Norway, butter was one of a suite of commodities, including cows, cloth, and grain, that functioned not only as media of exchange, but also as units of account, limiting the need for coin: in thirteenth- and fourteenth-century Norwegian sources, the value of butter was expressed as *laupa* (a 'basket' with a volume of *c.*16.2 litres), relative to *kýrlag* (the value of a good cow) or *baugr* (*c.*1.5 marks of silver). It is highly probable that such capital wealth was preferred over coin, since it could be easily converted into vital consumables necessary for survival during difficult times such as famines (Skre 2011, 72). If usefulness as money depends on social and environmental context, then butter had obvious value, being a rich source of energy and protein that is easily preserved.

Unlike for Norway, the use of butter as a form of commodity-money in Viking Age Orkney cannot be proved. Yet following the dramatic decline in evidence for large-scale circulation of silver in Scotland after the eleventh century (Graham-Campbell 1995, 62; Critch 2015), it seems likely that Quoygrew's farmers would have found trade in commodities to be their most convenient alternative. Indeed, beginning *c.*990, hoards from Scandinavian Scotland demonstrate an increasingly narrow range of silver media, with no further deposits dated beyond *c.*1065. Based on weight, so-called 'ring-money' accounts for the greatest proportion of hoard material during these years, as the number of coin finds from the same period represents a significantly smaller bullion value. Furthermore, 'ring-money' from these later hoards is dramatically debased—examples dated *c.*990–1065 typically contain only 40–60 per cent silver, whereas examples from the earlier Skaill hoard (*c.*950–70) often exceed 90 per cent silver (Critch 2015). Without widespread circulation of silver in the region, or an adequate standard of material, Orcadians likely relied upon other supplementary media of exchange. Even with the emergence of coinage, the adaptability of commodity-money makes it likely that it was not abandoned in the later medieval period (Gullbekk 2011). Certainly, the Orkney rental of 1492, described above, confirms that butter tax continued to be levied some years after the transfer of Orkney to Scotland in 1472, despite the fact that the Scottish crown had been producing its own coin since 1136 (Thomson 1996; Bateson 1997, 39).

The Archaeology of Butter Production: Dairying Strategies at Quoygrew

It is clear from the historical evidence that butter had tremendous market potential once the necessary trade routes for its distribution began to take shape in the eleventh century. Its dietary benefits, multifunctional nature, and, most importantly, required use in *skat* payments, all suggest that butter production took place at rates high enough to satisfy far more than local need. Thus, while direct archaeological evidence is rare, one must accept that, to some extent, site assemblages represent production strategies designed to meet such ends. How is one to interpret evidence from a site like Quoygrew, which would have been expected to pay *butter skat* to local elites? How might one begin to render butter visible archaeologically?

One must look first to zooarchaeological evidence from domestic animals. From the wider European perspective, it is obvious that cattle and sheep bone assemblages from Orkney have a distinct character. O'Connor's survey of collections *c.*AD 1000, spanning northern Europe from Ireland to the eastern Baltic, dubs cattle 'the tractors of pre-industrial Europe', apparently slaughtered for meat as adults after years of pulling the plough (2010, 10). However, amongst this selection of largely urban sites, those included from Orkney—Buckquoy and Skaill (Deerness)—stand out, with cattle and sheep specimens typically outnumbering other domesticates, such as pigs, by ratios as high as 3:1. A high frequency of young calf mortality also accompanies these numbers (O'Connor 2010, 7, 11–13).

Within the North Atlantic research context, debate has focused on the relation of high neonatal cattle mortality to dairying strategy. McCormick (1998) suggests that neonatal death could be attributed to a lack of adequate fodder, based on eighteenth- and nineteenth-century ethnography, as well as early Irish literature citing the need for the calf in order for lactation to occur. However, Vigne and Helmer (2007) do not dismiss the possibility that technologies may have existed as early as the Neolithic to facilitate the let-down of milk, or that one calf may have stimulated several cows. Looking specifically at sites in the Norse-influenced areas of Atlantic Scotland, Mulville et al. (2005) favour the notion of intended early culling, believing early ethnographers may have been dismissive of husbandry practices that would have appeared strange from their southern perspective. Furthermore, differential survival of lambs and calves at some sites weakens an argument based on environmental determinism. In fact, Mulville et al. (2005, 174) cite wild northern sheep populations with lower rates of early death than managed populations. It appears conclusive that deliberate culling played some role in a dairying husbandry strategy. In fact, it may imply a husbandry practice inherited from pre-Viking local practice (cf. Smith 1994; Bond 1998; 2007)—unlike in Atlantic Scotland, it is not typical of Viking Age and medieval Scandinavia (e.g. Barrett et al. 2007; O'Connor 2010), nor of other Scandinavian areas of Britain and Ireland (e.g. O'Connor 2004; McCormick & Murray 2007; Dobney et al. 2007; Holmes 2014), but the tradition does appear to have been later transplanted to Iceland (McGovern 2009).

Does Quoygrew fit a similar pattern? Excavations completed at the site between 1997 and 2005 investigated two settlement mounds, one coastal (known as the Fish Midden) and one *c.*50 metres inland (labelled the Farm Mound) (Fig. 14.2). Two structures and their associated middens provide significant insight into the day-to-day economics of eleventh- to thirteenth-century Quoygrew. House 5, built near the shore in the eleventh century, was occupied during Phase 2 (*c.* eleventh and twelfth centuries) of the site, and was most directly connected to fishing, as is evident from the extensive Fish Midden against its western gable. Refuse from House 5 also accumulated in the North and South Middens, both located along its long walls. Buildings broadly contemporary with House 5 are known from the Farm Mound—whilst not fully excavated, they may have formed the domestic core of the settlement in the eleventh and twelfth centuries. In Phase 3 (*c.* thirteenth and fourteenth centuries), a substantial new

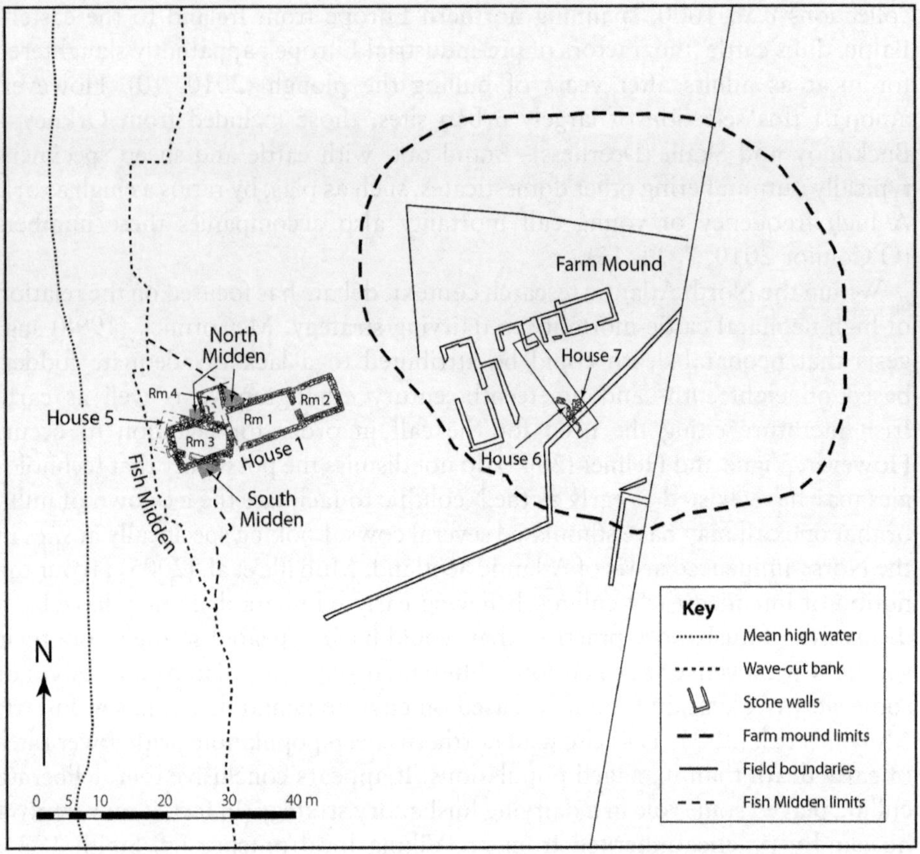

Fig. 14.2. Settlement features of Quoygrew discussed in the text (drawing by Lucy Farr, Dora Kemp and James Barrett).

dwelling with three rooms, House 1, was built over House 5 (Fig. 14.3). Room 3 within this structure was clearly a byre, including edge-set flagstones as stall dividers and a paved central drain (Barrett & Gerrard 2012). An earlier (tenth-century) baseline regarding economic activity at Quoygrew is provided by Phase 1 middens that have been excavated in the Farm Mound.

Analysis of mammal bone, mainly from the Farm Mound and Fish Midden, was completed by one of the current writers (JFH). Changes through time can be examined within the Farm Mound, between the early Phase 1 (tenth century) and later Phases 2 to 3 (eleventh to thirteenth centuries), with further eleventh- to thirteenth-century data from the Fish Midden. As established, mammal age-at-death estimates are crucial to understanding dairying—thus, a triple approach was taken in this area. First, each identified bone specimen was assigned a qualitative age estimate on an ordinal scale, based on size, texture, and fusion of long bone epiphyses: 'adult' (full-sized elements with smooth and solid textures), 'sub-adult' (just fused or in the process of fusing, with similar size

Fig. 14.3. Reconstruction of House 1 at Quoygrew as it may have appeared in the thirteenth century (drawn by Alan Braby).

and texture to adults), 'juvenile' (smaller, fairly robust, and smooth, with unfused epiphyses, but well-defined surfaces), and 'neonatal' (small, roughly textured, fragile, and porous, with unfused and poorly defined epiphyses). This qualitative system is imprecise, but maximizes the sample size available for intra-site comparison, particularly through time. It was consistently applied to the entire assemblage by a single individual (Harland 2012). Age was also assessed using the classic methods of epiphysial fusion of long bones (following Silver 1969; Moran & O'Connor 1994), and tooth eruption and wear (following Grant 1982; Payne 1973; 1987; O'Connor 1989; 1991).

Like most Orcadian sites of this period (cf. Harland 2006), cattle and sheep dominate. Within the Farm Mound, sheep are more numerous than cattle in Phase 1, at 34 per cent and 14 per cent of the mammal bone assemblage respectively. This difference decreases in Phases 2 to 3, with sheep at 24 per cent and cattle at 18 per cent. Within the contemporary Phases 2 to 3 of the Fish Midden, cattle (37 per cent) are instead more numerous than sheep (27 per cent). When combined with numbers for unidentified large mammals (likely cattle) and medium mammals (likely sheep), this trend is more evident. Large mammals represent only 23 per cent of the assemblage in the tenth century, while increasing to 32 per cent of eleventh- to thirteenth-century deposits in the Farm Mound and 43 per cent during the same period in the Fish Midden. Overall, this pattern

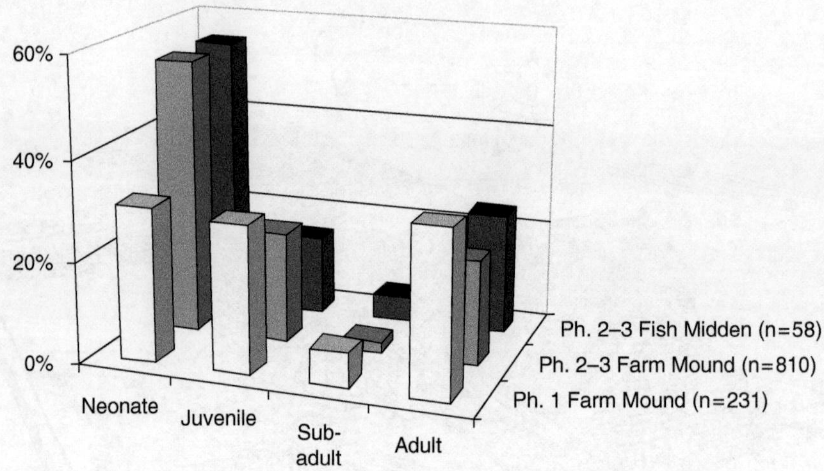

Fig. 14.4. Quoygrew cattle ordinal age categories based on the number of identified specimens (combining sieved and hand-collected bone finds) (data from Harland 2012).

suggests an increase in the usage of cattle through time, peaking in the eleventh to thirteenth centuries (Harland 2012).

With regards to ageing, the Quoygrew assemblage includes a very high proportion of fragmented neonatal specimens not represented within fusion or dental data—thus the need for broad ordinal categorization (Fig. 14.4). Using this method, over half the cattle from Phases 2 to 3 of both the Farm Mound and Fish Midden were neonatal, representing a change from Phase 1 where there was a higher proportion of juvenile and adult bones. This chronological pattern is statistically significant, likely representing a real increase in neonatal death from the tenth century through the eleventh- to thirteenth-century phases (Harland 2012). Moreover, it is important to emphasize that the use of both hand-collection and sieving during field recovery of the animal bones is likely to provide a sample under-representing small neonatal and juvenile elements. It was logistically impossible to sieve all the sediment excavated at Quoygrew. As it is, 1,964 samples, totalling 16,391 litres of sediment, were sieved using 4 mm or finer mesh.

Epiphysial fusion data from both phases of the Farm Mound suggests similar changes in age-at-death profiles (Fig. 14.5). For cattle, the percentage of fused epiphyses is low, even for early fusing elements. Furthermore, Phase 1 exhibits more fused epiphyses than the later periods, indicating that the age at which cattle were slaughtered decreased, beginning in the eleventh century.

Mandibles offer similar results (Fig. 14.6). While half the cattle in Phase 1 reached 'adult' stages by the later Phases 2 to 3, only half survived to the 'juvenile/ immature' stage. Almost 40 per cent of cattle in Phase 1 were considered 'elderly', decreasing to 10 per cent in Phases 2 to 3. Once again, the difficulty of recovering intact rows of teeth likely contributes to under-representation of young specimens. Overall, this pattern confirms the increase in neonatal cattle slaughter over time.

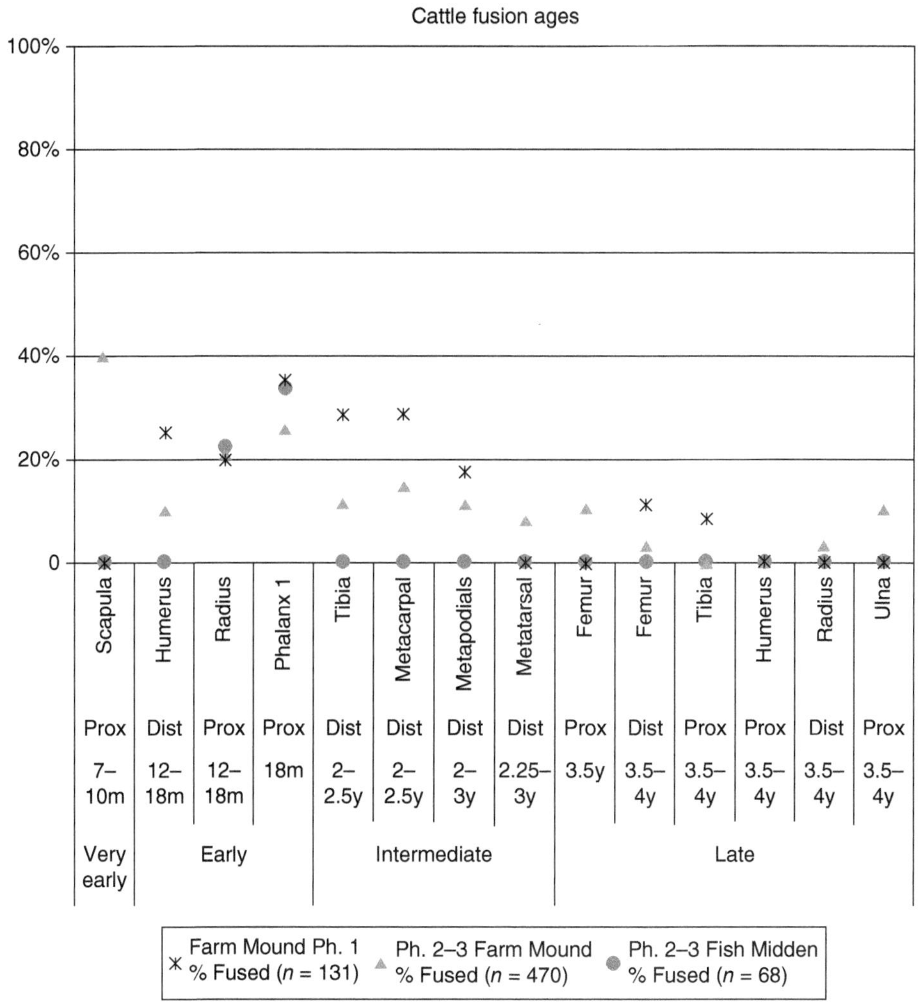

Fig. 14.5. Quoygrew cattle mortality profiles based on epiphyseal fusion (combining sieved and hand-collected bone finds) (data from Harland 2012).

It appears that a high proportion of all cattle were slaughtered younger than twelve to eighteen months, most notably in the eleventh to thirteenth centuries. The proportion of adults was low regardless of method, and given the higher likelihood of recovery for adult bone, it appears only a minority of Quoygrew's cattle reached maturity. This profile is consistent with that which Mulville et al. (2005, 179) propose for dairy production in the Northern Isles, with newborn calves killed to make greater quantities of dairy available for human consumption. Increases early in Phases 2 to 3 indicate an effort to intensify dairy production, whether for local consumption, rent, tax, tithe, or trade (Harland 2012).

The evidence from Quoygrew may offer further support for intensified dairying in the eleventh to thirteenth centuries. Increased production may have

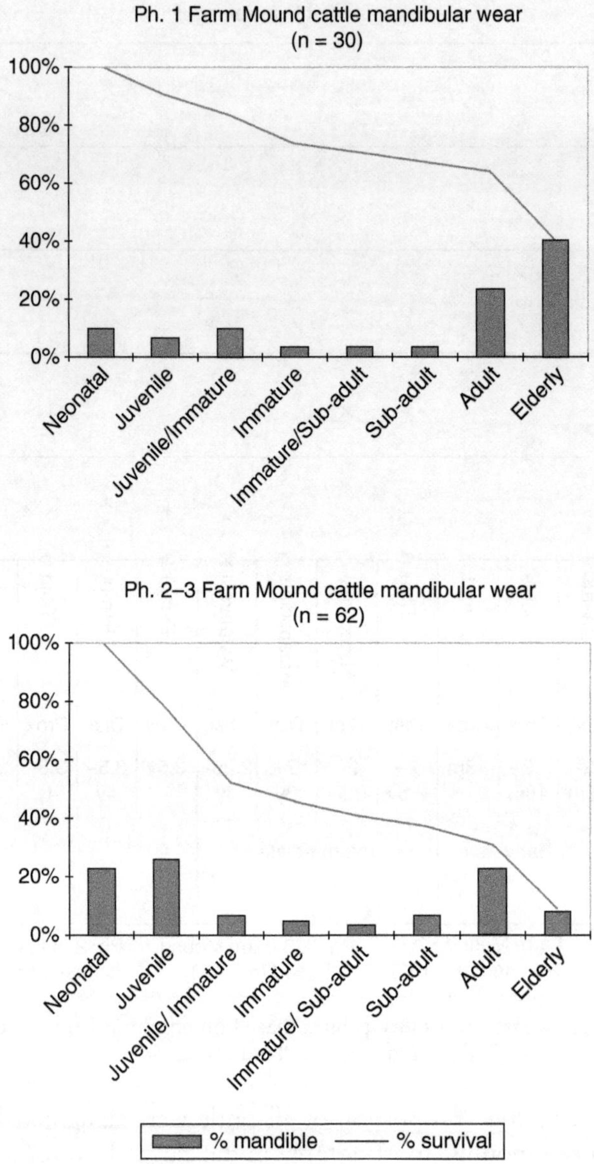

Fig. 14.6. Quoygrew cattle mortality profiles based on dental evidence (combining sieved and hand-collected bone finds) (data from Harland 2012).

necessitated higher-quality fodder, and in the relevant phases, large quantities of oats (including chaff and weed seeds) are found amongst botanical remains from byre flooring or manure, either unthreshed or incompletely threshed, as if left unprocessed as fodder. Earlier and later contexts contain higher quantities of carbonized oats in middens, implying they were preferentially dried for human consumption during these periods, with less used for fodder (Adams et al. 2012).

Similarly, $\delta^{13}C$ and $\delta^{15}N$ isotope ratios inform us about grazing—enriched $\delta^{13}C$ values indicate grazing on seaweed and/or fish products, while enriched $\delta^{15}N$ values indicate grazing on coastal vegetation and perhaps foddering with fish products. Caprine data shows enrichment of both values, with greater variability in Phases 2 to 3, implying grazing in increasingly variable environments. Cattle data, on the other hand, is consistent with animals grazed entirely on terrestrial vegetation. In summary, it appears possible that sheep were diverted to the shore, freeing inland grazing for cattle during the crucial phase of increased dairying (Barrett & Richards 2012).

Discussion

Overall, it appears that dairying played a significant role in the seasonal round at Quoygrew. Does this trend necessarily translate to butter production? If so, where was the butter going? First, one can argue that, given the known requirements of *butter skat*, production was not optional, but expected. During the periods of *skat* as a tax on cows, to possess cows meant to make butter, but unfortunately to speculate on the size of the herd, and thus the tax owed, would be to stretch the available data. Minimally, however, Quoygrew may represent one pennyland, and, if accurate, it would have owed one-third of a spann in butter (or *c.*50 lb) each season. This number does not include rent to either the bishopric or earldom, depending on its rental status within the township, or tithes to the church—all before supplying its own stores. Within this context, the archaeological evidence suggests that payment of *butter skat* would have been a significant motivator for intensified dairying at Quoygrew in the eleventh to thirteenth centuries.

To return to an earlier question, what was the intention behind such incredible amassment of butter, particularly for those elite collectors? To briefly touch on the artefactual evidence from Quoygrew, studies of style and raw material demonstrate many of its utilitarian stone objects, such as mica schist querns, Eidsborg schist hones, and some steatite vessels, were imported from Norway. They are particularly well represented in the eleventh and twelfth centuries (Batey et al. 2012). Similarly, residents at Quoygrew possessed fine combs of Scandinavian style and fabric, particularly during the eleventh to thirteenth centuries (Ashby & Batey 2012). Given the evidence for a boom in the fishery at Quoygrew during the same period, detailed elsewhere by Harland and Barrett (2012), it appears that trade relations between Orkney and Norway were strong, with Quoygrew benefiting either directly or indirectly. Overall, it implies a strong political and economic relationship with Norway during the period of Bergen's development, as well as a desire to maintain a distinctly Scandinavian identity (Barrett 2012a).

Finally, one must consider elites, known to have advanced taxation, as examples of those accumulating butter in vast quantities. While most Viking

Age and medieval sites in the Northern Isles have the distinctive neonatal slaughter signature, the Birsay area, associated with the earls of Orkney, is an exception (Harland 2006). Sites there include few or no neonatal specimens (see Noddle 1976–7; Hunter & Morris 1982; Rowley-Conwy 1983; Sellar et al. 1986; Rackham 1996). As an important political and religious centre, it is a likely destination for *butter skat*, where staples would have helped to finance imported trappings of elite life, such as textiles, weapons, building timber, and the services of stonemasons and poets (Barrett 2012a). That the period of intensified dairying at Quoygrew overlaps with the introduction of the earldom's pennyland system, as well as the growth of Bergen, is no coincidence.

To conclude, a culture of butter production as a dietary necessity in northern Europe, when met with local pre-Viking husbandry strategies in Scotland, provided the know-how and the market for increased production. Given the role of butter as *skat*, it appears that elites in particular targeted this market and fuelled production. However, in order to understand this development and better interpret the archaeological record, it is necessary to do so in conjunction with an understanding of contemporary political and economic history. Zooarchaeological records from the North reveal a significant role for dairying, and butter trade may be the key to their distinctive character.

ACKNOWLEDGEMENTS

The excavations at Quoygrew were mainly funded by Historic Scotland (now Historic Environment Scotland). The post-excavation analysis and writing were funded by the Arts and Humanities Research Board (now Arts and Humanities Research Council), the Cambridge Trust, and the Leverhulme Trust. We thank our friends and colleagues in Orkney for their logistical support, an anonymous reviewer for helpful comments on the text, and the McDonald Institute for Archaeological Research for permission to reproduce images from Barrett (2012b).

REFERENCES

Adams, C.T., S.L. Poaps, & J.P. Huntley 2012. 'Arable Agriculture and Gathering: The Botanical Evidence'. In Barrett (ed.), 161–97.

Anderson, J. (trans. and ed.) 1981. *The Orkneyinga Saga*. Edinburgh: Mercat Press.

Anderson, P.A. 1992. *Black Patie: The Life and Times of Patrick Stewart, Earl of Orkney, Lord of Shetland*. Edinburgh: John Donald.

Ashby, S.P. & C.E. Batey 2012. 'Evidence of Exchange Networks: The Combs and Other Worked Skeletal Material'. In Barrett (ed.), 229–43.

Barrett, J.H. 2007. 'The Pirate Fishermen: The Political Economy of a Medieval Maritime Society'. In *West Over Sea: Studies in Scandinavian Sea-Borne Expansion and Settlement before 1300*, ed. B.B. Smith, S. Taylor, & G. Williams, 299–340. Leiden: Brill.

Barrett, J.H. 2012a. 'Being an Islander'. In Barrett (ed.), 275–92.

Barrett, J.H. (ed.) 2012b. *Being an Islander: Production and Identity at Quoygrew, Orkney, AD 900–1600.* Cambridge: McDonald Institute for Archaeological Research.

Barrett, J.H. 2015. 'Maritime Societies and the Transformation of the Viking Age and Medieval World'. In *Maritime Societies of the Viking and Medieval World*, ed. J.H. Barrett & S.J. Gibbon, 1–13. Leeds: Maney/Society for Medieval Archaeology.

Barrett, J.H., L.R. Farr, D. Redhouse, S. Richer, J. Zimmermann, L. Sharpe, S. Ovenden, J. Moore, T. Poller, K.B. Milek, I.A. Simpson, M. Smith, B. Gourley, & T. O'Connor 2012. 'Quoygrew and its Landscape Context'. In Barrett (ed.), 25–46.

Barrett, J.H. & J.F. Gerrard 2012. 'The Quoygrew Sequence'. In Barrett (ed.), 47–96.

Barrett, J.H., A. Hall, C. Johnstone, H. Kenward, T. O'Connor, & S. Ashby 2007. 'Interpreting the Plant and Animal Remains from Viking-Age Kaupang'. In *Kaupang in Skiringssal*, Kaupang Excavation Project, Publication Series vol. 1, ed. D. Skre, 283–319. Aarhus: Aarhus University Press.

Barrett, J.H., D. Orton, C. Johnstone, J. Harland, W.V. Neer, A. Ervynck, C. Roberts, A. Locker, C. Amundsen, I.B. Enghoff, S. Hamilton-Dyer, D. Heinrich, A.K. Hufthammer, A.K.G. Jones, L. Jonsson, D. Makowiecki, P. Pope, T.C. O'Connell, T. de Roo, & M. Richards 2011. 'Interpreting the Expansion of Sea Fishing in Medieval Europe using Stable Isotope Analysis of Archaeological Cod Bones'. *Journal of Archaeological Science* 38: 1516–24.

Barrett, J.H. & D.C. Orton (eds) 2016. *Cod and Herring: The Archaeology and History of Medieval Sea Fishing.* Oxford: Oxbow.

Barrett, J.H. & M.P. Richards 2012. 'Feeding the Livestock: The Stable Isotope Evidence'. In Barrett (ed.), 199–205.

Bateson, J.D. 1997. *Coinage in Scotland.* London: Spink.

Batey, C.E., A.K. Forster, R.E. Jones, G. Gaunt, F.J. Breckenridge, J. Bunbury, & J.H. Barrett 2012. 'Local Availability and Long-Range Trade: The Worked Stone Assemblage'. In Barrett (ed.), 207–27.

Berggren, L., N. Hybel, & A. Landen (eds) 2002. *Cogs, Cargoes, and Commerce: Maritime Bulk Trade in Northern Europe, 1150–1400.* Toronto: Pontifical Institute of Mediaeval Studies.

Black, M. 1990. 'Survival Kit (16th century Seamen's Fare)'. In *Oxford Symposium on Food and Cookery 1989: Staple Foods Proceedings*, ed. H. Walker, 57–60. London: Prospect Books.

Bond, J.M. 1998. 'Beyond the Fringe? Recognising Change and Adaptation in Pictish and Norse Orkney'. In *Life on the Edge: Human Settlement and Marginality*, ed. G. Coles & C.M. Mills, 81–90. Oxford: Oxbow Books.

Bond, J.M. 2007. 'The Mammal Bone'. In *Investigations in Sanday, Orkney, Vol. 1: Excavations at Pool, Sanday*, ed. J. Hunter, J.M. Bond, & A.N. Smith, 207–27. Kirkwall: The Orcadian Ltd/Historic Scotland.

Cameron, E. (ed.) 1998. *Leather and Fur: Aspects of Early Medieval Trade and Technology.* London: Archetype Publications.

Candow, J.E. 2009. 'The Organisation and Conduct of European and Domestic Fisheries in Northeast North America, 1502–1854'. In *A History of the North Atlantic Fisheries, Volume 1: From Early Times to the Mid-Nineteenth Century*, ed. D.J. Starkey, J.T. Thór, & I. Heidbrink, 387–415. Bremen: Verlag H.M. Hauschild.

Carus-Wilson, E.M. 1962–3. 'The Medieval Trade of the Ports of the Wash'. *Medieval Archaeology* 6–7: 182–201.

Challinor, C. 2004. 'Butter as an Economic Resource in the Northern Isles'. In *Atlantic Connections and Adaptations: Economies, Environments and Subsistence in Lands Bordering the North Atlantic*, ed. R.A. Housley & G. Coles, 163–74. Oxford: Oxbow Books.

Crawford, B.E. 2013. *The Northern Earldoms: Orkney and Caithness from AD 870 to 1470*. Edinburgh: John Donald.

Critch, A. 2015. '"How are Princely Gifts Repaid by your Powerful Friends?": "Ring-Money" and the Appropriation of Tradition in Insular Viking Politics, AD 900–1065'. PhD thesis, University of Cambridge.

DN (Diplomatarium Norvegicum), 1847–2011. Diplomatarium Norvegicum, vols 1 to 21. Oslo: Dokumentasjonsprosjektet. www.dokpro.uio.no/dipl_norv/diplom_field_eng.html.

Dobney, K., D. Jaques, J. Barrett, & C. Johnstone 2007. *Farmers, Monks and Aristocrats: The Environmental Archaeology of an Anglo-Saxon Estate Centre at Flixborough, North Lincolnshire, UK*. Oxford: Oxbow Books.

Earwood, C. 1991. 'Two Early Historic Bog Butter Containers'. *Proceedings of the Society of Antiquaries of Scotland* 121: 231–40.

Epstein, S.A. 2009. *An Economic and Social History of Later Medieval Europe, 1000–1500*. Cambridge: Cambridge University Press.

Fenton, A. 1976. *Scottish Country Life*. Edinburgh: John Donald.

Graham-Campbell, J. 1995. *The Viking-Age Gold and Silver of Scotland*. Edinburgh: National Museums of Scotland.

Graham-Campbell, J., S.M. Sindbæk, & G. Williams (eds) 2011. *Silver Economies, Monetisation and Society in Scandinavia, AD 800–1100*. Aarhus: Aarhus University Press.

Grant, A. 1982. 'The Use of Tooth Wear as a Guide to the Age of Domestic Ungulates'. In *Ageing and Sexing Animal Bones from Archaeological Sites*, ed. R. Wilson, C. Grigson, & S. Payne, 91–108. BAR British Series 109. Oxford: Archaeopress.

Gullbekk, S.H. 2011. 'Norway: Commodity Money, Silver and Coins'. In Graham-Campbell, Sindbæk, & Williams, 93–112.

Hansen, G. 2015. 'Bergen AD 1020/30–1170: Between Plans and Reality'. In *Maritime Societies of the Viking and Medieval World*, ed. J.H. Barrett & S.J. Gibbon, 182–97. Leeds: Maney/Society for Medieval Archaeology.

Harland, J.F. 2006. 'Zooarchaeology in the Viking Age to Medieval Northern Isles, Scotland: An Investigation of Spatial and Temporal Patterning'. PhD thesis, University of York.

Harland, J.F. 2012. 'Animal Husbandry: The Mammal Bone'. In Barrett (ed.), 139–54.

Harland, J.F. & J.H. Barrett 2012. 'The Maritime Economy: The Fish Bone'. In Barrett (ed.), 115–38.

Hayeur Smith, M. 2015. 'Weaving Wealth: Cloth and Trade in Viking Age and Medieval Iceland'. In *Textiles and the Medieval Economy: Production, Trade, and Consumption of Textiles, 8th–16th Centuries*, ed. A.L. Huang & C. Jahnke, 23–40. Oxford: Oxbow.

Holmes, M. 2014. *Animals in Saxon and Scandinavian England: Backbones of Economy and Society*. Leiden: Sidestone Press.

Hufthammer, A.K. 2016. 'Fish Trade in Norway AD 800–1400: Zooarchaeological Evidence'. In Barrett & Orton (eds), 221–30.

Hunter, J.R. & C.D. Morris 1982. 'Appendix: Excavation of Room 5 Clifftop Settlement Brough of Birsay 1973–4'. In *Pictish and Norse Finds from the Brough of Birsay 1934–74*, ed. C.L. Curle, 124–38. Edinburgh: Society of Antiquaries of Scotland.

McCormick, F. 1998. 'Calf Slaughter as a Response to Marginality'. In *Life on the Edge: Human Settlement and Marginality*, ed. G. Coles & C.M. Mills, 49–51. Oxford: Oxbow.

McCormick, F. 2008. 'The Decline of the Cow: Agricultural and Settlement Change in Early Medieval Ireland'. *Peritia* 20: 209–24.

McCormick, F. & E. Murray 2007. *Excavations at Knowth 3: Knowth and the Zooarchaeology of Early Christian Ireland*. Dublin: Royal Irish Academy.

McGovern, T.H. 2009. 'The Archaeofauna'. In *Hofstaðir: Excavations of a Viking Age Feasting Hall in North-eastern Iceland*, ed. G. Lucas, 168–252. Reykjavik: Institute of Archaeology.

Magnus, O. 1555/1996. *Description of the Northern Peoples*. London: The Hakluyt Society.

Martin, M. 1716/1981. *A Description of the Western Isles of Scotland*. Edinburgh: James Thin.

Moran, N.C. & T.P. O'Connor 1994. 'Age Attribution in Domestic Sheep by Skeletal and Dental Maturation: A Pilot Study of Available Sources'. *International Journal of Osteoarchaeology* 4: 267–86.

Mulville, J., J.M. Bond, & O.E. Craig 2005. 'The White Stuff: Milking in the Outer Scottish Isles'. In *The Zooarchaeology of Fats, Oils, Milk and Dairying*, ed. J. Mulville & A. Outram, 162–82. Oxford: Oxbow.

Nedkvitne, A. 1976. 'Handelssjøfarten mellom Norge og England i Høymiddelalderen'. *Sjøfartshistorisk Årbok* 1976: 7–254.

Nedkvitne, A. 2014. *The German Hansa and Bergen 1100–1600*. Cologne: Böhlau Verlag.

Nedkvitne, A. 2016. 'The Development of the Norwegian Long-Distance Stockfish Trade'. In Barrett & Orton (eds), 50–9.

Nielssen, A.R. 2009. 'Norwegian Fisheries *c.*1100–1850'. In *A History of the North Atlantic Fisheries, Volume 1: From Early Times to the Mid-Nineteenth Century*, ed. D.J. Starkey, J.T. Thór, & I. Heidbrink, 83–109. Bremen: H.M. Hauschild.

Nielssen, A.R. 2016. 'Early Commercial Fisheries and the Interplay among Farm, Fishing Station and Fishing Village in North Norway'. In Barrett & Orton (eds), 42–9.

Noddle, B.A. 1976–7. 'The Animal Bones from Buckquoy'. In 'Excavation of Pictish and Viking-Age Farmsteads at Buckquoy, Orkney', by A. Ritchie. *Proceedings of the Society of Antiquaries of Scotland* 108: 201–9.

O'Connor, T.P. 1989. *Bones from Anglo-Scandinavian Levels at 16–22 Coppergate* (The Archaeology of York 15/3). York: York Archaeological Trust.

O'Connor, T.P. 1991. *Bones from 46–54 Fishergate* (The Archaeology of York 15/4). York: York Archaeological Trust.

O'Connor, T.P. 2004. 'Animal Bones from Anglo-Scandinavian York'. In *Aspects of Anglo-Scandinavian York*, ed. R.A. Hall, D.W. Rollason, & M. Blackburn, 427–45. York: Council for British Archaeology.

O'Connor, T. 2010. 'Livestock and Deadstock in Early Medieval Europe from the North Sea to the Baltic'. *Environmental Archaeology* 15: 1–15.

Payne, S. 1973. 'Kill off Patterns in Sheep and Goats: The Mandibles from Asvan Kale'. *Anatolian Studies* 23: 281–303.

Payne, S. 1987. 'Reference Codes for Wear Stages in the Mandibular Cheek Teeth of Sheep and Goats'. *Journal of Archaeological Science* 14: 609–14.

Perdikaris, S. 1999. 'From Chiefly Provisioning to Commercial Fishery: Long-Term Economic Change in Arctic Norway'. *World Archaeology* 30: 388–402.

Rackham, D.J. 1996. 'Beachview, Birsay: The Biological Assemblage'. In *The Birsay Bay Project, Vol. 2: Sites in Birsay Village and on the Brough of Birsay, Orkney*, ed. C.D. Morris, 161–91. Durham: University of Durham, Department of Archaeology.

Rigby, S.H. 2005. *The Overseas Trade of Boston in the Reign of Richard II*. Woodbridge: The Boydell Press.

Rowley-Conwy, P. 1983. 'The Animal and Bird Bones'. In 'Trial Excavations on Pictish and Viking Settlements at Saevar How, Birsay, Orkney', by J.W. Hedges. *Glasgow Archaeological Review* 4: 109–11.

Sellar, T., S.M. Colley, A.K.G. Jones, & G. Turner 1986. 'Animal Bone Material'. In *Rescue Excavations on the Brough of Birsay 1974–1982*, ed. J.F. Hunter, 208–16. Edinburgh: Society of Antiquaries of Scotland.

Sephton, J. (trans.) 1994. *The Saga of King Sverri of Norway*. Dyfed: Llanerch.

Silver, I.A. 1969. 'The Ageing of Domestic Animals'. In *Science in Archaeology: A Survey of Progress and Research*, ed. D.R. Brothwell & E. Higgs, 283–302. London: Thames & Hudson.

Skre, D. 2011. 'Commodity Money, Silver and Coinage in Viking-Age Scandinavia'. In Graham-Campbell, Sindbæk, & Williams (eds), 67–92.

Smith, H. 1994. 'Howe: Animal Bone Report'. In *Howe: Four Millennia of Orkney Prehistory*, ed. B. Ballin Smith, 139–53. Edinburgh: Society of Antiquaries of Scotland.

Thomson, W.P.L. 1996. *Lord Henry Sinclair's 1492 Rental of Orkney*. Kirkwall: Orkney Press.

Thomson, W.P.L. 2008. *The New History of Orkney*. Edinburgh: Birlinn.

Urbanczyk, P. 1992. *Medieval Arctic Norway*. Warsaw: Semper.

Vésteinsson, O. 2016. 'Commercial Fishing and the Political Economy of Medieval Iceland'. In *Cod and Herring: The Archaeology and History of Medieval Sea Fishing*, ed. J.H. Barrett & D.C. Orton, 71–9. Oxford: Oxbow Books.

Vigne, J.-D. & D. Helmer 2007. 'Was Milk a "Secondary Product" in the Old World Neolithisation Process? Its Role in the Domestication of Cattle, Sheep and Goats'. *Anthropozoologica* 42.2: 9–40.

Wickler, S. & L. Narmo 2014. 'Tracing the Development of Fishing Settlement from the Iron Age to the Modern Period in Northern Norway: A Case Study from Borgvær in the Lofoten Islands'. *Journal of Island and Coastal Archaeology* 9: 72–87.

Williams, G. 2004. 'Land Assessment and the Silver Economy of Norse Scotland'. In *Sagas, Saints and Settlement*, ed. G. Williams & P.A. Bibire, 65–104. Leiden: Brill.

Woolgar, C.M. 2006. 'Meat and Dairy Products in Late Medieval England'. In *Food in Medieval England: Diet and Nutrition*, ed. C.M. Woolgar, D. Serjeantson, & T. Waldron, 88–101. Oxford: Oxford University Press.

Index

Diagrams, tables etc. are given in italics